GENERAL FOX CONNER

GENERAL FOX CONNER

Pershing's Chief of Operations and Eisenhower's Mentor

STEVEN RABALAIS

CASEMATE

Philadelphia & Oxford

First published in the United States of America and Great Britain in 2016.
Reprinted in 2017 and 2020 by
CASEMATE PUBLISHERS
1950 Lawrence Road, Havertown, PA 19083, USA
and
The Old Music Hall, 106-108 Cowley Road, Oxford, OX4 1JE, UK

Copyright 2016 © Casemate Publishers and Steven Rabalais

Hardcover Edition: ISBN 978-1-61200-397-9
Digital Edition: ISBN 978-1-61200-398-6

A CIP record for this book is available from the British Library

For a complete list of Casemate titles, please contact:

CASEMATE PUBLISHERS (US)
Telephone (610) 853-9131
Fax (610) 853-9146
Email: casemate@casematepublishers.com
www.casematepublishers.com

CASEMATE PUBLISHERS (UK)
Telephone (01865) 241249
Email: casemate-uk@casematepublishers.co.uk
www.casematepublishers.co.uk

Dedicated to the love of my life, Colleen
We Are One

CONTENTS

LIST OF MAPS

The maps in this work appear by courtesy of the American Battle Monuments Commission.

ACKNOWLEDGMENTS

Many wonderful people have generously given of their time and talent to bring this book to publication.

I express my sincere gratitude to Casemate Publishing for affording this previously unpublished writer the opportunity to tell the story of a forgotten giant of American military history. Tara Lichterman, Clare Litt, Ruth Sheppard, Nikolai Bogdonavic, and Hannah McAdams, as well as Steve Smith and Libby Braden before them, provided much patient and insightful guidance, for which I am deeply thankful.

Pam McPhail of Calhoun City, Mississippi made her impressive collection of information on General Conner available to me to begin my research. Members of the general's family, especially Norm MacDonald, Lori Conner, Drew Conner, and the late Macpherson Conner, allowed me access to precious family treasures, including Bug Conner's remarkable scrapbook. I sincerely hope that you have all found this book worthy of your trust in me. I also extend my thanks to Ginny Brandreth for her introductions to Norm, Mac, and also to Sam Black.

Professors Karl Roider and Bob Mann at Louisiana State University were both kind enough to read earlier drafts of this work and to offer their comments and ideas for improvement. I also extend my sincere gratitude to Dr. Roider for instilling in me, during my freshman year at LSU in 1978, a love of history that endures to this day.

I also appreciate the time and critiques given me by Billy Gunn, Carl Palmer, and Greg Probst—three talented men whose perspectives, and friendship, I value greatly. Martha Baker's guidance and suggestions, always made with sweet frankness (or is it frank sweetness, Martha?), have made this a much better book than it otherwise would have been. Angela Gagliano and Zella Lopez have also both devoted many hours of assistance in countless ways.

This book would not have been completed without the love and support of my family. My brother Rob has been with me on this project since the first research/road trip to Mississippi. Alecia and Randy were both kind enough to read my earliest efforts; they nonetheless urged me to continue. My dear daughters Lindsay, Lauren, and Amanda have each helped in ways I will always treasure—from locating obscure books at the LSU Library (a 19-year-old college student's dream, I'm sure) to helping me overcome computer challenges that most 8-year-olds can handle on their own. They must love me. I certainly love them.

The courage and determination of my late brother Ronnie has inspired me to see this work to completion, as have my memories of the enjoyment my mother (Maw-Maw Betty) found in having me read passages of the book to her as I wrote them. My father, Merrill Rabalais, who began his educational career teaching history, passed on to me his own love of the subject. Though all are now gone, each has continued to guide me. I also offer a special prayer of thanks to St. Francis de Sales—the patron of writers.

My deepest thanks go to my beloved bride, Colleen, whom I had the blessing to marry in 1986. I would never have begun this book, much less finished it, without Colleen's encouragement and support. She has also devoted countless hours of her own valuable time to researching, proofing, and otherwise bringing this work to completion. I was able to make this book a labor of love because of Colleen's love for me. My love for her transcends all things in my life.

Lafayette, Louisiana
March 2016

PROLOGUE

London, UK
July 4, 1942

The first Independence Day since Pearl Harbor was an eventful one for Major General Dwight D. Eisenhower, Commanding General of the United States European Theater of Operations.

On that day, almost 7 months after America's entry into World War II, the United States conducted its first offensive operations in Europe. American airmen launched what the general called "a bombing raid to celebrate July 4" against German air bases in Holland. Eisenhower, who had been appointed to command 11 days earlier by Army Chief of Staff George C. Marshall, had never before ordered men into action. Before the mission, he visited the American crews to wish them luck. He also talked to the survivors who made it back to base. For the first time in his career, the general could count casualties directly attributable to his own orders.[1]

Apart from his command duties, Eisenhower was also busy that Saturday introducing himself as the smiling and optimistic face of the American military presence in beleaguered Britain. More than 2,000 people passed through the receiving line at a reception hosted by the American ambassador. Later that evening, Eisenhower met with his general staff to discuss matters of supply for the American military force he planned to build. Eisenhower had inherited the staff; he had concern over its suitability for the task ahead.[2]

Eisenhower, therefore, had much on his mind that Independence Day in 1942, as he penned a letter to his mentor:

> Dear General,
>
> More and more in the last few days my mind has turned back to you and to the days when I was privileged to serve intimately under your wise counsel and leadership. I cannot tell you how much I would appreciate, at this moment, an opportunity for an hour's discussion with you on problems that constantly beset me.

When I came to this job I was, of course, prepared to find that much of the advice given me would be colored, consciously or unconsciously, by the particular position of the individual involved, and by his conception of what his advice would mean to his own personal fortunes. But, discounting this normal human failing, I find it difficult at times to separate the wheat from the chaff among opposing views, presented, I believe, with full honesty of purpose. Right now, aside from the old question of making firm agreements with allies, many of these arguments involve internal organization–the same problems that you faced twenty-five years ago, and which have been the subject of bitter debate among some of our very able officers ever since ...

I do not expect an answer to this letter, and certainly do not want to bother you with matters for which, you may be certain, I'll soon have answers. I hope they will be right. But, recently, I've been so frequently struck by the similarity between this situation and the one you used to describe to me, that I thought you might like to hear something about it ...[3]

Eisenhower's letter was not addressed to George Marshall, the man most responsible for his elevation to command. Nor did he write to either Douglas MacArthur or John J. Pershing, both of whom he had served before the war. Instead, this glimpse into Eisenhower's state of mind, as he assumed his first significant command, was written to retired Major General Fox Conner—a figure now forgotten in American history.

As Pershing's chief of operations for the American Expeditionary Forces (AEF) during World War I, Fox Conner directed the development and successful deployment of American combat forces in France. Pershing considered Conner to have been "a brilliant soldier" and "one of the finest characters our Army has ever produced." Pershing paid tribute to Conner by telling him: "I could have spared any other man in the AEF better than you."[4]

Fox Conner commanded Dwight Eisenhower when both were stationed in the Panama Canal Zone in the 1920s. Despite having been part of the high command that had helped win the "War to End All Wars," Conner held the then-unorthodox view that the American Army would fight a second war in Europe within two decades. Conner imparted that belief to his protégé Eisenhower and transformed him from a struggling young officer facing a court-martial into one of the Army's rising stars.

The influence of Conner upon Eisenhower's career is best described by Eisenhower himself. "In sheer ability and character," wrote Eisenhower of Conner, "he was the outstanding soldier of my time." Eisenhower believed that Conner had "more influence on me and my outlook than any other individual, especially in regard to the military profession." He paid tribute to his mentor by writing: "In a lifetime of association with great and good men, he is the one more or less invisible figure to whom I owe an incalculable debt."[5]

Conner has become an "invisible figure," to use Eisenhower's phrase, partly by his own design. Unlike many of his World War I comrades, Fox Conner did not write a memoir. He also directed a former aide to burn his personal papers. Nonetheless, through analysis of archival records and surviving personal letters, as well as from the writings of those whose lives and careers were affected by Fox Conner, the complete story can now be told of the life and career of this remarkable officer, whom Dwight Eisenhower considered "the greatest soldier I ever knew."[6]

The story begins, amid the ashes of the Civil War, in Calhoun County, Mississippi.

CHAPTER I

CALHOUN COUNTY

He had always thought in terms of war.
—Virginia Conner, 1951

His work in the family's north Mississippi cotton patch done for that day in the mid-1880s, young Fox Conner waited at the family's hearth. The boy watched as his father moved toward the fireplace by lightly touching the table, chairs, and other objects that defined his surroundings. Robert Conner settled into a comfortable place and began to reminisce. Fox listened, spellbound, as the blind man told his stories of war.[1]

Robert spoke of his part in April 1862's Battle of Shiloh, where more than 23,000 men were killed, wounded, or missing after just two days of close-quarter fighting in heavy rain and mud. Soldiers who had been countrymen the previous year looked each other in the eye as one slew and the other was slain, often with bayonet or sword; the kind of killing that made hands, and rage, bloody. Robert Conner fought at Shiloh until Union gunfire ripped open his leg. Robert survived to fight again at Chickamauga and Chattanooga in late 1863, but thousands did not—including Robert's friend, Private Jesse Fox. Like his Fox ancestors who had died fighting the British during the American Revolution, Jesse Fox lost his life at Shiloh in the service of his fledgling nation.[2]

Fox Conner also heard how the Civil War had ended for his father. Shot through the head and eyes outside Atlanta in 1864, Robert Conner was left bleeding upon a battlefield he could no longer see. Robert nonetheless heard the roar of cannon and the moans of the wounded.

He could also smell the aftermath of battle in the heat of a Georgia July. While collecting the dead, the Yankees found Robert Conner and took him to a hospital. The Northern men he had been trying to kill had saved his rebel life. But the darkness remained. The sights of battle—of men killing other men—were the last things ever seen by the man who came to be known as "Blind Bob" Conner.[3]

Fox Conner understood that war could be tragic. But he was irresistibly drawn to it; Fox begged his father to tell him more.[4]

Robert Herbert Conner told his son what war was actually like. Born in 1843, Robert had joined the Confederate Army at the outset of the Civil War in 1861. Before the war, the intelligent and well-educated Conner had a penetrating gaze, set in a face with a square jaw and tightly drawn lips that presented an air of seriousness. The war took Robert Conner's sight, but not his will. After his release from a Union hospital, Robert returned to his father's cotton farm near Slate Springs in isolated Calhoun County, Mississippi. There, Robert Conner began to rebuild his life. He learned to grade cotton by feeling it between his thumb and forefinger; he became a cotton trader.[5]

Blind Bob, however, also had the insight to recognize that his education provided an advantage upon which to build his future.

Robert Conner became a teacher at the Slate Springs Academy. Fuller Fox, the younger brother of the slain Jesse Fox, founded the school in 1872. Fuller welcomed his fallen brother's Confederate comrade. Other members of the Fox family also taught at the academy, including Nancy Hughes Fox, Fuller's older sister. Known as Nannie, she was in her early 30s, and still unmarried, when Robert Conner joined the faculty. The two began a romance. They married on December 30, 1873.[6]

Nannie gave birth to their first child, a son, on November 2, 1874 at Slate Springs, Mississippi. His name symbolized the union of two families devoted to both military service and education. Nannie Fox and Robert Conner named their son Fox Conner, with no middle name.

As the eldest son of a blind father, Fox Conner grew up quickly in the mid-1880s. In springtime, Fox's mule-drawn plow creaked through row after row in the family's 600-acre cotton field. His young arms and chest strained to control the gray beast that normally felt a man's weight pulling back against it. In summer, Fox walked those same rows, often barefooted, as he picked cotton. Some days, a hundred pounds went into the burlap sack he wore upon his back. Every boll mattered. Without the money from cotton farming, the growing Conner family could not survive on the meager salaries of two teachers in rural Mississippi.[7]

But as Fox Conner bore his burden in the cotton field, his daydreams carried him to fields of battle far away from Calhoun County. In Fox's mind, his back carried a soldier's pack rather than a burlap sack. Instead of stumbling behind a plow, he was marching behind a caisson. Even when raking manure in the Mississippi heat, Fox saw the pungent piles as the opposing lines of two armies; he maneuvered them with his rake as a general would move his divisions upon a map.[8]

Once the harvest was in and the weather turned cool, Fox went to his father's schoolhouse instead of his cotton field. Robert Conner became superintendent of the Slate Springs Academy after Fuller Fox left the school to practice law. Fox flourished at the school and rose to the head of his class. Blind Bob Conner could hear his son's intellect grow. But with a school term of only five months and a curriculum focused upon the rudiments of reading and writing, Fox Conner needed more than the Slate Springs Academy could provide. To meet the need, Robert and Nannie Conner continued their son's education at home.[9] More importantly, Fox Conner learned to teach himself.

Around the age of 10, Fox subscribed to *The Youth's Companion*, the leading American weekly subscription magazine of the late 19th century. The magazine was no mere compilation of children's tales. With the slogan "For all the Family," its articles on an array of subjects—from fiction, poetry, and history, to theology, politics, and science—were written for both older children and for adults interested in becoming better-educated citizens. Literary giants such as Henry Wadsworth Longfellow, Louisa May Alcott, Alfred, Lord Tennyson, Emily Dickinson, and Harriet Beecher Stowe each published stories in the magazine, as did British Prime Minister W.E. Gladstone, future Supreme Court justice Oliver Wendell Holmes, future President Theodore Roosevelt, and many others.[10]

The Youth's Companion fed Fox Conner's appetite to learn. He and a friend won a contest for selling subscriptions to the magazine. For his prize, Conner chose a book on American history. The passages that interested him most involved his nation's battles and the men who fought them.[11]

The articles in *The Youth's Companion* were written to be read aloud, and Fox eventually began to tell the evening stories in the Conner home to his sisters, Mary and Nannie Gus, and to brothers Manly, Rush, and Fuller. Sometimes he recited poetry. Mostly, he shared stories of scientific discovery and far-off exploration that transported them all to places beyond the fields of Calhoun County. His mother and father enjoyed the evenings too. Their eldest son Fox was becoming a teacher.[12]

The common thread that wound through the articles in *The Youth's Companion* was the premise that reunited America was exceptional among the world's nations, and that its citizens had a duty to excel as well. With a circulation of nearly 500,000 weekly, *The Youth's Companion* served, in the late 19th century, the same function that radio, television, and the internet have provided to subsequent generations of young Americans: a mass medium that allowed people from different regions of the country to form a common, if idealized, image of their nation. *The Youth's Companion* influenced the reconciliation of Northerners and Southerners into a single national identity once America emerged from the divisiveness of postwar reconstruction and actually began to reunite. The magazine's most enduring legacy—The Pledge of Allegiance—by which millions of American children from Montana to Mississippi to Maine have begun their day for more than a century, was created by the magazine's writers and published in 1892.[13]

That same year, Fox Conner turned 18, and he made a pledge of his own.

Fox had been pondering what his life's work would be. One option was to follow in his father's footsteps and become head of the family's farm, and possibly its community's school as well—both noble occupations. Undoubtedly, he could have served his family well by staying in Calhoun County to continue his father's and mother's work there.

Fox Conner, however, felt called to service of a different type. His boyish fascination with war had never waned; it had intensified as he continued to read about history's great generals and momentous battles. Fox also respected family tradition. His Fox ancestors had fought and died for their young country during the American Revolution, when the nation's future was in doubt. His father and his Uncle Jesse had done the same for their country, albeit with a different outcome. Fox Conner likewise embraced *his* country—the reunited nation of Northerners and Southerners that *The Youth's Companion* fostered. As his forebears had done, Fox Conner vowed to serve his country as a soldier.[14]

While Fox owed his fascination with warfare to the stories of his enlisted father, he also understood that generals, not foot soldiers, made history. Fox was determined to become an officer. He also sought a higher education. He wanted a lot for a poor farm boy whose parents could not afford to send him to college.[15]

But Fox Conner also had a plan.

The United States Military Academy at West Point, New York afforded the perfect opportunity for Fox Conner to achieve his twin goals of a college education and an officer's commission. Significant hurdles, however, separated him from his objective. Only members of Congress or the president had the power to appoint a young man to West Point. Also, only one cadet from each congressional district could attend West Point at a time. Because cadets normally needed at least four years to graduate, the opportunity for appointment from a congressional district generally arose only once every four years. Even if a vacancy existed, and if the necessary appointment could somehow be obtained, each appointee then had to pass rigorous physical and academic examinations before being allowed to enter the academy.[16]

In formulating his strategy, Fox realistically assessed the assets available to him. Work on the farm had made him a lean and muscular young man who could easily meet whatever physical requirements West Point might have. Fox also trusted the educational foundation laid by his parents, and which he had furthered through his own reading. Conner believed he could compete academically; those that he could not outthink, he could outwork.[17]

But the obstacle of securing the necessary political appointment to the United States Military Academy still loomed large. Fox Conner saw one possible route from Calhoun County to West Point, New York—a path that passed through the nearby town of West Point, Mississippi.

In 1893, Fox Conner's Uncle Fuller was a man on his way up. After leaving the Slate Springs Academy, Fuller Fox established his law practice in West Point, the county seat of nearby Clay County, Mississippi. Fuller Fox also plunged into Mississippi politics; he became a state senator, a delegate to the 1892 Democratic national convention that nominated Grover Cleveland for president, then United States Attorney under President Cleveland.[18]

Just as Fuller Fox had helped Robert Conner make the transition from army to civilian life two decades earlier, so did he open the door for his nephew to enter military service.

Hernando De Soto Money, a former Confederate Army officer, represented northern Mississippi in Congress. Representative Money was a controversial figure. Another Mississippi politician once accused Money of taking a bribe from railroad interests. In the ensuing fight between the two men, Money's accuser threw a law book that struck the congressman in the head. H.D. Money had his enemies, but he also had his friends, including Fuller Fox. An astute politician, Money recognized the value of association with Fuller Fox, who eventually became both a congressman himself and a candidate for governor of Mississippi.[19]

Congressmen normally made appointments to West Point a year in advance of admission so that the appointee could adequately prepare for the academy's difficult academic entrance examinations. In May 1893, however, an opening unexpectedly arose for a young man from Congressman Money's district to join the class that would enter West Point the following month. Fuller Fox let H.D. Money know that his nephew wanted to go.

That was all it took.

On May 31, 1893, Congressman Money appointed Fox Conner of Slate Springs, Mississippi, to the West Point class that would convene in two weeks—provided he could pass the entrance exams.[20]

Conner's plan had succeeded. He would have the opportunity to pursue the life he had daydreamed of as he had worked the fields and read his stories. Fox Conner also received a valuable introduction to the effect that a powerful sponsor could have upon a young man's career.

CHAPTER 2

WEST POINT

We got sabers the other day so we ride with these now. A fellow
begins to feel pretty high ranking when he gets his saber.

—Fox Conner, 1897[1]

Fox Conner entered the gray and granite world of the United States Military Academy on June 15, 1893.

Having been appointed only two weeks before admission, Conner first faced the task of passing West Point's entrance examinations in reading, writing, spelling, history, geography, and arithmetic. As Conner took his tests, he trusted that the educational foundation laid by the Slate Springs Academy and his parents would be good enough.

It was not.

On June 19, 1893, West Point's Academic Board met and found candidate Fox Conner "not duly qualified for admission to the academy" due to deficient marks in grammar and arithmetic. An 1893 academy report noted the high failure rate of young men who had been appointed so near to the admission date. "The wonder is how some of these young men ever came to be selected to represent their districts at West Point," the report bemoaned. More charitably, the committee also recognized that most candidates required at least 6 months of preparation for the entrance tests, and that "many fail who might have succeeded had they had the benefit of the time for preparation."[2]

Bearing the weight of failure for the first time in his life, the pride of Slate Springs went home. But he did not abandon his dream.

Having failed only two subjects, Conner remained eligible for re-examination. Back in Calhoun County, Conner immersed himself in study for the next nine months. He drew upon all he knew and all that he could teach himself. On March 19, 1894, he travelled to New Orleans to retake the tests that would determine his future.

Conner passed his tests. On June 15, 1894, he again reported to Reception Day at the academy with 108 other appointees who hoped to become members of the West Point Class of 1898.[3]

Conner and his new classmates stood with heels together and arms straight down at their sides as sweat began to soak their Sunday suits in the summer sun. Cadets in gray uniforms spoke to the new men sharply and impersonally, with Northern accents much different from the familiar drawl of Calhoun County. Conner quickly recognized that a chasm separated plebes like him from the upperclassmen who barked at them.[4]

After keeping the new men at attention well past the point of comfort, the upperclassmen sent them inside one of the buildings. Without ceremony, the plebes shed their civilian clothes and put on their uniforms. The men inside loaded the newly gray-clad plebes with their bedding and belongings, then briskly marched them to their barracks, much as Conner had driven the gray beasts in his family's cotton fields.

In West Point's culture, as Conner wrote in a June 16 letter home, he and his fellow plebes were indeed no more than "beasts" to be tamed.

Conner had begun "Beast Barracks"—the initial three-week indoctrination of plebes. Conducted by upperclassmen with little faculty supervision, Beast Barracks essentially amounted to a hazing spree by upperclassmen.

Hazing took many forms. Upperclassmen "braced" Conner, by forcing him to stand for prolonged periods in an exaggerated position of attention: his palms turned outward to force the shoulders further back with his chin tucked down and abdomen sucked in making it hard to breathe. "They make you get your shoulders back until the back of it is full of wrinkles," Conner wrote his parents. "A fellow's bones ache so he can scarcely move after one of these drills."

West Point "yearlings," cadets who had just completed their own plebe years, hazed with zeal. Yearling corporals, assigned the tasks of instilling discipline in the newly arrived beasts, were especially harsh. Corporal William Connor singled out the new man from Mississippi. "The cadets who have namesakes in the new cadets … are worse on them than any others," wrote Fox. "They do this because they want the standing of their name kept up."

One of Conner's classmates described the hazing in 1894 to have been "very bad and really brutal." Fox Conner did not complain. "I don't care how hard they are on me as it will straighten me and develop me generally," Conner wrote his parents; he added that he liked academy life "even better than I had expected."

From Beast Barracks, Conner went into his first summer camp.[5] Each summer, incoming plebes, and the cadets who had just finished their first and third years, lived in tents on The Plain—the elm-lined parade ground leading down to the Hudson River. Despite its pleasant-sounding name, summer camp presented plebes like Conner with "the most trying time of the entire course," as one West Point instructor put it, in which first-year men were "divested nearly of all pleasure." Yearling corporals bellowed as the plebes ran, did calisthenics, and went on marches of up to 15 miles a day in the summer heat. Apart from the physical training, plebes also tended to camp latrines and performed other menial tasks for upperclassmen to instill the practice of obedience to superiors.

A greater challenge faced Cadet Conner once classes began on September 1, 1894.[6]

Conner's first-year courses included algebra, geometry, trigonometry, and surveying, as well as English and French. West Point grouped cadets into sections of twelve to fifteen men for each subject, based upon academic performance. The sections constantly changed after weekly exams held in each course; better-performing students rose while struggling cadets dropped. Failure in a single class normally led to dismissal from the academy or, at best, being "turned back" to the next class with the taint of having failed—a stigma Conner already bore.

An October 6, 1894 letter to his parents reveals Conner's sense of academic inadequacy as he struggled with the curriculum in his plebe year:

> If anything I have ever said, and I fear it has, has caused you to regret and reproach yourself for not giving me better opportunities, I am sorry for it, for I know that you have borne much worse fortune than you were able and that I did not use the opportunities I had in the right way. I am to some extent overcoming the habit of making my mistakes.

First-year men like Conner also wrestled with isolation from family and friends. Except for a furlough home after their second year, cadets remained at the academy for the entire four-year course. Through his letters home, however, Conner maintained contact with his loved ones in Mississippi.[7]

Each Sunday, after attending mandatory church services, Conner used his day off to write his family. His letters mostly described the ordinary details of life at the academy, ranging from comments on the weather and food of New York, to the fortunes of the West Point football team, to one of his classmates being court-martialed for refusing to go to church. Conner frequently ended his letters with lighthearted notes to his youngest sister, 10-year-old Nannie Gus. Conner shared with Nannie Gus one unusual experience in which, while horseback riding in his free time, he encountered two traveling minstrels with bagpipes and a monkey. Conner thought the monkey "was very much ashamed of the company he was forced to keep."

Conner's letters also kept his educator-parents apprised of his academic progress. By the end of his first year in early June 1895, one-third of the 109 men who had begun the course the previous summer had either resigned or been discharged. Conner, however, finished his plebe year ranked thirty-first of the remaining seventy-one cadets. After having failed the entrance examination in arithmetic in June 1893, Conner finished his plebe year ranked nineteenth in mathematics. He finished thirty-eighth in French—a subject that would factor in his future.[8]

On June 12, 1895, the academy held graduation ceremonies, which included Recognition Day for Conner's class. Nearly a year after arriving as beasts, Conner and his classmates themselves became yearlings. The men who formerly hazed and harassed them welcomed their fellow upperclassmen with smiles, handshakes, and slaps on the back. Fox Conner was even free to address William Connor by his first name.[9]

Fox returned to The Plain for his second summer camp, this time as a yearling. When not harassing plebes, Conner found time to return to a favorite pastime. The academy's library, with its high ornate ceilings and finely carved reading tables, provided a literary oasis. Conner began to read historical fiction. Among the leather-bound books on the library's mahogany shelves was *The Last Days of Pompeii*, written by the British author Sir Edward Bulwer-Lytton. *The Last Days of Pompeii* was a full-length novel of nearly 400 pages, which used the genre of historical fiction, presented in an action-adventure format, to describe the history of Pompeii and its destruction. Conner wrote home that he found it "one of the best books I ever read." That summer, he also read *Les Misérables* and *Ivanhoe*.[10]

Conner held his position in the class his second year, despite the increased difficulty of the curriculum, which included differential and integral calculus, analytical and descriptive geometry, French and Spanish, and military engineering such as bridge building.[11] Fox's West Point experience also helped him build bridges of a different sort.

Having lived in rural Mississippi, Fox Conner had little or no exposure to people from other parts of the United States. His early letters home, for example, referred mostly to fellow southerners, such as his fellow Mississippian Marcellus Spinks, Robert Maxey from Arkansas, and his roommate Alvan Read from Louisiana. Whether comparing the hominy of West Point to the grits back home, or writing Nannie Gus about the treats that "possum time" would bring her, Conner was thoroughly a Southern country boy when he entered West Point. He later joked that he was probably the only cadet who ever went to West Point barefooted.[12]

The ordeal of their plebe year, however, created strong ties among the seventy-one cadets who had survived it. Conner formed friendships with young men from across the country, such as Pennsylvanians William Nesbitt and Robert Davis, Henry Butner of North Carolina, Herbert Lafferty of Colorado, Chauncey Humphrey of Kansas, and Malin Craig of Missouri. The academy kept the cadets at West Point for two years before allowing a visit home in order to instill a common identity. Malin Craig was the grandson of a Union general; Fox Conner the son of a Confederate private, but as they worked and studied and marched together for meals at Grant Hall, they began to form a common bond as *American* officers. If Fox Conner perceived any irony in taking his meals at a mess hall named for the general who had commanded Union troops at Shiloh—where his uncle was killed and his father wounded—he made no mention of it.[13]

Conner also did his share of walking with his classmates. Cadets walked "punishment tours" to atone for demerits.[14] Wearing his full-dress uniform and carrying his weapon, Conner and his fellow "area birds" marched in the academy's central area during precious free time, going back and forth across the courtyard for hours at a time.

In his second year, Conner received 111 demerits. Only two men in the upper half of the class had more demerits, and most had far fewer. Malin Craig and Robert Davis, by comparison, had fifteen and thirty-six, respectively. Conner's two primary problems were tardiness and smoking. Academy regulations prohibited any use of tobacco. Tactical officers, known as "tacs," strictly enforced the tobacco regulations and often played a cat-and-mouse game to detect furtive smokers such as Conner, who had smoked since age 14.

As 1895 turned to 1896, Conner walked the academy's central area in the cold of a New York winter, his fingers numb and snow crunching underfoot. Once the weather began to warm at the academy, Conner's thoughts increasingly turned to Slate Springs, and to the family he had not seen in nearly two years. Fox Conner was ready for his furlough home.[15]

In June 1896, Fox Conner returned to Slate Springs for the summer. Apart from writing that he was looking forward to coon hunting, Conner left no record of the events of his furlough. Presumably, he followed the advice of one publication of the time to "prepare a lengthy and possibly exaggerated story" about his experiences at West Point and to "(not) fall in love if you can help it."[16]

When Conner returned to West Point in late August for the 1896–97 term, he wrote home that his return to the academy was "simply awful," and that he "had nothing to do but get homesick."[17] His studies, however, soon filled that void.

West Point's third-year curriculum emphasized scientific subjects on which Conner had received no prior schooling, such as anatomy, physiology, analytical mechanics, astronomy, chemistry, electricity, magnetism, geology, mineralogy, and the physics principles of wave motion. According to one West Point instructor, third-year studies were "the most trying and difficult part of the academic course."[18]

In January 1897, the class learned the results of mid-year examinations which, according to Conner, were "rather disastrous to our class." Two of the leading students in the Class of 1898, Malin Craig and Robert Davis, were both found to have been of "questionable proficiency" in chemistry. Conner's roommate Chauncey Humphrey and four others found deficient in that subject faced dismissal from the academy.[19]

Fox Conner, however, had a breakthrough semester.[20] Conner's high grades catapulted him to the first section of his class, a goal to which he had striven since his plebe year. His letters home in the spring of 1897 reported that he was holding his place in the upper echelon.

As he had done at home in Slate Springs, Conner continued to share knowledge with his family. He explained to his educator-parents what he was learning about the movement of light and sound waves through the atmosphere. The traits of an educator also appeared in Conner's letters to his two youngest siblings. He told Nannie Gus to "pay more attention to capitals & to the number of your verbs. Do that and you will soon be a fine letter writer." He complimented his younger brother Fuller's use of the word "absconded" in one letter.[21]

While Conner remained a faithful correspondent with his family in Mississippi, the climate and geography of New York began to distance Fox Conner from the place of his birth.[22]

From Trophy Point at West Point, where The Plain meets the Hudson, Conner could look northward. Tree-covered mountains with names like Storm King, Breakneck Ridge, and Bull Hill rose from the river, framing a view of the blue-green Hudson Highlands that rolled in the distance. The mountains beckoned. On weekends, Conner explored the highlands, alone with the sounds of birdsong and the soft fall of hooves on dirt trails. As he absorbed the cool solitude, the broiling cotton fields of Calhoun County seemed a world away. Conner wrote Nannie Gus that he found the mountain air "so pure and fresh and dry that it doesn't' seem to me that Mississippi air deserves to be called by the same name."[23]

By the end of Conner's third year, his affinity for the mountains, and position in the class, were both well established. His high grades, coupled with a near-halving of his demerits from 111 to 69, propelled Conner from thirty-first to fourteenth in class ranking.[24]

Conner attended his last summer camp on The Plain, then began his final year of classes in September 1897. Conner's graduation profile in *The Howitzer* yearbook portrayed a serious young man. His motto was "steadfastly purposing to lead a better life." Malin Craig's, by comparison, was "Well said; that was laid on with a trowel." Among the comments made of Conner were that he "wears perfumery on his handkerchiefs, and tobacco on his other paraphernalia" and "from his pay of $45 per month he always saves $90." The generally humorous poem honoring the fifty-nine graduates of the Class of 1898 also memorialized Conner's more reserved attributes:

> In the South, in Mississippi, there was born some years ago,
> In that region of plantations of the cotton and the hoe,
> One who's now a Ninety-Eighter, and a factor for her honor,
> Never subject to faux prattle, but is subject to Fox Conner.[25]

Conner advanced steadily through his final year's studies in civil engineering, military engineering, ordnance and gunnery, drill regulations, law, and history—a subject much under-emphasized in West Point's engineering curriculum of the time. He wrote Nannie Gus: "Graduation seemed a long way off when I reported here as a beast. I hardly dared to hope that I could graduate. Now I am hoping and making day dreams about how high I will graduate."[26]

Not everything, however, went smoothly for Conner in his last year at West Point.

The academy organized all cadets into four "companies," lettered A through D, with each cadet having a rank from private to captain. In his final year, Conner served as a sergeant in Company A, led by its captain, Malin Craig.[27]

In the fall of 1897, Company A received a new tactical officer to enforce discipline in the company.[28] The new "tac" himself had been the top graduate of the West Point Class of 1886; he knew all the cadet tricks, including the places where men hid to smoke. He enforced regulations to the point of excess, and Conner's demerits rose sharply in his final year. In addition to his habitual infractions for smoking and tardiness, Conner also received demerits for violations such as profanity and not bathing on schedule.

In a letter home, Conner referred to his new tactical officer as a "skisoid." The cadets also gave the new tac a different nickname related to his prior service as commander of an African-American cavalry troop. In time, the epithet "Nigger Jack" became softened to "Black Jack," but in 1897, First Lieutenant John J. Pershing was loathed by the men of Company A, who decided to strike back.

As a tactical officer, Pershing also enforced academy regulations during mealtimes. One day, Lieutenant Pershing entered the dining room at Grant Hall amid the low din of dozens of different conversations and the plinking of knives and forks on plates. But as Pershing strode down the center aisle, cadets stopped talking in mid-sentence. All movement ceased. Silence smothered the room, leaving only the sound of the lieutenant's boots echoing upon the floor.[29]

John J. Pershing had received the ultimate cadet insult—The Silence. For The Silence to succeed, all members of each of the four companies, from captains down to privates, had to be complicit, including Company A's sergeant, Fox Conner.

Relations between Pershing and the men of Company A only worsened in 1898. One cadet hatched a scheme to cause a bucket of water to fall onto Pershing, which resulted in the entire company being placed under arrest.[30] But as Company A pondered its next move in the clandestine battle with its tactical officer, hostilities of a far more serious nature erupted south of the nation's border.

On February 15, 1898, amid growing tension between the United States and Spain over America's support of Cuban revolutionaries, the American battleship *Maine* exploded in Havana Harbor, killing 260 sailors. A powerful and immediate urge for revenge arose across the United States. The *New York Journal* captured the nation's sentiment: "REMEMBER THE MAINE! TO HELL WITH SPAIN!"[31]

On April 25, 1898, the United States declared war on Spain. Like others in the nation, the cadets at West Point greeted the outbreak of war with "cheers" and "joy." The Secretary of War ordered the West Point superintendent to graduate the Class of 1898 immediately, without further study or testing. That evening, after a final parade in a downpour of rain, the men of the Class of 1898 were mustered into the Army as second lieutenants. Fox Conner requested cavalry duty. The Army instead assigned him to the artillery service.[32]

By the time Conner joined the long gray line of academy graduates, only fifty-nine remained of the original 109 young men who had sweated at attention on Reception Day in June 1894. Of the four Mississippians in the Class of 1898, Conner ranked the highest at seventeenth, followed by Marcellus Spinks at twentieth, Ira Welborn at thirty-ninth, and David Stone at the lowest or "goat" ranking in the class.[33]

The new lieutenants joined the officer corps of a tiny Regular Army of around 28,000 men stationed in widespread frontier posts. Spain had 80,000 soldiers in Cuba alone. At no time in its history had the United States entered a war with an army so small in relation to its population. President William McKinley issued a call for 125,000 volunteers to fight the Spanish in the Caribbean and also across the Pacific in the Philippine Islands. In response, more than a million Americans from across the nation sought to enlist. With the officers needed to lead those men in short supply, an immediate opportunity arose for the Class of 1898 to go to war.[34]

When they had begun their studies four years earlier, the Class of 1898 chose crimson as its class color.[35] That selection proved prophetic.

Since childhood, Fox Conner had longed to lead men in battle. His opportunity was now at hand.

CHAPTER 3

BIDING TIME

Q: Has he availed himself of his opportunities for improvement professionally?
A: Yes, to an unusual degree.

—Fox Conner's 1914 Efficiency Report[1]

Once the United States declared war on Spain in April 1898, most of the small Regular Army, including West Point's most recent graduates, went to assembly camps near the Gulf of Mexico for deployment to Cuba. Others reported to Pacific coast bases for an invasion of Spain's territory in the Philippines. Conner, however, did not figure into the Army's plans for either the Cuban island or the Philippine Islands.

He headed instead to Rhode Island.

On May 26, 1898, Second Lieutenant Fox Conner reported for coast artillery duty at Fort Adams on Narragansett Bay near Newport.[2] When not on guard against the unlikely event of a Spanish invasion of the upper Atlantic coastline, Conner served as a training officer for the volunteers and militiamen from New England who reported to Fort Adams in response to President William McKinley's call to arms.

Eager for battlefield service, Conner sent three requests to the Army Adjutant General's Office for transfer to a cavalry unit. His regimental commander approved each request, but no transfer orders ever came. While many of his classmates went off to war, Fox Conner stayed in New England, teaching other soldiers and watching the water. All he could see was a missed opportunity.

The United States military routed Spain. On May 1, 1898, the American Navy defeated its Spanish counterpart at Manila Bay, which opened the Philippines to occupation by American forces. In Cuba, the Navy blockaded the Spanish fleet in Santiago Harbor while the Army advanced on the city. Santiago fell on July 17 after Colonel Theodore Roosevelt and his Rough Riders, supported by a cavalry troop of African-Americans commanded by Black Jack Pershing, captured high ground known as the San Juan Heights. Spain sought an armistice, which went into effect on August 12, 1898.

The armistice suspended combat, but it did not end the war. As treaty negotiations with Spain dragged on through the autumn of 1898—longer than the fighting had lasted—the United States prepared to resume hostilities. The Army removed its heavy coast artillery guns from installations such as Fort Adams and shipped them to Cuba for use as siege weapons. Conner and his battery moved south as well in late September. After training at Fort Wheeler near Huntsville, Alabama, Conner and his men reported to Savannah, Georgia: a port of embarkation for soldiers being deployed to Cuba. They arrived on November 20.

For nearly a month, Conner worked to keep himself and his men ready as they awaited orders to ship out. Then word arrived in mid-December.

Spain and the United States had signed the Treaty of Paris on December 10, 1898. Cuba gained its independence as an American protectorate. In the Pacific, Spain sold the Philippines to the United States. The "splendid little war," as American Secretary of State John Hay termed it, had ended. Fox Conner had missed the Spanish–American War.

Conner eventually made it to Havana, Cuba in January 1899 as part of the American occupation force.[3] The Spanish left Havana without incident; they also left the city in disarray. Occupation troops maintained order and helped establish local government authority. Conner also worked to implement the American policy of buying rather than confiscating the weapons of the former Cuban rebels. He noted that the government frequently returned the guns to their prior owners once they joined "Rural Guard" units formed to maintain order in the countryside. "Reminds me of arming the Indians," Conner wrote home.

By 1900, American citizens had resumed travel to Cuba. That year, an adventuresome 21-year-old woman from the Hudson River Valley town of Ossining, New York went to Havana to visit an aunt and uncle stationed with the occupation force. By her own description, Virginia Brandreth was "never known for either style or beauty." Known to her family as "Bug," Virginia was fashionably full-figured, with dark brown hair worn in curls. She smiled with a broad grin that made her eyes narrow almost to a squint. Often speaking in a loud voice, a habit formed by talking with her hearing-impaired father, Bug Brandreth made an impression on most people.

But not Fox Conner.

Bug first saw Fox as he made his rounds through Havana on horseback with a fellow officer. Conner's tanned face and blue eyes, both features accentuated by his all-white uniform, captivated the young woman. She snapped a picture with her Kodak. Conner, however, did not stop to visit with his admirer, as most young officers would have done. With an air that Bug thought conceited, Conner continued on his way. Bug learned that other young women had likewise been spurned by the young officer. Bug wrote in her memoir that Conner had developed a reputation as "the woman hater" of Havana.

Bug Brandreth returned to Ossining while Fox Conner stayed in Cuba. As the work of the occupation force wound down in mid-1900, Lieutenant Conner awaited orders for his next assignment. By then, the American Army was embroiled in a vicious guerrilla war in the Philippines against rebels who had no intention of submitting to a different Western overlord.

Many of Conner's classmates fought in the conflict known as the Philippine Insurrection, including eight who died there. Conner's former West Point tac, John J. Pershing, won fame in the Philippines for displaying a combination of military and diplomatic skill in subduing Muslim warriors who had declared *jihad* against Americans on the island of Mindanao.

Fox Conner's orders, though, sent him to Washington, D.C., where he served garrison duty at Washington Barracks from August 1900 through early October 1901. Conner helped soothe his disappointment at again being passed over for combat by retreating into reading at the base library, where he studied works on artillery theory and other literature. On January 25, 1901, Conner received promotion to the rank of first lieutenant; on September 23, he became Captain Conner. The examining board that promoted Conner to captain less than a year after his previous advancement in rank noted the marked improvement in his level of artillery knowledge.

That same year, Conner suffered from malaria, most likely contracted while serving in Havana. A much more pleasant effect of Conner's Cuban service also manifested during his time at Washington Barracks.

In the year since Bug Brandreth's return to New York, she had kept on her bedroom dresser the snapshot she had taken of Fox Conner in Cuba.[4] When Bug learned that Fox was stationed in Washington, she resolved to meet the aloof young man. In what she described as a "planned attack," Bug travelled to Washington in early March 1901, ostensibly to visit her friend Cornelia Knox and to attend the second inauguration of President McKinley. Bug then finagled an invitation to a tea party at Washington Barracks, in the hope that Conner might attend. Recalling that the young officer had shown her no interest in their previous encounter, Bug devised a strategy: "If he refused to meet me," she wrote in her memoir, "I would sprain my ankle and fall at his feet."

Her contingency plan proved unnecessary. According to Bug, it was "love at first sight." The romance between Fox Conner and Bug Brandreth proved the adage of opposites attracting. As Bug finally talked with the man she had only imagined from the photograph, she learned that the behavior she had mistaken for arrogance was more a product of shyness in social settings. Bug found herself more attracted to Fox's quiet sturdiness and polite drawl than she had been to his blue eyes. Equally so, Bug made conversation comfortable, in a way Fox had not known before, which encouraged him to put aside his books and give romance a try.

Bug stayed in Washington for three weeks. She and Fox saw each other daily, but always in the company of others in that era of chaperonage. On her last night in the city, the two found themselves alone on a beach beneath one of the city's old sea walls. As they strolled on the soft sand, Fox summoned the courage to put his arm around Bug's shoulder. Being much shorter, Bug nestled under Fox's arm. She waited for her beau to stop and turn toward her, But Fox kept walking. "You fool," Bug thought. "Why don't you kiss me?"

They parted the next day. Fox saw Bug off at the train station, but not before taking care of unfinished business. As she was leaving, Fox gave Bug their first kiss.

The couple met the following week in New York City. They spent a rainy afternoon circling Central Park in a horse-drawn carriage, savoring the opportunity to be alone. That evening, Fox met Bug, her mother, and her sister for dinner. The Brandreth ladies then attended a military drill exhibition at Madison Square Garden in which Conner and his men participated. Bug could hear Fox shouting commands over the sounds of bugles and rolling caissons, as he maneuvered his battery of horse-drawn field artillery through intricate turns and alignments. The performance thrilled Bug, who memorialized her evening with a poem:

> You may talk about Napoleon,
> Grant and Kaiser Bill;
> But I tell you they're not in it,
> When Conner leads the drill.
>
> Blow the bugles, beat the drums,
> Let martial music thrill;
> Sure 'tis the finest sight on earth,
> When Conner leads the drill.

In May, Bug returned to see Fox in Washington. During a twilight cruise on the Potomac River, Fox noticed that Bug was shivering in the evening chill. He suggested a hot toddy to ward off the cold. Then the couple had a second drink. The alcohol placed Conner at greater ease as he began to put into words the emotions that had swirled within him for weeks. "That was his undoing," Bug wrote in her memoir. "Before the effects wore off, he asked me to marry him!"

Bug said yes. The couple then faced the matter of telling her father.

"I will never allow any daughter of mine to marry in the Army," Bug's father had long proclaimed. Franklin Brandreth presented the picture of Yankee prosperity, having inherited his father's patent medicine business as well as his fortune. Brandreth, who had been a colonel in the New York State militia, believed that army life offered a woman nothing but hardship, so he had forbidden his three daughters from even attending social functions at which young officers would be present. Now his daughter was betrothed to one.[5]

Fox Conner travelled to Ossining on July 4, 1901 to meet Colonel Brandreth at Cliff Cottage, the family's two-story Victorian manor. The beautifully bound books that filled the Cliff Cottage library, where the nearly deaf Brandreth spent much of his time, caught Conner's attention. To Bug's great relief, the two men liked each other immediately. Fox wasn't much on small talk. Colonel Frank couldn't hear anyway. They both loved books and they both loved Bug. That was enough.

In November 1901, to be closer to Bug, Conner secured a transfer to Fort Hamilton in Brooklyn, New York, where he took command of the 123rd Coast Artillery Company. Fox also began to form a close relationship with Bug's family. When the Brandreths invited him to their hunting camp in the Adirondack Mountains of northern New York, he gladly accepted.

What Conner saw there awed him.

The estate, known as Brandreth Park, covered more than 42 square miles in sparsely populated Hamilton County, New York. The property's jewel, Brandreth Lake, gleamed with 900 acres of clear water, which reflected the images of surrounding Adirondack Mountains twice as high as those that had captivated Conner at West Point. Trails wound through the woods to smaller ponds. The Brandreth family's complex of cabins, named Camp Good-Enough, dotted the edge of the main lake. As at Cliff Cottage, Colonel Frank kept his camp stocked with books. Conner found the combination of lake and literature irresistible.

Fox enjoyed the taste of affluence that neither his profession nor his own family could provide. In the mountains near West Point, Conner had begun to leave his Mississippi life behind. In the Adirondacks, the Brandreth way of life pulled him away forever.

Fox Conner joined the Brandreth family in an evening wedding at Cliff Cottage on June 4, 1902. The marriage of Colonel Brandreth's daughter made the society pages of the *New York Times*.[6] Bug's maids of honor included her Washington accomplice, Cornelia Knox. Captain George Barney, with whom Conner had served in both Rhode Island

and Cuba, acted as his best man; Conner's West Point classmate Marcellus Spinks also stood in the wedding.

Conner and Spinks were the only Mississippians there. Perhaps the cost and difficulty of travel from Calhoun County to New York exceeded what Blind Bob Conner and his family could manage. Bug seemed to view it differently. "Fox's family had completely ignored me," she wrote. "I imagined they were horrified that their son, a dyed-in-the-wool rebel, was to marry a Yankee."

The reality of having married into the Army soon confronted Bug Conner. Instead of a honeymoon, she and Fox immediately returned to Fort Hamilton, a place Bug found "most unattractive."[7] To maintain a semblance of her carefree days at Cliff Cottage, Bug played her beloved violin, as she had done in the music room of her father's mansion. Still, the echo that resonated most through Bug's new home was Colonel Frank's warning about the hardships of life as a military wife.

Bug eventually adjusted to life as an army wife. The sounds of children then began to fill their home at Fort Hamilton. Daughter Betty Virginia Conner arrived November 21, 1903, followed by a son, Fox Brandreth Conner, born June 23, 1905. Not surprisingly for a woman who preferred to be called "Bug," she nicknamed the children "Betsey" and "Tommy."

Although their years at Fort Hamilton brought contentedness to the young Conner family, Fox grew restless in his profession. He later wrote that he had "little or no interest" in his coast artillery duties. To fill the time, Conner continued to read works at the Fort Hamilton library on subjects ranging from artillery regulations to military law.[8]

Those solitary and scholarly pursuits led to Fox Conner's first significant professional opportunity.

In 1903, Congress enacted military reforms proposed by Secretary of War Elihu Root. The new legislation created a general staff system, headed by a chief of staff, to better coordinate Army operations. Secretary Root also established schools at each post, where officers could receive basic instruction in the theories and practices of warfare. Root also founded specialized schools for infantrymen, engineers, artillerists, and other branches of service. Those officers who exhibited "the most aptitude and intelligence" were to be recommended by their superiors for the two-year General Service and Staff College at Fort Leavenworth, Kansas. Atop the Army's new educational system, Root also created the Army War College in Washington, D.C. to study military strategy, national defense policy, and to conduct war planning.

As Fox Conner continued his professional studies at the Fort Hamilton garrison school, his academic aptitude came to the attention of the post commander, Colonel George Greenough. The colonel considered Captain Conner "studious, very competent, and hardworking." In Conner's 1905 Efficiency Report, Colonel Greenough gave Conner "excellent" ratings in all categories. Greenough further noted that the captain would be "well adapted" for service in the newly created General Staff Corps once he received the proper training. "Captain Conner is a very thorough man," Greenough wrote in 1905; he added that Conner "should be given opportunity."

That opportunity arose in the summer of 1905 when the Army's chief of artillery assigned Fox Conner directly to the second-year Staff College phase of the Leavenworth program—which focused upon training for high command service—without Conner's prior attendance at either his artillery branch school or the first year of the Leavenworth course. The school's commandant, Brigadier General J. Franklin Bell, doubted that officers such as Conner, who had not attended the first year of the course, had a fair chance to succeed in the second phase of the course.

Through his seven years of service, Fox Conner had never gotten the opportunity to distinguish himself in battle. His intellect, however, ultimately placed Conner in position to compete for a spot among the Army's new elite.

On August 20, 1905, Fox Conner reported for duty at Leavenworth's General Service and Staff College.[9] Fort Leavenworth also housed the United States Disciplinary Barracks where convicted military personnel served their prison sentences. At times, students such as Conner appeared to have the more difficult existence.

In an effort to simulate the pressure under which staff officers would have to function during war, the Staff College heaped more work upon the students than most could accomplish in a day. Anxious to avoid the stigma of failure, Conner and his fellow officers drove themselves by working late into the night.

Leavenworth's "applicatory method" drew heavily upon military history to analyze the quandaries faced by an army's high command and to devise solutions under rapidly changing conditions. Students learned, through map exercises, to plan and control the movement of troops from afar. In 1905, the American Army lacked accurate military maps of the United States, so Conner and his classmates worked with German maps of the Lorraine area of France made during the Franco-Prussian War of 1870–71. Leavenworth also imported the German Army's five-paragraph format for field orders, which created a uniform method of communication from headquarters down to field units. As one student later put it, the Leavenworth-trained staff officers at all levels of command "learned to speak the same language."

Leavenworth also emphasized the importance of foreign language. The head of the Leavenworth language department acknowledged the "severe strain" of the language course. After Conner attended to his daily work, which included up to five hours a day in classroom language lessons, he spent hours each evening repeating the French phrases his gramophone scratched out. Bug recalled that in the spring of 1906, before she forced him take a break, her husband had pushed himself to the point that he "did not know what he was doing" and "could not recognize anyone."

Fox Conner graduated from the Staff College on July 2, 1906; he ranked second in his class. Conner also began to establish his credentials as a military scholar in 1906 when he published an article that critiqued a book about a pivotal battle in the Russo-Japanese War of 1904–05. General Bell, despite his earlier reservations concerning Conner's prospects, recommended that the War Department assign the captain to the Army War College to complete his education.[10]

The Army, though, sent Conner's to Fort Riley, Kansas, where he reported in July 1906 as the lone staff officer for a field artillery unit. The schoolmaster's son also found himself at the head of his own classroom at Fort Riley's School of Application for Cavalry and Field Artillery. Brigadier General Theodore J. Wint, commanding general of Army forces in the region, observed field maneuvers that Conner had helped plan and conduct in the summer of 1906. The general noted with approval the "particular exactitude" that characterized Conner's planning. "It is but just," wrote General Wint, "to reserve more conspicuous notice for Captain Fox Conner."

Conner also worked with Captain John Hartman of the cavalry to introduce an experimental Leavenworth-style applicatory course to teach the veteran troopers and artillerymen at Fort Riley. Colonel E.S. Godfrey, Fort Riley's commandant, praised the "zeal and abilities" of Conner and Hartman, but he nonetheless concluded that the duo's "theoretical instruction was out of place at this practical school." Godfrey recommended that the applicatory course be discontinued. Conner's aptitude, however, soon found a more fitting application.

By April 1907, Conner's former Leavenworth commandant, J. Franklin Bell, had risen to the position of Army chief of staff. Despite the protest of Colonel Godfrey at Fort Riley, General Bell transferred Conner to the Army War College in Washington, D.C. In addition to joining the incoming 1907 class, Conner also served as the field artillery's representative to the War College section charged with strategic studies and planning.[11] General Bell directed Conner to help devise the tactical problems to be studied at the upcoming War College program, even though Conner himself had not yet attended the course. Among other things, the 1907/08 War College studied the possibility of a Pacific war between the United States and Japan. Wargaming consistently resulted in America's loss of both Hawaii and the Philippines.

After he completed the War College course in 1908, Conner stayed at the college for the next three years as an instructor. Two different War College presidents, Brigadier Generals W.W. Wotherspoon and Tasker Bliss, each praised Conner's abilities as an educator. Officers senior in rank to Conner began to attend his War College courses, a situation Conner found unsettling. For example, Lieutenant Colonel Hunter Liggett, an officer with a wealth of field experience and 19 years more service than his teacher, attended Conner's 1910 class. For one complex exercise, Conner assigned his West Point classmate Malin Craig to work as Liggett's assistant. The working relationship between

Liggett and Craig that began in Conner's War College class would prove beneficial in the coming years.

While at the War College, Conner continued to establish his credentials as a leading American artillerist. The U.S. Field Artillery Association named Conner to its executive council. He helped draft the Army's field artillery regulations and served on a board of officers that made recommendations for modernizing the Army's artillery. In May 1910, Conner published an article, "Field Artillery in Cooperation with the Other Arms." Additionally, Conner improved his French language skills at the War College and he also learned to read German in order to study original works by the artillery theorists of Europe's two most potent armies. Generals Wotherspoon and Bliss each commented favorably upon Conner's foreign language skills.

Most importantly, Generals Bliss and Wotherspoon—each of whom would eventually serve as Army chief of staff—recognized Fox Conner's potential for service at the highest levels of command. Conner also formed productive relationship with younger War College officers such as Major John McAuley Palmer. At the War College, Conner and Palmer shared a disdain for working with foreign battlefield maps. "We groused bitterly," Palmer recalled, "because we had to use German maps of the Franco-German frontier in the area around Metz."

Their 4 years at the War College in Washington brought momentous events to the Conner family. Fox's father died on January 21, 1908 at the age of 64. Robert Conner's headstone bore the inscription: "Here Lies A Confederate Soldier." The grave monument for Blind Bob Conner also proclaimed: "Whereas I Was Blind Now I See." Fox and Bug Conner also welcomed another daughter, Florence, born on Halloween in 1910.[12]

As Conner's War College assignment neared completion in 1911, several career options opened.[13] He declined military attaché positions in Mexico and Turkey. At Bug's urging, Conner accepted a position on the West Point faculty so that the young Conner family could be nearer to Bug's parents and to Brandreth Lake. But as the Conners made plans to return to Fox's alma mater, they learned that he had said yes too quickly.

An opportunity arose for Conner to serve one year in a French artillery regiment and to thereafter attend *L'École Supérieure de Guerre*, the

French war college. Conner, however, had already given his commitment to return to West Point. Once again, as when Colonel Greenough had initially recommended him for general staff service, Fox Conner found himself the beneficiary of an older officer's sponsorship: General Wotherspoon, who recognized the value that the assignment in France would have to the young artillery captain's career, intervened to have a different officer sent to West Point so that Conner could go to France.

★ ★ ★ ★ ★

As Fox Conner and his family traveled to France in July 1911, a young man from Abilene, Kansas began his own journey through the military profession. Dwight D. Eisenhower, known as "Ike," had hoped to attend the United States Naval Academy. A Kansas senator sponsored a competitive exam to select his appointees to the service academies. Eisenhower did not receive the appointment to Annapolis, but the senator offered him the chance to go to West Point instead. Ike gratefully accepted the opportunity to receive a free college education and to play football.[14]

★ ★ ★ ★ ★

On October 1, 1911, Fox Conner reported for duty with the French 22nd Field Artillery Regiment based in Versailles, France.[15] The family lived in a hotel across from the grand Palace of Versailles, then moved to a rented home around a mile away. From mornings that began with the aroma of freshly baked croissants, to evenings enjoying the inebriating sweetness of white Barsac wine, Fox and Bug embraced French culture, and especially the delights of nearby Paris.

Conner's French language skills blossomed, in part because he and Bug employed a live-in housekeeper, Marie, who spoke no English. By 1912, Conner had become fluent in French; he was able to argue in French with a bank teller over the bank's check-writing practices. As was his habit, Conner also spent evenings ensconced in his study, where he developed an appreciation of French literature—of a sort. Bug learned from Marie that in addition to reading works by French military theorists, Fox also indulged in risqué French books of the type banned in the United States.

Most importantly, Fox Conner gained insight into the French military. He learned of France's pride in the *"soixante-quinze,"* the 75mm field artillery piece capable of firing up to twenty rounds per minute without the necessity of resighting the gun after each shot. Conner also came to understand the shame that permeated the French Army over its defeat in the Franco-Prussian War, which resulted in France's loss of the provinces of Alsace and Lorraine in 1871. Despite the passage of four decades, France's desire for revenge—and for recapture of the lost provinces—still smoldered.

As Conner served with the French Army in 1912, the War Department unexpectedly summoned him home before he could attend the French war college. Congressional opponents of Secretary Root's reforms, concerned that the General Staff Corps would become an isolated oligarchy, passed the "Manchu" legislation, which limited officers below the rank of major to a maximum of four years of general staff duty during any 6-year period of service.[16] At the time of the law's enactment, Conner had been on general staff service for nearly five years. The War Department therefore "Manchu'd" the Conners home on July 24, 1912.[17]

After an extended leave at Brandreth Lake through late November 1912, the Conner family headed west by train for Fox's second tour with the 6th Field Artillery at Fort Riley.[18] The Conners met another officer also travelling to Fort Riley. Bug recalled that the young cavalry officer sat with a stony expression and with a fearsome saber across his lap. He spoke, however, with a high and squeaky voice. That voice, among other traits, came to distinguish Lieutenant George S. Patton. The two officers and their wives formed a lasting friendship.

The Conner family spent a pleasant 1913 at Fort Riley, where Fox commanded an artillery battery. In January 1914, amid growing tension between the United States and its southern neighbor, the 6th Field Artillery received orders to deploy on the Mexican border. A thunderstorm hammered Fort Riley as the regiment scrambled to ready its equipment, animals, and men for the 800-mile journey southward to El Paso, Texas. As Conner dug through his attic to find his gear, he heard his 10-year-old daughter Betsey bawling in fear that her newborn pet guinea pigs would drown in the storm. Fox ran outside, as driving rain pelted him, to rescue the tiny creatures and calm his daughter's fear.

Conner sweated through the summer of 1914 on the Texas–Mexico border, where temperatures often exceeded 100°F. No record exists of his unit being involved in any hostile action. But while Captain Conner and his men uneventfully defended their border, his former comrades in the French Army were steadily retreating from theirs.

In early August 1914, war erupted across Europe.[19] Great Britain, France, Belgium and Russia (joined by Italy in 1915) formed the "Allies" who went to war against the "Central Powers." led by Germany and the Austro-Hungarian Empire. France launched a long-planned offensive into Alsace-Lorraine to recover its lost territory. Germany easily stopped the French advance; it then attacked through Belgium to invade France. The German Army overran the French, British, and Belgian forces in its path and moved to within 30 miles of Paris before French troops, under the command of French General Joseph Jacque Joffre, stopped the Germans at the Battle of the Marne in early September 1914. With neither side able to achieve quick victory, the opposing armies dug into a system of trenches that ran from the English Channel to the Swiss border, from which they began a deadly war of attrition along the Western Front of the conflict known as the Great War.[20]

Fox Conner followed the events of September 1914 from a hospital bed in Texas, wherein he endured the alternating high fever and teeth-chattering chills of a recurrence of his malaria. Once recovered, Conner took command of a battery in the 5th Field Artillery Regiment, based at Fort Sill, Oklahoma.[21] Conner spent his first Christmas away from Bug and the children when his battery was deployed to the Mexican border in Arizona from December 1914 through late January 1915.

While at Fort Sill, Captain Conner also taught at the Army's School of Fire for Field Artillery located there. The school's commandant, impressed by Conner's abilities as an educator, recommended that Conner succeed him as head of the school. Also in 1915, Conner published an article in the *Field Artillery Journal* that the journal editors considered to be "of a highly controversial nature." Conner critiqued an article by a fellow artillery officer on the technical subject of "lost motion and jump" in American field artillery guns. Conner labeled the article's conclusions "worthless" and "misleading." He cited French artillery theorists and the example offered by the French *soixante-quinze* field gun to argue that the American artillery-man deserved better weapons than those which the Army was providing.

While at Fort Sill, Conner also worked on weapons development. He participated in early efforts to employ aircraft for artillery spotting. Also, in July 1915, Conner served on a board of officers sent to a Caterpillar tractor factory in Enid, Oklahoma, to assess the suitability of its equipment for military purposes. The board favorably reported on the potential utility of vehicles using tracks, rather than wheels, to move across difficult battlefield terrain.

In Europe, the battlefields had indeed gotten difficult for the Allies. On the war's Eastern Front, Germany routed Russia in several battles in 1915. With Germany's attention focused eastward, the French, British, and Belgians undertook major offensives against entrenched German positions on the Western Front, which succeeded only in generating massive Allied casualties, particularly to troops under the command of France's "Hero of the Marne," General Joseph Joffre.

The United States remained officially neutral; however, public opinion in America steadily tilted toward the Allies after a German submarine torpedoed the British ocean liner *Lusitania* in May 1915. More than a thousand civilians, including 128 Americans, had perished. As the possibility of American involvement in the war began to grow, the War Department needed trained observers to monitor how the war was being fought. In late 1915, with his two-year Manchu field service obligation satisfied, the War Department ordered Captain Conner to return to France as a wartime observer. Conner's experience in the French Army, his French language skills, and his knowledge of the artillery doctrines of both France and Germany made his an ideal selection as Washington's eyes and ears on the Western Front, where neither side could do much more than rain artillery shells upon each other's trenches.

Conner left Fort Sill on November 21, 1915, Betsey's 12th birthday. One of the rare surviving letters between Fox and Bug reveals the heavy heart with which he left his family. "I am not ashamed to say," Fox confided to Bug, "that I have been furtively wiping my eyes all the morning." Fox closed the letter to his "Blessed Bug" by telling her: "I love all of you more than you can imagine. Kiss all my babies."

As Conner's train headed toward Washington, the ache in his heart gave way to a sharp pain in his right lower abdomen.[22] The pain abated, so Conner pressed on to Washington, rather than detraining to see a doctor. That decision nearly cost Fox Conner his life.

Once in Washington, Conner underwent emergency surgery. Physicians determined that his problem had begun as acute appendicitis. The pain had lessened after his appendix burst, but infected pus from the ruptured appendix had permeated his abdominal cavity. A potentially fatal peritonitis condition then developed. According to Bug, Fox's surgeons had little optimism about saving his life.

Conner survived, but he remained hospitalized for more than 6 weeks. As the Germans and French began their titanic clash at Verdun in February 1916, Conner could again only read about the war from a hospital bed. After three months of convalescence, Conner returned to duty as an instructor at Fort Sill on March 8, 1916.

While the European war remained a foreign news story to most Americans in early 1916, a much more direct threat arose on the nation's southern border. On March 9, Mexican insurgents under the command of Francisco "Pancho" Villa crossed the border and killed seventeen Americans in a raid on Columbus, New Mexico. Earlier in the year, Villa's forces had also killed American civilians in Mexico. Not willing to wait for Villa's next move, President Woodrow Wilson ordered the Army to launch a "Punitive Expedition" to enter Mexico and capture or kill Villa.[23]

President Wilson named one of his brightest generals to lead the incursion into Mexico: John J. Pershing. In a controversial move a decade earlier, Theodore Roosevelt had promoted Black Jack Pershing, over 762 superior officers, directly from captain to brigadier general. For the Mexican operation, Pershing selected several of the Army's most promising young officers to accompany him, including George Patton.

Fox Conner, though, stayed in Oklahoma and continued to teach other soldiers as his contemporaries, once again, left to fight in a foreign land.

By 1916, Conner had been a captain for nearly 15 years. Although he had passed the exam for promotion to the rank of major in April 1913, no vacancies for an artillery major had opened. In mid-1916, however, a spot came available for a major on the staff of Army Inspector

General E.A. Garlington. To avail himself of Conner's artillery expertise, Garlington offered Conner both the position and the promotion. Fox accepted. In July 1916 Major Conner and his family left Fort Sill for the Inspector General's bureau in Washington, D.C.[24]

Conner eventually made it to Mexico. In August 1916, he accompanied his former War College President Tasker H. Bliss, then serving as the Army's assistant chief of staff, on an inspection of Pershing's forces. Conner took the occasion to visit with his friend Patton, who had gained notoriety for killing a Mexican general and returning to base with the dead commander strapped to the hood of his car. While on the border, Conner also conducted a "curtain of fire" exercise in November for National Guard artillery forces stationed near Brownsville, Texas.

★ ★ ★ ★ ★

Fox Conner spent much of November and December 1916 at Fort Sam Houston in San Antonio, Texas, which served as a training facility for National Guard troops. The fort also housed the headquarters for the Army's Southern Department, whose chief inspector, Lieutenant Colonel Eli A. Helmick, worked closely with Conner to improve the readiness of the guardsmen being sent to the border.[25]

Also assigned to Fort Sam Houston in late 1916 was First Lieutenant Dwight D. Eisenhower, who had graduated from West Point in 1915 despite what he termed a "staggering catalogue of demerits."[26] Using language strangely similar to Bug Conner's description of Fox in Cuba, the wife of one officer at Fort Sam Houston considered Lieutenant Eisenhower to have been "the woman hater" of the post; nonetheless, the woman introduced her young friend Mamie Doud to the lieutenant from Kansas.

Eisenhower had applied to join Pershing's Punitive Expedition, but he was not selected. Instead, Eisenhower served as an inspector and instructor of National Guard infantry units at Fort Sam Houston. Despite the similarities of their assignments, as well as their demeanor toward the opposite sex, Major Conner and Lieutenant Eisenhower did not meet during the six weeks they were both at Fort Sam Houston in late 1916.

The careers of Fox Conner, Eli Helmick, and Dwight Eisenhower would, however, eventually intersect.

★ ★ ★ ★ ★

By February 1917, the American military venture into Mexico had ended without the capture of Pancho Villa, but with stability having been restored to the border. That same month, though, American–German relations markedly deteriorated.

In early February, Germany announced that it would sink, without warning, any ships—including American vessels—suspected of aiding the Allied war effort. Then on February 28, President Wilson revealed the contents of an intercepted telegram from German Foreign Secretary Arthur Zimmerman, who had proposed a German–Mexican alliance under which Mexico would declare war on the United States and recover Texas, New Mexico, and Arizona if victorious. The news moved American sentiment to the brink of war. When German submarines torpedoed three American vessels without warning in March 1917, killing fifteen American sailors, the die was cast.[27]

On April 2, 1917, President Wilson went before Congress to obtain a declaration of war against Germany on the grounds that "the world must be made safe for democracy." The measure moved rapidly through Congress. On April 6, 1917, the United States declared war against the European superpower.

As the United States entered the Great War in April 1917, Major Fox Conner was a 42-year-old officer with only limited troop experience and a worrisome history of health problems. Unlike many of his contemporaries, Conner had not seen combat in Cuba or in the Philippines or in Mexico. Despite his knowledge of artillery doctrine, he was not on duty with an artillery unit at the war's outset, nor was he a member of the General Staff Corps for which he had received specialized training.

The American Army would certainly need competent inspectors as it attempted to mobilize for the worst war the world had yet seen. The safe bet would have been that Fox Conner would again remain home while his compatriots went off to France.

But then France—or at least the embodiment of the French Army—came to America for a visit.

CHAPTER 4

GETTING STARTED

It would seem that there has hardly been enough appreciation shown for the value
of this first work, and the spirit in which the American General Staff conducted it.
—French Major Edouard Réquin, 1919[1]

The message that the nation was at war reached American naval vessels, at sea and in port, within five minutes of President Woodrow Wilson's signing the war resolution on April 6, 1917. At berths along America's coastlines, warships greeted the news with the deafening bellow of wide-open steam horns. As the bass tones resonated across the water, the higher pitched whistles of smaller watercraft, including boats on the Potomac River in the nation's capital, joined the cacophony. Bug Conner recalled that Washington, D.C. "teemed with excitement" that Good Friday.[2]

As word spread across the nation, people rushed from their homes and shops to gather at town halls and churches. Newsboys carried the extra editions of the day's newspapers. William Randolph Hearst's *New York American* of April 6, 1917 featured a soaring eagle spanning the width of the front page with the headline "WAR WITH GERMANY" borne upon its wings. Across the continent, the April 6 *Tacoma Times* headline proclaimed: "U.S. IS IN IT AT LAST!"

Few in America, though, understood what the United States had actually gotten into.

America entered the war on the side of an alliance veering toward defeat. On the Eastern Front, a string of German victories and the rising tide of Bolshevik revolution had forced the abdication of Russian Czar

Nicholas II in March 1917, which left the alliance's eastern power on the verge of collapse. War weariness also beset America's new French and British allies. More than a million French lives had been lost on the Western Front since 1914. In April 1917, mutiny had erupted in the French Army after a failed offensive produced 130,000 more casualties for only minimal gains in territory.[3]

As Fox Conner put it: "Bleak indeed were the Allied prospects—except for America!"[4]

In Conner's view, the American declaration of war "gave the Allies new hope at a time when hope was bitterly needed." France's Hero of the Marne, Marshal Joseph Joffre, concurred. He wrote in his memoir that America's involvement offered "a ray of hope" that "pierced the gloom which enveloped us." By April 1917, though, Joffre no longer led the French Army. After the heavy losses of 1915 and 1916 had failed to produce any significant change on the Western Front, the French government removed Joffre from command. With little need for the marshal's services in Paris, France dispatched its national hero to Washington in late April to discuss—and influence—America's initial plans for participation in the war.[5]

Great Britain also sent a delegation to Washington. As the United States began planning to participate in its first coalition war since the American Revolution, the British and French vied for the position of primary influence upon their new American allies. The British initially held the advantage of a common language with the United States. The war, however, was in France. American planners at the Army War College recognized that the United States Army would have to land at French ports, be transported on French railroads, live on French land, and otherwise coordinate a myriad of details with the French government. The War College, therefore, needed a liaison officer to communicate effectively with the Frenchman Joffre and his staff.

Fox Conner's fluency in French, plus his year of service in the French Army, made him an ideal selection. As one of the few American officers with both Leavenworth and War College training, Conner also grasped the issues that confronted the American high command. Fox Conner, therefore, received his first wartime assignment when the War

Department appointed him the liaison officer between America's War College planners and Joffre's delegation.[6]

Joffre captivated the American public.[7] Conner accompanied him to New York City in May 1917. More than 25,000 people jammed into Battery Park in lower Manhattan to see the 65-year-old French marshal, whose big belly and bushy white eyebrows and moustache reminded some of a grandfatherly French peasant. In Washington, D.C., "Papa" Joffre addressed the United States Senate. When he uttered a single phrase—"*Vivent les Etats Unis!*"[8]—senators abandoned decorum and "yelled like college boys at a football game." Joffre knew he had clout in America. He intended to use it.

In meetings with the Americans, Marshal Joffre got to the point: both the British and French were running out of men, so unless America supplied a quick infusion of soldiers into the trenches, the war would be lost once Germany turned its full weight westward after finishing off Russia. "Lavish with advice," as Conner put it, Joffre thought that Americans should be drafted directly into the French and British Armies—a concept Conner strongly opposed. Joffre refrained from raising the idea publicly only after the War Department vehemently rejected a similar British proposal.

Instead, Joffre suggested that the United States send a single division of its own troops to France, under an American commander, "to show as soon as possible the American flag upon the French front." Joffre emphasized the positive effect the sight of American soldiers would have upon the dangerously low morale of both the French military and citizenry. As liaison officer, Conner took Joffre's idea to the War College, where Lieutenant Colonel John McAuley Palmer served as one of America's primary war planners. Conner and Palmer, who had worked together at the War College in 1911, immediately recognized the fundamental problem with Joffre's proposal to send an American division to France.

The United States had no divisions.

Although American military doctrine considered the division to be the primary tactical unit to be employed in large-scale warfare, America entered the Great War with no fighting organization larger than a regiment.[9] As Conner described it, the American Army had mostly functioned as a "police guard" on the Mexican border and in America's foreign territories; the separate regiments had almost no experience working together as components of a larger force. Also, the United States had neglected to modernize its artillery, despite the recommendations of the 1911 board on which Conner had served. "We never prepared in time of peace," Conner said, "the material we knew we would need in time of war." Major Edouard Réquin of Joffre's staff bemoaned that "it was nothing less than astounding to see in what a state of military unpreparedness the United States had undertaken to enter the war."[10]

John McAuley Palmer also suspected an ulterior motive behind Joffre's idea to send a vanguard American division: in Palmer's view, Joffre doubted the American public's resolve to bear the hardships of war, and he believed that only the loss of America's sons in the Western Front's trenches would cement its commitment to defeating Germany. "He wanted us to send a division abroad at once," Palmer wrote of Joffre's proposal, "and the sooner it shed blood, the better."

Despite Palmer's reservations, President Wilson embraced Joffre's idea. So did Wilson's secretary of war, Newton D. Baker. A self-described pacifist, Secretary Baker hardly fitted the mold for someone tasked with overseeing America's involvement in a war that had already killed millions. According to one American general, Baker "knew little about the business of war."[11]

Secretary Baker ordered the War Department to form a division for immediate deployment to France. The task of planning that division fell to the Army War College, where Palmer and his colleagues again turned to the French for guidance. As liaison, Conner worked closely with Palmer and with Major Réquin and Colonel Louis Remond of Joffre's staff to structure a prototype for the American divisions to be formed. Rather than merely copying the French model of a 12,000-man "triangular" division, composed of three infantry regiments, Conner and the War College planners devised a larger 18,000-strong "square" division that would contain four infantry regiments grouped into two separate brigades.[12]

Through his work in structuring the square American division, which was designed to take advantage of America's superior manpower resources by adding a fourth regiment, Fox Conner made his first imprint upon the American Expeditionary Forces—or AEF—as the force became known.

The discussions between Joffre's staff and the War College, in which Fox Conner participated as liaison, also led to another far-reaching decision. On Major Réquin's recommendation, the War College proposed that Wilson immediately send a commanding general to Europe to establish an American presence and to begin creation of the transportation, supply, and training systems that would have to function before the American Expeditionary Forces could fight. Wilson and Baker approved the proposal. They then turned to selection of that commander.[13]

Major General John J. Pershing's professionalism during the Punitive Expedition into Mexico had impressed both President Wilson and Secretary Baker. At age 56, Black Jack Pershing remained fit and lean, with graying hair that augmented the air of competency about him. No less than during his "tac" days at West Point, Pershing's stern visage asserted authority. The general also exuded confidence—a trait much needed to boost Allied morale. Shortly after receipt of the War College proposal on May 10, Secretary Baker appointed Pershing commander-in-chief of the AEF. Baker then directed Pershing to depart for Europe, with a staff, as soon as possible.

But assembly of a staff was no simple matter.[14] Fewer than 5 percent of the Army's officers had received staff officer training at either Leavenworth or the War College. Due to statutory restrictions, the entire War Department general staff consisted of nineteen officers at the war's outset. Fox Conner accurately described the General Staff Corps as "a name rather than a living thing" at the time the United States entered the Great War. "To anyone having even a cursory knowledge of the task which confronted us," Conner said, "this poverty of staff officers is the strongest indictment we can make of our lack of preparedness."

Pershing first selected James G. Harbord to be his chief of staff. The two had served together as cavalry officers in the Philippines, where Harbord had impressed Pershing with his "ability, his resourcefulness, his faculty for organization, and, above all, his loyalty." Within two weeks, Pershing had assembled his staff of 187 people, including officers, enlisted men, civilian clerks, and translators. Pershing named John McAuley Palmer the AEF's assistant chief of staff for combat operations. Pershing also chose men who had served him well in Mexico, including George Patton, whom Pershing included on his staff as an aide-de-camp.

Fox Conner, who had been promoted to lieutenant colonel on May 15, 1917, had no reason to think Pershing would select him for service in France.[15] According to Bug Conner, the two men barely knew one another. They had not met since West Point 20 years earlier. Also, Black Jack Pershing surely recalled "The Silence" and other insubordinate behavior directed at him by Conner and the other cadets of West Point's Company A. Conner could only hope that Pershing's memory of those events had dimmed.

But Pershing did remember Fox Conner—in a positive light. Years later, Pershing wrote of the "high regard" he had for Conner as a West Point cadet and of the "promise of a brilliant future" Conner had shown at the academy.

More importantly, Pershing needed a trained general staff to direct the millions of American soldiers who would eventually serve in France. None of Fox Conner's primary professional attributes—Leavenworth and War College training, service in a French regiment, fluency in the French language, knowledge of German military theory, and mastery of both American and French artillery doctrine—had been of any particular use in either the Philippine jungles or the Mexican desert. Pershing, however, recognized that in the colossal war of millions, being waged against Germany, in France, where artillery dominated the battlefield, the AEF needed the unique qualifications that Fox Conner offered.

As such, in AEF General Order No. 1, issued May 26, 1917, General Pershing included Lieutenant Colonel Fox Conner on the staff that would go to France to establish the nucleus of the General Headquarters of the American Expeditionary Forces. Pershing made Conner, who was still formally assigned to the Inspector General's bureau, an assistant to AEF Inspector General André Brewster. As one of fifty-nine officers selected by Pershing, Conner joined an elite group formed from less than 1 percent of the Army's officer corps.

★ ★ ★ ★ ★

Among the remaining 99 percent of Army officers was Captain Dwight Eisenhower of the 19th Infantry Regiment, headquartered at Fort Sam Houston, Texas.

The 19th Infantry formed a part of the Army's Southern Department, which Black Jack Pershing had commanded until his elevation to AEF commander-in-chief. Eager to put his West Point training to use in commanding troops, Captain Eisenhower hoped Pershing would select his regiment to be among the first to see action. Pershing did choose four regiments from the Southern Department to form the "square division" that Conner and his War College Colleagues had devised. The 19th Infantry was not among them.

Rather than going to Europe, Captain Eisenhower went to Leon Springs, Texas as the regimental supply officer for the newly formed 57th Infantry Regiment. Eisenhower wrote that he was "crushed" when he learned that he would not go to France.[16]

★ ★ ★ ★ ★

Fox Conner's orders directed him to report on May 28, 1917 to Governors Island, off the southern tip of Manhattan, where the British ocean liner RMS *Baltic* waited to transport Pershing and his staff to Europe.[17] To maintain secrecy, the War Department ordered members of Pershing's staff to travel in civilian clothing and with no indication of military rank on their baggage. They were to identify themselves simply as members of the "D.E. McCarthy party." While on his way to New York under similar orders, George Patton had dinner on the evening of May 26 with his friends Fox and Bug Conner in Washington, D.C.

The next day, for the first time in his 19-year military career, Fox Conner went off to war.

Profound sadness had accompanied Conner's 1915 departure from his family, when he had left Fort Sill to serve as a neutral nation's military observer. In 1917, his journey posed greater personal risk. Conner understood that he would travel, through submarine-infested waters, as a legitimate military target aboard an unarmed passenger ship. Conner's orders to report immediately to New York, under conditions of secrecy, also prevented his sharing of farewells with his two oldest children, who were away at boarding school. Even Fox's last glimpse of Bug at the train station provided no comfort. "I waved and waved," he wrote Bug the next day, "but I could not make you see me." Instead, Mrs. Conner simply turned away as the train carried her husband off.

But Conner knew that he was leaving with his wife's support. Bug and he both understood the significance of his assignment on Pershing's staff. "I felt very strongly," Mrs. Conner wrote, "that Fox, who had devoted his entire life to the study of war, was not left behind." Fox told Bug: "You are certainly a soldier's wife. If every woman sends her loved one to war as you did, it is won already."

Despite the orders for discreet travel in civilian garb, Conner allowed himself one formality: in addition to luggage, Conner carried his officer's sword, which reached past his waist when stood on its tip.[18] Bug thought it her husband's way of "announcing to the world where he was he headed." Conner's indiscretion was far from the worst among the "McCarthy" party. Some appeared in uniform. Others placed the letters "AEF" on their luggage. The most notable breach of secrecy belonged to Pershing's orderlies, who, according to one observer, delivered the commander-in-chief's luggage "emblazoned with General Pershing's name so prominently that you could read the letters across the street."

One security precaution did succeed. When the *Baltic* cast off from Governors Island on a windy and rainy May 28, 1917, it did so without either Black Jack Pershing or his staff aboard. Instead, after the great liner had sailed out of sight, and once the danger of a hidden bomb had passed, Pershing and his staff boarded a side-wheel harbor steamer, the *Thomas Patten*, to rendezvous with the *Baltic* in eerily named Gravesend Bay off the coast of Brooklyn. As the *Patten* chugged southward through The Narrows separating Brooklyn from Staten Island, the boat passed Fort Hamilton, where Fox Conner's journey to general staff duty had begun with the recommendation of Colonel Greenough.

The *Patten's* skipper fought choppy waves, whipped by a stiff south-easterly wind, to bring his smaller craft alongside the *Baltic* in Gravesend

Bay. The liner's crew then ran a gangplank to the smaller vessel's top railing, which the passengers used for a slippery and nerve-wracking transfer onto the liner. Once all made it across safely, the *Baltic* entered the Atlantic as the rain continued and darkness fell.

George Patton noted the "heavy fog" that shrouded the *Baltic's* departure. Apart from describing the weather, "foggy" also best described the collective conception of the AEF staff as to exactly what it was supposed to do next. In Pershing's words, when the War Department "went to look in the secret files where the plans to meet the situation that confronted us should have been found, the pigeon-hole was empty."

Apart from emphasizing that "the forces of the United States are a separate and distinct component of the combined forces, the identity of which must be preserved," Secretary Baker's orders to Pershing provided little specificity.[19] Pershing and his staff would have to figure it out on their 11-day voyage across the North Atlantic. Harbord wryly observed that "officers whose lives have been spent in trying to avoid spending fifteen cents of Government money now confront the necessity of spending fifteen millions of dollars—and on their intellectual and professional expansion depends their avoidance of the scrap heap." "It is doubtful," Conner said, "if we had on April 6, 1917, one single officer who fully appreciated the necessity for the coordination of economic and military policy in modern war on a great scale."

As Pershing's chief of operations, John McAuley Palmer bore an especially heavy load. Although he had hoped the sea voyage would provide an opportunity for rest from the long hours of planning at the War College, Palmer discovered that the trip was "no pleasure cruise." Talk of German submarines permeated the conversations aboard ship, particularly once the passengers learned that the *Baltic* had narrowly avoided two torpedo attacks on its previous passage. Memories of the 1912 *Titanic* disaster added to the anxiety as the ship passed North Atlantic icebergs the size of mountains. Palmer became ill from immunization shots. Then Pershing detached Palmer's lone assistant, Major Hugh Drum, to conduct a study of available French ports, leaving Palmer to address singlehandedly what he termed "problems enough to busy a staff of twenty or more."

The chief of operations needed help. "Happily," Palmer recalled, "the selection of someone to replace Drum in the Operations Section did not take too many hours from my work."

"Fox Conner was my man," Palmer wrote. "I needed no prolonged period of trial to determine this." Palmer already knew of Conner's "substantial abilities" from their work together at the War College both before and since America's declaration of war. Palmer also considered Conner's knowledge of both the French language and the French Army to be highly valuable assets. Believing that Conner was "exceptionally well qualified" to carry out the critical planning functions required of the Operations Section, Palmer resolved to "pry him loose" from the Inspector General.

Palmer took his request to Chief of Staff Harbord, who warned Palmer of a potential problem with Conner's transfer to the Operations Section: Conner of the field artillery and the infantryman Palmer each held the rank of lieutenant colonel. Each arm of service, however, controlled its own promotions. If the artillery promoted Conner to colonel first, Palmer would then have to step aside and serve under the higher-ranking officer.

"If that should happen," Palmer told Harbord, "I would be very glad to change desks with Conner." He added: "I recommended him for the job because I believe that nobody else is so well fitted to serve in that capacity and I certainly would not revoke the recommendation even if it should prove prejudicial to my own fortunes." Palmer recalled that "Harbord smiled somewhat at my high-minded speech but agreed to let me have the man I wanted." According to Palmer, "Fox Conner soon proved his worth many times over in the Operations Section."

Drawing upon Conner's artillery expertise, Palmer first assigned Conner to outline the AEF's artillery needs. Conner succinctly summed up America's capability at the war's outset: "We had no guns and we had no possibility of making any guns within less than a year." Conner continued to hold the view, set forth in his "highly controversial" 1915 *Field Artillery Journal* article, that the French 75mm field gun provided a superior weapon to its American-made counterpart. More practically, the French guns were already in France. In what Palmer considered an "excellent paper," Conner recommended adoption of the *soixante-quinze* as the AEF's primary field artillery weapon. In one of the few decisions made aboard the *Baltic*, Pershing concurred. The recommendation proved sound. "As it turned out," Conner recalled, "of the main calibers, not one American-made gun was received by the AEF."

The *Baltic* arrived in Liverpool, Great Britain on June 8, 1917.[20] After a brief reception by an honor guard that included wounded British war veterans, Conner and the others left by train for London. Apart from the dignitaries who greeted the Americans at the train station, most Londoners made no fuss over the arrival of the Americans. While Pershing attended ceremonial and diplomatic meetings over the next few days, Palmer and Conner visited the British War Office to observe a functioning wartime staff in operation. "The more we learned," Palmer wrote, "the more discouraged we became."

Palmer and Conner saw a bustling complex. Amid the tapping of telegraphs, the clicking of typewriters, and the din of dozens of conversations occurring simultaneously, hundreds of officers, supported by a thousand clerks, tracked and directed the operations of the divisions and corps that formed the British Expeditionary Force. Palmer lamented that, by contrast, "the whole Operations office for the AEF, officers, clerks and all, could ride comfortably in a single one of those funny little London taxis." Conner and Palmer also visited British training facilities for bayonet and poison gas warfare. A mock trench raid provided the two American officers their first glimpse of the combination of 20th-century technology and primitive barbarism that typified trench warfare on the Western Front.

After five days in Great Britain, the AEF staff crossed the English Channel by boat then took a train for Paris.[21] The Americans arrived in the French capital late in the afternoon of June 13, 1917. The welcoming delegation at the station included Marshal Joffre and his staff. Palmer recalled that Major Réquin and Colonel Remond, with whom he and Conner had worked closely in Washington, greeted the Americans like "long-lost brothers." Pershing described the reception at the Paris train station as "cordially informal."

Then they went outside.

The roar that greeted the AEF staff spanned a range of emotions, from sobs to laughter. Thousands jammed the streets, squares, balconies, and housetops along the two-mile route to Pershing's hotel in Paris, waving flags and banners of red, white, and blue—the colors of both the French *Tricolore* and the American Stars and Stripes. Showers of flowers and cheers of "*Vive l'Amérique!*" rained down upon the arriving Americans. Police lost control of the crowd. The citizenry of Paris surged into the street, hoping to see, or even touch, their American saviors. As the automobiles bearing Conner and the other Americans inched forward, people danced about in what Palmer described as "an orgy of delight." Women tried to enter the cars to bestow their gratitude. "It was most touching," Pershing wrote, "and in a sense most pathetic."

Pershing and his staff understood that the French public's hysteria reflected the desperation of a war-weary nation grasping at hope, particularly in the aftermath of the April 1917 French Army mutinies. Describing France's national psyche at the time of the AEF's arrival, Conner wrote that "discouragement ran like wildfire through her civil population as well as among her soldiers." To begin lifting French morale, Pershing ordered his staff officers to display a sense of optimism at all times; a positive attitude became "a matter of duty," as Conner put it. The American commander, however, had his own doubts. "Difficult to see how we are to meet the expectations of the French," Pershing confided to his June 14, 1917 diary.[22]

Determined to succeed, Pershing drove his staff to complete the blueprint for building the AEF in France.[23] The commander-in-chief added a few officers to Palmer's Operations Section, but the staff remained "far too small" in Réquin's estimation. With no office space available in Paris, Conner and his AEF colleagues moved into converted residences on Rue Constantine, near the French War Ministry. Men, maps, and manuals filled cramped rooms, where Pershing's staff worked on stacks of boxes rather than desks. Pershing, who frequently failed to adhere to a daily schedule, worked his assistants late into the evenings. "The work imposed upon the few staff officers who had accompanied me," Pershing recalled, "was very heavy."

Years later, Fox Conner told a War College audience that "the pressure of work on the few officers constituting [the Operations Section] in the summer of 1917 was terrific." He added that the officers who endured that period "may be excused for being impatient with excuses of lack of time."

Conner and the others at the newly established AEF headquarters in 1917 also contended with nervous French officers looking over their shoulders. America's new allies, Conner recalled, "were very doubtful of what our military effort would be." Even Major Réquin, generally an admirer of his American colleagues, wrote that Pershing and his staff "had everything to learn regarding the European war." Concerned that the war would be lost while the inexperienced Americans learned how to build and control a large army, the French sought to take control of the AEF's operations. Having formed what Conner termed "this idea of our inability to organize and employ a large American Army under our own flag," the French renewed their earlier proposal that incoming American troops be inserted directly into the French Army.

Despite the crowded and harried conditions under which they worked, Pershing's staff produced results. Conner's first task involved negotiating with the French to obtain artillery—"one of the most difficult problems the AEF had to solve," Conner thought. He recognized that France's heavy losses in men had left the French with more guns than gunners. Conner therefore made arrangements to obtain more than a thousand of his favorite 75mm gun and around 300 of France's larger 155mm howitzers. Réquin noted that the agreement struck by Conner eventually resulted in American divisions receiving French artillery in preference to France's own divisions. "Had we not arranged to take advantage of this surplus capacity," Conner recalled, "we would not have had guns."[24]

Conner also continued the work he had begun in Washington to structure the AEF's combat divisions. He learned that a typical 12,000-man division fielded by the French, British, and Germans could usually not sustain an attack long enough to dislodge the enemy from well-entrenched positions. Conner recognized that the inability of either side to advance on the Western Front had produced a stalemate that "showed most of the characteristics of siege warfare." Pershing, however, did not intend simply to feed his men into the same trenches that had devoured the young British and French men before them. Instead, the American commander aimed to "force the Germans out of their trenches and beat them in the open."[25]

To that end, Fox Conner and Hugh Drum designed a distinctly American division that would contain nearly 28,000 men, which more than doubled the size of other divisions on the Western Front. Conner and Drum retained the same "square" division model—containing two infantry brigades, each formed from two regiments—that had been decided upon earlier in Washington. The two divisional architects created a massive division designed to outlast its opponent by inflicting—and absorbing—greater casualties before becoming exhausted.[26]

Conner also recognized that the AEF lacked a sufficient number of trained commanders and staff personnel. "The number of our trained staff officers," Conner recalled, "was very, very small." Conner reasoned that, with divisions twice as large as the norm, the AEF would require only half as many officers for command and staff positions. The men in charge of the divisions, however, would have to control fighting units much larger than those in which any of them had previously served. Calculations showed, for example, that an AEF division would require 30 miles of road space to move its men, animals, equipment, and supplies.

Conner and the Operations Section also began to study the issue of where the AEF would form and fight.[27] The Western Front ran in a generally southeast direction from the English Channel to the Swiss–French–German border. The British, concerned with protection of ports on the English Channel, manned the northern sector of the line with the help of Belgium's few troops. Determined to defend Paris and Verdun at all cost, the French massed their forces in the central area of the front.

To the south of Verdun lay the portion of Lorraine retained by France after the Franco-Prussian War, including the triangular German protrusion into the Allied lines known as the St. Mihiel salient. Unsuccessful French offensives in 1914 and 1915 had left the salient—and most of Alsace-Lorraine's valuable coal and iron resources—under German control. Since then, the area had become a quiet sector, which both sides used to rest and rebuild their divisions. According to Conner, the Germans were satisfied to keep it that way "because it kept the fighting

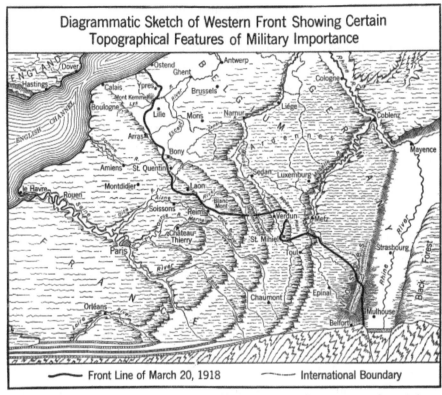

Map 1: Sketch of Western Front. Credit: The American Battle Monuments Commission.

out of Germany." The lightly held Lorraine region afforded the physical space necessary for the AEF to grow. The area could also be supplied from ports on France's western coast that were not already clogged by the needs of the French and British armies to the north.

Strategic considerations also pointed to Lorraine as the area for the AEF's eventual operations. Under Conner's analysis, the coal and iron deposits located in the German-controlled portions of Lorraine, as well as the rail lines running through the area, "bore much the same import-ance to the German cause as did Paris and the channel ports to that of the Allies." Conner reasoned that an American offensive into Lorraine would oblige the Germans to move troops to defend the area. Such an offensive "would not only relieve any enemy pressure in the north of France," Conner wrote, "but if successful might be expected to free the whole of northern France as a minimum result." As importantly, an attack into Lorraine would bring the war onto German soil.

Such an offensive in Lorraine would ultimately require an assault upon the German fortress at Metz—the area Conner and Palmer had extensively studied through map exercises at the War College in 1911. As the duo began to envision a grand American offensive into Lorraine, Conner and Palmer no longer "groused," as they had at the War College, about working with German war maps of Metz battlefields.[28]

France also wanted the AEF deployed southeast of Verdun. Eager to place the Americans near the lost provinces of Alsace and Lorraine—and as far away from British influence as possible—France offered Pershing the use of facilities in Lorraine. "But it was not likely," Conner wrote, "that the French had made their proposals in view of the employment of millions of Americans as a distinctive American force." Concerned that the facilities offered by the French would limit the AEF to forming small units suitable only for absorption into the French Army, Pershing sent Palmer, Conner, and three other officers to view what his allies were offering.[29]

On June 21, 1917, Conner and his fellow officers began their tour of the French bases. After inspecting eight proposed areas, the American delegation concluded that the facilities offered by the French, although far from ideal, suited the AEF's purposes. On June 25, Conner and his colleagues met with Pershing to recommend acceptance of the French facilities in Lorraine. As noted by Conner: "If we did not go there, we could not beat an army of several million anywhere else." More practically, the AEF had nowhere else to go.

The next day, elements of the American 1st Division, including 36-year-old Captain George C. Marshall, landed in France. As the 1st Division's operations officer, Captain Marshall would implement, at the divisional level, the plans Palmer and Conner were formulating at General Headquarters. On July 4, 1917, a battalion from the 1st Division's 16th Infantry Regiment paraded in Paris. The Americans marched to the grave of the Marquis de Lafayette, the Frenchman who had helped the United States win its independence. American Colonel Charles E. Stanton proclaimed: "Lafayette, we are here!" Conner thought the speech "of the greatest benefit to the French morale."[30]

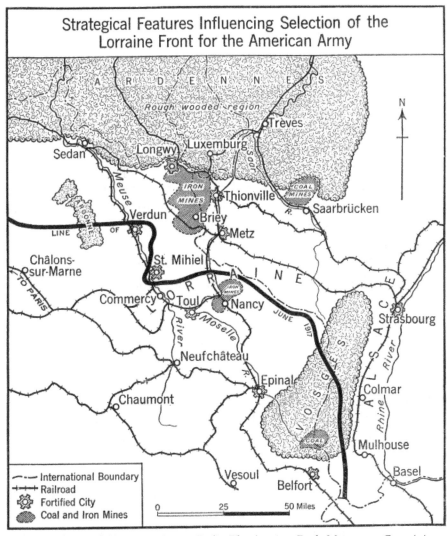

Map 2: Selection of the Lorraine Front. Credit: The American Battle Monuments Commission.

Also in the early summer of 1917, "to add to the joy of living," as Conner put it, a new group of American officers arrived at Pershing's Paris headquarters.[31]

The War Department dispatched a delegation of thirteen officers, led by Colonel Chauncey Baker of the Quartermaster Corps, to address most of the same organizational issues on which the Operations Section had labored since the *Baltic*. Conner and his overworked colleagues found themselves scrutinized not only by the critical French, but also by their recently arrived American comrades. Chief of Staff Harbord recalled that Colonel Baker's delegation, known as the "Baker Board," was "conscious of its official independence" and was at times "quite arrogant" toward Pershing's staff.

The presence of two groups of Americans, both charged with the same task, created further French doubt as to the competency of the AEF high command. Harbord also noted the "quiet amusement" expressed by the French that the new group's leader was a quartermaster—a position normally occupied in the French Army by lesser-talented officers.

Eventually, the Baker Board endorsed most of the plans already made by Pershing's staff. The "General Organization Project" that emerged from the Pershing–Baker conference envisioned formation of a million-man American Army in France by the spring of 1918. The conference adopted the 28,000-man square division structure proposed by Conner and Drum. The Baker Board further endorsed formation of a six-division corps structure consisting of four combat divisions and two additional divisions to provide supply services and replacements. The General Organization Project also established the basic framework for an army of 3 million by 1919. "Fortunately," Conner recalled, "we were able to gain the adherence of a majority of this commission to our plans."

Not everyone on the Baker Board, however, shared Fox Conner's views.

Colonel Charles P. Summerall, whom Harbord considered "the most articulate member" of the Baker Board, believed the proposed AEF divisions lacked adequate artillery strength, and Summerall "spoke out strongly" against Conner's proposed division structure. Harbord wrote that Summerall had "carried his argument as nearly to the limit of courtesy as I have ever seen an officer go and escape unrebuked."

Summerall recalled the exchange differently; he wrote that he had been "viciously attacked, personally and officially, by officers of the staff whom I hardly knew." Summerall believed he had replied only "with equal force and resentment." According to Summerall, Pershing asked the colonel to step outside. The commander-in-chief then attempted to persuade Summerall to arrive at a consensus with Conner. "Your staff is wrong," Summerall bluntly told Black Jack Pershing. Summerall recalled that Pershing then became "furious" and returned to the meeting without saying another word to him. "I felt I would not be allowed to return to France," wrote Summerall, "and that my part in the war was ended."

Conner's position on divisional artillery strength ultimately prevailed in the Pershing–Baker conference by a vote of sixteen to five. According to Harbord, though, memories of the acrimonious exchange between Conner and Summerall "lingered and affected official action for many years." Summerall made enemies that day, but he also developed a much more important ally. Just as Pershing had not allowed the personal affront of a West Point cadet to affect his judgment as to Fox Conner's suitability for duty on the AEF staff, he also looked past Charles P. Summerall's arrogance. Impressed with the colonel's abilities, Pershing asked the War Department to transfer Colonel Summerall to France for service in the AEF.

On July 11, 1917, Summerall and his colleagues left Paris. Harbord's diary reflected his glee at watching "Chauncey Baker and his crowd of picnickers" leave Paris. He added: "We shall now breathe more freely that they are gone." Not all of Pershing's staff, however, felt such relief.

Even before the Baker Board's arrival, Colonel John McAuley Palmer had struggled with the workload placed upon him as AEF chief of operations. The need to complete the section's studies hurriedly, and to then defend them against the second-guessing of men such as Charles Summerall, significantly exacerbated the strain. During the Baker–Pershing conference, Palmer could not concentrate. Confusion clouded his mind. As soon as Baker and his entourage departed, Palmer sought medical attention. The head of the AEF's medical staff diagnosed Palmer with "a classic account of a nervous breakdown, utter mental exhaustion from sustained overwork and worry." The physician ordered immediate rest. Pershing accordingly sent his chief of operations to Versailles for a two-week vacation.[32]

In Palmer's absence, the Operations Section forged ahead. In July 1917, Conner served on a board of officers that studied the tactics and weapons used on the Western Front, including the relative strengths and weaknesses of French and British tanks. Conner, who in 1915 had been one of the first American officers to assess the suitability of tracked vehicles for military purposes, favored a light tank designed by the French automaker Renault.[33]

While John McAuley Palmer recuperated, Pershing and Harbord reorganized the AEF's General Headquarters (GHQ) by creating five sections with distinct areas of responsibility. The head of each section was made an assistant chief of staff. Each section, as well as its leader, was given a designation that began with the letter "G": Administration (G-1), Intelligence (G-2), Operations (G-3), Coordination (G-4), and Training (G-5). The new staff structure, and particularly the creation of a separate section for training, lightened some of the burden borne by Palmer, whom Pershing retained as Assistant Chief of Staff for Operations (G-3). Pershing also increased the Operations Section's staff by adding Majors LeRoy Eltinge and Stuart Heintzelman, and Lieutenant Colonels Paul Malone and Kirby Walker. Like Charles Summerall, Colonel Kirby Walker had impressed Pershing by his service on the Baker Board. The G-3 section also began to borrow the services of the 1st Division's operations officer, Captain George Marshall.[34]

Palmer returned to duty as chief of operations in early August of 1917. Despite his resolution to take Sundays off and to exercise more, Palmer quickly fell back into habits of excessive work and worry. By mid-August, Palmer again recognized that his mind was working "very slowly because there was little steam left in the boiler." When another medical examination found enlargement of his heart and low blood pressure, the AEF physicians declared Palmer medically unfit for duty. The devastated Palmer presumed he would be invalided home. Instead, Pershing placed Palmer on sick leave and ordered him to spend two months at Cannes on the French Riviera. As Harbord put it, John McAuley Palmer had been "Canned."[35]

With the 1st Division already in France, and the 2nd, 26th, and 42nd Divisions scheduled to arrive later in the year to form the initial American battle corps, the AEF's Operations Section needed effective leadership. In Fox Conner, Pershing had a solid option. As Palmer's top assistant, Conner had extensive knowledge of the plans already made by the section. In addition, Conner had achieved the rank of colonel on August 5, 1917, and he possessed sufficient rank for the position. Also, dating back to the voyage of the *Baltic*, Chief of Staff Harbord had envisioned that Conner might one day replace Palmer as AEF chief of operations—an idea Palmer had endorsed.

Pershing, however, did not choose Fox Conner for the interim position. Instead, he selected the new man from the Baker Board—Colonel Kirby Walker.

Pershing left no record as to why he chose Walker over Conner for the interim G-3 position. Both Walker and Conner had received promotion to colonel on the same day. Both were Leavenworth graduates, although Walker had not attended the War College as had Conner. At age 50, Kirby Walker was more experienced than the 42-year-old Conner. Walker had also been a West Point classmate of Palmer.

Another factor might have been Conner's work in mid-August 1917. As Palmer went on his extended leave to the Riviera, Fox Conner, Hugh Drum, and LeRoy Eltinge were absorbed in a detailed analysis of the AEF's strategic options. Pershing may have preferred that his most experienced operations officer remain focused upon completing that critical task.[36]

Whatever the reason, on August 25, 1917, Colonel Kirby Walker became acting AEF chief of operations. If Fox Conner felt any personal or professional disappointment at having been passed over—particularly in favor of a member of the Baker Board—he left no record of it.

While Conner's job remained the same, he and the others at GHQ did have a change in scenery in the late summer of 1917.

Having long outgrown the cramped rooms on Rue Constantine, Pershing and his staff left Paris in early September for Chaumont, a city of 15,000 in the high country of the picturesque Haute-Marne region of France.[37] Located around 150 miles southeast of Paris, Chaumont offered a headquarters location much nearer to the anticipated American front in Lorraine. The move also created distance between the American high command and the Frenchmen in Paris who still wanted to control it.

Fox Conner and George Patton drove together to Chaumont. Once the urban boulevards of Paris were behind them, the duo jolted down the poplar-lined stone roads of rural France. They drove through villages of ancient stone cottages, and by fields of grain ripening in the late-summer sun, before a flat tire stopped them. Once they got back on the road, Conner and Patton continued over the rolling and forested hills of the Haute-Marne, steadily climbing toward Chaumont, until their car engine developed a cylinder failure. The automotive problems galled Patton, who commanded the headquarters mechanics and chauffeurs. The previous year, Patton had killed an enemy commander in Mexico. To that point in the Great War, however, Captain Patton had done nothing more than oversee mechanics who could not keep his car running long enough to make it to the new AEF headquarters. Patton, who considered himself "nothing but a hired flunkey," yearned for a more active role in the war.[38]

Conner and Patton made it to Chaumont. They motored down the tree-lined Avenue du Fort Lambert, with its broad and shaded promenade in the center, until they arrived at the gated compound that enclosed the Damremont Barracks. Situated on a high crest overlooking the Marne Valley, the four-story stone buildings, with their many chimneys and rooftop features, gave Pershing's new AEF headquarters an almost chateau-like appearance.

The AEF staff settled into its new surroundings and got back to work. On September 25, 1917, the Operations Section submitted its detailed analysis entitled "A Strategical Study on the Employment of the AEF Against the Imperial German Government." The study, covering twenty-one single-spaced pages, assessed the options and anticipated actions of all combatant nations on the Western Front, including those of Germany, Great Britain, France, Italy, and the United States.[39]

Conner, Drum, and Eltinge projected that the impending defeat of Russia would enable Germany to move approximately 700,000 seasoned troops for a major offensive in the spring of 1918 against either Italy in the south, or against the Western Front. Given France's war-weariness and the spring mutinies in the French Army, the authors believed that Germany was more likely to attack the Western Front in order to "cause the collapse of the French nation, either by defecting its army, or by inflicting such losses therein as to render it powerless." Conner and his cohorts thought that a German attack against the city of Nancy, located near the cradle of the AEF in Lorraine, offered Germany its greatest chance of success.

The strategic assessment also concluded that Germany's extra men from the Eastern Front would not create a manpower advantage for Germany any stronger than that which the Allies had enjoyed for the prior 2 years without achieving a breakthrough. The operations staff members considered it "doubtful" that Germany would prevail—provided the British and French coordinated their operations, and if the teetering French stayed in the war. Conner, Drum, and Eltinge expressed the opinion that the Allies should therefore operate on the defensive in 1918 while the AEF developed into a force strong enough to launch a decisive offensive in 1919.

Regarding America's participation, Conner and his colleagues apprised Pershing that shipping shortages would preclude the United States from fielding the million-man force that the General Organization Project had anticipated would be in France by the spring of 1918. They projected that only around 500,000 men, a "minimum force" suitable for only minor operations, would actually be available. The authors told Pershing that the AEF would nonetheless have to enter the fight in 1918, primarily to boost French morale. In frank terms, Conner, Drum, and Eltinge expressed their concerns that it "certainly would be difficult to hold the French to the war if they realized our inability to lend them early material support."

The three planners recommended elimination of the St. Mihiel salient in Lorraine as the initial objective for American operations in 1918. Warning against a "piecemeal waste" of American troops by incorporation of smaller units elsewhere within the Allied armies across the Western Front, the Operations Section recommended that Pershing concentrate America's available divisions south of St. Mihiel, where they could continue to train as cohesive units and also stand ready as an Allied reserve force in the event of a German breakthrough during the anticipated German spring offensive. "The part the United States plays in 1918," the officers wrote, "should be no more than is necessary to satisfy public opinion and to prepare for the 1919 offensive."

Conner, Drum, and Eltinge also addressed America's military options for 1919. They expected the AEF, by then, to have in place a "decisive force" of 1,272,858 men, organized into five corps. The three planners reiterated the Operations Section view that the AEF should attack toward Metz in Lorraine while the French and British simultaneously attacked in their sectors to the north. In discussing potential objectives for 1919, the strategic assessment analyzed the entire Western Front, from the English Channel to Switzerland, including the area of the Argonne Forest, which the study considered to be "a serious obstacle" to offensive operations. Conner and his colleagues found "little of strategical importance" in the area of the Argonne. They concluded that "the only advantage to be gained from an advance in this section would be the re-occupation of French territory which has little relation to our objective."

The September 25, 1917 Strategical Study formed the basis for all subsequent American planning studies during the war. Although the study bore the initials of Fox Conner, Hugh Drum, and LeRoy Eltinge, Conner was not on duty when his two colleagues submitted the study. He was again in a hospital.[40]

Conner's 1915 ruptured appendix and resulting peritonitis left scar tissue in his abdomen, which eventually wound around his intestines to produce a potentially fatal bowel obstruction. Surgeons operated on September 18, 1917 to free the obstruction. Pershing's aide, Major Robert Bacon, noted in his diary that the surgeons had operated "just in time." Bug Conner later wrote in her memoir that it was "nip and tuck as to whether Fox would make the grade."

George Patton checked on his friend Conner following the surgery. Patton wrote that as Conner began to awake from the ether, he (Conner) yelled out: "I know what pane [sic] is for I have had three children and you bet your life I am not going to have any more!" Bug Conner was in her husband's thoughts, if not his presence.

Conner remained hospitalized for 6 weeks in the autumn of 1917. The loss of both Palmer and Conner threw the Operations Section into disarray. "Things are very much in need of a leader in your Section,"

Harbord wrote Palmer on September 20. He added: "To lose you and Fox Conner at the same time is a severe blow."[41]

British journalist Charles à Court Repington of *The London Times* visited Chaumont in early October 1917. His diary provides a glimpse into the functioning of Pershing's staff while Palmer and Conner were gone. He described Pershing's staff as "taken aback by the immensity of the problem before them" and "largely ignorant of the practical side of soldiering." In Repington's view, the Americans were "groping their way about in the dark" and did "not yet understand what a General Staff means." Amid his generally scathing comments, Repington wrote that the still-hospitalized Fox Conner was "an efficient second" to Colonel Walker in the Operations Section.[42]

In mid-October, Conner got some company in the hospital when George Patton fell ill with jaundice, which Patton thought was caused by "excessive fish eating." Their hospitalization together provided the two friends further opportunity to discuss Patton's career options.[43]

Still dissatisfied with his headquarters duty, Patton had applied to Pershing in early October for a transfer to the newly established AEF Tank Corps. Conner, who had recently studied the use of tanks on the Western Front, advised against the move. Instead, Conner urged Patton to take command of an infantry battalion, which would be accompanied by promotion to the rank of major. Patton wrote his wife Beatrice on October 26 that he felt "sure of being a major very soon," and that he could easily obtain the gold oak leaf insignia worn by officers of that rank. "Col. Conner has a lot he will give me when I need them."

Despite Conner's advice, Patton eventually followed his instinct and gambled on the Tank Corps. To Patton, it was "apparently a thing of destiny." Pershing granted Patton's request and appointed him director of the AEF's light tank training school. In that position, George Patton began to develop the theories and strategies of armored warfare for which he would become famous more than two decades later. Although Patton had not heeded his friend's advice, Fox Conner helped Patton obtain the land he needed for the tank school training grounds. The tanks

Patton worked with were the Renault light tanks that Conner had recommended.

★ ★ ★ ★ ★

Captain Dwight Eisenhower found much less success in his own efforts to change his wartime duties.

Dissatisfied with his duties as a supply officer in the United States, Eisenhower repeatedly sought a transfer to a combat unit. The War Department instead reassigned him to duty as a training officer. Eisenhower was on training duty and away from his wife Mamie when their first child, Doud Dwight Eisenhower, arrived on September 24, 1917.

Eisenhower continued to apply for overseas service. The commander of a machine-gun battalion scheduled for shipment to France "heartily endorsed" Eisenhower's application for reassignment to his unit. The War Department instead sent what Eisenhower later described as a "curt reply" that he should "obey orders and in effect let the War Department run the war." Eisenhower's run-in with the War Department would not be his last.[44]

★ ★ ★ ★ ★

Fox Conner left the hospital on November 5, 1917. He returned to an AEF headquarters in mourning.

Two days earlier, the American Army had suffered its first combat deaths. Company F of the American 16th Infantry Regiment, while in training with a French division, held the line in a quiet sector near Bathelémont, east of Verdun. In the darkness of the early hours of November 3, 1917, German troops conducted a successful trench raid against the American position. Corporal James Gresham was shot through the eye. Private Merle Hay had his head smashed in. Private Thomas Enright died of multiple bayonet wounds and a slashed throat. In July, these men had been among the Americans who had marched in Paris that glorious day when Colonel Stanton proclaimed: "Lafayette, we are here!" At their burial in November, their French divisional commander, in a moving plea, asked that their remains be "left here, left to us forever," so that Frenchmen in generations to come could "bring

to their graves the tribute of their respect and of their gratefulness."
Pershing reportedly wept.[45]

More ominously, by the time Conner left the hospital, the overall
strategic posture of the Allies had gravely deteriorated. As anticipated,
Russia had collapsed. The new Bolshevik regime of V.I. Lenin proclaimed a unilateral armistice in late October, which effectively ended
the war on the Eastern Front. The Central Powers had also routed the
Italians at the Battle of Caporetto in late October, taking 275,000 Italian
prisoners, many of whom had gladly quit the war. France and Great
Britain, fearing that a total collapse of their southern ally would allow
a decisive number of German troops to be brought against the Western
Front, agreed to send eleven divisions to shore up the reeling Italians.[46]

On November 5, AEF Chief of Staff James Harbord directed the
Operations Section to "confidentially consider the possibility of the AEF
being compelled by events in Italy to take a place in the line at once."[47]
Harbord sent his memorandum to a section still suffering from a void in
leadership. In late October, Pershing had transferred Kirby Walker from
the Operations Section to the position of head of the AEF's military
police. With Walker gone, and with both Palmer and Conner still on
medical leave, Lieutenant Colonel LeRoy Eltinge became the section's
third leader in as many months.[48]

John McAuley Palmer did his best to return. When he learned of the
crisis that faced the Allies, Palmer insisted on a repeat medical examination in hope of being cleared to return to duty. His physicians, though,
advised that Palmer should only work in a non-pressured position in
which he could control his workload and increase his daily exercise.
Those medical restrictions effectively ended John McAuley Palmer's
tenure as Pershing's G-3. Still hoping that Palmer would eventually
return to full health, Pershing assigned him to develop a course to teach
incoming divisional staff officers. But with the American 26th Division
having recently landed in France, and the 2nd and 42nd divisions soon
to arrive, Pershing needed an effective leader in his Operations Section.[49]

Once before, Black Jack Pershing had passed on selecting Conner to
head the Operations Section. Pershing did not make the same mistake
twice. On November 5, 1917, the day Fox Conner left the hospital,

Pershing appointed the 43-year-old colonel from Mississippi acting chief of operations for the American Expeditionary Forces.[50]

Six months earlier, Conner had been on mundane duty as an inspector. The combination of Palmer's misfortune and Conner's own perseverance placed Fox Conner in position to direct the development and deployment of an army that would number in the millions and play a decisive role in the deadliest war humankind had fought to that time. In James G. Harbord's opinion, Conner "probably had no superior as an operations chief in the Allied armies. How much he contributed to the success of the AEF has never been adequately stated." In time, historians would label Conner "the genius of operations," and "the brains of the AEF."[51]

Fox Conner, though, had yet to earn these high accolades in the bleak days of early November 1917. He first had to bridge the chasm that existed between the expectations and the reality of what the AEF could accomplish.

CHAPTER 5

THE WAR WITHIN THE WAR

The Germans were frankly scornful of our ability to exercise any real influence in the war. The German idea appeared to be: first, that we could not create a large army; second, that even if we could organize a large force we could not transport such a force to Europe; third, that even if we did succeed in transporting a large force to Europe it would not fight … Our Allies were almost as incredulous as were the Germans as to our ability to realize such a program.

—Fox Conner, 1918[1]

On November 5, 1917, Colonel Fox Conner settled in behind John McAuley Palmer's former desk at AEF headquarters in Chaumont. As Conner pored over the memoranda and studies prepared by his G-3 colleagues during the 6 weeks of his hospitalization, the interim chief of operations quickly grasped the fundamental problem before him: more than 90,000 American troops had arrived in Europe. America's French and British allies, struggling to keep Italy and themselves in the war, clamored for Pershing to do something—anything—with his fresh troops. Yet, more than 6 months after entering the war, the AEF remained an ineffective force that had made no impact on the battlefield.[2]

The United States faced momentous decisions in late 1917: would Pershing heed his beleaguered allies' pleas to send American soldiers in small units to be "amalgamated" within existing British and French divisions before the war was lost in 1918, or would the American commander hold his troops to form the nucleus of the million-man army that American planners such as Fox Conner had envisioned as the key to actually winning the war in 1919? Through his numerous studies, reports, and memoranda, Fox Conner provided the behind-the-scenes analyses and advice that drove John J. Pershing's decisions—often bringing Conner into conflict with colleagues both within and without the AEF.

Conner's first action as interim operations chief was to reply to Chief of Staff Harbord's inquiry as to whether the Italian collapse at Caporetto necessitated any change to the AEF's strategic plan. On November 6, 1917, one day after leaving the hospital, Conner projected that Italy's defeat was "possible but not yet probable," and he counseled against alteration of the AEF's plans. More practically, Conner told Harbord that no American units were sufficiently prepared for combat and that events on the Italian Front were not so grave as to justify the "desperate measure of employing our troops before they are ready." Conner also reiterated his concern over France's willingness to continue the war. He therefore recommended that the Intelligence Section conduct "a propaganda in the French press," to emphasize the financial and food assistance being provided by America.[3]

Conner also recognized that in its victories over the Russians and the Italians, Germany had found a way to return movement to the battlefield. Concerned that Germany would utilize the same tactics in an offensive into Lorraine, Conner warned, in a November 9 memorandum, that the immobile AEF troops near the front lines were "sure to suffer disaster," as had the Italians at Caporetto. He urged that efforts be "redoubled" to improve mobility of the AEF's combat units.[4]

The acting chief of operations then submitted, at Pershing's request, a more detailed "Strategical Study on Possible Course of War" on November 15, 1917.[5] Conner estimated that the loss of Italy—which he considered "probable" at that point—would free at least thirty-five German and Austro-Hungarian divisions for service on the Western Front. Conner advised that the additional enemy divisions would provide the Central Powers with a sufficient manpower advantage to potentially succeed in an offensive against the Western Front in the spring of 1918.

Given the nearness of the AEF's Lorraine training areas to the Swiss border, Conner also expressed concern, in the November 15, 1917 Strategical Study, over the possible entry of Switzerland into the war.

Noting the propaganda efforts to prepare the Swiss public for entry into the war, Conner observed that Switzerland could mobilize "an excellent offensive force" of at least ten divisions, which would more than offset the minimal American force positioned in Lorraine. In language that appears strange in the modern geopolitical context, the November 1917 study warned: "The entry of Switzerland into the war would be critical and should be prevented at any cost."

Despite the possibility of negative developments in Italy and Switzerland, Conner continued to advise Pershing that the Allies could successfully stop the expected enemy offensive. The key, Conner thought, was the formation of "perfect unity of action" by the available French and British forces, despite what he termed in a subsequent memorandum the "suspicions" and "ulterior motives" that drove each nation's policies toward the other. Noting the impracticality of continuing the war if France made peace, Conner also reiterated the need for optimism within the American Army. "Should rumors that we are not in the war wholeheartedly gain color," Conner wrote, "French, and probably British, morale would be deplorable."

Conner's November 15, 1917 study also stressed the importance of raising the number of American troops in France. "Any increase in the shipping program of our troops," he wrote, "is a guarantee of ultimate success." The slow pace of transporting American troops led to an early test of Fox Conner's authority as interim operations chief.

The General Organization Project submitted in July 1917 envisioned a six-division corps structure. By November, however, elements of only four American divisions—the 1st, 2nd, 26th, and 42nd—had arrived in France, with 20,000 more men needed to bring those divisions to full strength. Conner therefore proposed grouping the existing American forces into a smaller corps structure to be composed of only three combat divisions, with one of the existing divisions to be broken up to serve as the source of replacement and labor troops for the other three.[6]

In a November 10 memorandum, Conner addressed the issue of which division to dismantle. The 1st and 26th divisions had been in France the longest and had received the most combat training. The 2nd Division, a hybrid formed from Regular Army and Marine Corps regiments, contained a solid base of professional soldiers. Also, the risk of an intra-service dispute with the Navy existed if its marines became relegated to replacement or labor duty for Army troops. This left the 42nd Division, formed from National Guard units. The separate elements of the 42nd had just begun to arrive in France, and had received the least training of all the divisions. Conner, therefore, recommended that Pershing convert the 42nd Division into the replacement and labor division.

Conner's recommendation revealed his political naïveté. Secretary of War Newton D. Baker had created the 42nd Division from state militia units throughout the United States so that men from across the nation could enter the war as quickly as possible. To command the division, Baker had named Major General William Mann, the politically connected head of the War Department's Militia Bureau. Major Douglas MacArthur, who had assisted Baker in forming the division, became its chief of staff.

Mann and MacArthur used their political influence, particularly with Secretary Baker, to thwart Conner's plan. To generate sympathetic publicity for the guardsmen, Major MacArthur also leaked information to journalist Herbert Corey concerning clothing shortages in the division. In response to political pressure from Washington, Pershing directed Conner to conduct "a review of the question" of designating the 42nd Division as a replacement division.

Conner reconsidered the issue. He arrived at the same conclusion.

In a November 22 memorandum to Chief of Staff Harbord, Conner argued: "If the drafted National Guard is to be a reliable asset in this war, it must be treated without special privileges." Conner emphasized that if the division commander and staff succeeded in overriding GHQ's authority, "it would become increasingly difficult to utilize the National Guard counter to their desires." Conner urged his superiors to back his position: "The decision in this case is fundamentally important. It will probably establish the policy relating to employment of National Guard divisions for replacements."

The astute Harbord recognized that Conner's position, while logical, would draw Pershing into a political conflict he was likely to lose, particularly since the 42nd Division was Secretary Baker's own creation. On Harbord's advice, Pershing rejected Conner's recommendation. The 42nd Division remained intact. Pershing instead designated the next National Guard division slated to arrive, the 41st, to serve as the replacement division.

The 42nd Division became one of the most successful American combat units of World War I. Douglas MacArthur became a decorated field commander and the youngest division commander in the AEF. At least one of MacArthur's biographers, Frazier Hunt, contended that MacArthur also became Fox Conner's enemy.[7] "There were unquestionably certain members of the GHQ who blamed the whole affair on MacArthur and never forgave him for what they considered his interference," Hunt wrote in 1954. "Among these high staff officers that had this feeling were Pershing's G-3 … Fox Conner." Hunt considered Conner part of "the little GHQ crowd that had never been quite reconciled toward the brilliant young MacArthur." Other historians have also noted MacArthur's perception that he was disliked by the men he called "the Chaumont crowd."

None of Conner's existing writings provide information on whether he took Pershing's rejection of his advice, or the dispute with MacArthur, as personally as Frazier Hunt claimed. In a 1957 interview, George Marshall labeled as "nonsense" Hunt's theory that Conner later influenced him to view MacArthur negatively. Also, Pershing's decision did not reflect a repudiation of his G-3's judgment or ability. On December 18, 1917, at John McAuley Palmer's insistence, Pershing dropped the word "acting" from Conner's title. The 43-year-old colonel from Mississippi became the AEF's Assistant Chief of Staff for Operations in his own right.[8]

The dispute regarding the 42nd Division was only the beginning of the power struggles between the AEF's General Headquarters and its division commanders. In December 1917, Pershing removed General Mann from command of the 42nd Division. Pershing also sacked the commander of the 1st Division, Major General William Sibert. According to George Marshall, who served as Sibert's operation's officer at the time, the AEF's headquarters and field officers were "wholly out of sympathy with each other" in late 1917. Marshall, who noted the tendency of the Chaumont officers to parrot Pershing's stern demeanor, recalled that the GHQ staff members "had become very severe and they didn't know what they were being severe about."[9]

As chief of operations for the American Army's first coalition war since the Revolutionary War, Fox Conner also frequently found himself at the center of disputes between the AEF and its allies. He later termed those intra-Allied struggles "the war within the war."[10]

As 1917 drew to a close, 176,655 American troops had arrived in France—far fewer than the half-million men whom Conner and the Operations Section had deemed necessary for even minor combat operations. Conner remained "very much alarmed" over what he termed the "exceedingly disappointing" pace of transportation of the American Army. Seeking to capitalize on America's need to move men to Europe more rapidly, Great Britain offered to ship a number of American infantry battalions, but with significant strings attached: the men would be trained by the British, for service in British divisions, and under British command—essentially the same proposal for amalgamation of smaller American units rejected by the United States at the beginning of the war.[11]

On December 16, 1917, despite the temptation of additional British shipping, Conner recommended that "the British proposals be politely refused." He warned that an agreement to place American battalions into the British Army would result in "straining our relations with the French to the breaking point." In Conner's view, acceptance of the British offer would also result in "frittering our power away" by shipping American troops that the AEF would probably never recover. He pointed out that any later attempt to use the French transportation system to move either the men or their equipment "would be met with the various difficulties and obstacles which the French are such masters in politely presenting when they care to do so." Pershing concurred, and he declined the British offer.

British emissaries in Washington also lobbied President Wilson to reverse Pershing's decision to deploy the AEF in Lorraine. Great Britain preferred to see the American Army formed between the British and French sectors so that the AEF could support both allies. On January 1,

1918, Harbord directed Conner to again address the subject of where the AEF should be formed, "not only from the standpoint of strategy but including political considerations."[12]

On January 7, 1918, Conner delivered another detailed "Strategical Study" to Chief of Staff Harbord.[13] Conner reiterated his previous assessment that the anticipated German offensive would involve a "war of maneuver," for which the AEF was still not prepared to play any significant role. Conner also held firm to his belief that "our real mission lies in 1919," when the AEF would conduct a decisive offensive from its positions in Lorraine. "From a purely strategical point of view," Conner told Harbord, "our present plans, including the location of our troops during training, are correct for both the year 1918 and that of 1919."

Conner then addressed how "the political situation" should affect America's decision on whether to move the AEF to a position between the British and French Armies. Conner balanced the anticipated benefit of increased British morale against the negative effects that such a decision would have upon Franco-American relations. He told Harbord: "We are on French soil, and must use French facilities and it would appear that we must get along with the French unless we should decide to turn all our forces over unreservedly to the British." Conner also counseled against allowing the possibility of stronger postwar economic relations with Great Britain to affect selection of the American sector. "The war must be won," Conner reminded Harbord, "before an after-the-war commerce can be established."

The AEF stayed in Lorraine. Regarding Great Britain's continuing offer to transport American troops, provided they serve in the British Army, Conner wrote: "If it is possible for the British to transport additional troops to be trained in the rear of their lines, it should be possible for them to transport additional troops to join our own army wherever that army may be." Nonetheless, Conner recognized the "deep anxiety" of the British regarding the German spring offensive. He also understood that the American Army could not conduct its grand offensive in 1919 if the Allies collapsed in 1918.

Conner therefore devised a plan.

He acknowledged on January 7 that "the opportunity to obtain additional shipping was too great to be lost," and proposed a solution to accommodate both British and American interests:

> the British should be plainly told that our ability to conduct an offensive in 1919 depends on increasing the rate of transporting, equipping and homogeneously training our troops in such a way as to not fritter them away. If the British are equally frank and represent that the possibility of continuing the war until 1919 is dependent on putting some of our troops in rear of the line then a certain number of complete [emphasis in the original] divisions should be brought over on British shipping and supplied in rear of the British front with British resources. Such action should not, however, be taken without at least the passive consent of the French.

Conner's January 7 proposal led to adoption of the "6 Division Plan" of January 30, 1918. Great Britain agreed to transport and supply six entire American divisions, rather than only the infantry battalions it actually wanted. The British further agreed to train American soldiers in accordance with the AEF's training methods and to use French guns when training the AEF's artillery. Under Conner's 6 Division Plan, after a ten-week training period in the British sector, the various elements of the American divisions would be united and sent to Lorraine for service in the AEF. In this manner, the British secured the services of American troops to act as an emergency reserve, while the AEF found a way to move six complete divisions to Europe.[14]

Colonel Conner also continued to address the readiness of the American forces already in Lorraine. On January 6, 1918, Conner directed a memorandum to the AEF's chief of coordination—his former West Point nemesis William D. Connor—outlining the activity needed to enable the 1st Division to enter the line as a complete unit. On January 15, Conner also gave Pershing his recommendations for officers to serve as regimental commanders in the 1st Division; among them was Lieutenant Colonel Robert J. Maxey, his West Point classmate.[15]

On January 19, the 1st Division entered the line south of St. Mihiel under the command of Major General Robert Lee Bullard. The following day, Pershing opened the headquarters of the American I Corps, under the command of Major General Hunter Liggett, who would assume field command of the first American battle corps in Lorraine, once its component divisions had been properly trained and assembled. In early February, the AEF also established headquarters for the American II Corps, to control the divisions that would serve in the British sector under the 6 Division Plan.[16]

Pershing, who wanted his Chaumont staff officers to develop a better working relationship with their corps-level staff counterparts than they had enjoyed with the AEF's divisional officers, sought Conner's advice on naming chiefs of staff for the corps commanders. Recalling the successful result of his having teamed Hunter Liggett and Malin Craig at the War College in 1910, Conner recommended his friend and former West Point classmate Craig for the position as Liggett's I Corps chief of staff. Conner also suggested his Operations Section colleague George Simonds for the same position in II Corps. Pershing accepted both recommendations.[17]

Relations between Chaumont and the AEF's divisional commands, however, remained strained. George Marshall recalled that as he went about his work as the 1st Division's operations officer, there were usually "four or five observers from GHQ standing at one's elbow to watch how it was being done." Marshall said this practice "did not tend to quiet the nerves and promote the assurance of the division staff during their novitiate."[18]

On February 9, as Conner and others from headquarters inspected 1st Division positions near the town of Seicheprey, he noticed the familiar rumble of artillery fire, as he had heard on countless firing ranges before. This time, the whining of the projectiles grew louder with the passing seconds. Then the earth around him began to explode in gouts of dirt and rock that rained down as thunderous concussions shook the ground around him.[19]

The artilleryman Conner was on the wrong end of an artillery barrage.

Men scurried to find cover in shell holes. Ever the artillery student, Conner walked slowly to watch how the Germans plotted their shots. The lesson came at a price: Conner felt the sting and rip of hot metal in his face and neck. Blood from his neck soaked his uniform. Concerned about a possible severed jugular vein, fellow officer Henry Smither tried to apply a tourniquet to Conner's neck. The AEF chief of operations heard one of his comrades ask: "Is Conner going to bleed to death?" Another quipped: "Well, if he doesn't, Smither will choke him to death!"

Neither calamity happened, although Conner spent the next 5 days in a hospital for treatment of shrapnel wounds. He earned a Purple Heart for his wounds received at Seicheprey.

After returning to duty in mid-February 1918, the chief of operations resumed his work of forming the American corps in Lorraine.[20] On February 17, Conner reported that the 1st, 2nd, 26th, and 42nd divisions would each be ready for front-line service by the end of May 1918. The next day, he proposed that the AEF "insist" on June 1, 1918 as the date when its divisions would form "a purely American force under American command alone." Fox Conner and William Connor then jointly submitted a memorandum to Harbord on February 19; it urged Pershing to secure a formal agreement from the French to turn over the St. Mihiel area to the Americans so that the AEF could begin construction of the supply depots and other facilities needed to support a significant offensive.

Aware of the anxiety that continued to permeate French and British planning for the impending German offensive, Conner continued to counsel against allowing the "extreme pessimism" of America's allies to dictate when the AEF would be deployed. He also warned: "The French Command has every intention of postponing to the last possible date the establishment of a real homogeneous American Army under the exclusive command of Americans." He again urged Pershing to take a firm stand. "The sooner the French mind (including staff officers) is disabused of our submission to such an idea the better for all concerned."

In his February 17, 1918 memorandum, Conner worried that the shipment of American troops continued to lag. He and others in the AEF, therefore, had reason for optimism when, in March 1918, one of their own became Army chief of staff in Washington. Major General Peyton C. March, who had served as commander of the AEF's artillery forces in France, pledged that shipping would be his top priority. Secretary Baker appointed General March to succeed Tasker H. Bliss, whom President Wilson appointed as America's representative to the

"Supreme War Council" formed by the Allied governments to better coordinate intra-Allied strategy. James G. Harbord described Peyton March as "a live energetic man, full of energy and aggressiveness." Although sometimes abrasive, Peyton March produced results, and he understood the task before him. In a newspaper interview shortly after his appointment, March declared: "I propose to get the men to France if they have to swim."[21]

★ ★ ★ ★ ★

Captain Dwight Eisenhower was ready to dive in.

In February 1918, the Army assigned Eisenhower to Camp Meade, Maryland, where Fox Conner's classmate and fellow Mississippian, Colonel Ira C. Welborn, commanded tank units being trained for service in France. Eisenhower's hopes soared in March 1918 when he received orders assigning him to command of one of the tank battalions scheduled for deployment. Anxious to avoid any mishap, Eisenhower made detailed plans for the battalion's departure, including a trip to New York to inspect the harbor facilities from which his men would board the ship.

In March 1918, the tank battalion sailed for Europe without incident, but also without Eisenhower. Colonel Welborn considered the captain too valuable as a training officer to be spared for combat duty. Instead, Welborn sent Eisenhower to establish a tank training facility at Camp Colt, an "old, abandoned camp site in Gettysburg, Pennsylvania, of all places," as Eisenhower put it.

As the men he had trained went off to war, the captain settled into his next training assignment. Eisenhower's disappointment eased when his wife Mamie and their infant son, nicknamed "Icky," joined him in Gettysburg.[22]

★ ★ ★ ★ ★

In Europe, Germany's spring offensive continued to loom large in mid-March 1918. Although the Central Powers had failed either to knock Italy out of the war or to lure Switzerland into it, Germany had nevertheless amassed on the Western Front an army Fox Conner termed "by far the most formidable force which the world had ever seen."[23]

Despite having been wounded in February, Fox Conner continued to inspect the American troops serving in front-line positions in Lorraine. On March 18, he submitted a memorandum to his GHQ colleagues that outlined a number of deficiencies in the AEF's front-line units; these included shortages in such essential equipment as motorized transportation, field kitchens, telephones, and mobile electric equipment needed to provide lighting at divisional headquarters. Mindful that America's allies considered the AEF high command incompetent, Conner observed: "In some cases, the shortages have been such as to make our appearance in French sectors very embarrassing."[24]

With the German attack on the horizon, Conner also warned in his March 18, 1918 memorandum: "So far the replacement system has not worked and we may very soon expect large calls for replacements." With the War Department still behind in troop shipments, Conner urged that troops serving in the AEF supply system be given combat training so that "men who must soon go to the front line trenches may have a reasonably fair show when they get there."

Also in mid-March 1918, a different Baker delegation visited France when Secretary of War Newton D. Baker crossed the Atlantic to make a first-hand assessment of the AEF's progress. Baker also met with French leaders, including General Ferdinand Foch, chief of staff of the French Army. Conner, who served as Baker's translator at the meeting, recalled Foch's basic message to the American Secretary of War: "For God's sake, hurry."[25]

Foch understood what was about to happen.

On March 21, 1918, while Secretary Baker was still in France, Germany launched Operation *Michael*.[26] General Erich von Ludendorff, architect of the successful German campaign in Russia, attacked the British in the Picardy region of France—the same area where Great Britain had waged its unsuccessful Somme campaign in 1916. Ludendorff planned to separate the French and British, drive the latter to the English Channel, then advance on Paris to win the war.

Ludendorff's seventy-six German divisions, which employed the same tactics as at Caporetto, overwhelmed the twenty-eight British divisions that opposed them in Picardy. In an area where little change in the opposing lines had occurred since 1914, Ludendorff broke through the British trenches and advanced nearly 35 miles in 8 days. "Very few had imagined the possibility of such complete success," Conner wrote shortly after the war.

To drive the wedge between the British and French, Ludendorff then pushed toward the French city of Amiens, a critical transportation hub located approximately 80 miles north of Paris. Conner described Amiens as the "neck of the bottle" through which the roads and rail lines connecting the French and British sectors passed. Conner thought that the fall of Amiens seemed "imminent," and that Ludendorff was poised to deliver "an all but fatal blow to the Allied cause."

The two principal Allied armies faced not only a physical rupture but also a strategic one. On March 24, the British commander, Field Marshal Sir Douglas Haig, called upon his French counterpart, General Philippe Pétain, to honor an earlier agreement to send twenty French divisions to the British front. Concerned over his ability to defend Paris, Pétain demurred. When Haig asked Pétain whether he understood that Ludendorff would separate the two armies unless French divisions moved to support the British, the French commander-in-chief simply nodded his head.[27]

Despite the dire conditions around Amiens, Fox Conner's view of the American Army's mission did not change. On March 25, 1917, as Ludendorff drove toward Amiens, Conner met with Pershing to discuss deployment of the AEF. Rather than suggesting that American troops go to the aid of Britain, Conner proposed to send the 26th and 42nd divisions to the left and right of the 1st Division in Lorraine, in order to create the American I Corps he had been planning for months. Noting that both divisions faced marches of several days, Conner also thought each would need 7 days of rest and would not be available until April 6 at the earliest—a leisurely pace, given the seriousness of the situation near Amiens.[28]

Later that evening, Pershing and Pétain discussed the possibility of forming the American corps proposed by Conner. The French commander rejected the idea on the grounds that too large a section of the front would fall under the defense of the inexperienced American divisions. The following day, Conner submitted a revised proposal to send the 42nd Division, under its own commanding general and staff, for service in a French corps and to place the 1st and 26th divisions beside each other in Lorraine. Pétain accepted the 42nd Division, but he continued to resist the idea of placing the 1st and 26th divisions in contiguous positions. With available troops at a premium, Pétain and Pershing could not reach agreement on deployment of either of the two longest-serving American divisions in France.[29]

The "perfect unity of action," which Fox Conner had identified as the key to the undermanned Allies' surviving the German offensive, was failing to materialize.

Recognizing its peril, Great Britain then took an unprecedented step. On March 26, 1918, the British commander Haig agreed to grant French General Ferdinand Foch authority to coordinate the operations of the British and French Armies on the Western Front. Foch quickly acted to strengthen the junction between the two armies by extending the French line northward into the British sector, which provided support to Haig while allowing Pétain to retain command of the French divisions. A week later, the Allied governments made Foch the supreme commander of all Allied forces on the Western Front.[30]

The Allies also turned to America for greater assistance. On March 27, the Supreme War Council, including the American representative, General Bliss, issued its "Joint Note 18." The council called upon the United States to ship only infantry and machine-gun troops and to allow their "temporary service" in the French and British armies. Secretary Baker, while still in France, endorsed the idea of "preferential transportation" of infantry and machine-gun units, but he made it clear that Pershing would control where the troops would serve. On March 28, in a grandiose gesture, Pershing told Foch: "Infantry, artillery, aviation, all that we have are yours; use them as you wish." The Allied supreme commander sent the American 1st Division, under its own commander and staff, to serve in a reserve role south of Amiens. He also sent the 2nd, 26th, and 42nd divisions to non-contiguous areas of Lorraine to replace French divisions being transferred northward to the Amiens fighting.[31]

Fox Conner understood the spirit of Pershing's offer; he neverthe-less viewed the March 28 agreement as "an entire disruption of our plan" for establishing an American force in Lorraine. In an April 1 memorandum, Conner outlined the negative consequences of Joint Note 18, particularly upon the AEF's already-weak ability to supply and reinforce its troops. He warned that the delay in forming complete divisions that would result from implementation of Joint Note 18 would impair the ability of AEF division commanders and their staffs to gain needed experience. Conner summed up his view: "It is further evident that delay of this nature postpones final success." Pershing, thereafter, recommended that the War Department give a limited application to Joint Note 18, under which the infantry and machine-gun units of only four divisions, together with replacements, would go to France ahead of the other components of those divisions.[32]

Ludendorff's Operation *Michael* advanced to within 12 miles of Amiens but could not take the city against the combined French and British defenses marshaled by Foch. The German commander also faced difficulty in supplying his troops across terrain devastated by both the 1916 British offensive and by Operation *Michael* itself. On April 5, as German casualties neared a quarter-million men, Ludendorff ordered a halt to the offensive. Despite its early success and gain of territory, Germany had failed to separate the French and British armies, either physically or strategically.[33]

The next day, April 6, 1918, marked the first anniversary of America's declaration of war. It was lost on no one that an entire year had come and gone without any significant American participation.

The Allies understood that Ludendorff, more delayed than defeated, would draw upon Germany's superior manpower reserves to replenish his force and renew his offensive. With Operation *Michael* having claimed 160,000 more men from its already depleted army, Great Britain sent its ambassador to the United States, Lord Reading, to appeal directly to President Wilson for a broader application of Joint Note 18 than Pershing and Conner were willing to give it.[34]

In response to Lord Reading's request for 360,000 American infantry-men and machine gunners over a 3-month period, the president replied that the United States would "send troops over as fast as we could make them ready," which Reading interpreted as a firm agreement. Neither Baker nor Pershing knew about the Wilson–Reading meeting. When two British generals appeared at Chaumont to discuss transportation arrangements to transport the AEF's troops, Baker and Pershing cabled the president for instructions. Wilson replied that no specific agreement had been reached and that "details are left to be worked out."

Pershing turned to Fox Conner to tend to those details.

On April 6, Conner submitted his analysis of Lord Reading's plan. Conner summarized his view: "No action in rejecting this proposal can be too energetic." He pointed out that the 360,000 men sought by the British would constitute the infantry and machine gunners needed for 21 divisions and that the remaining components of those divisions would not arrive until well into 1919. Conner argued that acceptance of Lord Reading's proposal would "end all hope of seeing an American Army in the war."

Conner's analysis also reflected a fundamental mistrust of his allies. Given his recent experience in having the French resist the contiguous deployment of even two American divisions in a quiet sector, Conner stated: "Familiarity with past events forces us, willingly or unwillingly, to the conclusion that both the British and the French are determined to delay in every possible way the organization of a purely American force under American command." Given the vague language of Joint Note 18 that the American battalions would "eventually" be returned to the AEF, and the reality that the British had only limited and dwindling manpower reserves, Colonel Conner also doubted that Great Britain would ever release the American units. He thought it would be "at least as easy to resist incorporating our soldiers with the British as it will be to secure the return of our units once we have brigaded them with the British."

Further analyzing the positions of the Allies, Conner wrote: "The British and French, actuated by the highest motives, are convinced that we are incapable of handling large forces." Conner considered this position "mortifying": "If we are incapable then the war is lost, for neither our people nor our soldiers will consent to the indefinite virtual drafting of our men under foreign colors."

Conner also framed his April 6, 1918 analysis within the context of whether the United States would act, and be accepted, as a world power equal to the British and French. Regarding Lord Reading's proposal, Conner wrote:

> ... acquiescence in such a plan delivers over 360,000 officers and soldiers to foreign commanders, down to include the regiment, but leaves us unable to evade ultimate responsibility. There is no precedent for such a plan in all the history of equal [emphasis in the original] nations. Great Britain did not even follow such a course with her dependencies—Canada, Australia and New Zealand—but formed contingents from those countries in complete divisions and Army Corps.
>
> Even though such piecemeal employment of our forces should against all precedent result in a tactical victory, America would not accomplish her object. America must have a voice in the peace councils if a peace satisfactory to her is to be formulated. She will have no such voice if her forces are used up by putting her battalions in French and British units.

On April 9, Conner submitted a proposal to provide the British with half of the American infantry and machine-gun troops they desired, without crippling the efforts of the AEF to form an independent army. He proposed that the British ship 60,000 American infantry and machine-gun troops in April, May, and June, while American shipping would transport the artillery, supply, and other auxiliary units of those divisions. The troops brought in British shipping would be trained by the British and would serve in British units if needed in an emergency; they would then be returned to the AEF, after three months, to be united into complete American divisions. Eager to obtain the men it could, Great Britain agreed to the plan, but only for April.[35]

Conner's April 9 memorandum recognized that the priority given to shipment of the troops Great Britain needed meant that transportation of other servicemen needed by the AEF would have to be delayed. Of significance to the career of Captain Dwight Eisenhower, Conner noted: "Since difficulties of obtaining matériel render it impossible to hope to equip them within the next three months, we may at once postpone the arrival of all tank personnel."[36]

Conner's intra-Allied struggles were not limited to the British. On April 9, he met with French Brigadier General Camille M. Ragueneau, the French Army's chief representative at Chaumont.[37] According to Conner's account, Ragueneau insisted that the American infantry battalions sent earlier to French divisions for training purposes should remain with the French for an "indefinite" period of time. Conner bluntly told General Ragueneau that the United States had "no intention of leaving our units indefinitely in foreign divisions." Conner further pointed out that "German papers had already commenced a propaganda" denigrating the ability of the Americans to fight on their own.

General Ragueneau also touched a nerve when he told the Leavenworth and War College graduate Conner in the April 9 meeting that the French high command "did not see the possibility" of the AEF forming "competent staffs" to control the incoming American troops. According to Conner, Ragueneau argued that although "France had no men left ... she had trained staffs, and that was what was needed"— without considering the possibility that France was running out of men *because* of its commanders and staffs.

While Conner and Ragueneau verbally sparred at Chaumont on April 9, 1918, more serious fighting resumed to the north.

With the combined Allied forces still massed in Picardy, Ludendorff attacked northward on April 9 along the Lys River and into the Flanders region of Belgium. In Operation *George*, Ludendorff planned to drive the British Army northward to the English Channel and capture the ports of Calais and Dunkirk. Like Operation *Michael* in March, Operation *George* achieved great initial success, as Germany drove a deep wedge into the British and Belgian lines in Flanders. Understanding the necessity of holding the Channel ports, the British commander Haig issued dramatic orders to his troops on April 11: "With our backs to the wall, and believing in the justice of our cause, each one of us must fight on to the end."[38]

On April 12, Conner sent Supreme Commander Foch a message from Pershing, offering the services of the American 1st Division. "There is no reason why this division should not take its place actively wherever you desire to place it," the message read. "In case you consider it urgent, this division could go in at once." Conner also acted to create another fighting division by combining elements of the two AEF replacement divisions then in France, the 41st and 32nd divisions.[39]

As British casualties mounted during Operation *George*, Pershing and his staff met with British officials in London from April 22 through April 24.[40] The issue of amalgamating American units into the shrinking British divisions dominated the discussions. British representatives at the meeting surprised Pershing with a cable from Lord Reading in which he claimed that President Wilson had made a written commitment to monthly shipments of 120,000 infantrymen and machine gunners for four months—an even larger number of men than Conner had objected to on April 6. Refusing to believe that either Wilson or Baker would have made such an agreement without notifying him, Pershing ignored Lord Reading's cable.

The American commander did agree in the April London Conference to modify Conner's 6 Division Plan to allow for the priority transportation in May of the infantry and machine-gun troops of the divisions already scheduled for service with the British. In return, Great Britain agreed to transport the artillery and other services of the divisions "immediately thereafter." In effect, Great Britain agreed to provide nearly twice as much shipping as it had previously offered, prompting AEF Chief of Staff Harbord to ask: "Where has such an amount of shipping been? ... Why has it needed a menace to the Channel ports to make it available?" Conner had raised a similar question in his January 7 Strategical Study concerning the good faith of the British in making shipping available to the AEF.

Like Operation *Michael* before it, Operation *George* stalled because of the same combination of stout Allied resistance and difficulty in supplying front-line attack units. On April 29, Ludendorff halted the second phase of his offensive. Germany had gained ground, and had inflicted another 120,000 casualties upon the withering Allied armies, but had failed to accomplish its larger strategic objective of capturing the Channel ports. Conner's 1917 prediction—that effective Allied unity of action could overcome Germany's advantage in troop strength—was proving correct.

The AEF had again played no significant role in stopping Ludendorff's spring offensive, although the American 1st Division at least moved closer to the fighting. On April 25, 1918, the division moved up from its

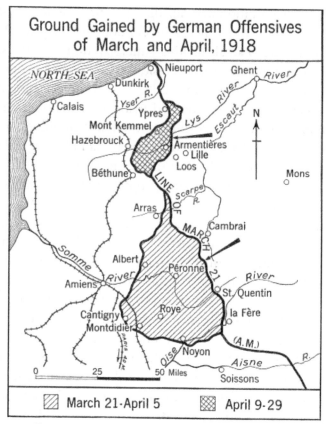

Map 3: *German Offensives of March and April 1918. Credit: The American Battle Monuments Commission.*

reserve position on the Amiens front to relieve a French division on the front line, south of the village of Cantigny. As the AEF's premier division entered the front line of an active sector for the first time, Fox Conner fretted that the unit might still be "below the standards of experience, training and discipline which should be attained before men are called upon to submit to the ordeal of modern battle."[41]

The British and French likewise remained gravely concerned over their own abilities to persevere. By Foch's estimate, the Germans still had 200 divisions on the Western Front, to only 162 for the Allies. The supreme commander also estimated that Germany could bring in another 600,000 men as replacements.[42] With the United States as the only source of matching manpower, Pershing and his staff fought yet another intra-Allied amalgamation battle in May.

The Supreme War Council met in Abbeville, France on May 1–2, 1918.[43] General Foch, irked at France's exclusion from the London Conference in April, demanded a share for France of the American infantrymen and machine gunners being shipped to Europe. Conner recalled that the British and French debated the issue of where the incoming Americans would go "in a manner that seemed to imply that the American Commander-In-Chief had no voice in the matter."

But Pershing made himself heard.

In words that echoed Conner's studies of December 16 and January 7, the American commander argued that it was foolhardy to "fritter away" American strength by hurling thousands of untrained soldiers into the path of the German Army, particularly when the AEF already had complete divisions in France that were trained and available to fight.

At the May Abbeville Conference, Pershing agreed to extend, through June 1918, the priority on shipment of American infantry and machine-gun troops, as Conner had originally proposed in his April 9 study. Under the Abbeville Agreement, however, Pershing retained control over where the American troops would go for training and initial service. He also secured the right to decide when the units would be returned to the AEF for formation into American divisions. The American commander also wrested from the Supreme War Council a significant declaration: that "an American Army should be formed as early as possible under its own Commander and under its own Flag."

Following the Abbeville Conference, Conner continued making plans for that independent army. His May 7, 1918 memorandum assigned female codenames for the forty-seven divisions and six corps the AEF expected to form. Conner gave the name "Virginia" to the 89th Division, to be formed of men drafted from Kansas and other Great Plains states where he and his Virginia had spent enjoyable days. Conner monitored the movement and training of the elements of the 4th, 28th, 30th, 35th, 77th, and 82nd divisions being sent to the American II Corps in the British sector pursuant to the 6 Division Plan. Ever mindful of the need to establish America's independence in the control of its troops, Conner told II Corps Chief of Staff George Simonds: "You will control the date of entry into the line of the American units." Conner also worked with the French high command to have the American 2nd Division sent to a reserve position in an active sector near Paris.[44]

Conner worked in May 1918 from a Chaumont GHQ swirling with change. Pershing honored a promise to James G. Harbord and reassigned his chief of staff to field service. General Harbord took command of the Marines that formed the AEF's 4th Brigade, one of the two brigades of the 2nd Division. Harbord wrote that his departure from Chaumont "came as a shock to many of those who had been at GHQ since the beginning."[45]

To replace Harbord, Pershing selected James McAndrew as his new chief of staff. The 55-year-old McAndrew, a veteran of the wars in Cuba and the Philippines, had also served as commandant of the Leavenworth Staff College and as president of the Army War College. Since October 1917, McAndrew had served as head of the AEF Staff College at Langres, and he had overseen the training of many of the men who would serve in staff positions in the regiments, brigades, and divisions being formed. Pershing also appointed LeRoy Eltinge, one of Conner's top assistants in the Operations Section, to the newly created position of deputy chief of staff.[46]

No evidence exists to suggest that Pershing considered Fox Conner for either the chief of staff or deputy assignments. But with Harbord gone to the field, and McAndrew and Eltinge in new positions in Chaumont, Conner provided needed continuity in American high command as it strove toward the objective of forming the AEF into an equal partner in the Allied coalition.

That goal appeared within reach by mid–May 1918. Seeking to capitalize on the Supreme War Council's Abbeville declaration that an independent American Army be formed "as early as possible," Pershing met with French General Pétain in Chantilly, France on May 19 to establish a specific sector for the AEF. Pétain agreed to turn over the Woëvre region of Lorraine[47]—including the St. Mihiel salient—"as soon as circumstances permit." Pershing pressed Pétain for specificity as to what the "circumstances" would be, resulting in a written agreement from the French commander that the Americans would "definitely" take over the Woëvre sector once four complete American divisions were in the line, with two in reserve.[48]

With the 1st and 2nd divisions deployed in separate French corps in active sectors to the north, Conner prepared a schedule for deployment of the other six AEF divisions that were in various states of readiness. Under Conner's May 24, 1918 plan, the National Guardsmen of the 26th and 42nd divisions would be ready for front-line service by June 22. The Regular Army troops of the 3rd and 5th divisions had begun arriving in April and May, and Conner projected that these divisions would become available by mid-August. Conner also expected the 32nd and 41st divisions, then in training near the Swiss border, to revert to their original roles as replacement divisions. Under Conner's May 24 schedule, even if both the 1st and 2nd divisions remained in the areas around Amiens and Paris, the American I Corps could take over the Woëvre sector by mid-August 1918—or sooner if Foch returned the 1st and 2nd divisions earlier.[49]

On May 25, Conner met with General Ragueneau, who gave tentative French approval of the proposed deployment schedule. Conner's May 25 memorandum acknowledged that his plan would have to be altered "if an emergency so demanded."[50]

That emergency still threatened. The Allies understood that Ludendorff had no option but to commit his full reserves to complete the conquest of the British and French before American troops arrived in sufficient number to erase the manpower advantage that Germany still enjoyed. Conner recalled that "various people had predicted an attack on every locality between Switzerland and the North Sea," but that no one really knew where Germany would next strike. Would the German commander seek to finish off the British in Flanders or, instead, attack French lines weakened by Foch's movement of more than fifty French divisions to support the British?[51]

With American battalions spread throughout the Allied ranks, and the AEF's two best divisions serving near the middle of the Allied line, the time was drawing near for the AEF to fight, regardless of where Ludendorff next attacked. Since arriving in France, Fox Conner had focused primarily upon the design, formation, and preservation of the American Army, without actually employing it in combat.

That was about to change.

CHAPTER 6

FIGHTING WITH THE FRENCH

*General Pershing, as top commander, operated very largely through his
operational staff—that was General Fox Conner, who was the head
of the G-3 organization—so far as fighting was concerned.*
—George C. Marshall[1]

At AEF headquarters in Chaumont, Fox Conner fielded telephone calls
on May 28, 1918 in what one observer described as a "bewildering suc-
cession."[2] Staff officers and clerks scurried to decode and deliver to the
chief of operations the jumble of information that each new message
brought. The sounds of phones ringing and being slammed down blended
with the incessant hum of voices and the percussion of boots on the floor.

Well to the north of Chaumont, more American boots marched to
battle. After months of planning and waiting, the AEF had finally joined
the fight.

Since April 1918, when the American 1st Division had entered the
line near Amiens as a component of the French X Corps, German
artillery had harassed the Americans from high ground near the village
of Cantigny. In mid-May, the French corps commander had approved
an American attack to take Cantigny. The 1st Division's operations
officer, Captain George Marshall, served as the primary planner for that
operation. As AEF chief of operations, Conner kept a watchful eye on
Marshall and his preparations, which included construction of a replica
of the Cantigny defenses against which the division practiced its attack.[3]

Satisfied with his division's readiness, Major General Robert Lee
Bullard set May 28, 1918 for the AEF's attack on Cantigny. On May 27,

three battalions of the 28th Infantry Regiment began moving into position to spearhead the operation. Fox Conner's West Point classmate, Lieutenant Colonel Robert J. Maxey, commanded the regiment's 2nd Battalion.

But while the AEF focused its attention on its three battalions near Cantigny on May 27, German Field Marshal Ludendorff chose the same day to unleash thirty divisions against the Allies in a resumption of his grand offensive against the Western Front.

In Operation *Blücher*, Ludendorff sent his superior force against seven tired Allied divisions holding the Aisne River less than a hundred miles northwest of Paris. In the third phase of his 1918 offensive, Ludendorff attacked the Aisne as a diversion, designed to draw French divisions away from the British sector and back toward Paris. The German commander planned to then turn his attack northward to complete his conquest of the weakened British Army in Flanders.[4]

Fox Conner acknowledged that the AEF had not anticipated the attack on the Aisne and that the French were "absolutely surprised" by it. By noon on May 27, Ludendorff had crossed the river and advanced in the direction of Paris. The reeling French forces fell back in the same direction—exactly as the German commander had planned.[5]

Ludendorff's attack on the Aisne created a quandary for the AEF. Bullard wanted to proceed with the well-rehearsed attack on Cantigny, scheduled for the next morning. But the French X Corps, including the artillery designated to support the American attack, planned to meet the Germans on the Aisne Front on the afternoon of the 28th. Not wanting to lose the opportunity to gain the AEF's first experience on the battlefield, particularly given the extensive preparations, Pershing decided to proceed, even though the French warned that only limited artillery support would be available.

At 5:45 a.m. on May 28, as Conner and the others at GHQ in Chaumont waited for news, French artillery supporting the 1st Division began an intense bombardment of Cantigny. Flashes of bursting shells illuminated clouds of poison gas, smoke, and dust that roiled skyward from the village. At 6:45 a.m., the American battalions left their trenches and attacked in waves, as practiced. Conner's liaison officer at the

1st Division, Lieutenant Colonel Walter Grant, reported that the infantry advanced "as if it were at inspection—really splendid." Within an hour, Maxey's battalion had occupied Cantigny with minimal casualties. Grant told Conner: "The fight came off practically exactly as planned."[6]

At AEF headquarters, Conner and his Operations Section colleagues basked in the satisfaction of success.

The moment was short-lived.

As Conner continued to monitor developments at Cantigny, the door to his office burst open. French General C.M. Ragueneau rushed in. Worry marked the face and voice of the French high command's chief representative at Chaumont as he lamented: "*C'est terrible! C'est affreaux! Les Boches sont arrivés au Marne. Au secours!*"[7]

Once the German Army bridged the Aisne, French defenses began to collapse. Ludendorff easily crossed two more rivers, the Vesle and the Ourcq, and also captured the strategic rail junction at Soissons. More than 60,000 Frenchmen surrendered before the German onslaught. Although Ludendorff had attacked the Aisne as a diversion, the French Army's disarray prompted the German commander to change plans. Instead of turning north to fight the British in Flanders, Ludendorff converted his attack into an all-out drive to capture Paris. He therefore sent his full force toward the Marne River—the last natural obstacle before the French capital—where France and Germany had fought their pivotal 1914 battle.

According to Fox Conner, once the peril to Paris became evident, "something akin to panic seized that city."[8] The AEF chief of operations therefore understood Ragueneau's consternation as the agitated Frenchman stood before him. Obeying Pershing's directive for Americans to exude optimism, Conner met the French general's anxious plea with soothing reassurance. According to Major Lloyd Griscom, who witnessed the meeting, Conner told Ragueneau: "Don't you worry too much. We'll help you out. That's what we're here for." Conner then proposed to send the American 2nd Division to a front-line position to confront the Germans. According to Griscom, Conner "calmed his excited visitors as if they had been children."

Ragueneau, who contended that France faced "the greatest emergency of the war," pleaded for more men. Conner confided to Griscom: "I

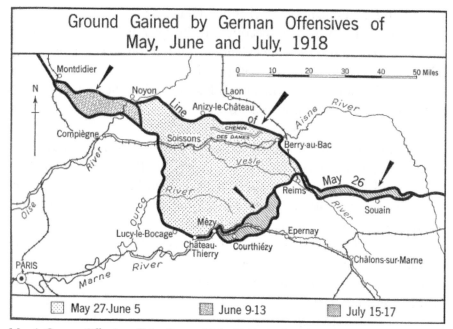

Map 4: German Offensives of May, June and July, 1918. Credit: The American Battle Monuments Commission.

don't know when to believe 'em. One minute they're on the crest of the wave and the next at the bottom of the lowest trough." The chief of operations also complained that the French were "bothering the life out of us trying to persuade us to put our half-trained divisions on the front line."

The individual battalions of the American 3rd Division had been in France only since April 1918. The deployment schedule tentatively agreed to by Conner and Ragueneau on May 25 did not envision the 3rd Division entering the line until mid-August.[9] But when Ragueneau, with "tears in his eyes," as Griscom described him, gave Conner the full details of the French Army's dire situation on the Marne, Conner relented; he agreed to also send elements of the 3rd Division into the fight as well.

Conner telephoned the headquarters of the 3rd Division. The snippets of conversation quoted by Griscom reveal the surprise that met Conner's decision to deploy the division well ahead of schedule: "Can you have your division ready tomorrow morning to go into the line? ... Yes, I know you haven't had any trench training ... Yes, it's an emergency ... The French will get you there ... How about it?" Griscom recalled that Conner hung up and announced, "Everything is arranged."

On the afternoon of May 28, Chief of Operations Conner ordered the 3rd Division: "Have all infantry, machine guns, signal troops, trains, and hospitals ready to entrain on May 31 or as soon thereafter as transportation can be furnished." Conner's directive that "infantry will probably be used in small units" for service with the French—a practice he detested—demonstrated the exigency of the situation on the Marne.[10]

Having secured the services of both the American 2nd and 3rd divisions, Ragueneau left Conner's office on May 28 in what Major Griscom described as "the seventh heaven of joy." But when Fox Conner returned his attention to the 1st Division at Cantigny, he learned that American casualties were beginning to mount.

Among those killed in action was his West Point classmate Robert Maxey.

Once the French corps moved to the Aisne and withdrew its suppressing artillery fire from the Cantigny operation, German batteries began to rain deadly fire upon Maxey's battalion. Caught in the open with little area for shelter, Maxey, whom Conner had recommended for a field command, tried to hold his troops together amid the torrent of mortar rounds that decimated his men. Shrapnel shredded Maxey's neck. Bleeding profusely, Maxey insisted on being taken to Colonel Hanson W. Ely, commander of the 28th Infantry Regiment, to make a final report. Robert Maxey, who lost his life on the first day of the AEF's first major attack, became the first and only member of the West Point Class of 1898 to perish in combat during the war.[11]

Maxey's 1st Division comrades fought off seven German counterattacks over the next 4 days. In a postwar study of American operations, Conner wrote: "The Germans were determined at all costs to counteract any moral effect which an American success, coming just at the first moment of Allied depression over the enemy's great success on the

Aisne, might have." On May 29, Colonel Ely reported the condition of his 28th Infantry Regiment as "pounded to hell and gone." But Fox Conner and Hugh Drum had designed the large AEF divisions to outlast their opponents in prolonged combat. On May 30, battalions from the 16th and 18th regiments relieved Ely's troops to continue the fight at Cantigny.[12]

By May 31, the 1st Division controlled Cantigny and the surrounding heights, but at a cost. In 4 days of fighting, the division suffered more than a thousand casualties, including almost 200 killed. Germany lost almost twice as many men. The 1st Division had performed as Conner had planned, in both absorbing and inflicting casualties. Fox Conner acknowledged that the capture of Cantigny was of "minor importance" militarily; nonetheless he thought that the 1st Division's success in its debut operation "was of the greatest possible value in that it demonstrated to our Allies and to the enemy the value of American troops in the offensive." Of particular importance to Conner, who had borne his share of French and British condescension in the preceding months, the Cantigny operation "greatly increased the respect for American troops among our Allies as well as among the Germans."[13]

Farther east, events on the Marne River gave the AEF an opportunity to enhance its new reputation.

By the end of May, Ludendorff's Aisne offensive had driven a 30-mile-deep salient into the Allied line, with the leading point of the advance reaching as far as Château-Thierry on the Marne River, less than 50 miles from Paris. On May 31, Conner and Pershing met in Chaumont to discuss events on the Marne. Conner thought that "the future seemed darkest" at that time, as more than a million people had begun to flee Paris and the surrounding areas.[14]

Conner worked with Ragueneau and the 3rd Division's staff to coordinate the division's supply and transport to Château-Thierry for service with the French XXXVIII Corps. Upon arriving, battalions of the 3rd Division demolished the bridges across the Marne, then repelled several German efforts to cross the river. As Conner described it in his wartime Notes on Operations: "Wherever the soldiers of the 3rd Division appeared, there too the German advance broke on the rocks."[15]

The French also sent the American 2nd Division, including James G. Harbord's Marine Brigade, to block the road between Château-Thierry and Paris. Harbord described the French troops he encountered as a "motley array which we read characterizes the rear of a routed army." In one of the more memorable sayings to emerge from the war, one Marine officer, in response to a French suggestion that the Americans join in the French withdrawal, replied: "Retreat hell. We just got here." Harbord likewise proclaimed: "We will dig no trenches to fall back to. The marines will hold where they stand."[16]

The Marines indeed held at Château-Thierry. But even as the 1st, 2nd, and 3rd divisions proved their mettle at Cantigny and Château-Thierry, Fox Conner and his Chaumont colleagues continued to wage the Battle of Amalgamation against their French and British allies regarding the hundreds of thousands of fresh American troops arriving in France.

On May 29, as Conner dealt with the details of the 3rd Division's hasty deployment to the Marne, he also addressed French General Philippe Pétain's request that the AEF leave its infantry battalions in French divisions through September 1918, when the next class of French conscripts would complete its training. In a memorandum to AEF Chief of Staff James McAndrew, Conner pointed out that such an agreement would send incoming Americans to the front with only 4 months of training so that the French recruits could receive 6. Conner urged his superiors to reject Pétain's proposal and to "insist" that the French Army send a "considerable proportion" of its own inductees to the front with the same amount of training as the Americans.[17]

Conner wrote his May 29 memorandum in preparation for the Supreme War Council meeting held in Versailles on June 1 and June 2, 1918. Conner accompanied Pershing to the Versailles conference, which the AEF chief of operations considered "one of the most interesting and most tempestuous" of the intra-Allied conferences.[18]

As anticipated, Pershing clashed with his allies over one of the issues identified in Conner's May 29 memorandum: whether the United States should shorten the training period for its troops so that French conscripts could receive greater training. The British, French, and Americans agreed at Versailles to shorten the training period for all new recruits.

The focus of the Versailles conference centered on Foch's request that the United States alter its shipping schedules to send only infantrymen and machine gunners for immediate use in French and British divisions. The supreme Allied commander sought 250,000 such troops in June and an equal number in July. Pershing refused, citing the AEF's critical shortages in artillery and other services. With Conner at his side to provide information and advice during the heated session, Pershing eventually agreed to send 170,000 infantrymen and machine gunners in June, together with 80,000 troops of other services. The ratio would change to 140,000 and 110,000 in July. Foch promised to provide Pershing with French artillery, aviation, and other support that the AEF would be unable to provide for itself under the agreement.

In a post-conference memorandum to the AEF chief of supply, Fox Conner acknowledged that the Versailles agreement was "a compromise which had to be made between the desirability of building up all parts of the AEF progressively and the imperative necessities of strengthening the combatant forces of the Allies." Because of the Versailles conference, however, the AEF would continue to face a significant imbalance between its infantry forces and their supporting units, including tanks.

★ ★ ★ ★ ★

As the War Department continued to suspend the transportation of tank troops to France, Major Dwight Eisenhower's command at Camp Colt in Gettysburg swelled to more than 10,000 men during the summer of 1918. Eisenhower recalled that he mostly worked to "prevent the dry rot of tedious idleness." In June, the War Department sent Eisenhower his first actual tanks to use in training—three Renault light tanks stripped of their guns. Before then, Eisenhower had done his best to simulate tank warfare by having his men fire machine guns from moving trucks.

Moreover, the Army provided little guidance as to what Eisenhower was supposed to teach his tankers-in-training. "Our chief source of information in 1918 came from newspapers," Eisenhower recalled, "and we had to use our imaginations." The War Department, for instance, did not provide Major Eisenhower with the 58-page study, *Light Tanks,* authored by George Patton, which summarized what Patton had learned as head of the AEF's light tank training school in France.[19]

★ ★ ★ ★ ★

The Versailles conference also produced an unexpected boon for the AEF. To strengthen the defense of Paris, Foch proposed to transfer several French divisions from Lorraine to the capital region, and to replace those with the American divisions serving in the British sector pursuant to the 6 Division Plan. British Field Marshal Sir Douglas Haig, who had been the beneficiary of Foch's coordination during the first two phases of Ludendorff's attack, agreed to the plan. Each commanding general designated a representative with full authority to arrange the transfers. Pershing chose Conner.

On June 3, Conner met with his British and French counterparts at General Pétain's headquarters. Conner recalled, in a postwar lecture, that "each staff officer had full power, and within an hour all details were settled." Those details included "almost every conceivable thing," from the selection of the particular divisions for transfer, down to logistical details pertaining to exchange of rifles and food for horses. The British agreed to release five of the divisions sent to them under the 6 Division Plan: the 4th, 28th, 35th, 77th, and 82nd divisions. With the goal of forming an independent American force ever on his mind, Conner saw to it that the French deployed the American divisions in areas where other American divisions were already located for training.[20]

The AEF moved a step closer to establishing its first functional corps when, on June 6, Pétain agreed to give the American I Corps control of the Château-Thierry sector, where both the 2nd and 3rd divisions were deployed. Also on June 6—a date that would become associated with a more famous American attack in France 26 years later—the 2nd Division began a bitter 3-week battle of attrition that placed Conner at the center of controversy.

German troops occupied the *Bois de Belleau* (Belleau Wood), a copse of trees north of the 2nd Division's line near Château-Thierry. Approximately 1,000 yards wide by 3,000 yards deep, Belleau Wood was not on the highway to Paris and had little strategic significance;

however, the French wanted the woods retaken. The task fell primarily to Harbord's 4th Brigade.[21]

The Marines advanced at 3:45 a.m. on June 6. The lead platoons waded through wheat fields to approach the woods. Just as the outline of the trees became discernible against the darkness, the forest erupted into thousands of red and yellow muzzle flashes that sent death whirring toward the Marines. The thunder of artillery joined the rapid hammering of the German machine guns as American Marines fell by the hundreds. Those not hit by bullet or shrapnel dove for protection. Understanding that the open ground provided no sanctuary, platoon leaders urged their men forward. Above the pandemonium of gunfire and explosions, Sergeant Daniel Daley bellowed: "Come on you sons-of-bitches, do you want to live forever?"

Many didn't live past the day. The United States Marine Corps suffered 1,087 killed, wounded, or taken prisoner on the first day of the Belleau Wood attack. Not until Tarawa in World War II would the Marines lose as many men in a single day.

For the next 4 days, the Marine Brigade slowly advanced into Belleau Wood against positions made naturally strong by dense stands of trees, steep ravines, and massive boulders. Harbord's men fought back several counterattacks and suffered constant shelling. By June 10, the brigade had taken the southern half of the woods—but with losses of more than 2,000 men. Those who survived neared exhaustion; some simply fell asleep during the incessant bombardment.

On June 11, Harbord sent two messages to Major General Omar Bundy, the 2nd Division's commander, urging him to send help for the Marines. Bundy turned to Chaumont for the reinforcements.[22]

No relief came.

According to historian Frank Vandiver, "Fox Conner, in one of his rare lapses, decided things were not really bad in the woods." Author Laurence Stallings, who was wounded at Belleau Wood while leading a Marine platoon, wrote that Conner's "idiotic" remarks had "infuriated" James G. Harbord.[23]

Fox Conner's decisions regarding the American troops at Belleau Wood therefore warrant scrutiny.

Throughout the 2nd Division's operations in Belleau Wood, Conner remained at Chaumont and received reports from his liaison officer to the division, Walter Grant, who had served him well at Cantigny. Major Robert C. Richardson, Chaumont's liaison with the French XXI Corps in which the 2nd Division served, also sent reports to Conner.[24] However, Richardson and Grant did not provide consistent assessments of the Marine Brigade's condition, nor did Harbord. For example, Richardson told Conner in a June 12 telephone conversation that Harbord's brigade needed to be relieved "just as soon as possible." On the same day, though, Grant reported that he had met with Harbord three times and that "on none of these occasions did he (Harbord) mention the fact that he desired his brigade relieved."[25]

To clarify the matter, Grant spoke again with Harbord on June 13 to ask for a "candid expression of his opinion" on whether the 4th Brigade needed to be removed. Grant relayed to Harbord the information received at Chaumont indicating that that Marines were "near the breaking point." Grant reported back to Conner that Harbord had "scouted any such idea, stating that their morale was unimpaired, but that physically they were tired out." Grant also spoke to several 2nd Division officers who provided the same assessment: the division could remain in place if the length of its line were shortened to enable the formation of a rear echelon where individual battalions could go for a short rest. Conner had already asked Ragueneau, on June 11, to send either the American 42nd Division or a brigade of the 4th Division to shorten the 2nd Division's line for this purpose. Richardson also told Conner on June 13 that the French corps had its own plan for providing relief to the American division.[26]

Furthermore, on June 12, the 2nd Division's chief of staff, Colonel Preston Brown, had reported to Conner that "it is now believed that the *Bois de Belleau* has been completely cleaned out of enemy detachments," which suggested that the fighting was near its end. Bundy reported the same to the French corps commander on June 13.[27]

Stallings and others have accurately quoted Fox Conner when he told Major Richardson on June 13: "The reports we have show that conditions are not very bad. Do nothing further in the matter."[28] Conner's assessment, however, must be analyzed within the context of the reports he had received indicating that the fighting in the woods was almost over, that the Marines needed rest rather than removal, and that help from the French was on the way.

Larger policy issues concerning the AEF's role in the Allied coalition also influenced Conner's decisions regarding relief of the 2nd Division at Belleau Wood.

On June 9, Ludendorff had begun the fourth phase of his offensive. With French forces having been drawn back to protect Paris, the German commander attacked northward to unite his positions in the Amiens and Marne salients. On June 10, the French high command issued a directive: "In the present situation, frequent reliefs are entirely out of the question; everyone must contribute to his full capacity without thought of fatigue." Eager to demonstrate that the AEF could bear the same rigors of fighting as the French, Conner told Richardson on June 13 to inform the French XXI Corps that the question of relief of the 2nd Division was "entirely in their hands and that we think anything they do in that way is all right."[29]

Fox Conner also recognized that the fighting at Belleau Wood had acquired symbolic significance beyond the tactical importance of the forest itself. German prisoners captured on June 12 had revealed that the Germans were sending their best troops into Belleau Wood to inflict a "moral defeat" upon the inexperienced American Army. On June 8, the German commander in the region, General Böhm, had told his troops that they were fighting at Belleau Wood primarily to defeat "the Anglo-American claim that the American Army is equal or even the superior of the German Army."[30] Fox Conner understood that no other American divisions were available to relieve the 2nd Division; withdrawal of the division from the woods would hand Germany a propaganda victory it had not earned on the battlefield.

Conner, therefore, decided on June 13 to leave the 2nd Division in place.

Fox Conner's grasp of grand strategy provided scant comfort to Harbord's 4th Brigade when, on June 14, the Germans turned to mustard gas to force the Marines from the *Bois de Belleau*.

German chemical engineers had designed mustard gas (dichloroethyl sulfide) to burn rather than asphyxiate. First used by the Germans in 1917, the chemical got its name from the strong odor of mustard that accompanied the gas as it burst forth from artillery shells to smother the battlefield in burning poison. The stench faded long before the poisonous effects of the gas did, which promoted premature removal of gas masks and even greater injury. Mustard gas permeated clothing and leather. It also seeped into the surrounding ground and vegetation, such that an exposed soldier who remained in the area continued to ingest the poison days after a gas attack.[31]

Mustard gas was therefore an effective weapon against a stubborn enemy, such as Harbord's Marine Brigade, that could not be otherwise dislodged from a position.

On the morning of June 14, the Germans saturated American positions with more than 8,500 artillery rounds, including mustard gas shells.[32] The last sight seen by Marines too slow in donning their gas masks was of a mist moving toward them. Then the gas burned their eyes shut. Panicked men stumbled in the darkness; those who could see at all recoiled at the sight of their blackened, burned, and blistered hands. If anything was heard over the barking of one's own burned lungs trying vainly to cough up the poison within, it was the sound of comrades shrieking and crying. One Marine private gassed at Belleau Wood wrote: "The human senses reeled into oblivion before such an attack."[33]

The mustard-gas attack on June 14 claimed more than 700 victims from Harbord's already depleted force. Still, the Marines held the southern half of the woods.

On June 15, Conner's liaison Walter Grant relayed Harbord's concern that the morale of the still-unrelieved brigade was "on pure nerve and is liable to snap." Grant also warned Conner of French concerns over a possible German counterattack, but he also pointed out that no assault was likely for a few days, since the mustard gas posed an equal hazard for any German soldiers entering the area. Conner recognized that the imperative need to rest the 2nd Division, and an opportunity to do so, had both arrived.

On June 15, the French corps sent one of the American 3rd Division's brigades to the right of the 2nd Division, while battalions of the French 167th Division took up positions on the left. These reinforcements allowed the 2nd Division to shorten its line and to establish rear areas where its exhausted troops could rest for several days without withdrawing the division altogether. On June 16, Grant reported to Conner that "relief last night passed off without incident ... All feel much better this morning."[34]

Fortunately for the 2nd Division, the German attack forecast by French headquarters never materialized. On June 25, with the Marines having rested for more than a week, Harbord's brigade began its final attack to clear the woods. By the morning of June 26, the Marines had driven the remaining Germans from Belleau Wood.

The AEF had prevailed in the test of wills that was at the heart of the contest over the *Bois de Belleau*.

During the Belleau Wood fighting, the 2nd Division outlasted four separate German divisions sent against it. As at Cantigny, the large AEF division structure had proven its value, but the 2nd Division was spent. Since the harrowing days of late May, Harbord's 4th Brigade had lost more than 5,000 men killed, wounded, or captured. The 3rd Brigade, which formed the other half of the 2nd Division, also suffered more than 3,000 casualties, mostly in the 23rd Infantry Regiment, commanded by Conner's former Chaumont colleague, Colonel Paul Malone.

On June 25, Colonel Malone transmitted a message to Conner through liaison officer Major Walter C. Short.[35] Malone stressed the "absolute, imperative necessity" of withdrawing the entire 2nd Division before it was destroyed. Short told Conner that Malone was "very emphatic about this proposition and wanted me to present the matter to you personally." On June 26, AEF Deputy Chief of Staff LeRoy Eltinge made Conner aware that General Liggett, whose American I Corps was to include the 2nd Division, also thought the division needed to be withdrawn.[36]

The matter of relieving the 2nd Division, however, remained entangled in the intra-Allied struggles between Chaumont and the French high command over control of American divisions.

By mid-June, the American 26th and 42nd divisions were ready to enter front-line service. Both divisions had sent staff officers to establish headquarters in the Château-Thierry region, where Pétain had agreed on June 6 to form the American I Corps. On June 16, Conner and his West Point classmate Malin Craig discussed arrangements for Craig's I Corps staff to assume control of all American forces in the Château-Thierry region.[37]

Pétain, however, refused to send either of the fresh American divisions to the Château-Thierry sector. Pétain thought the 26th Division should go to Amiens and that the 42nd Division should serve in the Champagne region of France, where he expected Ludendorff's next attack to come. Additionally, Pétain refused to release either the 2nd or 3rd divisions from the French corps in which they served. In essence, although Pétain had agreed to form an American corps near Château-Thierry, he would not send any American divisions to form it.[38]

Conner addressed the issue of French control of American divisions in a June 22 memorandum. Conner's tone reflected irritation over what he viewed as a French breach of the June 6 agreement to form the American I Corps. "It appears to me," wrote Conner, "that this is a deliberate move to prevent, or at least postpone, the formation of an American corps." In Conner's view, there was "no doubt but that a very considerable element among the French commands and staffs are [sic] as determined as ever to block anything looking to the formation of higher American units." Conner noted two factions among the French: one that had "never abandoned the idea of drafting Americans into French units," while the other "considers the morale of the French so poor at present as to necessitate the dispersion of American troops in the effort to bolster up failing French morale."[39]

Cognizant of the role of American public opinion, however, Conner pointed out in his memorandum that American morale was also at stake:

> So far, the American people are deluded in the belief that we really have an American sector, or sectors, which are controlled by Americans. This delusion cannot be kept up indefinitely. We are also face to face with another fact—many of our officers, and, it is believed, soldiers are distinctly disgusted with French tutelage. Officers and, it is understood, newspapermen are constantly asking whether or not we are ever to have American corps and an American army.

Conner had good reason to believe that Pétain was purposefully delaying the formation of an American corps, despite his earlier agreement to do so. In a June 19 memorandum to the French generals serving under his command, Pétain stated that the American units had been "placed at our disposal for an indeterminate period," with no reference to the imminent formation of an American corps. Pétain also set forth his views on the "prerogatives" of the French generals, noting that "no change will be made in the organization of the American units without previous authorization by the French General-In-Chief to whom also will be referred all difficulties that may arise."[40] That Pétain sought to make himself, rather than Pershing, the final arbiter of matters pertaining to organization of the American units, was revealing.

Conner's June 22 memorandum urged Pershing to "demand" that Pétain activate the American I Corps within 10 days and to form the corps entirely with American divisions. Conner also recommended that Pershing regain both the 1st and 42nd divisions for service in I Corps in the Château-Thierry area. "We have 800,000 troops in France," Conner wrote, "and the Commander-In-Chief is in a position to make the reasonable demands implied by the above."

On June 24, Pétain again agreed to activate the American I Corps— but with only the American 2nd and French 167th divisions in it.[41] As such, when Conner received the messages from Short and Eltinge on June 25 and 26, which emphasized the need to withdraw the 2nd Division from the front, the AEF still had no other available American division in the area with which to accomplish that relief.

Conner continued to press the issue with General Ragueneau at Chaumont until, on June 29, the French high command relented and agreed to send the American 26th Division to the Château-Thierry sector. After having been on the front line for more than a month, the 2nd Division began its withdrawal to a quiet area, once the National Guardsmen of the 26th Division began to arrive on July 4. The same day, General Liggett assumed tactical command of the American I Corps, formed by the American 2nd and 26th divisions, plus the French 167th Division. Fox Conner, whose long-range plans called for an American corps structure formed of six American divisions, remarked that the "result was by no means fully satisfactory." Conner's persistence, though, had played a prominent role in bringing to life the AEF's first functioning battle corps.[42]

As chief of operations, Conner's duties in the summer of 1918 also went well beyond the details of the relief of a particular division or the formation of a single corps.

On June 18, as the number of Americans in France approached 1 million men, Conner and eight other officers met with Pershing to formulate plans for expanding the American Army to 3 million men by the spring of 1919. Pershing wrote: "The group of officers to whom I outlined the enlarged program were those upon whom the additional burden would fall the heaviest." Conner devised a comprehensive schedule under which 1,862,000 additional American troops would be shipped through May 1919—enough to form sixty-six complete divisions. Conner then accompanied Pershing to a June 23 meeting with General Foch and French Premier Georges Clemenceau, in which Pershing agreed to recommend an even more ambitious expansion to eighty divisions by April 1919 and to 100 divisions by July 1919.[43]

On July 10, Pershing and Conner also met with the Allied Supreme Commander Foch and his chief of staff, General Maxime Weygand. Pershing began the meeting by again calling upon Foch to create a distinct American sector under American command. Conner's account of the meeting quoted Foch's agreement that America had "the right to have her army organized as such," and that "the American Army must be an accomplished fact." But Foch, who remained concerned that Ludendorff would soon again attack, would not commit to release the existing American divisions from service in French corps. In his summary of the meeting, Conner wrote: "All in all, the impression gained by the undersigned was that General Foch was not favorable to the idea of establishing an American sector of any degree of permanency prior to October 1."[44]

At the July 10 meeting, Foch and Pershing also instructed their principal assistants, Weygand and Conner, to arrive at an agreement as to where several newly arrived American divisions would go for training. Conner persuaded Weygand to send the incoming American 29th, 37th,

89th, 90th, and 92nd divisions to quiet areas in Lorraine, where five other AEF divisions—the 5th, 32nd, 35th, 77th, and 82nd—were nearing the end of their training. Weygand also agreed that the American troops would be "trained under purely American methods," a point that Conner had emphasized in his June 22 memorandum. Conner also prevailed upon Foch's chief of staff to send the five older American divisions for service in the additional American corps that he planned to bring into existence.

Also in their July 10 meeting, Foch outlined for Pershing and Conner his views on future combat operations. According to Conner's Notes on Operations, all conferees "believed certain" that Ludendorff would next attack in the Champagne region of France. Confident that the Allies would again contain the German attack, Foch had begun planning a major counteroffensive against the Marne salient to take place later in the summer. Foch expected the veteran American divisions to participate, but as components of different French corps. The supreme commander made no reference to any action against the St. Mihiel salient in Lorraine, which Conner had long-targeted as the area for the AEF's first full-scale offensive.

Looking to 1919, Foch outlined plans for a coordinated attack by the British, French, and Americans along a continuous front from the English Channel to the Meuse River, but with only a diversionary attack against the St. Mihiel salient. Foch concluded the meeting by asking Pershing to study the plan.

As was his practice, Pershing asked Conner to supply the analysis.

In a detailed memorandum submitted July 14, 1918, Conner wrote that he suspected an ulterior motive in Foch's insistence that American troops remain under the command of French corps commanders. Conner's conversations with both Weygand and Foch had led the AEF's chief of operations to form the "very distinct impression" that the two French generals doubted "the ability of both the French and British to attack unless carried along by the enthusiasm of Americans acting in the same region against common objectives." Conner thought it "unwise to associate our troops with troops who could only be drawn into an attack by our immediate presence."[45]

Conner, therefore, again urged Pershing to "insist" that Foch create an American sector, under Pershing's command, "without delay." Writing that the lack of designated American front was "no longer tolerable," the chief of operations urged his commander to take a firm stand: "America must now [the emphasis is Conner's] be assigned a permanent sector which can be developed in our own way in accordance with our national characteristics."

Colonel Conner also expressed doubt regarding the wisdom of General Foch's overall strategy, which did not include Conner's proposed Lorraine offensive. The AEF chief of operations remained convinced that capture of the enemy's coal and iron resources in the Briey region of Lorraine provided the surest route to victory over Germany. "Since her vitals are in Lorraine," Conner reasoned, "the simplest method is to take the most direct route to that region." He also questioned the strategic value of operations west of the Meuse River, where the difficult Argonne Forest lay.[46]

Despite Ferdinand Foch's masterful management of Allied operations since he became supreme commander in March 1918, Fox Conner believed that Foch's strategy contained "no reasonable prospect of final victory during 1919." In his July 14 memorandum, Conner wrote that the supreme commander's plan offered only "the certainty of prolonging the war."

Also in mid-July 1918, Conner acquired a talented new assistant in Chaumont—Lieutenant Colonel George Marshall. Weary of staff work, Marshall had earlier applied to the 1st Division's commanding officer, General Robert Lee Bullard, for reassignment as a regimental commander in the division. Citing Marshall's "special fitness" for staff work, Bullard denied Marshall's request for field service, but he acknowledged that his G-3's talents were better suited to a bigger stage. Fox Conner agreed. As one Marshall biographer put it: "Conner had long had his eyes on Marshall."[47]

On July 13, 1918, George Marshall reported for duty in Conner's Operations Section. Marshall faced an adjustment to what he termed the "strange atmosphere" of Chaumont. As his new colleagues discussed the broad details of planning an army of millions, Marshall found himself in a "different world" from divisional headquarters, which concerned itself much more with how Chaumont's directives affected soldiers in the field. Marshall wrote of the different viewpoints of the GHQ and field officers: "Each man was living in his own little world, ignorant to a surprising degree of all that occurred elsewhere."

Conner assigned his new assistant a room in the house where he and Deputy Chief of Staff LeRoy Eltinge lived. Undaunted by Foch's views on the role of the AEF in future operations, Conner also assigned Marshall to begin planning an attack on the St. Mihiel salient.

Conner's attention soon returned to the Marne salient when, on July 15, Ludendorff resumed the offensive. As anticipated, Germany attacked in France's Champagne region, near the city of Reims, hoping to cross the Marne and resume the drive on Paris. According to Conner, the French high command knew the "hour and minute" the attack would come.[48]

Across the Champagne Front, the well-prepared Allied defenders wrought heavy losses upon Ludendorff's tired force. By July 18, Ludendorff's fifth offensive was through. So were Germany's hopes of winning the war in 1918.

Foch recognized that the opportunity had arisen to strike before Ludendorff could regroup; he therefore decided to immediately launch the counteroffensive he had discussed with Pershing and Conner on July 10. With the bulk of Ludendorff's force on the southern face of the Marne salient, Foch rapidly assembled a force on the salient's more lightly held western face. The Allied supreme commander included in his attack force the American 1st Division, well rested since its Cantigny victory 6 weeks earlier. Foch also called upon the 2nd Division, only 2 weeks removed from Belleau Wood.[49]

In a confidential briefing to journalists given later in the war, Conner provided insight into the difficulty of moving the 2nd Division back into the line on such short notice. "The necessity for putting that division in arose very suddenly," Conner said. "It simply had to go in." With only 30 minutes' notice, troops piled into trucks for the trek on dark and muddy roads clogged by both motorized and horse-drawn traffic. Once the trucks got as close as they could, the troops double-timed, in

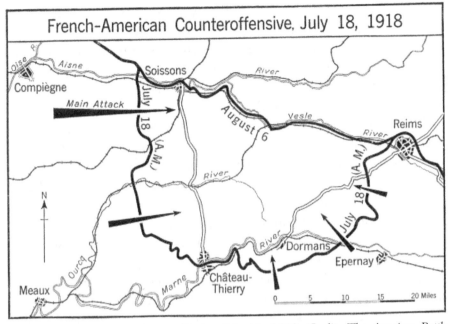

Map 5: French-American Counteroffensive, July 18, 1918. Credit: The American Battle Monuments Commission.

a driving rainstorm, to arrive in position for attack. Men arrived before their machine guns did. The division had no plan for how to care for its wounded. "No arrangements had been made, or could have been made under the conditions," Conner told the reporters.[50]

Foch grouped the American 1st and 2nd divisions into the French XX Corps, together with a division of "fanatical Moslems from Morocco," as James G. Harbord admiringly termed the troops from France's North African colony. At 4:30 a.m. on July 18, the Americans and Moroccans spearheaded Foch's counteroffensive against the Marne salient's western face. The combined force overwhelmed the German defenders in the salient. In 4 days, the XX Corps advanced 7 miles in the type of open-warfare operation that Pershing had long envisioned. By July 21, the Allies had captured the heights south of Soissons as well as the rail lines supplying German forces at Château-Thierry and other areas farther south.

In Conner's view, the Allied victory at Soissons had "turned the tide and marked the end of all German offensive efforts." Germany's Chancellor Georg von Hertling concurred. Writing of the successful Allied counteroffensive at Soissons, he wrote: "On the 18th even the most optimistic among us understood that all was lost. The history of the world was played out in three days."

The success of the 1st and 2nd divisions at Soissons, and also that of the 3rd, 26th, 32nd, and 42nd divisions, which subsequently attacked the southern face of the Marne salient to drive Ludendorff northward, again proved the military value of the large AEF divisions which had been built to inflict and absorb greater casualties than their opponents.

But the toll in American lives was beginning to mount.

The 1st, 2nd, 3rd, 26th, 32nd, and 42nd divisions reported casualty lists of more than 32,000 men killed, wounded, or captured during the July counteroffensive. The 1st Division alone suffered more than 7,000 casualties in its 4 days of battle. Conner noted that "not one was a prisoner." The Soissons operation killed or wounded each of the lieutenant colonels in three of the 1st Division's four regiments. In one regiment, every lieutenant colonel lost his life, thus raising the question of how America would have fared in its next world war had Lieutenant Colonel George Marshall gotten the field command in the 1st Division he had sought.[51]

At Chaumont, though, Fox Conner and his colleagues viewed the casualty figures through the filter of their allies' experiences of 4 years of trench warfare, in which hundreds of thousands had lost their lives for the gain or loss of territory measured in mere yards. Conner maintained confidence in his calculus of swapping men for miles of territory: "We had lost over 30,000, but the results were commensurate," Conner wrote in his Notes on Operations. Speaking to reporters about the 2nd Division's operations, in which the division lost 4,000 men in 2 days of fighting at Soissons, Conner reflected the Chaumont mindset that Marshall and others found discomfiting: "In the long run," Conner said, "the difficulties of the division were nothing compared to the results which were accomplished."[52]

The successes and struggles of the AEF in the Marne salient provided fresh impetus for the AEF to seek greater control over America's troops.

Fox Conner particularly objected to the lack of American control over matters of supply of troops in the field and care for the Americans wounded while serving in French units. Conner, who considered it "imperative" that American troops be assembled into an independent force, went with Pershing to meetings with Foch and Pétain on July 21 and July 22, 1918. Pershing and Conner again urged the two French generals to create an independent American sector under Pershing's direct command.[53]

Their efforts finally bore fruit. The Frenchmen said yes.

On July 24, 1918, Pershing announced the formation of the American First Army, to be formed of six American divisions grouped into two corps. Pershing, who planned to serve as both First Army commander and AEF commander-in-chief, created a separate First Army staff. Colonel Hugh Drum, Conner's RMS *Baltic* colleague and co-architect of the large AEF divisions, became First Army's chief of staff. In the following days, Drum and Conner realigned the available American divisions to send the 4th, 26th, and 32nd to Hunter Liggett's I Corps in the southern areas of the Marne salient. Robert Bullard took command of the new American III Corps in the area around Soissons, to be formed by the 3rd, 28th, and 42nd divisions.[54]

Also on July 24, Foch issued orders that Fox Conner had long awaited: the Allied supreme commander ordered the AEF to begin plans for an attack against the St. Mihiel salient in Lorraine—plans which Conner and Marshall had already begun to devise.[55]

Conner envisioned what he termed a "nut cracker operation," designed to "pinch out" the St. Mihiel salient by simultaneous attacks against both the southern and western faces of the triangle. In addition to Marshall, Conner also assigned Walter Grant of the Operations Section to devise the battle plans. According to Marshall's biographer Forrest Pogue, however, the "chief impetus" for planning the AEF's debut offensive came from Fox Conner.[56]

Conner also worked with First Army chief of staff Hugh Drum to manage the myriad of arrangements necessary to transport more than a half-million American troops into position in Lorraine, including the use of French road space to move the American divisions by night.

Conner recalled that America's troops were "dispersed from Switzerland to the English Channel" and that coordination of the staff work from GHQ down to the division level "was in itself and extraordinary task."

Conner also recognized that the Abbeville and Versailles agreements had left the AEF "woefully deficient" in artillery, tanks, air support, and anti-aircraft guns needed for a successful offensive at St. Mihiel. The chief of operations therefore addressed the "exceedingly complex" intra-Allied staff work necessary to have the French live up to their earlier promises to provide those forces and to place them under American command for the upcoming St. Mihiel offensive.

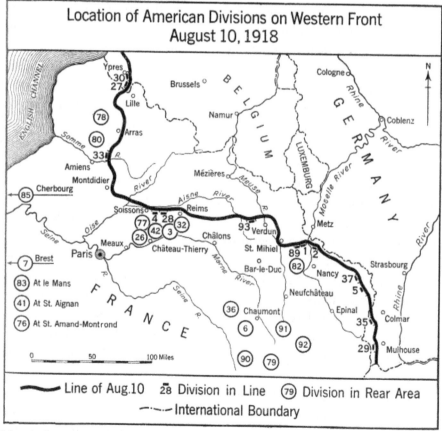

Map 6: American Divisions on the Western Front, August 1918. Credit: The American Battle Monuments Commission.

On August 3, 1918 Conner submitted a plan for twelve American divisions to make a primary attack on the western face of the salient while a smaller French force attacked from the south. With Conner's August 3 analysis providing the "basis for discussions," Pershing and his chief of operations—recently promoted to the rank of brigadier general—met with Foch on August 9 in Sarcus, France. The Allied supreme commander approved the preliminary plans. Foch also agreed to move three American divisions from the British sector even though, the day before, Field Marshal Haig had commenced a major counteroffensive to drive the Germans from the Amiens salient.

By mid-August, the Operations Section's plan for St. Mihiel had evolved into a twenty-division offensive, involving sixteen American divisions, with four French divisions in support. On August 16, Conner sent First Army Chief of Staff Hugh Drum a memorandum identifying the American divisions that would participate. On August 18, at the height of Britain's offensive in the Amiens salient, Conner directed the American II Corps in the British sector to transfer the 33rd, 78th, and 80th divisions to Lorraine, "last two at once. 33rd no later than the 25th instant." Colonel George Simonds, II Corps chief of staff, told Conner on August 23: "If you had hit them for the five (divisions) instead of the three, they would have turned them loose."[57]

The conclusion of Simonds' August 23 memorandum reveals the behind-the-scenes power Conner had come to wield as the AEF's chief of operations. Referring to Major General George Read, commanding general of II Corps, Simonds told Conner that Read was "absolutely dependable," and would "carry out what you want," even though Read outranked Conner by one star. As one AEF general noted, Fox Conner had risen to the "inner circle of the inner circle" at Chaumont.[58]

Also in late August 1918, Conner's Operations Section lost one of its most dependable members. On August 20, the 2nd Division's new commander, Marine Corps Major General John A. Lejeune, asked George Marshall to take command of the division's 23rd Regiment in the upcoming St. Mihiel offensive. "Not being my own master," Marshall recalled, he referred Lejeune to General Conner. After the two generals met, Conner told Marshall "to pack up and leave within the hour." According to Marshall, "It seemed too good to be true, but in the next sentence he explained that I would not go to the 23rd Infantry." Instead, Conner sent Marshall to Hugh Drum's First Army staff at Ligny-en-Barrois to continue making plans for the St. Mihiel offensive. As with the Soissons operation the previous month, Marshall's indispensability as a staff officer prevented his assignment to combat duty. As consolation, and on Conner's recommendation, Marshall received promotion to colonel in late August.[59]

As Conner and his Operations Section remained immersed through the end of August in planning the AEF's first full-scale offensive, Ferdinand Foch paid Black Jack Pershing a visit at First Army's headquarters at Ligny on August 30.[60]

The Allied commander-in-chief delivered stunning news.

Foch had changed his mind, not only about the St. Mihiel offensive, but also about formation of an independent American Army.

With Germany on the defensive and in disarray, Foch told Pershing that he planned to launch, in 1918, the continuous front offensive he had initially planned for 1919. As he had outlined on July 10, Foch wanted the AEF to attack between the Meuse River and the Argonne Forest to capture the strategic rail lines connecting the cities of Mézières and Sedan. In Foch's view, any action east of the Meuse—including an attack at St. Mihiel—would have to be limited to a diversion. The supreme commander further shocked Pershing when he said that all available AEF divisions would be reincorporated into two separate French armies to participate in the attacks.

Pershing would have none of it. He at last took the firm stance that Fox Conner had been advocating for months. In his memoir, Pershing described this exchange with Foch:

"Marshal Foch," Pershing said bluntly, "you have no authority as Allied Commander-In-Chief to call upon me to yield up my command of the American Army and have it scattered among the Allied forces where it will not be an American Army at all."

"I must insist upon the arrangement," Foch persisted.

"You may insist all you please," Pershing retorted, "but I decline absolutely to agree to your plan. While our Army will fight wherever you may decide, it will not fight except as an independent American Army."

Foch pointed out that the American Army lacked sufficient artillery and air support for an attack on the St. Mihiel salient. Pershing demanded that France honor its earlier agreement to supply those forces. According to Pershing's account, the argument intensified as both men rose from the table, their glares revealing the fury that decorum would not allow their voices to show.

In a veiled insult, Foch asked Pershing: "*Voulez-vouz aller à la bataille?*"[61] "Most assuredly," Pershing shot back, "but as an American Army and in no other way."

Foch, whom Pershing described as "very pale and apparently exhausted," gathered his maps to leave the August 30 meeting; he implored Pershing to at least study the plan.

At 10:30 p.m. on August 30, Pershing telephoned Chaumont to summon Conner and McAndrew to meet him at Ligny. Pershing's two chief advisors left immediately and arrived at First Army headquarters at 2:30 a.m. on August 31. Conner, Pershing, and McAndrew immediately began to analyze Foch's proposal. Working through the night, the three generals then drafted a response that balanced the legitimate desire of the United States to have its more than 1 million men formed into an independent American Army against the reality that the AEF, which remained dependent upon French resources, was still a junior partner in the alliance.[62]

Fox Conner had long-recognized the importance of Allied "unity of action." The AEF's August 31 reply therefore began by acknowledging Foch's authority, as Allied supreme commander, to decide matters of military strategy. The letter then highlighted the logistical difficulty that an attack on the Sedan–Mézières rail lines would present for the AEF. The American high command, nonetheless, agreed to accept the supreme commander's decision to deploy the AEF in the area between the Meuse River and Argonne Forest, if Foch so insisted. Pershing also proposed to cancel the St. Mihiel operation altogether if Foch would provide neither the time nor resources for its success.

The American generals, though, refused to yield on Foch's proposal to re-amalgamate the American divisions into the French Army. "I can no longer agree to any plan which involves a dispersion of our units," Pershing wrote Foch. "There is one thing that must not be done and that is to disperse the American forces among the Allied Armies."

In essence, the August 31 letter jointly drafted by Pershing, Conner, and McAndrew informed the Allied supreme commander that although the AEF would dutifully play its role in the Allied partnership, the time had arrived for America to be made a full partner.

On the evening of August 31, Pershing sent Conner and McAndrew to Foch's headquarters to deliver the American response. The duo met with Foch's chief of staff Weygand. Conner recalled to a journalist several years later that "strong English and French phrases punctuated our discussion," as Weygand emphasized the need to maintain the offensive against the withering German Army. Foch read Pershing's letter, then asked McAndrew and Conner to return the next day to receive his reply. The two American generals did so. Without discussing details, Foch simply invited Pershing and his two top assistants to join him and Pétain at a meeting the following day.[63]

On September 2, Pershing, Conner, and McAndrew met with Foch and Pétain. Pershing recalled that the cordial atmosphere at Foch's headquarters differed markedly from that of their previous August 30 meeting. Foch's primary aim was to have twelve to fourteen American divisions attack in the zone between the Meuse River and Argonne Forest, with the rail lines between Sedan and Mézières as the objective. Pershing agreed. The American commander wanted, above all else, for those American forces to operate as an independent army under his command. Foch agreed.

The Allied supreme commander then asked Pershing whether the American Army still wished to attack at St. Mihiel. Pershing, Conner, and McAndrew withdrew to a separate room to discuss the matter. Their maps showed that German forces in the St. Mihiel salient would threaten the flank and rear of their Meuse–Argonne attack. The American generals, therefore, decided to eliminate the salient, despite having a smaller force than Conner and Marshall had planned upon. Foch consented. The supreme commander also promised to provide French troops and matériel to support the operation. He also agreed to delay his grand offensive until the end of September to allow the American Army to attack St. Mihiel around September 10.

Pershing's September 2 decision to maintain the St. Mihiel operation in addition to the Meuse–Argonne attack was momentous. The AEF lacked sufficient divisions to conduct two entirely separate offensives. To accomplish the dual operations, the newly formed American First Army would begin the St. Mihiel offensive and, while the battle was underway, begin transferring its divisions to the Meuse–Argonne Front. Pershing acknowledged that he had committed the AEF to the "gigantic task" of undertaking two separate offensives, on fronts 60 miles apart, within the same month, and with an army barely in existence. "History gives no parallel of such an undertaking with so large an army," Pershing noted in his 1931 memoirs.[64]

The two policy objectives Conner had long sought—the formation of a large, independent American Army and an attack against the St. Mihiel salient—would soon become reality. So would the unwanted appendage of the Meuse–Argonne offensive, which threatened to overwhelm both. Fox Conner faced an operations nightmare. To meet the challenge, Conner and his fellow AEF planners devised what military historian Russell Weigley described as a "complex of plans" that became "the greatest single achievement of American staff work in France."[65]

Those plans included a bit of subterfuge.

CHAPTER 7

OUR SEAT AT THE TABLE

From September 26th to November 11th (1918), the Germans employed 46 divisions in attempting to defend the Meuse–Argonne sector. This was 25% of the enemy's entire divisional strength on the Western Front.

—Fox Conner, Notes on Operations, 1918[1]

By 1918, the Argonne theatre of war had lost most of its importance, with most major offensives unfolding further west; for that reason here and there the strengths were substantially reduced.

—French informational plaque in the Argonne Forest, 2010

Colonel T. Bentley Mott served as John J. Pershing's liaison at Ferdinand Foch's headquarters. On August 31, 1918, Mott directed a handwritten and confidential letter to Fox Conner. "I have heard it repeatedly stated about these headquarters," Mott warned the chief of operations, "that "everybody [the emphasis is Mott's] was talking of a projected attack in the Woëvre." Mott reported conversations in which French officers, who were "not in a position where they should know anything," had asked him if it was true that the Americans planned to attack at St. Mihiel with fourteen divisions. Mott had merely deflected the questions, but Chaumont's eyes and ears at Foch's headquarters registered concern over the security of the AEF's plans for the St. Mihiel offensive.[2]

By the time Mott's letter arrived in Chaumont, Fox Conner was already engaged in a top-secret effort to deal with the problem.

At least since the days of Julius Caesar, invading armies have attacked through the Belfort Gap—a plateau between the Vosges and Jura mountains in upper Alsace, where Germany, Switzerland, and France meet. At the war's outset in 1914, French forces attacked through the gap and briefly occupied the city of Mulhouse before being driven back. In 1916, the Germans sought to divert French defenses from Verdun by feigning an attack through the Belfort Gap. In 1917, the French had suggested Belfort to Conner as an area where the AEF might be deployed.[3]

In mid-August 1918, the French commander Pétain had suggested to Pershing that the AEF undertake a campaign of deception to make the Germans believe that the Americans would attack in the Belfort Gap in Alsace rather than at St. Mihiel in Lorraine. On August 22, Pétain approved plans "relative to spreading false intelligence." Pétain also notified the French commander in Alsace that the AEF planned to send Fox Conner, George Marshall, and Walter Grant to the area for the "purpose of spreading the rumor than an offensive is being prepared in that region."[4]

Pershing, however, did not limit his deception to the enemy; he also directed Conner to mislead even the generals of the AEF as to where the American attack would occur.

In late August 1918, Pershing and Chief of Staff James McAndrew met with Colonel Arthur L. Conger of the AEF Intelligence Section. The three devised a scheme to allow plans for an entirely fictitious attack in the Belfort Gap to fall into the hands of German spies. Pershing asked Conger whether anyone else in the AEF needed to know about the secret. Conger replied that Conner, as head of the Operations Section, would have to generate certain orders necessary to give the feint plausibility. "Very well," Pershing told Conger, "then there will be just four; you, General Conner, General McAndrew and myself, and I do not want any other soul to know that this attack will not actually be carried out except us four." Conger then met with Conner to involve him in the plot.[5]

Major General Omar Bundy commanded the American VI Corps. Bundy had commanded the 2nd Division at Château-Thierry and Belleau Wood, but had since fallen out of favor with Pershing. In preparation for the St. Mihiel offensive, Pershing had elevated two of Bundy's fellow divisional commanders—Joseph Dickman of the 3rd Division and George Cameron of the 4th—to command the newly formed IV and V corps that would participate in the upcoming attack. Bundy, however, received command of the VI Corps, which essentially functioned as a training unit for newly arrived divisions.

Omar Bundy was therefore available, and sufficiently dispensable, to become the primary dupe in what became known as the "Belfort Ruse."[6]

On August 26, Conner issued orders attaching Bundy's VI Corps to First Army. Then, on August 28, Conner sent Bundy a memorandum directing him to "proceed, with such members of your Staff as you may consider absolutely necessary, to Belfort and prepare detailed plans for an attack in that region." Conner told Bundy: "It is believed that the enemy has been misled by the massing of our troops around Neufchateau and that the attack can be conducted by seven divisions in first line."

Conner informed Bundy that the 35th, 36th, 78th, 79th, 80th, and 91st divisions would participate in the operation. He also told the corps commander that "a reconnaissance party of three officers from each of these divisions is being ordered to Belfort to report to you on August 30th." To preempt Bundy's questions, Conner informed him that to maintain "the feature of surprise," no troops would be massed in the area until immediately before the attack and that artillery preparation would be kept to a minimum. Conner concluded by emphasizing to Bundy "the necessity for secrecy," while hoping that the opposite would occur.

Conner also issued orders on August 28 to the commanding generals of the seven divisions instructing each to send staff officers to "report to Major General Omar Bundy at the *Grand Hotel du Tonneau d'Or* at Belfort before noon on August 30th." Conner also told the generals to "personally warn these officers as to preserving silence as to their mission while in Belfort."

Arthur Conger of the AEF Intelligence Section attended the August 30 meeting at the *Grand Hotel*. With Belfort so close to the German border, a meeting of an American corps commander and more than twenty officers in a local hotel was bound to attract the attention of German intelligence agents. While at the hotel, Conger dropped a crumpled carbon copy of the fictitious plan into a wastebasket in his room. Conger then left the room unlocked and took a walk for 5 minutes. When he checked the wastebasket upon his return, Conger found the discarded plan was missing. German spies had taken the bait.

Bundy and his VI Corps staff continued to plan the Belfort offensive in what Arthur Conger described as "dead earnest"; they never suspected that their planning was in vain. On September 1, General Bundy reported to Conner on the results of his personal reconnaissance of the Belfort Gap, observing that "now is a most propitious time for launching an attack in this region." Conner's deception of Bundy continued even after the September 2 compromise between Pershing and Foch which scaled back the St. Mihiel attack and added the Meuse–Argonne offensive. On September 4, with the St. Mihiel offensive 8 days away, and as the American divisions began to move into position for the attack in Lorraine, Conner directed Bundy to enlarge the scope of his plans in Alsace and to proceed "in as active a manner as possible."

To further the hoax, Conner also directed radios in the Belfort area to send increased transmissions in code. Tanks went out at night to make fresh tracks for German aerial reconnaissance to observe the next morning. The AEF leased office space in Belfort.

But as Conner continued to deceive Bundy and the seven division commanders, staff officers in the involved divisions became alarmed. Instead of moving toward Belfort in Alsace, the daily orders from Chaumont moved the divisions farther away, which created concern over whether Conner and his staff had committed "some frightful blunder" in their orders. Unbeknownst to the division commanders and staffs, their men were actually moving northward toward Foch's Meuse–Argonne attack.

The Belfort Ruse succeeded.

The Germans moved three divisions from St. Mihiel in Lorraine to Mulhouse in Alsace to defend against an attack through the Belfort Gap. On September 10, two days before the St. Mihiel offensive began, German intelligence reported: "It is still not clear whether the attack is planned to be made only in Alsace or only in Lorraine or simultaneously in both places." Even on the day of the St. Mihiel attack on September 12, the French military mission in Berne, Switzerland reported a "state of nervousness of the German command" in Alsace, including plans for the evacuation of Mulhouse in case of an attack.

The Belfort Ruse also helped produce uncertainty and delay in the German high command that greatly aided the American attack at St. Mihiel. Ludendorff had ordered an evacuation of the salient in advance of an "enveloping attack." But the German commander in the area, General Max von Gallwitz, did not recognize until September 10 that the AEF would attack both the western and southern faces of the salient. Even then, Ludendorff only "requested" that von Gallwitz begin his withdrawal. Still not perceiving the seriousness of the threat, von Gallwitz did not begin his withdrawal from the salient until the night of September 11. "It is true," von Gallwitz later acknowledged, that "we did not consider the commencement of the attack as imminent as it later turned out to be."

The delay cost the Germans dearly.

At 1:00 a.m. on September 12, the St. Mihiel offensive that Fox Conner had envisioned for more than a year finally erupted.[7] A massive bombardment from nearly 3,000 artillery pieces caught the withdrawing Germans in the dark on open roads rather than in sheltered positions. As Conner put it, von Gallwitz's "orderly evacuation was thrown into the utmost disorder."

As dawn rose on the 12th, the American First Army commenced Conner's "nut cracker" operation. The AEF's more experienced divisions led the way. General Dickman's IV Corps, formed by the 1st, 42nd, and 89th divisions on the front line, with the 3rd Division in reserve, attacked the southern face of the St. Mihiel salient at 5:00 a.m. The 2nd, 5th, 82nd, and 90th divisions, which comprised General Liggett's I Corps, also advanced against the southern side of the salient. At 8:00 a.m., the western handle of the nutcracker began to squeeze the Germans. General Cameron's V Corps, which contained the 26th Division and half of the 4th plus a French division, attacked the salient's western face. Three divisions of the French II Colonial Corps also assaulted the point of the triangle near the town of St. Mihiel.

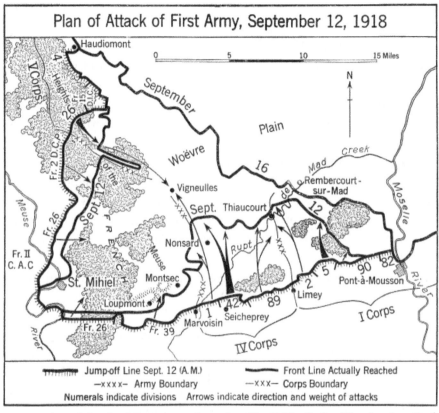

Map 7: Plan of Attack of First Army, September 12, 1918. Credit: The American Battle Monuments Commission.

Germany's transfer of three divisions to Alsace to defend the anticipated attack in the Belfort Gap left von Gallwitz with only eight and a half tired divisions in the St. Mihiel salient. To cover their withdrawal, the German defenders relied heavily upon what Conner described as a "great mass and variety of artificial works, the main feature of which was an elaborate system of wiring." In some areas, the barbed wire ensnarled more than seven miles of territory. Conner recognized that the previous three years of inactivity in the salient had left the obstacles "old and badly kept up." To break through the wire, Pershing deployed his tanks, including the light tanks of George Patton's 304th Tank Brigade. Pershing also employed a new technique of having the infantry units cut the wire as they advanced, assisted by small detachments of engineers.

"In an irresistible dash," Conner wrote in his wartime Notes on Operations, "the American soldier went over, under, and through the wire which had held up the Allied advance for four years." Nearly 1,500 planes, which Conner and Drum had obtained from the French and British, provided what Conner noted to have been "perhaps the most important air concentration the Western Front ever saw." The attacking divisions overwhelmed von Gallwitz's forces in the salient and achieved all objectives ahead of schedule. Early in the morning of September 13, Cameron's V Corps from the west linked with Dickman's IV Corps from the south. As Conner put it in his notes, "the salient was pinched out" on the attack's second day, and the St. Mihiel Front "was reluctantly permitted to stabilize."

Fox Conner never wavered in his belief that the AEF should have kept going at St. Mihiel to capture Metz and the strategic coal and iron reserves in the Briey Basin. As he put it in one wartime press conference: "The going was good!" When Pershing called off the attack on September 13, German forces were still withdrawing toward defensive positions that had not been fully prepared. George Marshall had "no doubt" that the AEF could have captured Metz by September 14. Dickman and MacArthur also thought the attack should have continued. In his postwar section report, Conner registered "great disappointment" that the needs imposed by Marshal Foch's Meuse–Argonne strategy had prevented the AEF from achieving "much greater success" at St. Mihiel.

German Field Marshal Ludendorff also thought the AEF could have won "a much greater and more decisive victory if their initial success had been exploited with more decisiveness and firmness of intention." Publicly, the Germans downplayed the St. Mihiel results by emphasizing that they had already planned to withdraw from the salient. German Army Chief of Staff Paul von Hindenburg, however, acknowledged that a "severe defeat" had occurred on September 12. The German commander von Gallwitz later submitted a detailed analysis of "the reasons for the failure of that day."

Von Gallwitz's failure yielded spectacular success for John J. Pershing in his debut as commander of an army in the field. In less than two days of fighting, the American First Army captured 200 square miles of territory, 13,251 prisoners, 466 heavy guns, 752 machine guns, and much other matériel needed by the dwindling German Army. At no time since the war's outset had the Allies regained so much ground in so little time, but the success came at the cost of 11,000 Allied troops killed, captured, or wounded in those fewer than 48 hours of fighting. Conner thought the casualties were "remarkably light," considering that more than 600,000 Allied troops had participated in the offensive.

Fox Conner believed that First Army's victory at St. Mihiel had proven to his still-doubting allies that the AEF high command could skillfully control large bodies of troops in combat. Significantly, Conner also thought that the AEF's successful assault on "defenses on which four years of labor had been spent" had instilled a "sense of power" in the American high command and troops. In Conner's view, "the American infantryman had learned that wire without fire was no obstacle, and that, given a superiority of fire, he could, with his own resources, cross any wire however deep and thick."

Conner's belief regarding the AEF's prowess would soon be tested between the Meuse River and the Argonne Forest.

Even before the fighting at St. Mihiel had ended, First Army had begun implementing George Marshall's plan to concentrate its divisions for Foch's offensive to capture the German rail lines between Sedan and Mézières. From west to east, I Corps under General Liggett would have the 77th, 28th, and 35th divisions for the attack into the Argonne on the western side of the front. Cameron's V Corps planned to attack the center of the German line, including the small mountain named Montfaucon, with the 91st, 37th, and 79th divisions. Robert Bullard's III Corps, formed by the 80th and 33rd divisions, plus half of the 4th, would operate on the eastern side of the front, along a hilly area known as the Heights of the Meuse. Few of the divisions had previously been in combat; four of them (the 35th, 79th, 80th, and 91st) had been part of the Belfort Ruse.[8]

The movement of more than a half-million men and 900,000 tons of ammunition and other supplies choked the three available French roads.

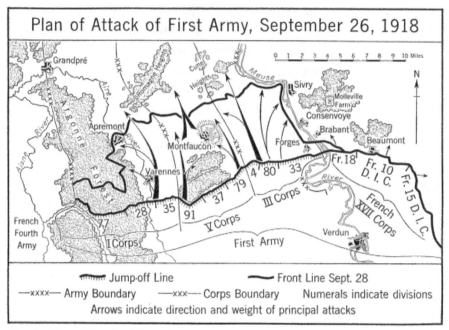

Map 8: Plan of Attack of First Army, September 26, 1918. Credit: The American Battle Monuments Commission.

Marshall described the congestion by pointing out that the seventy-two heavy guns of a single division occupied more than nine miles of road space and that 2,000 such artillery pieces had to be moved. To ensure secrecy, all movement took place at night. Fox Conner observed in his Notes on Operations that the AEF's concentration of troops for the Meuse–Argonne operation was "one of the most delicate and difficult problems of the war."[9]

As the American Army trudged in the darkness toward its second major offensive of the month, consequences of earlier compromises made with the Allies began to manifest. In a September 15 memorandum to Chief of Staff McAndrew, Conner pointed out First Army's critical shortages in machine guns, ammunition, ambulances, rolling kitchens, animals, "and practically everything else pertaining to combat divisions." Conner relayed the concerns of the AEF supply organization that it was "reduced to the breaking point" by the needs of First Army's dual offensives. Conner also warned McAndrew of the lack of trained replacements.[10]

Conner understood that the need for replacements would arise, given the significance—and difficulty—of the task Foch had assigned to the AEF. The German commander in the area, General Georg von der Marwitz, likewise considered the rail lines in the area of Sedan to have been "the life artery" of the German Army on the Western Front. In his Notes on Operations, Conner wrote that capture of the rail lines between Sedan and Mézières would produce "utter ruin" to the German Army. To defend the vital rail lines, von der Marwitz relied upon several heavily fortified defensive positions in front of them, including the powerful *Kriemhilde Stellung*, which also formed part of the primary German line of defense known as the Hindenburg Line.[11]

Map 9: *German Defense Organization in the Meuse-Argonne Region. Credit: The American Battle Monuments Commission.*

In describing First Army's task, Conner noted that the German wire, trenches, and machine-gun emplacements were "virtually continuous" to a depth of more than 12 miles. As at Belleau Wood, the AEF would confront dense woodlands and steep ravines in the Argonne Forest. From the high ground of Montfaucon in the center of the attack, as well as from the Heights of the Meuse on the right, German artillery would keep the Americans under constant crossfire. Before the AEF would even arrive at the major German defensive positions, the inexperienced American divisions would first have to cross no-man's-land which, according to Conner's notes, was "as worthy of all the name implies as any spot in the Western Front."

The mostly untested AEF divisions also had to overcome a critical decision made by Brigadier General Harold B. Fiske, the AEF chief of training. Despite the difficulty of the upcoming battle, General Fiske ordered many staff officers away from their divisions to attend previously scheduled training courses at the AEF staff college at Langres. In a 1930 letter to Pershing, George Marshall leveled his "most severe criticism" at Fiske's decision: "The staffs of these inexperienced divisions were absolutely scalped a few days before the assault," Marshall wrote, "in order that the next class at Langres might start on scheduled time." Marshall wrote further that he "always thought General Fox Conner, Hugh Drum and General Nolan should have determinedly opposed General Fisk [sic] at this moment, particularly Conner and Nolan."[12]

But Fox Conner did not.

As evidenced by GHQ's decision to assign mostly second-tier divisions to accomplish what it knew would be a highly difficult operation—and to then "scalp" those divisions shortly before battle—the men at Chaumont did not expect much to result from the Meuse–Argonne offensive. They certainly did not foresee the offensive as a potentially war-winning operation. The American high command essentially viewed the operation as the price to be paid to Foch for allowing both the formation of an independent American Army and the successful St. Mihiel offensive. "No one dared," Conner wrote in his postwar study of American operations, "to express the opinion that the final victory could be won in 1918." Instead, the AEF maintained its focus on 1919.[13]

"After successfully adjusting a thousand and one difficulties," Conner wrote in his Notes on Operations, "and after having foreseen the other thousand and one necessities which confront staffs," the eight-and-a-half front-line divisions arrived in place in time for the September 26, 1918 attack. Marshall's plan had succeeded in maintaining secrecy, aided by what Conner described as "successful ruses" east of the Meuse River. Four days before the attack, Ludendorff had considered it "improbable" that the lightly trained American divisions moving to the area would be called upon to lead an attack. Instead, the German commander continued to think that the Americans would resume the attack toward Metz, where the AEF's better divisions continued to hold their positions.[14]

Again, as at St. Mihiel, the German high command misjudged the situation.

The American Meuse–Argonne offensive began with a tremendous artillery bombardment shortly before midnight on September 26, 1918.[15] In 3 hours, First Army fired more artillery rounds than both sides had expended in the 4 years of the American Civil War. One artillery officer in the 35th Division, Captain Harry S. Truman, wrote home that his battery's cannon got so hot from repetitive firing, that the gun barrels boiled the wet gunnysacks used to cool them.

Then the American infantry attacked across the 20-mile front stretching from the Argonne to the Meuse. This time, the Germans were not withdrawing as they had at St. Mihiel. As the American infantrymen attempted to cut their way through miles of barbed wire, enemy troops emerged from the shelters that had protected them from the earlier artillery barrage. German machine guns and artillery then began to annihilate the Americans, who were often massed against the wire with no place to seek cover. As First Army's advance stopped, inexperienced division commanders and staff continued to push more troops forward, which "merely fed the men to the machine guns," as an Inspector General's report put it. Traffic snarls on destroyed roads prevented the evacuation of wounded men.

Among the American casualties on the first day of the attack was Lieutenant Colonel George Patton. With his tanks unable to advance, Patton located some lost infantrymen and began to lead them forward when a bullet from a German machine gun tore into his left thigh. The upward trajectory of the slug left an exit wound "just at the crack of my bottom," as Patton described it to his wife Beatrice. Patton also relayed his doctor's amazement that the bullet had not damaged any nerves or arteries in the area. He attributed his survival to "fate."

Elsewhere across the Meuse–Argonne Front, the AEF's fate looked bleak. Pershing's plan called for the capture of Montfaucon on the first day of the attack and an advance of 10 miles to breach the *Kriemhilde Stellung* by the second. Neither happened. Instead, the green American divisions were bled white in a battle that the AEF was clearly losing.

"Day and night," Conner wrote in his Notes on Operations, "the attack continued without interruption." Pershing and his First Army staff began to replace the mauled divisions with the more experienced units that had seen such great success at St. Mihiel. Meanwhile, Pershing's separate GHQ staff at Chaumont, including Conner, kept their focus on 1919. On September 29, 1918, as the AEF's offensive teetered on the edge of failure, Conner submitted a detailed shipping schedule to increase the size of the AEF to eighty divisions and more than 4 million men by July 1919.[16]

The German commanders, however, understood the imminent peril they were beginning to face in 1918. In furtherance of Foch's strategy of simultaneous attacks along the entire Western Front, the French Army launched an offensive to the west of the Americans on September 27. On the 28th, the British began a third offensive. Ludendorff wrote on September 29 that he expected the Allies, "by reckless commitment of all available means," to "bring about the decision of the war." Recognizing the importance of the rail lines behind his position, von der Marwitz told his troops on October 1 that "the fate of a great part of the Western Front, and perhaps the very fate of our people" depended upon the German Army's stopping a breakthrough between the Meuse and the Argonne. He used the very rail system the Americans were trying to capture to send six fresh divisions to bolster the *Kriemhilde Stellung*.[17]

As the British and French offensives to the west each gained momentum, Foch and Pétain pushed Pershing for greater results from the independent army for which the American commander had so

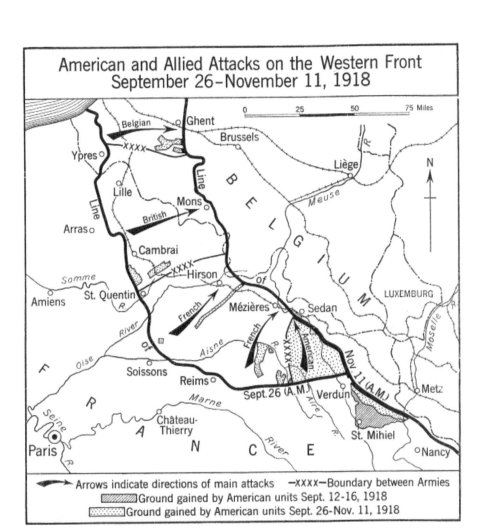

Map 10: Allied Attacks on the Western Front. Credit: The American Battle Monuments Commission.

strongly lobbied. On October 4, First Army resumed its attack with the 1st, 3rd, and 32nd divisions having replaced the 35th, 79th, and 37th. The veteran divisions, however, fared little better. "The resistance was desperate," wrote Conner, "and only small advances were realized." The 1st Division, under the command of the aggressive Charles P. Summerall, suffered more than 9,000 casualties in a week's fighting in the Argonne. Aware that his allies were having greater success to the west, Pershing resolved that he "had no course but to fight it out" between the Meuse and the Argonne. He continued to push his men forward against the deadly German positions.[18]

As the Meuse–Argonne battle grew in significance—for both Ferdinand Foch's strategy and John J. Pershing's prestige—Fox Conner began to take on a greater role in the operation.

Conner worked with Liggett's I Corps staff to plan an attack by the 82nd Division on October 7. The complex operation successfully drove the Germans from strategic positions in the Argonne that had held up the left side of the American advance. By October 10, the entire Argonne Forest was under American control.[19]

The formidable *Kriemhilde Stellung*, though, remained intact east of the forest. As Pershing continued to slam his forces against the heavily fortified German line, Conner directed the allocation of artillery, motor transportation, and other resources. "I was the one," said Conner in postwar testimony, "who knew that a certain division would probably go into battle on a certain date, or before another division. So this question came to me almost daily." He added: "We were always short [of equipment] and it fell to me to determine the priority of equipment."[20]

Conner also addressed the AEF's critical lack of infantry replacements—a problem he had foreseen in his September 15, 1918 memorandum. "By mid-October," Conner recalled in a postwar report, "the situation was desperate." First Army was short around 45,000 men due to the combination of heavy fighting and an outbreak of influenza among the troops. Unable to locate replacements elsewhere, Conner disbanded seven newly arrived divisions (the 31st, 34th, 38th, 39th, 76th, 84th, and 86th) and sent their untrained men directly to the front-line divisions as replacements. Decades later, Conner acknowledged the move as having been "a wasteful, inefficient way to gain replacements," but he added: "It was the only possible way to get enough of them in time."[21]

Also in mid-October, with the AEF having grown to more than a million men, Pershing divided his force into two separate field armies.[22] On October 12, Hunter Liggett took command of First Army in the Meuse–Argonne sector, while Robert Lee Bullard became commander of Second Army, formed by the American divisions east of the Meuse

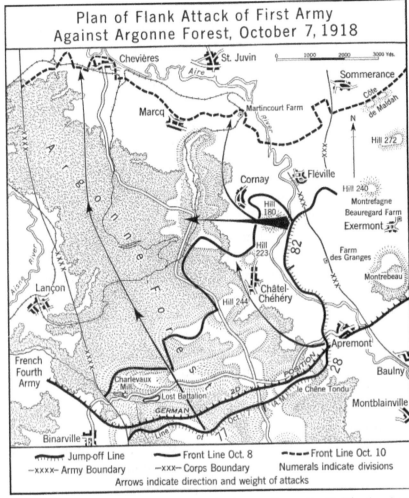

Map 11: *Flank Attack of First Army against the Argonne Forest. Credit: The American Battle Monuments Commission.*

River. Pershing maintained overall control of both armies as AEF commander-in-chief.

Having relinquished command of First Army, Pershing also reverted to having a single staff. Years later, George Marshall wrote of how "frantic" Pershing's dual staff system had made Conner. "Even the most serious movie always includes its lighter touches," Marshall wrote Conner in 1934, "and I have to laugh when I think of your diatribes prior to October 12th." George Marshall also benefitted from the AEF's reorganization when Liggett appointed him to the position of First Army's G-3. Hugh Drum remained First Army's chief of staff.

Pershing and Liggett also made changes atop First Army's field command structure. Joseph Dickman succeeded Liggett as I Corps commander on the left side of the front. Charles Summerall took command of V Corps in the center of the line. John Hines replaced Bullard as III Corps commander on the right side.

On October 14, the reorganized First Army resumed its attack and continued to grind slowly forward. On October 16, the 32nd and 42nd divisions finally broke through the *Kriemhilde Stellung* more than 2 weeks behind schedule. Frustrated by the lack of progress of other divisions, Pershing relieved three division commanders in mid-October, including Major General Clarence Edwards, who had commanded the 26th Division since its arrival in France.[23]

By late October, as the French and British offensives to the west continued to succeed, Pershing and his staff began to recognize that Foch's strategy to end the war in 1918 might actually work. Acutely aware of the AEF's poor showing—and that jockeying among the Allies for postwar influence had begun—Pershing dispatched Fox Conner to meet the press and to tell the AEF's side of the story regarding its contribution to the Allied cause.[24]

On October 22, 1918, Conner met with around fifty accredited news correspondents and censors at press headquarters in Bar-le-Duc, France.[25] McAndrew also attended the press conference, but Conner did most of the talking. Speaking "informally and extemporaneously," the AEF chief of operations began by discussing the history of America's war effort since 1917. He then turned to the ongoing Meuse–Argonne operation and declared it "a very wonderful piece of work," of which "all Americans should be proud."

Conner displayed his aptitude for teaching. Using maps, he showed the reporters how the region between the Argonne and the Meuse formed the "pivot" or "neck of the bottle" through which the Germans were attempting to simultaneously withdraw their forces threatened by the British and French offensives to the west by sending them eastward to defend against the American attack between the Meuse and the Argonne. Employing a French phrase, he explained that the rail lines between Sedan and Mézières formed the vital *voie de rocade* (lateral transportation system) that the Germans had to protect in order to move men and supplies rapidly between the fronts.

Conner contended that the greater French and British advances to the west had been made possible by the AEF's bearing the brunt of the fighting at the all-important pivot. He explained that the enemy strategy was to hold their pivot "until the very last," and that the American front was where the German Army was making its last desperate stand. He told the reporters that the persistent American attacks to capture the Sedan–Mézières rail system had drawn more than thirty German divisions from other areas to the Meuse–Argonne sector; these divisions, he explained, included "some of the best" that Ludendorff had left, and also most of his reserves. He told the reporters that the Germans had defended the area with "everything that anybody could possibly devise."

Not missing the chance to make the case for his own preferred strategy, Conner also described how the American attack along the Meuse River threatened the strategic Briey iron basin in Lorraine, which Conner had long considered the key to Germany's ability to remain in the war. "If the Briey basin is ever lost to the German," said Conner, "the time of his ultimate downfall is reduced by just that much."

Turning to the subject of casualties, Conner acknowledged: "Of course we have had losses. We have had heavy losses." He candidly informed the journalists that each of the divisions was losing up to 2,000 men a day, and that he was sending divisions back into the fight with far less rest than the men required. "You can't let up," Conner argued. "In order to keep up the push constantly, all the time, you have got to keep divisions in longer than we would like to." He pointed out that the French, British, and Belgians were doing the same. "I think that the men feel they are doing the right thing in bucking it and there is no feeling among the troops that they are not able to keep it up while they are accomplishing things." He added: "It is pretty hard on the division that is in there but this is a war, not [of] a division, but of millions of men."

Conner's remarks also reflected a fundamental change in his own thinking as to the wisdom of the Allied strategy of attacking the area between the Meuse and the Argonne. In July 1918, Conner had counseled Pershing that Foch's plan provided "no reasonable prospect for final victory during 1919" and offered only "the certainty of prolonging the war." By late October, however, Conner had come to view matters differently: "I have a great and abiding faith that we are doing the right thing," Conner said. He emphasized that the AEF had "to keep it up because there is every reason to believe that that will result in ending the war in the shortest possible time, also with the least possible loss of life."

One of the correspondents in attendance, Thomas M. Johnson of *The Sun* (New York), recalled that he and his fellow reporters were "following closely General Conner's pencil as it pointed here and there on our big map that covered the whole wall." He wrote that "General Conner had given us a phrase, '*voie de rocade*,' that struck our imaginations. We used it often."

More importantly, Conner's remarks had helped to instill a positive view of the war in the minds of the journalists reporting upon it. In his 1928 book recounting his experiences as a wartime journalist, Johnson wrote that Conner's briefing "had a great influence" on subsequent news reports. As Johnson put it, following the October 22 news conference, he and his fellow journalists "started a campaign to sell the Meuse-Argonne to the world."

Fox Conner then turned his attention to finishing the AEF's campaign to capture the Sedan–Mézières rail lines.

On October 23, Liggett suspended First Army's offensive to allow time to bring in fresh divisions for a new attack scheduled for November 1. Pershing assigned McAndrew and Conner to work with Liggett's First Army staff to plan what Conner termed "the great attack." The American commander-in-chief charged his two top assistants to "leave nothing undone that might cause us delay or failure."[26]

Pershing, McAndrew, and Conner remained at First Army's headquarters through the end of October. Conner and McAndrew focused on methods to correct the problems with transportation, communications, and coordination, which had plagued earlier phases of the attack. The respective staffs of GHQ and First Army also produced competing plans for the November 1 operation. Liggett ultimately adopted his own staff's plan.

Liggett and his staff did not always appreciate the presence of the men from Chaumont. The war diary of Liggett's aide, Pierpont L. Stackpole, reflected the tension between the two groups of officers. Stackpole recounted one incident in which Liggett reportedly told Pershing to "give us a directive and leave us alone." Another entry referred to the AEF commander-in-chief and his two most-trusted staff officers as "hanging around" First Army headquarters.

Despite the strain among Pershing, Liggett, and their respective staffs, Fox Conner's Notes on Operations indicate that First Army had "developed into a powerful and smooth running machine" by the end of October 1918. By contrast, Conner thought that the German Army was "ripe for disaster" and that the enemy's "will to resist had reached the breaking point." German soldiers had been surrendering in increasing numbers; their interrogations and confiscated letters revealed a growing sense of hopelessness. Tellingly, on October 26, 1918, Hindenburg and Ludendorff each tendered their resignations to the German Kaiser. The emperor retained Hindenburg but not his Western Front field commander Ludendorff. Germany's military maestro was out of the war.[27]

As signs of an Allied victory in 1918 continued to manifest, Foch summoned the Allied commanders to his headquarters on October 25 to discuss the armistice terms the Allies should demand. Conner accompanied Pershing to the conference. Pershing then submitted a letter to the Supreme War Council on October 30 in which he proposed that the Allies demand the unconditional surrender of Germany, rather than merely the suspension of fighting that would accompany an armistice. Historian John Ray Skates wrote that Conner "certainly concurred in (and he probably wrote) Pershing's recommendations."[28]

The Supreme War Council rejected Pershing's proposal for an unconditional surrender. French Premier Clemenceau called the idea "theatrical." British Prime Minister David Lloyd George dismissed the concept as being mere "politics" by the American general. The British commander Haig thought the Allies would be fortunate to secure an armistice at all, since he believed Germany capable of continuing the fight if its army could be successfully withdrawn and regrouped. For the remainder of his long life, though, Black Jack Pershing would argue that World War II would never have happened had his unconditional surrender proposal been adopted by the Allies.

Sir Douglas Haig had correctly observed that the German Army still needed to be defeated before its army was withdrawn; therefore, on November 1, the American First Army resumed its drive to capture the rail system between Sedan and Mézières.[29] Foch also sent the French Fourth Army, located to the left of the Americans, toward the rail lines with the same objective—to plug what Conner had termed the "neck of the bottle" before the German Army could escape through it.

The combined Allied force overwhelmed the exhausted Germans who held the last lines of defense in front of the rail lines. In his Notes on Operations, Conner wrote that the November 1 attack became "an onslaught that the enemy could not contain." German defenses began to collapse. The "retreat became a rout," as Conner put it in his notes. In his postwar report on AEF operations, Conner wrote that "the enemy's final break-up came with a rapidity that, before the middle of July, would have seemed incredible."

By November 4, First Army had advanced more than 12 miles and had driven the German Army across the Meuse River. Liggett then brought up heavy artillery to shell the German rail lines. Conner recognized that "the ultimate object of more than a month's continuous and desperate battle was now within reach." In James G. Harbord's 1936 description, "First Army had been responding in those last days like a racing car with Pershing's foot on the accelerator."

But as the AEF sped toward its objective, the men directing it lost control. They created what George Marshall termed "one of the bitterest contentions between American troops during the war." Conner and Marshall were both involved.[30]

Apart from the strategic value of the rail lines running through Sedan, the French also attached great emotional and symbolic importance to that city. In 1871, the final battle of the Franco-Prussian War had been fought at Sedan. France suffered a crushing defeat in which Prussian

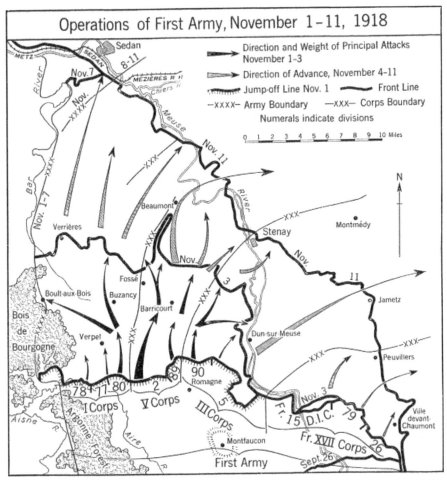

Map 12: Operations of First Army, November 1–11, 1918. Credit: The American Battle Monuments Commission.

troops captured French Emperor Napoleon III to end the war. In the resulting peace settlement, France also lost the city and most of Alsace-Lorraine. For more than 40 years, the French Army had yearned to avenge the shame of Sedan. Marshal Foch, who wanted Frenchmen to have the honor of recapturing the city, drew the boundaries between the French and American Armies to place Sedan into the zone of advance of the French Fourth Army.[31]

As the November attack progressed, however, the American First Army began to outpace its French allies, which left the western flank of the American Army exposed. Pershing, therefore, secured an agreement from French General Paul Maistre, who commanded the army group that included both the French Fourth and American First armies, to allow the American Army to disregard the previously established boundaries between the two armies and to move toward the northwest. While Pershing's ostensible purpose was to protect First Army's left flank, he had an ulterior motive: still stung by the disrespect shown to him and his army by the French, Pershing had decided to beat the French to Sedan in order to capture the city ahead of them.[32]

Thus was born the "Race for Sedan," which nearly wreaked disaster on the American Army.[33]

At 4:00 p.m. on November 5, Fox Conner travelled to First Army headquarters to deliver Pershing's order to take Sedan. Liggett and Drum were both away, so Conner met instead with First Army's chief of operations, George Marshall.

In a draft of his memoirs written a few years after the war, Marshall described the November 5 meeting as having been "a rather unusual interview." According to Marshall, after Conner and he had discussed the overall operations of First Army for around a half-hour, Conner then "suddenly" said: "It is General Pershing's desire that the troops of First Army should capture Sedan and he directs that orders be issued accordingly." Conner's abrupt pronouncement surprised Marshall. Noting that he and Conner were "on very intimate personal terms," Colonel Marshall dismissed General Conner's directive with a laugh and replied: "Am I expected to believe that this is General Pershing's order, when I know damn well you came to this conclusion during our conversation?"

"This is the order of the commander-in-chief, which I am authorized to issue in his name," Conner shot back to the junior officer. "Now get it out as quickly as possible."

Marshall, who recognized that Conner's directive would send the American First Army into the French zone of operations, continued to resist. In his memoirs, Marshall wrote that he "did not fancy making this drastic change" in plans without consulting either Liggett or Drum, his immediate superiors in the First Army chain of command; therefore Marshall "proposed a compromise" to allow time for him to discuss the matter with either Liggett or Drum. "General Conner was not enthusiastic over my attitude," Marshall later recalled, "but agreed to my proposal."

Marshall then complied with Conner's instructions and prepared an order for the American First Army to capture Sedan. To gain time to consult his superiors, Marshall secured Conner's permission to delay issuing the order until 6:00 p.m. The order that Marshall wrote, and which Conner approved, stated:

> 1. General Pershing directs that the honor of entering Sedan should fall to the First American Army. He has every confidence that the troops of the 1st Corps, assisted on their right by the 5th Corps, will enable him to realize this desire.
> 2. In transmitting the foregoing message, your attention is invited to the favorable opportunity now existing for pressing our advantage throughout the night.

Shortly before the 6:00 p.m. deadline, Hugh Drum returned to First Army's headquarters. Marshall informed the chief of staff of his meeting with Conner and showed Drum the proposed order. According to Marshall, Drum approved the order "without hesitation," but he added a final sentence: "Boundaries will not be considered as binding." Drum inserted the language to authorize the entry of American troops into the French zone. Marshall then telephoned the revised order to Joseph Dickman's I Corps on the left of the American line and to Charles P. Summerall's V Corps in the center. Satisfied with the authority of Fox Conner, their former Chaumont colleague, neither Drum nor Marshall informed the First Army commander General Liggett before transmitting the order to the two corps commanders.

Pershing, Conner, Drum, and Marshall had all intended the American I Corps, located on the western side of the American line—and therefore nearest to Sedan—to make the advance toward the French city. In directing V Corps to assist in the operation, the American high command meant for Summerall's corps to protect the eastern side of I Corps as Dickman turned his force. Charles P. Summerall, however, interpreted the order differently. In Summerall's view, the language addressing boundaries empowered him to ignore the previous lines of demarcation between the two American corps themselves. The aggressive Summerall accordingly decided to outrace Dickman's I Corps to the prize of Sedan.

The 1st Division, which Summerall had commanded until his elevation to corps command in mid-October, formed part of his V Corps. On November 6, Summerall personally delivered orders to his successor at 1st Division, Brigadier General Frank Parker, to "proceed at once in the direction of Sedan, operating at night as well as day." Parker's November 6 field order directed his division to "seize Sedan" even though two divisions of I Corps, (the 42nd and 77th), were much closer to the city.

As the 1st Division marched toward Sedan on the evening of November 6 and into the following morning, it marched directly across the fronts of both the 77th and 42nd divisions, just as one of the latter's brigades, commanded by Douglas MacArthur, was about to attack. Soldiers from the 1st and 42nd divisions exchanged fire—oblivious to the fact that they were shooting at their countrymen. The 1st Division suffered around 500 casualties. When MacArthur went forward to investigate the reports of "friendly fire," a 1st Division patrol, mistaking him for a German officer, detained him at gunpoint.

The 1st Division's 26th Infantry Regiment, commanded by Theodore Roosevelt, Jr., created additional problems when it moved further west and into the zone of the French Fourth Army. The French notified the American Corps commander Dickman that if Roosevelt's troops were not withdrawn within an hour, they would be fired upon. The American First Army commander, General Liggett, who did not learn of the order to take Sedan until he received the French protests, viewed the action as "a military atrocity." General Dickman was likewise "furious"; he wanted both Parker and Summerall to be court-martialed.

In his 1964 *Reminiscences*, Douglas MacArthur blamed the entire episode on the "ambiguous and extraordinary final sentence" of First Army's order. MacArthur attributed the order to the "prompting of General Fox Connor." He erred as to both the spelling of Conner's name and as to the actual author of the addendum.

Blame was plentiful. Pershing should not have attempted to beat his ally to such a symbolic destination. Conner should not have forced Marshall, in effect, to bypass Liggett with a drastic alteration of plans. Regardless of their friendship, *Colonel* Marshall should not have disobeyed the order of his superior officer—*General* Conner—to transmit Pershing's directive immediately. Drum should not have hurriedly appended such a vague phrase. Summerall should not have sent the 1st Division directly into the path of other American divisions. While Pershing, Harbord, Marshall, and others addressed the Sedan operation in their memoirs with varying degrees of candor, Conner took a different view. He made no reference to the Sedan incident in either his Notes on Operations or in his comprehensive report on the AEF's operations submitted shortly after the war. "The less said about the Race for Sedan the better," he told one fellow officer.

On November 8, Foch intervened to re-establish the original boundary between the French and American forces. Conner complied, then issued orders for First Army to turn aside so that the French could take Sedan. Instead of bringing the vindication Pershing had sought, the Race for Sedan had yielded only embarrassment. "As an illustration of the lack of team work, and an example of undisciplined inexperience," wrote James Harbord, "it justified much that our Associates thought and said of us."

Fortunately for the AEF, events elsewhere overshadowed the Sedan debacle. On November 6, 1918, after fighting for 40 days, First Army finally captured the Sedan–Mézières rail lines. With the loss of its vital *voie de rocade*, Germany also lost the ability to supply its troops on the Western Front or to withdraw them. In his 1919 postwar section report, Conner stressed the strategic significance of the operation. He pointed out that the German Kaiser would have "shortened his front by more than 150 kilometers [90 miles], and would have stood, with his own country intact, behind the most difficult part of the Ardennes" had the Americans not interdicted the Sedan–Mézières rail system. In Fox Conner's opinion, the AEF's November 6 victory "meant the end of all the German Armies in Northern France."[34]

The German high command concurred. On November 6—the same day the AEF captured the rail lines—German emissaries approached

Map 13: Ground Gained by First Army, November 1–11, 1918. Credit: The American Battle Monuments Commission.

Foch for armistice terms. As Conner put it in his Notes on Operations: "Two such coincidences are not the result of chance."[35]

In addition to its military collapse on the Western Front, the German Empire itself began to implode. In mass demonstrations in Munich and Berlin, protestors called for the Kaiser's abdication and an end to the war. Across Germany, "councils" of workers and soldiers sprang up, many headed by Bolsheviks. On November 3, forces loyal to the Kaiser had fired upon their mutinying comrades.[36]

Foch received the German peace delegation in the Compiègne Forest on the evening of November 7. The Allied supreme commander presented strict armistice terms: the immediate evacuation of all conquered territory including Alsace-Lorraine; the establishment of three Allied bridgeheads across the Rhine and into German territory; surrender of the German fleet and submarines; maintenance of the Allied naval blockade of Germany until a formal peace treaty was concluded; and payment of substantial reparations. Foch gave the Germans 72 hours to either accept or decline the terms. He would conduct no negotiations. Foch also denied the German request for a ceasefire during the period of deliberations.[37]

Conner, who thought the Germans might reject Foch's severe armistice terms, wholeheartedly agreed with Foch that the Allies needed to maintain maximum military pressure on the German Army until an armistice was actually signed. He explained in 1920: "A great many people believed that the German motive in asking for an armistice was to gain time." He also expressed concern as to "the possibility of treachery on the part of the German high command." Pershing concurred with his chief of operations. On November 8, the American commander sent a telegram to his corps commanders, directing them to "push to the limit any operations you had in prospect."[38]

One such prospective operation remained of distinct interest to Fox Conner—the offensive against Metz and the Briey iron reserves in Lorraine that he had long wanted to undertake.

On November 6, Pershing had received a request from Foch for six American divisions to join in a French attack into Lorraine. Pershing offered to send the 3rd, 4th, 28th, 29th, 35th, and 36th divisions, but only if the American forces served under General Bullard's Second Army command. Foch agreed. He set November 14 as the date for the attack. Except to note in his postwar report that such an attack "had been studied by General Headquarters as early as September 1917," Conner left no other record of his thoughts as the Allied supreme commander made plans to finish the war with an offensive into Lorraine—where Conner had always thought the war would be won.[39]

On November 9, Foch also ordered all Allied forces to continue their attacks vigorously: "The enemy, disorganized by our repeated attacks,

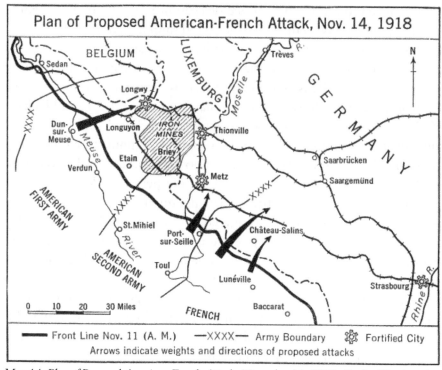

Map 14: Plan of Proposed American-French Attack, November 14, 1918. Credit: The American Battle Monuments Commission.

is withdrawing along the whole front. It is important to maintain and hasten our action. I appeal to the energy and initiative of the commanders in chief and their armies to secure decisive results." According to Conner, Foch's order had a threefold purpose: "First of all, to counteract the idea among the troops that the armistice had already been signed, or that it was certain that it would be signed; secondly, to take advantage of the existing situation so as to influence the German delegates to sign; and, thirdly, to take every advantage of the situation whether they signed or not."[40]

The men at Chaumont, therefore, continued to drive the AEF forward, including an attack by the 92nd Division that was moved up by one day. Fox Conner spent his time on November 9 and November 10 making plans for Second Army's attack into Lorraine, while waiting to see if the war would last long enough for the offensive to materialize.[41]

★ ★ ★ ★ ★

Fox Conner was not the only American soldier whose plans depended upon the war's continuation.

In late October 1918, Lieutenant Colonel Dwight Eisenhower received orders to sail for France as commander of the November shipment of tank troops being sent to France from Camp Colt. Eisenhower's commanding officer—Fox Conner's West Point classmate Ira C. Welborn—had offered to recommend Eisenhower for promotion to full colonel if he would agree to remain in the United States as a training officer. Eisenhower responded that he would prefer a reduction in rank if it would facilitate his getting into combat.

Eisenhower's ship was set to sail on November 18, 1918. However, as had also occurred to Fox Conner during the Spanish–American War 20 years earlier, Eisenhower would get no closer to combat than an order to proceed to a port of embarkation. "Fate, with the usual bad manners, intervened," Eisenhower wrote in 1967. "I had made no provision for the imminent German defeat."[42]

★ ★ ★ ★ ★

As Fox Conner put it, "all plans were interrupted on November 11th"—including his own plans for Second Army's offensive into Lorraine to capture the Briey iron mines.[43]

On November 10, German Kaiser Wilhelm II fled into asylum in the Netherlands. In Berlin, the socialist-led government that took power instructed the German peace delegation to accept Foch's armistice terms.[44] On November 11, 1918, in a rail car brought into a clearing in the Compiègne Forest, German diplomats signed the armistice agreement at 5:10 a.m.[45] Under the armistice terms, hostilities would cease at 11:00 a.m. Foch's staff notified Pershing at 6:00 a.m. An aide on Pershing's staff immediately transmitted Foch's message, verbatim, to the headquarters of First and Second armies. Conner, who had returned to Chaumont the preceding night, learned of the armistice shortly after 7:00 a.m.

Despite knowing that the armistice had been signed—and that 11:00 a.m. had been selected for the primarily poetic purpose of ending the war on the 11th hour of the 11th day of the 11th month—neither Conner nor any of his Chaumont colleagues directed the men of the AEF to stand down. Instead, the American Army continued to fight. According to figures produced by Conner after the war, the AEF suffered 3,912 casualties on November 11, including 268 Americans killed on the war's last day. In postwar testimony, Conner explained that the armistice was set to become effective "at," rather than "by," 11:00 a.m. He defended the continued fighting on November 11: "If you are in action against an enemy who, in the general mind of both military people and people at home, is a treacherous enemy, you take advantage of anything you can as long as it is legitimate to carry on warfare."[46]

The November 11 losses added to a total casualty list of 26,277 Americans killed, and another 95,786 wounded, in the final 6 *weeks* of the war. To place the number of deaths into perspective, the United States would suffer around 58,000 deaths in the 7 *years* of the Vietnam War. The Meuse–Argonne offensive, which historian Robert Ferrell correctly termed "the deadliest battle in all of American history," accounted for most of the losses in those 6 weeks of fighting.[47]

Fox Conner rationalized the number of killed and wounded by observing that the casualties were spread across twenty-two divisions which had successfully ground through the desperate resistance of a still-formidable German Army. "Viewed in the light of the results achieved," Conner wrote in his Notes on Operations, "the casualties were light." In his postwar Operations Section report, he described the Meuse–Argonne losses as having been "remarkably light."[48]

Not everyone shared that opinion, as Fox Conner would learn in time.

According to First Army's commander, Hunter Liggett, "the most impressive moment of the war" came at 11:00 a.m. on November 11, 1918 "when the infernal uproar which had been continuous for a long time suddenly gave place to a silence which was stunning."[49]

Fox Conner had done his part to make that peaceful stillness happen.

Conner had been one of the few select officers charged with form-ing an army of millions, overseas in a foreign land, when the United

Robert Conner as a Civil War soldier. (Macpherson Conner Collection)

The first known photograph of Fox Conner, c. 1876. (Norm MacDonald Collection)

The Conner family in the 1880s; Fox is standing behind his blind father. (Macpherson Conner Collection)

Conner's 1898 West Point graduation photo. (Macpherson Conner Collection)

The West Point courtyard c. 1898. (Macpherson Conner Collection)

The Class of 1898 at West Point; Conner is No. 31. (Macpherson Conner Collection)

1 Wheeler, D. P.
2 Murphy, W. L.
3 Berry, D. G.
4 Smith, C. S.
5 Hamilton, W. W.
6 Newbold, H. W.
7 Mead, F. E.
8 Cole, W. E.

9 Merrill, T. E.
10 Fleetus, W. W., Jr.
11 Brown, E. L.
12 Johnson, J. C.
13 Bearchey, E. N.
14 Cralle, G. M.
15 McGinnis, T. F.
16 Lyle, D. E. W.

17 Kmerls, B.
18 Read, A. C.
19 Scates, W. E.
20 Walton, R. F.
21 Lafferty, H. A.
22 Hammond, H.
23 Jordan, L. W.
24 Nesbit, W. F.

CLASS OF 1898

25 Fries, A. A.
26 Babcock, C. S.
27 McCloskey, M.
28 Otwell, C. W.
29 Kirchoner, K.
30 Gowen, J. B.
31 Conner, F.

32 Ingram, R. E.
33 Butler, H. W.
34 Maxey, R. J.
35 Spinks, M. G.
36 Boerge, F. C.
37 Kerth, M. C.
38 Nugent, G. A.
39 Exton, C. W.

40 Welborn, I.
41 Miller, H. W.
42 Davis, R. C.
43 Williams, A. E.
44 Gohn, J. F.
45 Stone, D. L.
46 Bricker, E. D.
47 Kerr, R. D.

48 Janda, J. P.
49 Henry, G. V.
50 Sewell, H. D.
51 Brown, J. I.
52 Bradford, J. H., Jr.
53 Humphrey, C. B.
54 Stephens, J. E.
55 Martin, E. H.

Carroll Armistead   Fox Conner
Picture I had of Fox for a year before we met

Conner in Cuba in 1900. This photo was taken by Fox's future wife, Virginia ("Bug") Brandreth who kept the picture on a dresser for a year before they actually met. (Macpherson Conner Collection)

(Below): Fox and Bug courting at Brandreth Lake in 1901. (Macpherson Conner Collection)

Mr. and Mrs. Franklin Brandreth

request the honour of

your presence at the marriage of their daughter

Virginia Grahame

to

Captain Fox Conner

of the United States Army

on the evening of Wednesday, the fourth of June

at seven o'clock

at Cliff Cottage

Ossining, New York

R.s.v.p.

An invitation to the wedding of Virginia Brandreth and Fox Conner, 1902. (Norm MacDonald Collection)

Fox, Bug, and their wedding party in 1902. (Macpherson Conner Collection)

Fox and Bug at Coney Island, c. 1902. (Macpherson Conner Collection)

Fox holding his daughter Betty ("Betsey") at her christening in 1903. (Macpherson Conner Collection)

Fox and Bug at Fort Riley, Kansas, 1906. (Macpherson Conner Collection)

Captain Fox Conner, probably at Fort Riley, Kansas, c. 1906. (Norm MacDonald Collection)

Fox's young family with his mother, Nannie Conner, c. 1909. (Macpherson Conner Collection)

Colonel Franklin Brandreth with his Conner grandchildren, 1911. (Macpherson Conner Collection)

(Left): Captain Conner at the Army War College in Washington, D.C., c. 1910. (Macpherson Conner Collection)

(Right): Conner with his ceremonial sword at the outset of World War I, April 1917. (Macpherson Conner Collection)

Conner with Colonel Remond of the French Mission, April 1917. (Macpherson Conner Collection)

Conner at his Operations Section desk during World War I. (Macpherson Conner Collection)

"Black Jack" Pershing and his wartime staff at Chaumont, 1918. Conner is to Pershing's immediate left. (Norm MacDonald Collection)

(Left): Conner and John J. Pershing in Paris leaving a 1919 conference. (Macpherson Conner Collection)

Conner (waving his hat) flanked by Pershing and Marshall, aboard the Navy launch that brought them to shore in New York Harbor after their return from France in 1919. (Norm MacDonald Collection)

(Right): Conner with Pershing and Secretary of War Newton Baker in New York, 1919. (Macpherson Conner Collection)

Pershing and his staff at the former State, War, and Navy Building in Washington, DC, 1919. Conner is to Pershing's immediate right. (Norm MacDonald Collection)

Conner, Pershing, and George C. Marshall at Brandreth Lake, 1919. (Macpherson Conner Collection)

The Ladyfish, *chartered by George Patton for his tarpon fishing trip with the Conners, 1921. (Macpherson Conner Collection)*

Bug Conner and her tarpon fish, 1921. (Macpherson Conner Collection)

Conner on horseback in Panama, c. 1922. (Macpherson Conner Collection)

(Left): Conner and his horse in Panama, c. 1922. (Macpherson Conner Collection)

Aerial view of Camp Gaillard, c. 1923. (Macpherson Conner Collection)

Photo of the Conner residence in Panama, c. 1924.
(Macpherson Conner Collection)

(Right): Conner holding baby John S. D.
Eisenhower, c. 1923. (Macpherson Conner
Collection)

Conner as Deputy Chief of Staff, c. 1926.
(Macpherson Conner Collection)

Fox and Bug Conner in Hawaii, 1929.
(Macpherson Conner Collection)

Conner (center) flanked by retired general Hunter Liggett and Lieutenant Trimble Brown in Hawaii,
c. 1928. (Macpherson Conner Collection)

General Conner reclining on the beach (in uniform), c. 1929. (Macpherson Conner Collection)

The Conners and Lieutenant Trimble Brown leaving Hawaii, 1930. (Macpherson Conner Collection)

Conner as commanding general of the First Corps Area, with full dress uniform and medals, c. 1934. (Macpherson Conner Collection)

Conner and Douglas MacArthur, c. 1932. (Macpherson Conner Collection)

Fox and Bug Conner with their children and their families at Conner's Corner in Brandreth Lake, 1936. (Macpherson Conner Collection)

(Below): Fox Brandreth "Tommy" Conner (Fox's son) at West Point, 1927. (Macpherson Conner Collection)

(Below): Macpherson Conner (Fox's grandson) at West Point, 1952. (Macpherson Conner Collection)

Conner in retirement with Bug at Brandreth Lake, c. 1942. (Norm MacDonald Collection)

View of Brandreth Lake. (Macpherson Conner Collection)

Conner, Pershing, and Harbord at a gathering of the Baltic Society, 1941. (Macpherson Conner Collection)

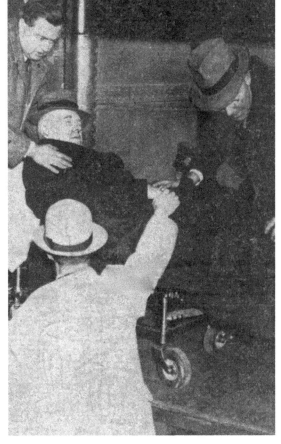

(Right): The injured Conner being taken off of the train in Utica, New York, 1941. (Macpherson Conner Collection)

(Right): A 1945 letter to Conner from George Patton regarding the Battle of the Bulge. (Macpherson Conner Collection)

HEADQUARTERS
THIRD UNITED STATES ARMY
OFFICE OF THE COMMANDING GENERAL
APO 403

13 March, 1945

My dear General Conner:

Your letter of February 11 has been just received.

We have just put across two more very nice shows, when we took Trier and then smashed through to take the whole Rhine from the 1st Army to Koblenz. This morning we are attacking, trying to get a break-through south of the Moselle. It is yet too early to determine what the results will be.

I am enclosing a brief account of the Bastogne Operation which may be of interest to you.

With affectionate regards to both of you, I am,

Devotedly yours,

G. S. PATTON, JR.

Major General Fox Conner
RFD 5
Hendersonville, N. C.
U. S. A.

Incl.
Copy, Bastogne Operation.

CRUSADE IN EUROPE

To
Maj. General Fox Conner -
    To whom I shall
always be indebted ———
with best wishes and
warm regard to him and
his entire family, from
their devoted friend
            Dke Eisenhower.
Dec. 1948.

Dwight D. Eisenhower's handwritten inscription to Conner on his 1948 book, Crusade in Europe. (Norm MacDonald Collection)

Conner in his Adirondack chair at his Adirondack cabin, c. 1950. (Norm MacDonald Collection)

States had lacked even one organized division at the war's outset. The "square" division, designed by Conner and Drum, allowed the AEF to take advantage of its primary strength—manpower in a war of attrition—while accommodating its lack of trained commanders and staff officers. As AEF chief of operations, Conner successfully managed the ad hoc deployment of available American forces, first to assist the Allies in defense of Ludendorff's 1918 spring attacks, then in taking the offensive in the summer and fall to end the war sooner than anyone had thought possible. Through the detailed and often taxing negotiations with America's French and British allies, Conner gained valuable insight into the practical difficulties of coalition warfare, which his nation—and a future protégé—would again face within a generation.

The few photographs made of Conner during the war depict an intently focused man who glared at the camera with pursed lips that bordered upon a scowl and with eyes that conveyed only aggravation at being disturbed from his work. According to Bug Conner, though, "Fox was perfectly happy all through the war." As the AEF's chief of operations, Fox Conner—who as a boy had imagined himself directing great armies in battle—had been able, in France, to achieve his childhood dream. Although none of Conner's wartime correspondence to his wife has survived to provide insight into his private thoughts, Mrs. Conner wrote that she had received "letter after letter saying that he had never enjoyed himself so much."[50]

Shortly after the war, the United States government awarded Fox Conner a Distinguished Service Medal. The citation lauded Conner's "masterful conception" of the AEF's mission as well as his "marked skill" in handling the complex details of organizing and deploying the American Army. France awarded Conner the *Croix de guerre* and also named him a Commander of the French Legion of Honor. The British, Belgians, and Italians also honored Conner, as did Panama—a nation that would factor into his future.[51]

Most importantly, though, Fox Conner had earned the admiration of his former West Point tac John J. Pershing. Twenty years after the war, Pershing would write his wartime chief of operations:

> Your broad conception of our task and your able counsel in planning our organization, as well as your clear vision of the strategy of our operations, stand

out vividly in my memory. None the less vividly do I recall your constant solicitude and aid in the trying days of battle and your unyielding support in times of difficulty with our Allies. Can I say more? Yes! One thing more. I could have spared any other man in the AEF better than you.[52]

At the war's outset in April 1917, Fox Conner had been an undistinguished major, in one of the least glamorous bureaus of the War Department, whose primary battles had been against health problems. Nineteen months later, he wore a general's star and sat in the inner circle that surrounded America's most powerful soldier since Ulysses S. Grant. At age 44, Conner was only midway through his career. With Pershing's sponsorship behind him, and another 20 years of military service ahead, Fox Conner stood poised to reach the pinnacle of his profession.

CHAPTER 8

HOME AGAIN

No. sir. That is your opinion and not mine. My opinion is that there were
no casualties the morning of November 11, or before that time, in the
American Army that were unnecessary.

—Conner Congressional Testimony, January 6, 1920[1]

Once the war ended, the AEF rapidly dwindled, both in size and in importance. Multitudes returned home to resume their lives. Fox Conner, however, remained in France to help direct the force that provided the United States a military presence in Europe as the war's victors carved and cast the old world order into something new.

Conner had been in the first group of American soldiers to land in France in June 1917. More than 2 years later, he was also among the last to leave. On September 1, 1919, Conner joined Black Jack Pershing aboard the *Leviathan*, a captured German ocean liner.[2] The week-long voyage to New York across the vast North Atlantic afforded Conner the opportunity to reflect upon events that had occurred since the November 11, 1918 armistice.

Some things had not changed. Conner and the French high command had continued to clash over control of American troops, whom the French wanted to put to work clearing and rebuilding France's devastated infrastructure. Some of Conner's decisions had also continued to incense AEF's field commanders, such as Charles P. Summerall, who blamed the "vipers at GHQ" for depriving his corps of the honor of leading American troops into Germany. Instead, the 1st Division had led the march on November 17, 1918, once First Army's chief of operations,

George Marshall, changed Conner's order to move his former divisional comrades into the vanguard. As had occurred in the Race for Sedan, Colonel Marshall knew that his friend General Conner would acquiesce. "He generously waived my ignoring of his orders," Marshall wrote in his memoirs, "and made no mention of the matter higher up."[3]

The months after the armistice had also forged a closer bond, personally and professionally, between Fox Conner and George Marshall. In January 1919, Conner had secured Marshall's return to the Operations Section in Chaumont, where the two officers had developed contingency plans for resuming the war if Germany refused to sign what all parties expected to be a harsh peace treaty. As other members of the Chaumont staff went home, Conner and Marshall gradually became Pershing's two top aides. On August 12, 1919, Pershing made Conner the AEF's chief of staff once James McAndrew returned to the United States.[4]

As the *Leviathan* plied the ocean waves on its westward voyage, Fox Conner also had time to ponder postwar disappointments. In November 1918, the War Department had denied Pershing's request to promote Conner to the rank of major general. Denied a second star, Conner remained a brigadier general until August 22, 1919, when the War Department had reduced his rank to colonel. The subject of Conner's rank had become one more source of strain between Pershing and Army chief of staff Peyton March.[5]

Conner's health, which had held up well through the stressful ordeals of 1918, had worsened in the winter of 1918–19, when he was hospitalized for more than 5 weeks with maladies ranging from influenza to tapeworms. When George Patton left for home in late February 1919, he wrote a farewell letter to his friend Conner in which he promised to visit Bug Conner and report on her husband's health, joking that he would make "no mention, however, of the able assistance you received from various Red Cross nurses while so frequently in hospitals."[6]

Conner could also look back upon more pleasant and productive memories of postwar France. After his release from the hospital on March 10, 1919, Conner had vacationed for two weeks on the French Riviera. Conner and his Operations Section staff then completed, in July, a comprehensive report on the AEF's military operations. The 112-page report, which became one of the earliest histories of the American Expeditionary Forces, provided a sanitized overview of the American Army's accomplishments. For example, Belleau Wood was simply noted as an area where the 2nd Division had fought; the Race for Sedan was not mentioned at all. In the Operations Section report, Conner stressed the war's "one great lesson"—which he feared was "soon to be forgotten" as the nation returned to peace: "The unprepared nation is helpless in a great war unless it can depend upon other nations to shield it while it prepares," a lesson he thought had been borne out by "every scrap of the history" of the AEF.[7]

The highlight of Conner's postwar service in France came on June 28, 1919, when he had accompanied Pershing to the Hall of Mirrors in the Palace of Versailles to witness the signing of the Treaty of Versailles. Among other provisions, the peace treaty required Germany to pay billions of dollars in reparations and to cede Alsace-Lorraine and other industrial regions to France. The terms also limited Germany to an army of 100,000 with no conscription or air force or submarines. Germany accepted sole responsibility for starting the war. The treaty also created a new League of Nations to establish the principle of collective security to maintain world peace.[8]

Amid the smiles and congratulations exchanged among the victors that day, Fox Conner felt uneasy. Having witnessed how the shame of defeat in the Franco-Prussian War in 1871 had fueled the desire for revenge in his French comrades, Conner doubted how long the words of a treaty would quell the warrior spirit of the militaristic—and humiliated—German nation.[9]

Mostly, though, in the nine months since the armistice had been signed, Fox Conner had simply longed for home. "Again and again he would write that the day was practically set," Bug Conner wrote in her memoir, "and then it would be postponed." After more than two years apart, Fox Conner missed his wife. "Every day brings an increasing realization of my luck and a sense of bewilderment as to why the Good Lord favored me so by giving you to me," Fox wrote Bug on June 2, 1919 to mark their 17th anniversary. "But I will be trying to write poetry directly.

The truth is that I love you to distraction and the near approach of [September] is driving me to madness."[10]

Fox Conner's wait ended when the *Leviathan* put into New York Harbor on the foggy morning of September 8, 1919.[11]

The first echoes of the cheering masses on shore reached the great ship as it emerged from the mist. Shore batteries fired salvos of salute. The ship's band began to play. Smaller watercraft, with pennants flying and horns wide open, pulled alongside the liner to escort it to shore; some used pumps to blast celebratory spouts of water high into the air.

Conner, Pershing, and Marshall watched the spectacle from the Navy launch that brought them to shore. Conner, who had not been able to exchange farewell waves with his wife when he had left the United States in 1917, used a telescope to find Bug on one of the nearby boats. Fox then joyously waved his hat, in a prearranged signal, to let Bug know that he had seen her.

Conner stepped off the boat's gangway and into a hero's welcome. Colorful confetti cascaded from Manhattan's office windows as cars carried Pershing and his staff to a reception at New York City Hall. On September 10, Pershing, on horseback, led a victory parade in the city. Conner, who rode closely behind his commander, halted to throw a kiss to Bug in the reviewing stand. George Patton complained to his wife Beatrice that it "would have been one hell of a parade if every man had done the same."

The Conners then accompanied Pershing on his southward journey by train to Washington, D.C. The train stopped frequently for Pershing—appearing much like a presidential candidate—to greet the throngs of people who filled train depots along the way. Following another parade on September 17 in the nation's capital, Conner then began to settle back into life with his family in the nation's capital.

Bug and their youngest daughter Florence had lived in Washington during the war, while the two older children, Betty (Betsey) and Fox Brandreth (Tommy), attended boarding school in Pennsylvania. During his father's two-year absence, Tommy Conner had drawn closer to his maternal grandfather, Colonel Frank Brandreth, whom he began to view as a father figure.[12] Conner's absence had also fostered a closer bond between Bug and her mother-in-law in Mississippi. In July 1919, "Mother Conner" had closed a letter to Bug by writing "I love, love, love every one of you." [The emphases are Nannie Conner's.] She also asked Bug to bring Fox down to Mississippi so she could "have a little pleasure crying and screaming over him!"[13]

Her son, though, had other plans.

In late September, Fox casually mentioned to Bug that he had invited Pershing and Marshall to her father's estate at Brandreth Lake in the New York Adirondacks. Fox spoke of the trip as if it had already been planned, but the news sent Bug's mind whirling. She knew that the camp had already been closed for the winter and that her father had not offered its use. Not wanting to miss her own opportunity to spend time with General Pershing, Bug "lied like a trooper," as she put it, and told Fox she was already working on the details. Bug then quickly assembled the help needed to host the most famous man in America at the family's mountain retreat.[14]

For three weeks in October 1919, Pershing, Marshall, and Conner enjoyed the solitude and autumnal beauty of Brandreth Lake.[15] Bug's two sisters, Paulina and Beatrice, joined them, as did a family friend, Elsie Robinson. All savored a campfire's warmth in the chilly mountain evenings as Pershing told tales of his service as a young cavalry officer. Some hunted deer in the mornings while others fished or strolled through forest paths dappled red, yellow, orange, and brown. Early in the trip, Marshall returned from the woods with a large buck. Pershing's hunting guide had fought in the AEF. Hunting success eluded Pershing until Bug's sister Paulina, an accomplished hunter who lived year-round at the lake, led the general on the last morning of the trip to a frosty beech knoll where he too felled a large deer.

According to family lore, Bug and her sister Beatrice also tried to snare the widower Pershing for their friend Elsie Robinson, but their matchmaking efforts went nowhere.

Snapshots of Pershing, Marshall, and Conner usually show each man scowling at the camera, but photographs taken during the lake stay show the three men grinning with wide and contented smiles. Decades after the trip, Marshall reminisced to the editor of his papers that his stay at

Brandreth Lake had been "very, very agreeable." No one enjoyed the trip more than Fox and Bug. In one picture of the group, Conner stood behind his shorter wife, holding her in a bear hug and crouching down so that his beaming face rested on Bug's left shoulder while her hands grasped his tightly to her body. In another shot taken moments later, while everyone else had resumed normal activities, Fox and Bug had remained in the same embrace.

While at Brandreth Lake, Pershing and his two principal assistants also worked to prepare the AEF commander-in-chief for testimony on a contentious political issue.

The United States had entered the Great War in an almost totally unprepared condition. To prevent a similar situation in the future, Secretary of War Newton Baker and Chief of Staff Peyton March proposed legislation to implement two fundamental revisions to America's peacetime military policy: maintenance of a half-million-strong peacetime army and, more controversially, three months of mandatory military service for all 19-year-old males. Some in the AEF had voiced their early support for the new policy, but Conner, who understood Pershing's political aspirations, had counseled his commander in January 1919 against embracing a policy that had little popular support. Conner and Marshall also considered the Baker–March bill flawed in several respects, most notably its failure to have created an organized army reserve.[16]

As Conner and Marshall prepared Pershing for his congressional testimony, they also had to manage Pershing's personal dislike of Chief of Staff March. The relationship between the Army's two leading figures, which had deteriorated as the war progressed, had become more strained once Congress bestowed the permanent four-star rank of General of the Armies upon Pershing while denying a similar honor to March, even though March was Pershing's superior in the statutory chain of command.[17]

By the time Pershing arrived in Washington from Brandreth Lake on October 31, 1919, the Baker–March bill was already in deep trouble.[18] Woodrow Wilson's Democrats had lost both houses of Congress in the 1918 mid-term elections. The Republican majority opposed the administration's military reorganization measure as a dangerous step toward creation of the type of militaristic society the nation had just gone to war to defeat. Democrats, fearing further political losses in the 1920 elections, had no appetite for becoming the party responsible for requiring all young men to join the army. President Wilson mostly left it to Baker and March to secure passage of their bill while he threw all his efforts into winning Senate ratification of American membership in the League of Nations. Wilson had crisscrossed the nation to make the case for league membership until he suffered a stroke on October 2, which left him—and his legislative agenda—significantly debilitated.

General March, who remained unpopular with Congress, testified for 23 days, but failed to persuade either legislative chamber as to the merits of his bill. Secretary Baker did not help when, to aid Wilson in securing ratification of the League of Nations treaty, he testified that a much smaller peacetime army could work just as well if America joined the league. By contrast, he told a Senate committee that the 500,000 men envisioned by the Baker–March bill would form only a "child's play army" without the collective security afforded by the League of Nations.

Pershing, flanked by Conner and Marshall at the witness table, began his 3 days of congressional testimony on Halloween Day 1919. Throughout his appearance before the joint Senate–House session, the General of the Armies freely consulted Conner and Marshall. According to Marshall, the Congressmen on the panel were "astonished" by how freely he and Conner contributed to Pershing's testimony.[19]

Pershing generally endorsed the concept of mandatory military service, but in an organized reserve force as Conner and Marshall had recommended. Pershing also testified that a standing peacetime army of 500,000 was unnecessary and too expensive. Instead, he suggested a force of around 275,000. In a 1944 letter, Marshall recalled Conner's "disturbed comments" as Pershing casually mentioned the force level of less than 300,000 men, which was far smaller than the three had discussed at Brandreth Lake. One senator formed the impression that Pershing "had not had time to study the problem thoroughly."

Pershing finished his testimony on November 2, 1919. Pershing also finished off the Baker–March bill. Congress adjourned without voting on the measure and decided to draft its own postwar military legislation.

The Senate also rejected Wilson's prized League of Nations treaty on November 19. As the era of isolationism dawned in the United States, Secretary Baker reflected that there were "unhappily, many things which this war has taught us but which we have not learned," as Conner, in his July 1919 G-3 report, had feared would occur.[20]

★ ★ ★ ★ ★

Two young officers did attempt to apply what they had learned during the war.[21]

In the autumn of 1919, George Patton and Dwight Eisenhower met at Camp Meade, Maryland. Patton commanded the remainder of the light tank brigade he had taken into battle in France. Eisenhower directed a battalion of heavy tanks which, like their commander, had not made it into the war. "From the beginning," Eisenhower recalled in his 1967 memoirs, he and Patton "got along famously."

The two officers shared similar views concerning the potential of armored warfare. Although prevailing Army doctrine limited the tank's role—and speed—to the support of advancing foot soldiers, Patton and Eisenhower each foresaw the tank's potential to become the spearhead of an independent and rapid-attack force. According to Eisenhower, Patton predicted in 1919: "I'll be Jackson, you'll be Lee. I don't want to do the heavy thinking; you do that and I'll get loose among our - - - - [sic] enemies, and really tear them to pieces."[22]

Patton and Eisenhower also became close personal friends. In their spare time, Eisenhower distilled gin while Patton brewed beer, which they enjoyed at "Club Eisenhower," their name for Eisenhower's quarters. Eager for advancement, the two officers also studied the exercises given students at the Leavenworth staff college. Mostly, though, Patton and Eisenhower talked tanks with "the enthusiasm of zealots," as Eisenhower put it. Dwight Eisenhower had found a good friend in George Patton— as he would learn in the coming year.

★ ★ ★ ★ ★

Fox and Bug Conner spent an enjoyable 1919 Thanksgiving with the Pattons at Camp Meade. Conner then joined John J. Pershing in early December on a cross-country inspection tour of military bases. As the 1920 election year neared, Pershing used the opportunity to give speeches, attend receptions, and generally act like a presidential candidate. At one stop, Black Jack Pershing even kissed a child.[23]

But as Pershing and his entourage met the public in late 1919, they encountered an increasingly discontented electorate. Rapid demobilization had led to high unemployment. Strikes disrupted the coal and steel industries. Some voters feared the spread of communism to the United States. More ominously for Pershing's political chances, disillusionment about the war had begun to pervade the nation. More than a quarter-million Americans had been either killed or wounded in less than 6 months of fighting in Europe's Great War; many in America had begun to ask the fundamental question: "For what?"[24]

Congress also began to tally the war's financial cost. The United States had spent more than 22 billion dollars from April 1917 through May 1919. To place that figure into perspective, one government publication estimated that the sum was "practically equal to the entire cost of running the United States Government from 1791 to 1914." To investigate how the money had been spent, Congress formed a Select Committee on Expenditures in the War Department. As hearings progressed, the congressmen began to scrutinize not only the cost, but also the conduct, of the war.[25]

Fox Conner took his turn at the witness table for 2 days beginning January 5, 1920.[26] Pershing's chief of operations testified before the Subcommittee on Foreign Expenditures chaired by Representative Oscar Bland, an Indiana Republican. Early questioning focused on efforts to find fault in the War Department's management of the domestic side of the war. Conner generally supported his Washington colleagues; he declined, for instance, to publicly criticize the War Department on matters pertaining to the pace of troop shipments and supply of troops.

The committee's questioning then turned to the AEF high command's decisions on November 11, 1918, the war's last day.

Representative Bland castigated Conner for not ordering American troops to cease fighting as soon as the armistice had been signed in the early morning hours of November 11. Bland, for instance, believed that the 92nd Division had been ordered to launch an attack after Germany had agreed to the armistice. Conner twice corrected the congressman to point out that the 92nd Division's attack had actually begun on November 10 and had already ended by the time the division received word that the armistice had been signed. Conner also explained that Chaumont's orders to its First and Second Army commanders were a verbatim repetition of Marshal Foch's orders to cease firing "at" rather than "by" 11:00 a.m.[27]

Tension between the two men grew as Congressman Bland, frustrated by Conner's defense of the AEF high command, began to tell Conner what he really thought of the "ambitious generals" who had caused a "purposeless waste of human life" on November 11. Conner responded in kind in their heated exchange:

Mr. BLAND:	I have taken this position: I have formed that at least in my own mind that if the officers themselves would have to bear the brunt of the shellfire that they would have been brought to the realization that it was unnecessary to sacrifice human life and it would not have been done.
Gen. CONNER:	Mr. Bland, if I may say so, the officers of the American Expeditionary Force had, I think, a much clearer conception and realization of what it meant to face shell fire than you can have, sir.
Mr. BLAND:	I do not know. I found a few of them who faced it and a great many of them who did not ...
Gen. CONNER:	... any imputation on the courage of the officers of the American Expeditionary Forces, from the commander-in-chief to the lowest appointed second lieutenant, is, in my opinion, unjust and unwarranted.
Mr. BLAND:	How many generals did you lose that day?
Gen. CONNER:	None.
Mr. BLAND:	You lost a lot of captains and a lot of lieutenants and a lot of non-commissioned officers ... But I am convinced that on November 11 there was not any officer of very high rank taking any chance of losing his own life, and I do not think you have cited any instances.
Gen. CONNER:	The statement made by you, I think, Mr. Bland, is exceedingly unjust and, as an officer of the Army, as an officer who was over there, I resent it to the highest possible degree, and I think, sir, I am entitled not to be put in such

	a position, appearing as I am before your committee and trying to give you, as I see it, the facts—the best opinion that I can; I think that it is not a proper time to state opinions that place me in a very difficult position, cause me to resent them, and considering the position I am in, I think that it would be well if you would ask me questions instead of making argument.
Mr. BLAND:	I will not listen to your lectures at all. You have stated, in answer to questions, and unsolicited answers, that you resent it. You have a right to resent it. The American people resent the loss of American lives on November 11, and it is our purpose to investigate that and to inquire why ... We have a right to question the motive, if necessary, of the men who occasioned this loss of life.[28]

Oscar Bland was not alone in his criticism of Fox Conner.

On January 8, 1920, the 92nd Division's artillery commander, Brigadier General John Sherburne, testified before Bland's subcommittee. Sherburne said he felt "absolute horror" at the "needless waste of life" that had occurred on the war's final day. In response to a question as to what he thought Second Army's commander, Major General Robert Lee Bullard, should have done to have prevented the casualties, General Sherburne replied: "General Bullard was not supreme. He was the man responsible to the inner circle of the inner circle, G-3 in Chaumont, who were giving him the orders."[29]

Sherburne elaborated: "Our army was so run that division and brigade and even corps commanders were piteous in their terror and fear of this all-pervading command by the General Staff which sat in Chaumont." He further explained that each division's chief of staff had "a direct line to Chaumont," and that division commanders would be "yanked out and put back" according to the wishes of GHQ. "No man's head was safe," Sherburne testified, "as long as the great triumvirate at Chaumont existed." He added: "I do not mean either General Pershing or General Bullard or General Liggett."[30]

When pressed by Representative Bland to identify the members of the dreaded "triumvirate," Sherburne gave only one name: Fox Conner.[31]

In Sherburne's view, Conner and his Chaumont colleagues were "theorists," who were "so wrapped up in their professional studies that they entirely forgot the human side" of war. Sherburne described the General Staff as behaving "much like a child who had been given a toy that he is very much interested in and that he knows within a day or two is going to be taken away from him and he wants to use that toy up to the handle while he has it."[32]

One of Conner's classmates from the West Point Class of 1898 joined in the criticism. Colonel W. Conrad Babcock, who commanded an infantry regiment during the Meuse–Argonne fighting, attended the January 1920 hearings. Colonel Babcock found it "sickening and depressing to hear officers like Brigadier General Fox Conner, my classmate, tell of the importance of our gaining a certain ridge or section of ground before the Armistice went into effect." Babcock asked: "What did these useless killings and injuries mean to officers who had never commanded men in battle, whose entire war experience was a war on paper, where the expenditure in human life was necessary but with which they had no experience, no responsibility, and apparently little sympathy?"[33]

Fox Conner was not the only Chaumont man to feel the sting of the backlash in public opinion.

In the spring of 1920, John J. Pershing entered the race for the Republican presidential nomination. He finished a dismal sixth in Michigan and did little better in Nebraska, despite having several ties to the state. Pershing then quietly bowed out of the race.[34] George Washington, Andrew Jackson, Zachary Taylor, Ulysses Grant, and Theodore Roosevelt each had become president after serving as the nation's most prominent soldier in a major war. The same would occur for Dwight Eisenhower following the next war. But in 1920, as the nation sought to put the Great War behind it, Black Jack Pershing never came close to the presidency.

Instead, Pershing returned to the AEF which, by mid-1920, had become reduced to a record-keeping organization with little to occupy the time of either a four-star general or his chief of staff. To give Pershing a function—and to insulate him from chief of staff Peyton March—Fox Conner devised a plan.

Conner proposed to transform the Army War College into an independent agency that would report directly to the secretary of war rather than to the Army chief of staff.[35] The college, which Pershing would head, would focus on war planning to prevent the nation's entering another major war without a plan for waging it, as had occurred in 1917. Under Conner's new agency, which was modeled upon the French *Conseil Supérieur de la Guerre*, the War College president (Pershing) would immediately become the Army's commander-in-chief in the event of war, and his staff would automatically become the general staff charged with executing war plans with which they were already familiar. Conner believed that creation of the new organization would prevent recurrence of the "grave defect" of sending the Army off to war with no plans and with no command structure already in place.

When Congress completed its work on the National Defense Act of 1920, Conner's War College restructuring plan did not make it into the legislation. In one memorandum, Conner proposed "executive action" to implement his planners-as-commanders concept, but the Wilson administration took no action to implement the policy.

Conner considered the National Defense Act of 1920 to have been, otherwise, "a very excellent bill." Congress authorized a 300,000-strong peacetime army, but with no requirement for mandatory military service. The act divided the United States into nine geographic "corps areas." Territorial commands in Hawaii, the Philippines, and the Panama Canal Zone were also created. Congress maintained the primacy of the chief of staff as the head of the Army, but it reduced the size of the general staff corps to ninety-three officers, far fewer than the 226 officers that Chief of Staff March had requested.[36]

As part of the nation's military restructuring effort, Secretary Baker also appointed Fox Conner and George Marshall to a board of officers tasked with restructuring the American Army's infantry divisions. The board ultimately recommended keeping the "square" AEF division structure devised by Conner and Hugh Drum during the war, but with a reduced size of 19,000 men. In recognition of both the drastically decreased size of the Army and the need for greater mobility, Conner and Marshall had recommended adoption of a much smaller 13,000-strong "triangular" division. Conner considered writing a minority report, but Marshall persuaded him to support the board's findings for the sake of unanimity.[37]

While the AEF division structure survived, the AEF itself did not. On August 31, 1920, the American Expeditionary Forces ceased to exist. So did Fox Conner's position as AEF chief of staff. Conner's title changed to "Chief of Staff to the General of the Armies" in early September 1920. But given the significant limitation on the number of general staff positions—and with Pershing having no real function in the Army—Fox Conner understood that his position had become untenable.[38]

In September 1919, Fox Conner had arrived home to a hero's welcome. A year later, he was essentially out of a job.

★ ★ ★ ★ ★

Uncertainty also affected the careers of Dwight Eisenhower and George Patton.[39]

In keeping with prevailing Army doctrine that limited the use of tanks to infantry support, the National Defense Act abolished the Tank Corps as an independent force; the legislation returned control of tanks to the infantry—a move that Pershing had endorsed in his 1919 testimony given with the assistance of Conner and Marshall. Referring to his and Patton's theories of armored warfare, Eisenhower wrote: "Our dream of a separate tank force was shattered."

Eisenhower, an infantryman, remained at Camp Meade and, again, became a football coach as he had been before the war. He applied for admission to the infantry school at Fort Benning, Georgia, but his commanding officer, Brigadier General Samuel D. Rockenbach, would not endorse his request. One Eisenhower biographer suggested that Rockenbach did not want to lose his football coach. Patton obtained a transfer back to the cavalry with orders to report in early October to Fort Myer, Virginia.

But before Patton left Camp Meade, he arranged a Sunday dinner that would forever alter the course of his friend Eisenhower's career.

CHAPTER 9

UNLIKE IKE

George Patton's influence on Ike was significant, but his greatest contribution to Ike's development was indirect, his role in bringing his friend under the tutelage of his true mentor, Brigadier General (later Major General) Fox Conner.

—John S.D. Eisenhower[1]

Camp Meade, Maryland offered few entertainment opportunities for the officers stationed there. Rows of simple wooden barracks lined the dusty, sometimes muddy, streets of the base, which had been cleaved from the surrounding woodlands in 1917 for a wartime training camp. Some officers posted at Camp Meade after the war, such as Dwight Eisenhower, had spent their own money to transform the austere structures into suitable family housing. Even something as ordinary as the arrival of a guest at the base provided a welcomed break from the monotony.[2]

Camp Meade was not the type of place normally associated with momentous events in a life. But in late 1920, Dwight Eisenhower met a visitor who would profoundly influence his future.

George and Beatrice Patton hosted their friends Fox and Bug Conner for lunch one Sunday in the autumn of 1920.[3] The Pattons also invited Dwight and Mamie Eisenhower to meet the general and his wife. In the afternoon, Conner asked the two younger officers to show him their tank-training facilities. As Eisenhower put it in his 1967 memoir, *At Ease*, the interest shown in their work by an officer of Conner's stature was "meat and drink to George and me."[4]

Eisenhower took the Conners for a ride in one of his tanks. The steel machine creaked and lumbered forward with tremendous noise and vibration. As the tank slammed into, and over, the uneven terrain of the training grounds, Bug Conner recalled in her memoir that she and Fox "nearly had our teeth jarred loose."

Patton and Eisenhower then took Conner to the base's repair shop. Immersed in the bouquet of the garage's gasoline and grease, the older officer found a chair and got comfortable. Conner, who had been among the first American officers to assess the feasibility of using tracked vehicles for military purposes, and who had helped select the tanks used by the AEF during the war, then began to ask questions, most of them posed to Eisenhower.

The three officers talked tanks until nearly dusk. Eisenhower recalled that as Conner left, he said little except that the discussion was interesting. In *At Ease*, Eisenhower wrote that Conner "thanked us, and that was that."

At the time, Eisenhower had not comprehended that he had just gone through a job interview.

As Fox Conner waited to learn whether he would remain on general staff duty or return to field service, he had begun to seek out a younger officer to serve as his assistant. When Conner asked Patton if he knew of any good candidates, Patton immediately thought of his Camp Meade colleague. "Ike Eisenhower is the man you want," Patton told Conner, "someday his name will be well known."

In late 1920, Dwight Eisenhower's name had also come to the attention of the Army's chief of infantry—but not in a positive light.

Eisenhower's article titled "A Tank Discussion" appeared in the November 1920 edition of the *Infantry Journal*. Eisenhower decried the prevailing Army view that the tank was a "freak development of trench warfare which has already outlived its usefulness." Instead he called for development of "speedy, reliable, and efficient engines of destruction," capable of much more than serving as moving shields for advancing infantry.[5]

While prophetic as to the eventual role of armor in the next war, Eisenhower's article provoked the ire of Major General Charles S. Farnsworth, the Army's Chief of Infantry, who also controlled the tank service. According to Eisenhower's memoir, General Farnsworth told

Major Eisenhower that his ideas were "not only wrong, but dangerous and that henceforth I would keep them to myself." Farnsworth also gave Eisenhower a clear instruction to not again publish articles in conflict with established infantry doctrine. "If I did," Eisenhower recalled, "I would be hauled before a court-martial."

Then a personal tragedy occurred at Camp Meade that dwarfed Eisenhower's professional struggles.

Around Christmas 1920, Eisenhower's three-year-old son, Doud Dwight Eisenhower (nicknamed "Icky"), contracted scarlet fever. As the boy's condition worsened, the Camp Meade physicians brought in specialists from nearby Johns Hopkins Medical School in Baltimore. Because of the highly infectious nature of the disease, the doctors quarantined Icky; neither of his parents could enter his sickroom. Eisenhower kept vigil at Icky's window while Mamie stayed home and prayed through the tortured hours. On January 2, 1921, with neither of his parents there to hold or comfort him, three-year old Doud Dwight Eisenhower passed away.[6]

Icky's death pushed his father to what Eisenhower termed, in a 1948 letter, "the ragged edge of a breakdown." Unfortunately for Eisenhower, other dark days awaited him at Camp Meade.

★ ★ ★ ★ ★

Fox Conner also suffered the loss of a loved one in the autumn of 1920. Nannie Fox Conner, who had given her eldest son much more than his name, died at age 77 on October 21, 1920. Nannie's devotion to Fox's education—as well as her brother's political influence—had both been indispensable to her son's entry into West Point. After his mother's death, Fox Conner's remaining ties to the state of his birth gradually dissolved. According to grandson Macpherson Conner, Fox gave his share of the inherited family farm to one of his sisters. After his mother's funeral, Fox Conner rarely returned to Calhoun County.[7]

Throughout late 1920 and into 1921, Conner continued to serve as chief of staff to Pershing, whose "General of the Armies" position was essentially ceremonial rather than functional. Conner also continued to advocate for adoption of a new military agency that would make war plans during peacetime and then automatically become a functioning general staff immediately upon the outbreak of war. Conner addressed the topic in an Army War College lecture on November 4, 1920. He also expanded upon the concept in an article published in the January 1921 edition of *The Cavalry Journal.*[8]

Conner's article, titled "The Relations That Should Exist between the War Department and Forces in the Field," called for the "absolute divorce" of the War Department in Washington from control of troops fighting in the field. Under Conner's proposal, the War Department would have the responsibility of mobilizing the nation's men, money, and matériel before turning those resources over to a separate "General Headquarters" organization, which would then implement, independent of the War Department's control, the plans that "GHQ" had already made. Under Conner's proposal, the head of the new organization would report directly to the president.

Conner drew upon military history—ranging from the Napoleonic Wars to the Crimean War to the American Civil War—to provide examples of how "interference" from distant war ministries had produced "deplorable results" on the battlefield. Conner's use of the word "interference" to describe civilian control of combat forces was revealing as to why Brigadier General John Sherburne, in his 1920 testimony to Congress, had labeled Conner and his Chaumont colleagues "as Prussian as any outside of Prussia"—a sentiment echoed by another fellow officer, Colonel Clarence Deems, who considered Fox Conner to have been "a Prussian in spirit."[9] Conner's 1921 article praised America's recently defeated German enemy for having had "the nearest approach, in modern times, to such an ideal system."

Published in January 1921, when many in the nation had come to view the Great War as a mistaken foray into European affairs that should never again be repeated, Conner's article also emphasized the need for America to plan for another major war similar to the one America would fight 20 years later. Conner foresaw the formation of a "combination [of enemies] powerful enough to bring a great war to our shores." He predicted that such an alliance of enemy powers would probably fight a war in multiple theaters across the world, and he stressed the strategic importance of holding America's bases in Hawaii and Panama.

Conner's proposal to diminish the War Department's power, in favor of a separate agency with authority to plan and command, found a surprising new supporter—the nation's new secretary of war.

Following Republican Warren G. Harding's election to the presidency in November 1920, John J. Weeks succeeded Newton Baker as secretary of war.[10] Secretary Weeks also inherited the problem of dealing with the difficult relationship between John J. Pershing and Army Chief of Staff Peyton C. March.

On April 21, 1921, Weeks told the *New York Times* that he planned to appoint Pershing to head a scaled-down General Headquarters organization that would study all war plans being made by the Army War College and be prepared to implement the plans immediately should the nation again go to war.[11] Weeks also explained that Pershing's position would be "separate and independent" of the chief of staff's position and that he would report directly to President Harding. Conner was not referenced in the article, but in all substantive respects, Secretary Weeks had described the agency outlined by Fox Conner in his article in *The Cavalry Journal* and in his prior memoranda to Pershing.

Critics pointed out that the proposed new structure sought to vest Pershing with duties that already belonged, by law, to Chief of Staff March. The *Army and Navy Journal* observed: "Complete disruption of the present system seems inevitable, at least at the top." Secretary Weeks soon backed away from the idea. Weeks announced instead that he would simply appoint Pershing as chief of staff once March retired on June 30, so that Pershing could legally form the core group of planners that would immediately take command of the Army in the field.

Pershing and Conner continued to bide their time in the summer of 1921 until March's term as chief of staff expired. With little else to do, Fox Conner went fishing.

In mid-June 1921, Fox and Bug Conner joined George and Beatrice Patton aboard the *Ladyfish*, a 75-foot houseboat Patton had chartered for deep-sea fishing off the Florida coast.[12] Patton, a devoted tarpon fisherman, supplied the rods and reels. When Virginia Conner asked Patton if he would save her if she fell overboard, Patton replied: "Not by a damn sight; but you bet I'd go after the reel. Those reels cost $94.35 apiece."

In her 1951 memoir, Bug took delight in pointing out that she had caught ten tarpon to her husband's one. She also out-fished Patton by one tarpon, which galled the competitive young officer. Bug also provided a glimpse into what she termed the "lovable and sensitive side" of the man who would later achieve fame as "Old Blood and Guts." One evening on the boat, Patton composed the poem "Florida" to commemorate the trip. The opening and closing stanzas read:

> Where the land slips off in sand and marsh
> And the trees grow in the sea;
> Where the tarpon leap, and the catfish weep,
> Come south and play with me.
> ...
> Where the mangrove shoots its crazy roots
> To build lands in the sea
> Where the pelicans dive, and the fish hawks thrive,
> Come south and happy be.

The two couples sailed to Key West, and then to Havana, where Miss Virginia Brandreth had first become infatuated with the young officer from Mississippi. By early July 1921, when Conner returned to duty in Washington, Peyton March had retired, and John J. Pershing was the Army's new chief of staff.

Pershing appointed Conner to a seven-member board of officers tasked to make recommendations for reorganization of the Army's command structure.[13] Pershing's first AEF chief of staff, James G. Harbord, chaired the board. Other members included John McAuley Palmer, Conner's original AEF Operations Section chief, and Robert C. Davis, Conner's West Point classmate.

Conner chaired the subcommittee on "Nucleus for General Headquarters in the Field in the Event of Mobilization," on which Palmer also served. On July 13, Conner submitted the subcommittee's report, which reiterated his call for creation of a war-planning section that would immediately become a functioning command organization in the event of war. In most substantive respects, the subcommittee's report reflected Conner's earlier writings on the subject, but with one major difference: with Pershing rather than March as chief of staff, Conner no longer advanced the idea of an agency independent of the chief of staff's office.

In August 1921, Pershing also restructured the general staff corps.[14] His new team resembled the AEF's wartime Chaumont organization. Pershing appointed James G. Harbord to the newly created deputy chief of staff position. As the second-highest-ranking officer in the Army, and Pershing's chief assistant, the deputy chief of staff controlled the day-to-day operations of the Army. Harbord moved into Peyton March's former office and assumed many of his administrative duties. Although Fox Conner had served as Pershing's chief of staff for two years, no evidence exists that Pershing gave any consideration to appointing the 47-year-old Conner to the powerful deputy chief of staff position.

Pershing also appointed trusted AEF subordinates to positions as assistant chiefs of staff to oversee sections bearing the same "G" designations used at Chaumont: Personnel (G-1), Intelligence (G-2), Operations (G-3), and Supply (G-4). For instance, Fox Conner's former West Point corporal, William D. Connor, returned to the position of the Army's G-4, as he had been in France during the war. Fox Conner had likewise rendered distinguished service as the AEF's G-3 during the war. Pershing, however, chose someone else to be his chief of operations in Washington.

Pershing's 1921 GHQ reorganization also created an entirely new section—the War Plans Division—to provide the planning and command organization for which Fox Conner had been advocating for more than a year. As the primary architect of the concept, Conner was an obvious choice to head the new organization.

But Fox Conner did not receive that appointment either.

Instead, Pershing ordered Conner to take command of an infantry brigade stationed in the Panama Canal Zone.[15]

Bug Conner recalled in her memoir that a number of her friends came to "weep and say that it was a dirty trick to send us to such a dreadful place."[16] No evidence exists, though, to suggest that Pershing intended to send one of his closest aides into exile in the Central American jungle. Several factors probably underlay Pershing's decision to send Conner to Panama.

The National Defense Act of 1920 retained the same "Manchu Law" that had cut short Conner's prewar posting to France in 1912.[17] During peacetime, no officer could serve in the general staff corps for more than 4 years before rotating to field service for 2 years. Conner had last served with troops in January 1915, and he had remained on general staff duty since the armistice in November 1918. Given that Conner would soon be required by law to return to field service, Pershing may not have wished to place the important new War Plans Division under the control of someone who would soon have to leave it.

Also, as Conner himself had recognized in *The Cavalry Journal* article earlier in the year, America's ability to operate as a multi-hemispheric power rested heavily upon holding the Panama Canal, particularly once budget cuts forced the Navy to scrap plans for a two-ocean fleet. Defense of the Canal Zone required close Army–Navy coordination and cooperation. Furthermore, when Pershing inspected the canal's defenses in 1920, he became concerned over the adequacy of the zone's coastal artillery defenses. Conner's early service as a coast artillery officer, plus his 2 months of study at the Naval War College in 1908, suited him well for the unique requirements of the Panama mission.[18]

Conner's new assignment also illustrated the reach of the pendulum's swing against the military in postwar America. In 1921, Congress lowered the authorized enlisted strength of the Army by almost half— from 280,000 to 150,000 soldiers; it also reduced the officer corps by 1,000. Conner, who had regained the rank of brigadier general in April 1921, was available to take command of a brigade.[19]

As importantly, Conner needed time in the field for his own professional development, after more than 6 years away from troop service. According to Pershing's biographer Frank Vandiver, "rumors reached Pershing of army dissatisfaction with general staff officers too long absent from troops, hence out of touch with reality." Based upon the harsh comments made of Conner the preceding year by fellow officers such as

Sherburne and Babcock, Conner may well have fallen into this category. A tour of duty in a difficult field command would therefore benefit Conner's career, as well as his reputation.[20]

★ ★ ★ ★ ★

After he received his Panama assignment, General Conner contacted Major Dwight Eisenhower and offered him the opportunity to go to Panama as the brigade's executive officer. As Conner's chief assistant, Eisenhower would manage the day-to-day operation of the unit. Dissatisfied with service in the postwar tank corps—and eager to leave the post where he had experienced the tragedy of his son's death—Eisenhower gratefully accepted Conner's offer.[21]

However, Eisenhower's commanding officer at Camp Meade, Brigadier General Samuel D. Rockenbach, opposed Eisenhower's reassignment on the grounds that the move would deprive his tank school of one of the Army's few trained tank officers. The War Department denied Eisenhower's request for a transfer. In his *At Ease* memoir, Eisenhower left his readers with the implication that Rockenbach's opposition presented the primary obstacle to his going to Panama.[22]

In the autumn of 1921, though, Dwight Eisenhower faced a much larger problem.

Army regulations allowed an officer and his family to either live in government-supplied housing, or to receive "commutation" (reimbursement) of expenses for a private dwelling, but not both. For a few months in 1920, while Eisenhower and his wife had refurbished their quarters at Camp Meade, their son Icky had lived with relatives in Colorado. Eisenhower nonetheless submitted a claim for $250.67 in commutation of expenses for "quarters, heat and light" related to Icky's care in Colorado.[23] Eisenhower signed a sworn claim form in which he certified: "Neither I, my family, nor anyone dependent on me has occupied public quarters, nor been furnished heat and light by the United States during the period for which commutation of heat and light is charged"—a clearly erroneous statement, given his and Mamie's occupancy of the government-owned premises at Camp Meade. The Army reimbursed him the full amount of the claim.[24]

In June 1921, when Eisenhower learned that another officer had been disciplined for receiving a similar reimbursement, he disclosed to the Camp Meade inspector his own receipt of the commutation money. Eisenhower took the position that since he and his wife were essentially living "in the field," and since he had spent his own money to make the Camp Meade quarters suitable for an infant, his claim for reimbursement was justified. He also requested an accounting so that he could repay the money if necessary.

Eisenhower's case went from the Camp Meade inspector, to the inspector at Third Corps Area headquarters (which had jurisdiction over Camp Meade), and finally to the desk of the Army's acting Inspector General in Washington, Brigadier General Eli Helmick. Each inspector concluded that Eisenhower had illegally drawn the expense reimbursement. On July 6, 1921, General Helmick wrote the Army adjutant general that Eisenhower's reimbursement was "clearly unauthorized," and that the major had signed a sworn certificate "well knowing" that the contents were false. Inspector General Helmick referred the case back to General Rockenbach at Camp Meade with the recommendation that Dwight Eisenhower "be brought to trial upon charges based upon the facts as developed."

Rockenbach disagreed that Eisenhower's offenses warranted a court-martial; instead, he delivered a verbal reprimand to Eisenhower. Rockenbach also ordered him to repay the $250.67. Eisenhower repaid the money on July 19, 1921; he assumed that would settle the issue. But when Inspector General Helmick learned of the light punishment, he reported to the adjutant general on August 25 that "no disciplinary action has been taken against this officer by the responsible military authorities at Camp Meade." Helmick recommended referral of the case back to Third Corps Area authorities for "appropriate disciplinary action."

On September 19, 1921, Eisenhower received correspondence from the Third Corps Area headquarters, which advised him that the matter remained under investigation. The letter also "duly warned" Eisenhower "of his constitutional rights in the premises." On October, 4, the corps inspector issued his own report: Eisenhower's sworn statements made in support of the commutation claim had been "false and untrue." The corps inspector concurred with General Helmick that Eisenhower should be brought to trial. On October 5, 1921, General Rockenbach at Camp Meade received orders from corps headquarters to proceed, on an expedited basis, with the court-martial of Major Dwight D. Eisenhower.

★ ★ ★ ★ ★

Fox Conner, who had spent his career in the artillery and general staff corps, had never served in an infantry unit, much less commanded one, as he would do in Panama. Conner therefore attended the Army's infantry school at Fort Benning, Georgia, to which he reported on October 1, 1921.[25] Conner was at Fort Benning when he learned of Eisenhower's court-martial predicament. Given Eisenhower's straits, Conner had to quickly decide what to do about the man he had asked to be his chief assistant in Panama.

Conner decided to stand by his executive officer.

On October 6, 1921, the day after Rockenbach received orders to proceed with the court-martial, Conner wrote his assistant a letter that began with the salutation, "My Dear Eisenhower."[26] Conner told the struggling young officer that he was "more than glad" that Eisenhower had accepted his offer to go to Panama. Conner also informed Eisenhower that he had written Chief of Infantry Charles Farnsworth to arrange for Eisenhower's transfer. Despite General Farnsworth's earlier reprimand of Eisenhower over the issue of tank doctrine, Conner conveyed no concern: "I hardly expect any great trouble in getting the order," he wrote. In a display of paternalism that would recur in their relationship, Conner also told Eisenhower: "I decided it was best not to wait until you could be consulted."

Conner's letter also informed Eisenhower that another influential insider was working on his behalf: "I wrote on the 4th to Col. G.C. Marshall, Aide to Gen. P, asking him to steer the matter." Conner also suggested, "it might be advisable for you to drop in on Col. Marshall, State, War and Navy Building, Room 270, and tell him your desire to go, or if you cannot get into the city, to telephone him."

In later years, Eisenhower and Marshall would each write that they first met in 1930; no documentation exists that Eisenhower either met or spoke with George Marshall in 1921.[27] However, given Eisenhower's precarious situation at the time, it is also plausible that he did as he was told by Conner and at least called Marshall, with neither Eisenhower nor Marshall wishing to refer to the embarrassing matter in later accounts written after both men had attained prominence.

Conner's influence began to change the course of the case. On October 24, Brigadier General Harry F. Hodges, commander of the Third Corps Area, intervened in the proceedings. Despite the recommendation of his own corps inspector that Eisenhower should be court-martialed, General Hodges recommended against bringing Eisenhower to trial. However, Inspector General Helmick refused to drop the matter. On November 1, Helmick wrote to Army Adjutant General Peter C. Harris (Helmick's West Point classmate), to insist that Eisenhower be tried on the charge of making a "false and fraudulent" claim. General Helmick also called for an expanded investigation into whether Eisenhower had improperly claimed other expense reimbursements.[28]

The adjutant general's office issued a memorandum on November 16, 1921 regarding Major Eisenhower, but not the one Helmick had sought. Conner and Marshall had indeed "steered" the matter through the Army's bureaucracy—directly to the office of Chief of Staff John J. Pershing, whom George Marshall continued to serve as an aide. In a memorandum, titled "Request of Fox Conner for Brigade Adjutant," the adjutant general's office simply informed Pershing that Conner "desires the detail of this particular man because he knows of his efficiency and because he is due for foreign service." The memorandum made no mention either of the several investigations conducted into Eisenhower's commutation claim or of the Army Inspector General's insistence that Eisenhower be court-martialed. The memo simply informed the chief of staff of Conner's request. That was all Black Jack Pershing needed to know.[29]

Also on November 16, with the question of Eisenhower's fate safely in the hands of Pershing and Marshall, Fox and Bug Conner left for Panama.[30]

Conner's behind-the-scene maneuvering bore full fruit on December 14, 1921. In a remarkable memorandum to Brigadier General J.H. McRae, Assistant Chief of Staff for Personnel (G-1), Eisenhower's nemesis, General Helmick, reversed his fervently stated position and concluded: "The trial of Major Eisenhower is not recommended." Helmick wrote that he no longer believed Eisenhower's conduct reflected any "intent to defraud the government." Instead of a court-martial, Helmick suggested that Eisenhower only be "appropriately reprimanded by competent authority."[31]

General McRae, whose War Department office had been next door to Conner's, possessed the necessary authority. On December 14, the same day as Helmick's memorandum, McRae drafted a written reprimand to Eisenhower. "Your admitted ignorance of the law" and "failure to take ordinary precautions," McRae wrote Eisenhower, had led to the serious charges. McRae also informed the major that he would not be brought to trial, but that a copy of the written reprimand would be made a part of his permanent record, as it has been since.[32]

Shortly thereafter, Eisenhower received his orders to report to Panama.[33]

Eisenhower, in his *At Ease* memoir, glossed over the matter and wrote only that "the red tape was torn to pieces" by Conner.[34] The absence of further mention of the matter in the later writings of Eisenhower, Conner, Marshall, Helmick, and the other men involved leaves only conjecture as to *why* Fox Conner staked his prestige on a young officer he barely knew.

Conner, who had not served overseas during the Spanish–American War, may have empathized with Eisenhower, who, likewise, had missed combat during World War I. Conner had also been audited during the war; he had a larger amount of $583.26 suspended from his salary, with the matter being uneventfully resolved by the money being withheld from his pay.[35] Conner's own similar experience could have caused him to view the issue over Eisenhower's improper expense reimbursement with less gravity than did Inspector General Helmick.

Conner might have recalled the help he had received from senior officers, such as Colonel Greenough at Fort Hamilton and General

Wotherspoon at the War College, who had gratuitously assisted his own early career. Also, Conner and Helmick had known each other from their service together at the Inspector General's bureau in 1916 and 1917; it is possible that Conner may simply have called in a favor.[36]

More practically, Eisenhower had skills that Conner undoubtedly valued. As commander of Camp Colt during World War I, Eisenhower had managed the daily operation of a military installation with insufficient resources for the mission assigned to it—experience that would benefit the executive officer of a unit based in a remote location such as the Panama Canal Zone. Also, people whose opinions Conner valued thought highly of Eisenhower: in addition to George Patton's strong recommendation, Ira C. Welborn, Conner's West Point classmate from Mississippi, had recommended Eisenhower for a Distinguished Service Medal for his service at Camp Colt.[37]

Regardless of Conner's motivation, it is highly probable that Dwight Eisenhower would have faced a court-martial in late 1921 had Fox Conner not intervened. Based upon the uniform opinions of the three trained inspectors who had examined the case, Eisenhower would likely have been convicted, since he clearly did draw expense reimbursement for his son in Colorado while he and his wife occupied government housing at Camp Meade. As Helmick pointed out in his December 14 memorandum to McRae, the charge that Eisenhower had defrauded the government was "of the gravest character" for which he might have been "not only dismissed from the service, but imprisoned."[38]

It is difficult to imagine the history of the mid-20th century without Dwight Eisenhower, but an Eisenhower convicted of fraudulent conduct in the early 1920s would almost certainly not have become the Supreme Allied Commander in Europe during World War II, much less President of the United States in the 1950s.

When Fox Conner rescued Dwight Eisenhower's career in 1921, he changed the course of history. Conner would also change Eisenhower himself during their three years together in Panama.

CHAPTER 10

PANAMA

My tour of duty was one of the most interesting and constructive of my life. The main reason was the presence of one man, General Fox Conner.
—Dwight D. Eisenhower, 1967[1]

On December 8, 1921, Fox and Bug Conner, accompanied by daughters Betsey and Florence, arrived by ship on Panama's Caribbean coast. Tommy Conner remained in the United States to complete his education and to prepare for his own application to West Point.[2]

As the Conners waited at the dock to be escorted to the headquarters of the 20th Infantry Brigade at Camp Gaillard, toward the Pacific end of the Panama Canal, the post adjutant met them. Bug Conner recorded the following dialogue in her memoir, *What Father Forbad*:

> "Has my furniture arrived?" Conner asked the young officer.
>
> "Yes sir; but nothing has been unpacked, as everyone knew that as soon as the General knew where he had been ordered, he would do everything in his power to have his orders changed."
>
> "I usually go where I am sent," Conner replied sharply.
>
> "Well, you can't come over now," the adjutant persisted. "You'll have to go and stay at the Tivoli Hotel in Panama City."
>
> "I'll be over after lunch, "Conner snapped. "Have the official car meet me at the locks."
>
> The adjutant, in an uncomfortable predicament, confessed to his new commander: "I'm sorry, sir, but the official car is busy."
>
> "Have something meet me," Conner said as he dismissed his subordinate, "for I'm coming over."

The Conners travelled 47 miles by train to Panama City. A small commuter bus then took the family six miles to the Pedro Miguel Locks, one of the three sets of locks in the Panama Canal system. The new commanding general at Camp Gaillard, and his family, then walked the remaining half mile to arrive at their new post, which Bug considered "the only place on the wrong side of the canal." The family crossed the Panama Canal by walking a narrow path atop the locks; a rope provided the only railing. They hiked the rest of the way on a dirt road that had begun to crumble into the canal.

The officers at Camp Gaillard had not planned a welcoming ceremony for their new commander. Conner had to order the officer's mess to prepare a meal for the family. "It was a strange sensation," Bug Conner recalled in her memoir, "to land in a post that did not want us." Mrs. Conner and her daughters waited in the equatorial heat and humidity while her husband inspected the base. She felt as if "the jungle was about to swallow us all up."

Once General Conner returned, he tried to lift his family's spirits; he told them that their new home, which was built on stilts to protect the floors from dampness, would look quite pretty—once they painted over the mold. Betsey Conner thought that the house, with latticework surrounding the porch, looked like a birdcage.

Dwight and Mamie Eisenhower arrived at Camp Gaillard in early January 1922. Mrs. Eisenhower, who was again pregnant, had battled both morning sickness and seasickness on their ocean voyage to the tropics. Like the Conner family, the Eisenhowers crossed the canal by means of the narrow catwalk on top of the locks and then trudged hundreds of yards in the Panamanian heat to arrive at the base. Mamie Eisenhower's spirits sank once she saw their new home. According to Susan Eisenhower, her grandmother peered into the abandoned house and saw a mildewed interior teeming with insects, lizards, and snakes.[3]

Bug Conner came to the rescue. She warmly greeted the appalled Eisenhowers. Bug then took Mamie by the hand to walk the younger couple to the nearby Conner residence. By mid-January, the Conners' "birdcage" had been painted and refurbished with new fixtures and mahogany trim inside. General Conner had also created a grand library in one room. Bug assured the Eisenhowers that, with work and patience, their new home would become transformed as well.

Although Bug's encouraging words helped, Mamie's melancholy rapidly returned. She couldn't sleep the first night in her new home. The sound of a rat chewing on a chair leg kept Mrs. Eisenhower awake all night.

As Mamie Eisenhower began the task of cleaning house in January 1922, her husband and General Conner did the same with the 20th Infantry Brigade at Camp Gaillard.

Given the importance of the Panama Canal to America's ability to conduct military operations in both the Atlantic and Pacific oceans, a 1920 board of Army and Navy officers had identified defense of the canal as one of the nation's top three military priorities. However, by 1922, an isolationist Congress had reduced the size of the *entire* American Army to only 137,000 soldiers—less than half the force authorized by the National Defense Act of 1920. The Army's plan for defending the canal called for 47,000 troops. But by 1922, three-quarters of that force existed only on paper. Conner's "brigade" actually consisted of a single regiment (designated the 42nd Infantry) formed by Puerto Rican National Guardsmen.[4]

According to Bug Conner's memoir, poor morale, and lax discipline pervaded Camp Gaillard at the time her husband took command. In a 1987 letter, Betsey Conner recalled that the Puerto Rican troops were "completely native" and that they often did as they pleased while on duty. "If they were hot, they took off their shirts," Betsey wrote. "If their feet hurt on a hike, they'd take off their shoes." A 1921 Army surgeon general's report on Canal Zone troops noted a high incidence of venereal disease, alcoholism, and use of illegal drugs such as cocaine, marijuana, and morphine.

The brigade had also suffered from poor leadership. In Bug Conner's estimation, her husband's predecessor had been "eccentric, if not actually crazy." Additionally, the single-regiment brigade structure produced the anomalous situation in which separate brigade and regimental headquarters both commanded the same group of men. According to Bug Conner, the regimental commander, Lieutenant Colonel R.R. Wood, exhibited the "petty but extremely irritating" habit of ignoring her husband's orders.

According to then-Major Bradford Chynoweth, who commanded a battalion in the 20th Brigade, General Conner was a "dominant commander," who quickly asserted his authority over the troops at Camp Gaillard.[5] Conner issued detailed daily orders. As the general's chief assistant, Major Eisenhower learned to generate orders using the five-paragraph field order technique emphasized at the Staff College at Leavenworth. The sometimes unpleasant task of enforcing those orders also fell to Eisenhower, as the brigade's executive officer.[6]

In contrast to the genial and consensus-building style that would typify his World War II persona, the younger Eisenhower in Panama displayed a rigid and sometimes overbearing style that rankled Major Chynoweth and other younger officers. Chynoweth, who had been friends with Eisenhower since West Point, came to view the brigade's executive officer as a mere yes-man for Conner. In a 1967 monograph, Chynoweth recounted a conversation in which Eisenhower acknowledged his "guiding philosophy" for serving under Conner: "I forget my own ideas and do everything in my power to promote what _he_ says is right." Chynoweth asked: "Right or wrong?" Eisenhower purportedly replied: "The Commanding Officer is _never_ wrong with me." [Emphases are in the original.]

Conner also acted to increase discipline in the enlisted ranks. Nearby Panama City provided plentiful prostitution, which in turn produced the high rate of venereal disease that plagued the brigade. Conner attacked the problem by automatically imposing the maximum punishment upon any soldier who contracted a sexually transmitted disease. The rate of disease, and punishments, began to drop.

Conner also introduced a new training program for marksmanship, which he personally supervised. Rifle proficiency in the brigade rapidly climbed. In three companies, 100 percent of the soldiers qualified as expert marksmen. According to a 1922 _Infantry Journal_ article, unnamed "officers serving in the Canal Zone" (likely Conner and Eisenhower) considered the marksmanship scores "one of the most remarkable records ever made in the service." Conner credited his regimental commander.

"When compared with the records made last season," the general wrote Lieutenant Colonel Wood on March 3, 1922, "this year's scores show conclusively the results of hard work, devotion to duty, and intelligently directed effort on the part of your whole command."

Conner also interacted with his men on a daily basis as he made his rounds through the post on a horse named Old Bill. As Eisenhower put it, Conner "never abandoned the position—and no senior officer ever should—of being an instructor."

Once, Conner encountered some Puerto Rican soldiers on a work detail who did not know how to use a scythe to cut grass, so he dismounted and gave a demonstration. When a team of horses got a wagon stuck in jungle mud and would not move, despite the cursing and beating of their teamsters, Conner took the reins and calmed the horses; according to Eisenhower, Conner "just talked to them and they went right out of the mud." Similarly, Betsey Conner's 1987 letter recalled an instance in which her father worked with his troops to tame a gun-shy mule that bolted each time any cannon fired. Conner had the mule hitched to a sled loaded with rocks. When the guns resumed fire, the frightened beast kicked up a whirlwind of dirt as it tried to run but could not move. Eventually, the mule, like the men of the 20th Brigade, settled down under Conner's firm leadership.

In Betsey Conner's estimation, "Daddy really knew mules and horses and men." [The emphasis is in the original]. Conner briefly discussed his views on the relationship between a commander and his troops in the foreword to a 1922 book, titled *Principles of Command*, by Major Ralph Jones. Conner began with the premise, borrowed from an Alexander Pope poem, that "the proper study of mankind is man." He then addressed the importance, to a military commander, of a basic understanding of human psychology. Despite his view that "the usual text on psychology is so abstruse as to be understandable only to the professor," Conner nonetheless believed that "the motives which control the majority of men and the mainsprings which actuate those motives are comparatively simple and few in number." He then referred his readers to Major Jones's book to learn the fundamental principles of applying psychological principles to command of troops.[7]

Fox Conner's developing relationship with his executive officer Eisenhower afforded the general an opportunity to practice a bit of applied psychology of his own.

During one casual conversation, Eisenhower mentioned to Conner that he had lost interest in a former passion—the study of history. In his memoir *At Ease*, Eisenhower wrote that, as a young student, the subject had captivated him: "Hannibal, Caesar, Pericles, Socrates, Themistocles, Miltiades, and Leonidas were my white hats, my heroes." Eisenhower's high school yearbook had predicted he would become a history professor; however, West Point's emphasis on rote memorization of names and dates had caused Eisenhower to develop an "intense dislike" of history, which he still bore, seven years after leaving the academy.[8]

Conner, who had never lost his own boyhood love of history, said nothing in response to Eisenhower's comment about history. The general did, though, invite Eisenhower to visit the Conner residence that evening.

Once there, the two officers retired to the general's library. In a 1964 interview, Eisenhower recalled that Conner's collection of books on military history was "magnificent." Bradford Chynoweth had a similar recollection of Conner's "fine military library" at Camp Gaillard. Shelves of beautifully bound books, including works written in French and German, lined the walls of Conner's study. Eisenhower recalled that one shelf held nothing but works on Napoleon. More than 40 years after his service in Panama, Eisenhower told journalist Charles H. Brown that he could "still see" the bright red covers of the *Napoleon as a General* series.[9]

But Fox Conner did not speak to Eisenhower about Napoleon or any other great commander of the past, nor did he discuss the importance of history to the development of a well-rounded military officer.

Instead, Conner drew three novels from the shelves of his collection and handed them to his assistant. "You might be interested in these," Conner suggested in his quiet Mississippi drawl.[10]

Thus began what Eisenhower described in *At Ease*, as a three-year "graduate school in military affairs and humanities." In his 1986 work, *The Challenge of Command*, former West Point history professor Roger Nye cited the examples of what "Eisenhower had in Fox Conner, Napoleon in de Guibert, and Philip of Macedon in Socrates," as examples of how "a great teacher" can impart to a young officer the "insights and values" necessary for later success in high command. Professor Nye also lauded Fox Conner as "the most celebrated" example of a mentor—one whose "chief function is to cause his people to become better *learners*." [The emphasis is in the original.][11]

Eisenhower said as much of Conner, but in simpler terms: "He was my teacher." As Eisenhower phrased it, his commander was a "smart, patient man, and he decided that I ought to amount to something; so he was going to see if I would."[12]

Conner loaned Eisenhower three works of historical fiction—*The Exploits of Brigadier Gerard* by Sir Arthur Conan Doyle (of Sherlock Holmes fame), *The Long Roll* by Mary Johnston (granddaughter of Confederate General Joseph Johnston), and *The Crisis* by American author Winston Churchill (no relation to the more famous Briton of the same name.) Historical fiction, such as *The Last Days of Pompeii* and *Ivanhoe*, had sustained Conner's own interest in history while he was at West Point.[13] Conner accordingly began Eisenhower's reintroduction to history through novels that told the compelling stories of fictional characters against the backdrop of historical events, in the hope that the stories would hold Eisenhower's interest long enough for his love of history to reignite.

In *The Exploits of Brigadier Gerard*,[14] Eisenhower read of the harrowing adventures of Etienne Gerard, a cavalry officer in Napoleon's army. Gerard first earned Napoleon's trust by rescuing the emperor from two would-be assassins. While fighting Bonaparte's battles against the British in Spain, Gerard cleverly escaped from local guerrillas that had planned to kill him in a gruesome manner. During Napoleon's campaigns in the East, Gerard was nearly killed when struck in the head by a timber hurled from an exploded castle in Poland. As Conan Doyle spun the tales of Gerard's daring feats, the author not only traced the arc of Napoleon's rise and fall—a staple of military education at the time—but he also provided entertaining vignettes of Napoleon, his generals, and his enemies.

In Conan Doyle's 1896 work, written well after the Napoleonic Wars but before World War I, Eisenhower read of parallels between the two conflicts. For example, Napoleon's campaigns against the Prussians had involved places such as Soissons, Meaux, and Château-Thierry—battlegrounds on which the United States had recently fought in the Great War. Also, in one story, Napoleon sent Brigadier Gerard on a confidential mission through enemy territory, in the expectation that he and the disinformation he was bearing would fall into enemy hands, as Conner had done with Omar Bundy in the Belfort Ruse.

One of the book's recurrent themes, which may have particularly resonated with Dwight Eisenhower, involved the protagonist's sense that he had never been given the opportunity to realize his full potential. Brigadier Gerard nonetheless took solace that "although I was not able to write my name upon history, it is sufficiently well known by all who served with me."

Mary Johnston's *The Long Roll*[15] tells the story of Confederate General Thomas "Stonewall" Jackson through the experiences of his aide, Major Richard Cleave. The night before he left home, Cleave prepared for war by reading of the military campaigns of Hannibal, as Eisenhower had done as a boy. Also like Eisenhower, Major Cleave frequently took the brunt of complaints and criticism from fellow officers about the strictness of the general he served.

The Long Roll's plot unfolds through the course of several Civil War battles that remained important case studies for American officers in the 1920s. Eisenhower read how the man called "Fool Tom Jackson" at the beginning of the Civil War, became "Stonewall Jackson" at First Bull Run, and finally Robert E. Lee's "right arm" at the Battle of Chancellorsville, by a consistent pursuit of his objectives, without regard to whether he was loved or loathed by those he commanded.

The Crisis[16] traced the careers of two Union generals who had similarly risen from obscurity to greatness when opportunity arose: Ulysses S. Grant and William T. Sherman. As Conan Doyle had done with Napoleon's Etienne Gerard, and Johnston with Stonewall Jackson's Richard Cleave, the author Churchill made Sherman's aide, Stephen Brice, an important character in the book. Brice's story presented Eisenhower with a third example of how officers who had served history's famous generals had themselves enjoyed adventurous and fulfilling careers, even if history had never noted their names.

As Conner had hoped, his own aide, Eisenhower, greatly enjoyed the fictional accounts. Conner then asked Eisenhower: "Wouldn't you like to know something of what the armies were actually doing during the period of the novels you've just read?" When Eisenhower expressed interest, Conner went through his shelves and found detailed histories of the Napoleonic Wars and the American Civil War for his assistant to study.[17]

Eisenhower had passed to the next grade of his education.

As the two men went about their daily work, Conner began to pose questions to Eisenhower about his reading. Conner especially focused Eisenhower's attention on the decisions—good and bad—that history's great commanders had made. Why was a particular decision made? Under what conditions? What were the alternatives? How might a different decision have affected the outcome?

Conner's Socratic method—so different from West Point's emphasis on memorization—restored Eisenhower's appreciation of military history. "The upshot was that I found myself becoming fascinated with the subject," Eisenhower recalled in *At Ease.* He began to think more in terms of the *why* of history rather than merely the *what*, which in turn produced what Eisenhower termed "profound and endless results" for his professional development.

In a 1965 *New York Times* interview on the value of what he had learned from Fox Conner in Panama, Eisenhower also made the telling comment that studying history "helped me lose myself in my work." He had begun to focus on his career, in part, as a diversion from difficulties at home.

Bug Conner recalled that the Eisenhowers were not a happy couple during their first several months at Camp Gaillard. According to Bug, Mrs. Eisenhower "made no bones" about her hatred of Panama, with its bats, bedbugs, and flying roaches.[18] Bug Conner, who considered herself the post's unofficial marriage counselor, recalled that Mamie began to "wear down a path" to the Conner residence to pour out her sadness.

Mamie Eisenhower was also frequently ill during her pregnancy. Camp Gaillard had no hospital; only an infirmary managed by a Red Cross nurse. Mamie initially had planned to have her child at the camp infirmary, but she gladly accepted her parents' offer to bring her home so that the baby could be born in an American hospital. In the early summer of 1922, Mrs. Eisenhower left for Denver. Conner saw to it that Dwight was with Mamie when their son, John Sheldon Doud Eisenhower, was born on August 3, 1922. For weeks before and months afterward, though, Dwight Eisenhower lived alone in Panama. History became his companion; conversation with Conner his comfort.

Mrs. Eisenhower returned to Camp Gaillard in November 1922, with baby Johnnie. But Mamie soon fell back into a tropical malaise. She recalled that her "health and vitality seemed to ebb away" in Panama. Bug Conner also saw the Eisenhower marriage begin to waste away. "They were two people drifting apart," Bug recalled. "Ike was spending less and less time with Mamie, and there was no warmth between them." Granddaughter Susan Eisenhower wrote that Mamie might have suffered from postpartum depression aggravated by jealousy over the amount of time her husband spent with Conner while off duty. Eventually, Mrs. Eisenhower decided to return to the United States, despite the plea of her husband to stay in Panama.

Once again without his family, Dwight Eisenhower soothed his loneliness by losing himself in the lessons of history to which Fox Conner had led him.

In contrast to Mamie Eisenhower, Bug Conner appeared to have quite enjoyed her time in Panama.[19]

As the wife of the post's commanding general, Bug enjoyed a full complement of household servants, which created ample time for leisure. According to her daughter Betsey, Bug mostly spent her days playing the violin. Betsey recalled that her sister Florence had a pet squirrel, which would sit atop Bug's head as she practiced her Amati. In a 1952 letter to Bug, Mamie Eisenhower wrote: "If I close my eyes, I can hear you practicing your violin across the field between our houses at Gaillard."

Fox and Bug enjoyed horseback riding, as they had at Fort Riley a decade earlier. Mrs. Conner also took interest in the camp's young families. In addition to providing a sympathetic ear to couples who struggled with the isolation of Camp Gaillard, Bug also helped raise money for the base infirmary. Once, she persuaded two film stars who were making a movie in Panama to help her raise funds. Bug also regularly attended the camp's Friday night dance. Mrs. Conner wrote in her memoir that the young officers at Gaillard "considered that the regiment was disgraced if I ever sat out a dance."

Betsey Conner also found Panama—and one of its officers—very much to her liking.[20]

According to her mother, 19-year-old Betsey Conner had been as indifferent to romance as her father had been; Bug wondered whether Betsey, like her father, would "fall hard and fast" in love once she met the right man.

Captain Frank Vida, a young officer under Conner's command at Camp Gaillard, provided the answer to Bug's question.

Vida, who had served with distinction in the Great War, played the violin. Bug was delighted when the young captain accepted her invitation to visit the Conner residence to play duets. Mrs. Conner quickly learned, though, that Vida was more interested in Betsey than Beethoven.

Captain Vida proposed on the porch of the Conner residence one evening in February 1922, when the general was away on a fishing trip. Vida had apparently not asked his commanding officer for his daughter's hand. When Bug told her husband that she thought Betsey and Vida were engaged, Conner remarked that his wife "got the craziest ideas."

The sunset wedding of Betsey Conner and Frank Vida took place on January 23, 1923, in a small outdoor chapel built by the base carpenter in the hibiscus-hedged garden of the Conner residence. Betsey walked down the aisle on her father's arm, as the setting sun bathed the chapel in light filtered through windows of colored paper the carpenter had fashioned to give the appearance of stained glass. Bug described Betsey's face as "serene and radiant"; in contrast, she thought her husband "looked just as if he would like to commit suicide." Despite Bug's description, there is no indication that Fox Conner—never known for outward displays of emotion—had any objection to the marriage.

Conner's first grandchild, Fox Conner Vida, was born November 30, 1923 in New York City.

Betsey's two siblings had far different experiences in Panama. Florence Conner, who was 12 when the family arrived at Camp Gaillard, had little to entertain her in the isolated jungle outpost. She also developed what Bug described as "tropical ulcers" on her chin and legs, which persisted until her parents sent her back to the United States for treatment. The sores cleared up as soon as Florence left Panama.[21]

Tommy Conner's one visit to Panama in the summer of 1922 left him, as well, with unpleasant memories.[22] Tommy, who arrived during Panama's rainy season, struggled with the climate. "Sometimes when you stepped out of the house," Tommy Conner recalled, "it was more like swimming than walking." He also remembered that the tropical humidity drained him of energy. "Sometimes just lifting food or a drink to your mouth wore you completely out."

Tommy Conner's trip to Panama also revealed the distance that had developed between father and son.

Since 1917, when Fox Conner had gone off to war, and his son to boarding school in Pennsylvania, contact between the two had become increasingly infrequent. During the formative years of his adolescence, Tommy Conner had drawn closer to his grandfather, Franklin Brandreth in Ossining. Tommy later said that Colonel Frank had become "more like a father to me than my own father was." According to Tommy's son, Macpherson Conner, Fox and Tommy Conner "didn't have a relationship" in the early 1920s.

Tommy had visited his parents in Panama during the summer before his own plebe year at West Point. As explained by Macpherson Conner, Tommy never felt the same calling to a military life that had burned within Fox Conner as a boy in Mississippi. Tommy had actually wanted to attend the Massachusetts Institute of Technology (MIT). Bug Conner recalled in her memoir that as Tommy nonetheless prepared to follow in his father's West Point footsteps, he was "full of what he intended to do, only to find that his father was too busy to take any interest in his aspirations."

Bug's description of her husband's indifference toward their son's future stands in stark juxtaposition to Fox Conner's legacy as a teacher and mentor. But while Fox and Tommy coexisted in the early 1920s through what Bug, Tommy, and Macpherson Conner have all described as a tepid father–son relationship, the general began to form an almost familial bond with his executive officer in Panama. Fox Conner eventually came to occupy what Dwight Eisenhower described as a "place in my affections ... that no other, not a relative, could obtain."[23]

Bug Conner wrote that she "never saw two men more congenial than Ike Eisenhower and my husband." On weekends, Conner and Eisenhower went fishing offshore. During Panama's dry season, the two men spent hours on horseback, marking trails through the jungle so that the garrison could rapidly move men and equipment to defend against an amphibious invasion—a topic that would occupy much of Eisenhower's attention two decades later.

While out mapping trails, the two men often camped in the jungle. Just as "Blind Bob" Conner had instilled a love of history in young Fox through stories of war told in front of the family's Mississippi hearth, so did General Conner cultivate his executive officer's renewed interest in history through campfire conversations about the great campaigns of the past.

In a 1964 interview, Eisenhower said that he and Conner formed a "particularly close" relationship, to the point that the younger officer grew comfortable enough to debate the general vigorously on topics under discussion. "O God, we'd get into the hottest arguments," Eisenhower recalled. "We slept in the same tent. He was a heavy smoker—so was I, then—and we'd get up in the night and light a cigarette and go on talking."

Conner gradually led Eisenhower to a more advanced level of military study.[24] The general introduced his assistant to the writings of the 19th-century Prussian military theorist Carl von Clausewitz, whose *On War* remains an influential treatise on warfare. Eisenhower struggled to grasp the military maxims set forth by Clausewitz, so Conner had Eisenhower read the book three times to drive home the lessons. Conner would quiz Eisenhower as to what each Clausewitzian principle meant. In a 1966 letter, Eisenhower identified *On War* as the book that had most profoundly influenced his military career. George Patton recounted one

World War II debate over strategy in which Eisenhower became "very pontifical and quoted Clausewitz to us."

Eisenhower also continued to avail himself of Conner's military library. "No matter what time of day or evening," Eisenhower recalled, "I would walk across to General Conner's house to ask for another book from his library." According to Eisenhower, Conner took delight in his protégé's interest, and when Eisenhower found a book to borrow, Conner would usually offer him a second one.

Eisenhower fashioned his own study on the second-floor screened porch of his home. There, he analyzed, and refought on paper, the campaigns of Napoleon and Frederick the Great of Prussia. Having read Churchill's fictional accounts of Ulysses S. Grant and William T. Sherman in *The Crisis*, Eisenhower then read the memoirs of both generals. Additionally, Eisenhower studied the leading scholarly works of the time on the Civil War, including those of Matthew Forney Steele, Conner's own former history teacher.

Eisenhower also studied the recent war in which his mentor had played a prominent role. In 1944, Conner recalled that Eisenhower's "grasp of the lessons of the World War was superb." Utilizing Leavenworth's applicatory method, Conner and Eisenhower "war gamed" the battles of World War I to analyze mistakes made by the war's commanders. They debated the effectiveness of the delaying actions of Lee at the end of the Civil War and of Ludendorff at the conclusion of the Great War. Conner thought Ludendorff's strategy had been superior.

Eisenhower also found his commanding general to have been "a very interesting man in social and private life too." Eisenhower described Conner as "easygoing" and "down to earth." Eisenhower also recalled that Conner "had a mind like a steel trap" and that "the range and curiosity of his mind was [sic] not limited to military affairs." The two officers also began to discuss what Eisenhower termed "the long history of man, his ideas, and works."[25]

In their discussions, Conner sometimes quoted from Shakespeare to relate passages from the bard's plays of kings and conquests in earlier centuries to more contemporary conflicts and characters. Conner told his protégé: "In all military history, only one thing never changes—human nature. Terrain may change, weather may change, weapons may change ... but never human nature." Conner also introduced Eisenhower to the works of Plato and other philosophers, including the German Friedrich Nietzsche, whose writings would later be hijacked by Eisenhower's Nazi adversaries.

Eisenhower wrote in *At Ease* that Fox Conner was also "something of a philosopher" himself, and a "storehouse of axiomatic advice." Eisenhower wrote that he later quoted Conner "on hundreds, if not thousands, of occasions." According to biographer Stephen Ambrose, Eisenhower frequently used-two particular sayings he had learned from Conner: "Always take your job seriously, never yourself" and "All generalities are false, including this one."

"There was no question," Eisenhower said in a 1963 interview, "that Fox Conner got me started in better methods of preparing myself." Conner also took note of his assistant's new habits. "The work of the day was always first with him," Conner said of Eisenhower in 1944, "but his every spare moment was devoted to higher studies."

Eisenhower continued those studies once his wife and son returned to Panama later in 1923.[26] According to granddaughter Susan Eisenhower, Mamie's time apart from Dwight led her grandmother to recommit herself to her marriage and to life as a military wife. Mrs. Eisenhower also became more tolerant of her husband's evening studies although, as she pointed out in one interview, the couple sometimes "missed particularly nice parties because Ike was studying."

One party Eisenhower apparently missed took place in 1924, when Fox and Bug Conner hosted their friend, George Marshall, who passed through the Panama Canal on his way to service with an infantry regiment in China.[27] Marshall wrote that "Conner gave me quite a party in Panama—lots of champagne."

Conner had frequently told Eisenhower that George Marshall was "the ideal soldier" and "nothing short of a genius." Conner had urged his chief assistant to seek an opportunity to serve under Marshall. According to both Marshall and Eisenhower, though, the two men did not meet in Panama. Despite Eisenhower's renewed interest in military history, it is difficult to imagine that he would have missed the opportunity to meet

Marshall, particularly given the role Marshall had played in "steering" the matter of Eisenhower's assignment to Conner's command. In all likelihood, Eisenhower was on leave at the time of Marshall's visit to Camp Gaillard.

Conner particularly praised Marshall for his skill in working within the Allied wartime coalition, which Conner believed would eventually have to become reconstituted.[28] "One of the most profound beliefs of General Conner," Eisenhower recalled of their Panama discussions in the early 1920s, "was that the world could not long avoid another major war." In Eisenhower's words, Conner believed that another major European war was "written into the Treaty of Versailles," which "carried within it the seeds of another, larger conflagration." Tommy Conner likewise recalled his father's saying that Clemenceau and Lloyd George (the wartime leaders of France and Great Britain) had been "a pack of crooks" who "took Wilson for a ride" at Versailles.

Fox Conner also viewed Woodrow Wilson's concept that the nation had actually fought a "war to end all wars" as a "mere slogan of propaganda." In contrast to the isolationist sentiment then prevalent in the United States, Conner repeatedly told Eisenhower that American participation in another large-scale European war was "almost a certainty." Again reflecting his admiration for the defeated Germans, Conner told his assistant: "You can't take the strongest, most virile people in Europe and put them in the kind of straitjacket that this treaty attempts to do." According to Eisenhower, Conner also foresaw a future German–Japanese alliance, which he thought the Soviet Union might join as well.[29]

Conner and Eisenhower discussed in detail the techniques of managing a multinational military coalition—skills Eisenhower would come to master two decades later.[30] In discussing the observations of some historians that Eisenhower had been a "political general" during World War II, Tommy Conner said in a 1982 interview: "Father made him that way."

Conner explained to Eisenhower that any future allied commander would face the same resistance Marshal Foch had encountered during the Great War—such as Conner's own strong opposition to amalgamation of American soldiers—when attempting to control troops of a foreign nation. Conner stressed the need for allied nations to develop a command structure that vested the supreme commander with stronger powers than Foch had held. Conner also thought that the general atop the international coalition would need to be as much a boardroom conciliator as a battlefield commander. Therefore, Conner stressed the need for a future supreme commander to be skilled in the "art of persuasion." Eisenhower recalled that Conner would "get out a book of applied psychology and we would talk it over … How do you get allies of different nations to march and think as a nation?"

"There is no question of his molding my thinking on this from the time I was thirty-one," Eisenhower said in a 1964 interview. Eisenhower similarly recalled, in other interviews, that Conner "kept dinning into me that I had to prepare myself for command because the future of the nation depended on my readiness and that of men of my time." According to Eisenhower, "the necessity of being prepared for war was a product of something that just seeped into me from the teachings of this man."

In his 1924 evaluation of Eisenhower, General Conner rated his executive officer as "one of the most capable, efficient and loyal officers I have ever met." In a 1944 interview, Conner said of Eisenhower: "It was evident that he would go far."[31] Not everyone at Camp Gaillard, however, was as impressed with Eisenhower—or with his mentor, Conner.

Major Bradford Chynoweth wrote that Conner and Eisenhower "as a team were the most ineffective training command that I can remember."[32] In his 1975 memoir, Chynoweth wrote that the younger officers in Panama needed guidance, but "got none from brigade headquarters." According to Chynoweth, "Fox and Ike visited every unit on the training field every morning, looked sour, criticized, and condemned. Then they returned to their office where Fox gave Ike lectures on military history."

Chynoweth further wrote that "Fox Conner and Ike failed to gain positive results and made everyone restive." In Chynoweth's view, Conner and Eisenhower, neither of whom had commanded soldiers in battle during the war, reverted to the style of West Point upperclassmen toward plebes: "Breathe down their necks and bark at them. Be tough!" He recalled that his two fellow battalion commanders, both National Guardsmen, "caught hell from both Fox and Ike."

Similarly, Chynoweth recalled that Conner would become "very impatient and irritated," when others disagreed with him. He described one instance in which Conner became "red faced and furious" when the brigade's younger officers objected to a proposed modification of training regulations. Chynoweth also disliked Conner's "iron-handed centralized system" of command, and, especially, Conner's approach to courts-martial. According to Chynoweth, Conner "went all-out and ordered them what sentences to inflict." Chynoweth believed that Conner had imbedded a spy (not Eisenhower) among the officers serving on the court. According to Chynoweth, Conner said: "If you don't vote as I direct, I will know exactly who voted wrong."

Chynoweth also resented the reason for his assignment to Panama in the first place. Chynoweth's mother and Bug Conner had played music together when Chynoweth and Conner had both served in Washington, D.C. Chynoweth believed that Conner had him transferred to Panama in the successful hope that Bug Conner could be reunited with her former duet partner. "Such is petticoat politics, in the Army or out," wrote Chynoweth.

To place Chynoweth's remarks in perspective, his criticisms put Conner and Eisenhower in fine company. The curmudgeonly Chynoweth expressed similar levels of disdain in his writings for others under whom he served, including George Marshall, Douglas MacArthur, Joseph Stillwell, Joseph P. Kennedy, and Charles Summerall. By his own admission, Chynoweth had a "self-defeating attitude of criticism" and "reputation for being contentious." Regarding the necessity of junior officers being subordinate to their superiors, Chynoweth wrote: "There is a lesson in it. I never learned the lesson."

Also, Chynoweth's views of Conner were not entirely negative. "In administering the post as a social unit," Chynoweth wrote, "Fox Conner was grand." In later years, when Chynoweth attended the War College, he "felt honored" when Conner singled him out by name during an address. Despite his criticisms, Chynoweth also wrote of Fox Conner that he "liked and admired him, as a man," one assessment of Conner on which Chynoweth and Eisenhower agreed.

Without question, Dwight Eisenhower held his mentor in high esteem. In Eisenhower's 1948 World War II memoir, *Crusade in Europe*, the former Allied supreme commander (who had commanded such generals as Montgomery, Bradley, Patton, and many others), wrote that he considered Fox Conner to have been "one of the most accomplished soldiers of our time." In a 1964 interview, Eisenhower termed Conner a "born leader of men." He also described his time in Panama with Conner as "one of the most satisfying experiences of my life ... It was not only instructive but a great pleasure."[33]

But in September 1924, the one-on-one tutelage that Conner provided Eisenhower came to an end when the War Department recalled Conner to Washington, D.C. to become the Army's chief of supply.[34]

At a minimum, Conner's service in Panama allowed him to satisfy the requirement of the Manchu Law that general staff officers serve at least two years with troops. Conner was also able to add a field command, albeit of a partially manned brigade during peacetime, to his already considerable resume. As importantly, the daily routine of managing a large body of men in less than ideal circumstances of climate and facilities also provided Conner with practical experience he had not gained in France.[35]

Fox Conner left Camp Gaillard on September 2, 1924.[36] The farewell given the general by his troops suggests that not all of the men under Conner's command shared the negative views of Major Chynoweth.

Captain George Randolph wrote that the men of the brigade lined the canal, saluted, and held their salutes as the vessel bearing Conner slowly moved away. As the camp's band played "Auld Lang Syne," "Aloha," and other sentimental tunes, Conner stood alone on the ship's bridge and returned the salute of the Puerto Rican guardsmen he had commanded for almost three years. Captain Randolph, in what he described as a "gesture dear to the hearts of the emotional Latins," drew his sword, waved it above his head, and called three cheers for Conner. As described by Randolph, "the answering roars were the last sounds from Gaillard to reach the General's ears as the boat bore him down the canal."

So ended the only period in which Fox Conner and Dwight Eisenhower ever served together.

Eisenhower remained at Camp Gaillard and looked forward to his own reassignment. He hoped to attend the Army's infantry school at Fort Benning, Georgia. No doubt at Conner's urging, Eisenhower also applied for admission to the Command and General Staff School at Fort Leavenworth, which remained an essential rung to be climbed by any officer who aspired to high command service.[37]

Prior to leaving Panama, Conner endorsed Eisenhower's application to Leavenworth. Conner wrote that Eisenhower was "especially fitted to profit by the course." Conner, who had skipped his own branch school and gone directly to Leavenworth, thought Eisenhower capable of the same route. Conner pointed out that Eisenhower had "kept pace with the Benning course by special study and contact with recent Benning graduates," presumably Conner himself. In his 1924 efficiency report on Eisenhower, Conner again lobbied for his protégé's admission to Leavenworth "on account of his natural and professional abilities."[38]

Eisenhower received his orders soon after Conner's departure. Having high hopes of assignment at least to the infantry school at Benning, if not to Leavenworth, Eisenhower "came back to earth with a thump," as he put it in *At Ease*. The War Department reassigned him to Camp Meade, where he and his wife had suffered their darkest days following Icky's death. Eisenhower would again coach football, which he described as "the rut I had started to dig for myself a decade earlier."[39]

It may well have appeared at the time to Dwight Eisenhower that his graduate school with Fox Conner had led him nowhere. Soon, though, the seeds planted by Conner in Panama would come to fruition in his protégé's career.

CHAPTER 11

CLIMBING THEIR LADDERS

I loved the next three years and Fox hated them.
—Virginia Conner, 1951[1]

The Conners returned to the United States on September 8, 1924. After an extended leave at Brandreth Lake, where Fox celebrated his 50th birthday on November 2, he reported for duty in Washington, D.C. on December 1 as the Army's Assistant Chief of Staff for Supply (G-4).[2]

Much had changed in the Army's hierarchy since 1921, when Conner had last served on the general staff. By 1924, the nation had a new commander-in-chief. Following the death in office of President Warren G. Harding in August 1923, Calvin Coolidge had succeeded to the presidency; he then won election in his own right in 1924. President Coolidge retained John W. Weeks as his secretary of war.

In the Army itself, Chief of Staff John J. Pershing stepped down on September 13, 1924 once he reached the mandatory retirement age of 64. The still-influential Pershing engineered the appointment of Deputy Chief of Staff John L. Hines to become his successor, even though several other generals ranked ahead of Hines on the seniority list.[3]

Conner's G-4 section controlled the Army's financial and budgetary functions, as well as its supply, equipment, construction, and transportation services.[4] Bug Conner wrote that her husband's new position involved "the handling of funds for which he had no natural aptitude." In a January 6, 1925 lecture to the Army War College, Conner admitted that he had "no experience in G-4 and very little detailed knowledge of anything connected with G-4." He wondered aloud to his audience whether his appointment was intended to be "recompense before crossing the Styx for many sins of omission and commission."

Conner quickly became immersed in the details of the Army's finances. Not surprisingly for a man of words who studied Shakespeare and Nietzsche in his spare time, Conner considered the detailed analysis of numbers a "thankless" and "never ending" task. "In time of peace," Conner wrote, "almost all decisions are made from a money point of view." He elaborated: "The enemy does not exist, the limitations of time and space are of relatively minor importance, and all other obstacles shrink into insignificance when compared with the limitation on funds. The real problem of the War Department in peace is to secure the maximum amount of national defense with minimum appropriations."

The Army's appropriations had indeed become minimal during the Coolidge Administration.[5] Congress enacted spending cuts, which produced budget surpluses in each year of Coolidge's presidency and which reduced the postwar national debt by nearly one-third. For the fiscal year in which Conner assumed his G-4 duties, annual military appropriations had reached a postwar low of $256,515,279. To place this figure into perspective, the United States military had spent $2,000,000 *per hour* at the time of the Armistice in November 1918. Even by peacetime standards, the military budget represented a one-third reduction from the spending levels set following enactment of the National Defense Act of 1920. Confident that its foreign policy would prevent American involvement in another large-scale foreign war, the Coolidge administration had also shrunk the Army's size to around 133,000 men—only slightly more than the 100,000 men the Treaty of Versailles envisioned would neuter the much smaller nation of Germany.

As the Army's G-4, Conner gained a sobering appreciation of the Army's significant deficiencies in preparedness. In a June 20, 1925 address to the Army Industrial College, Conner told his audience that "war reserves are far more of a theory at present than a reality," and that "in some essential items our stock is zero or precious near to it."[6] Especially concerned about the Army's ammunition supply, most of which had been manufactured in 1918, Conner told his audience that "guns can't shoot theoretical paper ammunition" and that the situation would only worsen as the supply deteriorated further through use and obsolescence. "The cause is simple," said Conner. "We are not getting money to maintain our stocks; worse than that—we are day by day eating up our fat."

Conner also voiced concern to the Industrial College that the nation had become "deluded by our experience in the last war," in which the British and French had borne the brunt of fighting for more than a year while the American home front slowly mobilized for war. "Next time," Conner said, "we may have to be in at the beginning as well as at the end."

★ ★ ★ ★ ★

Fox Conner's 1925 reference to the "next" war—so out of step with the isolationist sentiment in the United States during the Roaring Twenties—echoed his Panama conversations with Dwight Eisenhower. Once both men had returned to the United States, they resumed their discussions. Conner also continued his efforts to ready his protégé for a leadership role once war did arrive.

In early 1925, though, Major Dwight Eisenhower did not appear destined for high command. As ordered, Eisenhower had returned to Camp Meade—and to football coaching—in the autumn of 1924. The team struggled through what Coach Eisenhower described as a "dismal record." Feeling stymied in his career, Eisenhower met with Chief of Infantry Charles Farnsworth in Washington, D.C. to again request assignment to the infantry school at Fort Benning, Georgia. General Farnsworth, who had scolded Eisenhower in 1920 for his article on tank doctrine, agreed to send the major to Fort Benning—but not as a student. Instead, Farnsworth ordered Eisenhower to command a tank battalion at Benning, where he would be in sight of the school doors he could not enter.[7]

After his disappointing meeting with the chief of infantry, Eisenhower paid a visit to his Panama mentor, whose office was down the hall from General Farnsworth's in the State, War, and Navy Building in Washington.[8] "I told Conner my difficulty," Eisenhower recalled in a

1964 interview.[9] Upon learning that that Farnsworth had refused to send Eisenhower to an advanced school, Conner declared: "I'm not going to stand for this." Eisenhower then received what he termed a "strange" telegram from his mentor:

> NO MATTER WHAT ORDERS YOU RECEIVE FROM THE WAR DEPARTMENT, MAKE NO PROTEST, ACCEPT THEM WITHOUT QUESTION SIGNED CONNER.

Conner's telegram, which Eisenhower considered "cryptic in the extreme," puzzled the young major. Eisenhower's wonder then turned to worry when he learned of the path on which his mentor had placed him: Conner had arranged for Eisenhower's transfer out of Farnsworth's infantry branch and into the Army's recruiting service. In *At Ease*, Eisenhower wrote that infantry officers considered recruiting duty "a rebuke a little less devastating than a reprimand," which would normally have provoked outrage. "But with my solid belief in Fox Conner," Eisenhower wrote, "I kept my temper."

Eisenhower also learned that Conner had in mind for him a goal more ambitious than the infantry school at Fort Benning.

Army Adjutant General Robert C. Davis, Conner's friend and classmate from West Point days, controlled the recruiting service. Army regulations allowed the adjutant general's department to send a few of its officers each year to the Command and General Staff School at Fort Leavenworth—the primary portal through which officers who aspired to high command had to pass. As a favor to Conner, Davis agreed to accept Eisenhower into his department. Davis then assigned Eisenhower to the Leavenworth program that would begin in August 1925. As Fox Conner had done 20 years earlier, Eisenhower would bypass his service branch's school and go straight to Leavenworth.

Conner's move made waves. "It sort of burned them up at the Chief of Infantry Office," Eisenhower wrote. One officer there bluntly told him: "You will probably fail." Eisenhower recalled receiving letters from his classmates warning him that he had "ruined" himself, and that he would not be welcomed back to the infantry. Eisenhower also worried about his readiness for Leavenworth. "This was like being sent to college without a secondary school education," Eisenhower wrote in *At Ease*.

When Eisenhower queried Conner as to the preparatory work he should undertake, Conner told his protégé to "quit worrying." Conner added: "You are better prepared for Leavenworth than any other man that has graduated from Benning because you have had to do the work required at Leavenworth." Conner reminded Eisenhower that they had operated Camp Gaillard in Panama as a field command; for 3 years he had drafted daily orders using the five-paragraph field order technique emphasized at Leavenworth. Conner told Eisenhower that he would "feel no sense of inferiority." He added: "If you fail, it will be your own fault."

According to historians Carlo D'Este and Timothy Nenninger, Conner's bureaucratic maneuverings were actually unnecessary since General Farnsworth had already submitted Eisenhower's name for attendance at Leavenworth.[10] While Eisenhower's move to the recruiting service may well have been a dangerous and unneeded gamble, it was the bet that Conner placed and Eisenhower embraced: "I was ready to fly," Eisenhower wrote, "and needed no airplane."

★ ★ ★ ★ ★

Airplanes were also much on Fox Conner's mind in the latter part of 1925.

Since the end of the Great War, Air Service officers such as Brigadier General William "Billy" Mitchell, had forcefully advocated for expansion of the nation's air force. The outspoken Mitchell had grabbed headlines in 1921 when he demonstrated that airplanes could sink a battleship. In 1923, Secretary Weeks appointed a board, chaired by Major General William Lassiter, to devise a proposal to upgrade American air power. The Lassiter Board set forth an ambitious plan to expand the Air Service, but provided no analysis of its cost. Frustrated by inaction on the Lassiter plan, General Mitchell took his case to the public in newspaper and magazine articles in which he became increasingly critical of the Army and Navy bureaucracies. Mitchell crossed the line in September 1925 when he denounced the "incompetency, criminal negligence, and almost treasonable administration" of the War Department. President Coolidge personally ordered Mitchell's court-martial.[11]

Against the backdrop of the controversy involving General Mitchell, Coolidge convened his own President's Aircraft Board in September 1925 to formulate a comprehensive military aviation policy.[12] Coolidge directed the board to report its recommendations by November, in order to coincide with Mitchell's trial. Unlike the Lassiter Board, the President's Board also addressed the hard realities of cost. As the Army's chief financial officer, Fox Conner provided that analysis.

"Upon even a casual examination," Conner told the President's Board in his October 16, 1925 testimony, "it is apparent that the one difficulty in putting into execution the provisions of the Lassiter Board program is that of finances." More plainly, he told the board: "It is purely a question of money."[13] Conner explained that the Army had already given its Air Service "first priority" and had "neglected and curtailed many necessary things in order to put every possible dollar" into upgrading the nation's air power. He explained further that the Air Service had received a 25 percent increase in funding from the previous fiscal year while the rest of the Army's operations had been cut in order to fund that expansion.

Conner estimated that full implementation of the Lassiter plan would cost at least $90,298,784.50, annually, over the following 10 years. He pointed out that the Army's total appropriations for fiscal year 1926 were only $260,757,250.00 and that 40,000 soldiers were living in "war-time shacks" because of the lack of funds to upgrade housing. Conner then made his point: "There would be little left of the rest of the Regular Army in the United States if the Lassiter Board program were put into effect without increasing total appropriations."

The board members questioned Conner concerning the differences between his cost projections and the lower estimated cost of $65,000,000.00 per year offered by the Army's chief of aviation. Conner explained: "When anybody in the War Department has a pet project that they want to see, they can always do it for a less amount of money than it costs when you put the thing down in a cold-blooded, realistic way." Representative Carl Vinson asked Conner whether his much higher estimate was a simple application of the political principle that "you ask for more than you generally expect to get." Conner responded: "That has not been true lately, Mr. Vinson. We have not expected very much and we have been met on that."

The President's Board ultimately recommended a five-year plan for aeronautical expansion. President Coolidge, in his annual budget message, requested an increase in total military appropriations to fund the program, as Conner had emphasized.[14]

While military aviation made progress, Conner continued his efforts to stem the deterioration in other parts of the Army. In a letter to "My Dear Georgie," Conner wrote his friend, George Patton: "I'm afraid the poor old Regular (Army) is in for hard sledding. Our whole trouble is one of money. I think we have ourselves largely to blame for we have, in the past at least, wasted a H—[sic] of a lot of money."[15]

In testimony given in December 1925, Conner again tried to focus congressional attention on the Army's ammunition supply.[16] Conner warned the nation's lawmakers that the nation's entire artillery stock was equivalent to the ordnance expended in just six weeks during the Meuse–Argonne offensive. "On that ammunition," Conner cautioned, "we shall have to depend, for the most part, for the first eleven months of a war." Conner also reported the inadequacy of ammunition hastily manufactured at the war's end in 1918, including "a number of cases where the bullet will not leave the gun."

In January 1926, Conner gave further congressional testimony in which he warned of the dire shortages in essential gear such as clothing, boots, leggings, and blankets.[17] Khaki, so ubiquitous in the next war, had been eliminated from the war reserve due to lack of funds. Conner reminded the subcommittee that, when the nation had attempted to rapidly mobilize for war in 1917, the draft had to be delayed because the inductees could not be properly clothed. The government, Conner emphasized, was repeating the same mistake made a decade earlier. "We hold nothing in reserve than can be procured immediately upon the outbreak of war in sufficient quantities," he told the lawmakers.

The man who in December 1924 had professed ignorance of supply matters had learned a great deal by 1926, when he wrote an article that provided a comprehensive overview of operations of his G-4 section.[18] Conner began the article by citing military history, particularly Napoleon's dictum that "an army travels on its stomach." In Conner's view, war had become "truly a struggle between whole nations in arms" that required "all the resources that scientific and engineering ability can devise and produce in this constantly developing industrial age." He again sounded caution as to the Army's financial constraints: "Only by the utmost economy in the expenditure of maintenance funds has it been possible to make one dollar do the work of two."

A parsimonious Congress paid little heed to Conner's requests for greater funding. In October 1925, though, lawmakers did approve Conner's promotion to the rank of major general—the highest peacetime rank that an officer, other than the chief of staff, could hold. Conner received a congratulatory letter from John J. Pershing, who had unsuccessfully sought Conner's promotion to that rank in 1918. "If I may say so," Pershing wrote, "I think it would have come a little earlier if I had remained as Chief of Staff."[19]

Conner's climb within the Army's hierarchy continued on March 9, 1926, when Chief of Staff John Hines appointed Conner to the deputy chief of staff position, as Hines himself had been while he served as Pershing's heir apparent.[20] Even before Conner's elevation to the Army's second-highest position, he had functioned as "acting" chief of staff in place of the often-absent Hines. Conner, for instance had accompanied President and Mrs. Coolidge to a wreath-laying ceremony at the Tomb of the Unknown Soldier to observe Armistice Day in 1925.[21]

Bug Conner wrote in her memoir that her husband frequently handled the duties of Chief of Staff Hines, whom Bug described as being "not very well." Historians such as Carlo D'Este and James J. Cooke confirm that Conner "all but ran the Army" in place of Hines, who was said to have been "frequently absent" and "not in the best of health after the war." Considering that General Hines lived to the age of 100, the references to his poor health may have been euphemistic. According to author Merle Miller, Conner's son, Tommy, recalled his father saying that General Hines was "far gone in drink."

Fox Conner may have also turned to alcohol to deal with the pressures of his new position. His grandson, Macpherson Conner, recounted family stories of his grandfather's seeking solace in Martinis to deal with the frustration created by the demands for increased military capability in the face of inadequate funding. According to Macpherson Conner, his grandfather would go home so red-faced with anger that Bug grew concerned about Fox's health. The social obligations of the deputy chief of staff's position also wore on Conner. Bug Conner recalled that her husband cautioned her "not to speak to people of note, as they usually sat on you." Another irritation for the West Pointer Fox Conner may have been that officers on duty in the War Department wore business suits, rather than uniforms, to accommodate the national de-emphasis of things military.[22]

As the general staff's second-highest officer, Conner continued to wrestle with the Army's financial woes. He devised a plan to raise money by selling bases he considered no longer of military value, including the Presidio near San Francisco. Conner also proposed the sale of Governors Island in New York Harbor, where he and the other members of the original AEF staff had assembled for their journey to France aboard the *Baltic* in 1917. In testimony to a Senate committee, Conner estimated that more than $80,000,000 would result from sale of the surplus properties—enough to put the Army's housing construction program "on easy street," as he put it.[23]

The *New York Times* acknowledged the "wrench to Army traditions" that would follow the sale of such venerable facilities as Governors Island, which then housed the headquarters of the Second Corps Area, commanded by General Charles P. Summerall. The newspaper nonetheless recommended that Congress "give patient and watchful consideration to General Fox Conner's proposal."

Conner's idea nearly backfired. Upon learning of Conner's view that Governors Island was no longer needed for military purposes, New York congressman Fiorello LaGuardia argued that the 1800 act by which the State of New York had ceded Governors Island to the United States government also provided for reversion to state ownership if the property became unneeded by the military. "There will be no sale of Governors Island," LaGuardia told the *New York Times*, "so the General Staff and real estate speculators had better forget it." The War Department dropped Conner's proposal.[24]

Deputy Chief of Staff Conner also continued to advocate for the increased funding needed to modernize America's air force. In 1926, Congress passed the Air Corps Act, which implemented the recommendations of the President's Aircraft Board, before whom Conner had testified the previous year. To secure the money needed to pay for the program, Conner told a Senate appropriations committee in 1926 that unless military spending was increased by $55,000,000 per year, implementation of the Air Corps Act would "ruin the Army beyond any hope of recovery." Appropriations increased, although not by as much as the deputy chief of staff had recommended.[25]

Conner also took on the task of revising the curriculum at West Point, where his son, Tommy, was a cadet. General Conner thought that West Point was "not sufficiently in touch with other institutions of learning," particularly in its emphasis upon engineering-related subjects at a time when few graduates actually became engineers. At Conner's urging, the War Department ordered a thorough curriculum review in 1926; very little changed.[26]

Conner also assisted George Patton's effort in 1926 to become the commandant of cadets at West Point. Two of Conner's more influential West Point classmates, Adjutant General Robert Davis and Chief of Cavalry Malin Craig, also supported Patton's candidacy. Despite the efforts of the illustrious alumni of the Class of '98, the commandant position went instead to the personal selection of the West Point superintendent.[27]

★ ★ ★ ★ ★

Although Conner was unable to aid George Patton's ambitions in 1926, his earlier efforts to advance Dwight Eisenhower's career succeeded magnificently.

"Fox Conner had been correct," Eisenhower wrote in *At Ease*. As his mentor had predicted, Eisenhower performed well in the rigorous Leavenworth program. Eisenhower discovered that he had indeed already mastered, through his work as Conner's executive officer, the essential staff officer skills taught at Leavenworth: assessment of the situation at hand, formulation of the method for addressing it, and communication of orders clearly and concisely. The Leavenworth course also continued to emphasize the lessons of military history, which Eisenhower had extensively studied in Panama under Conner's tutelage.[28]

As historian Robert Ferrell, the editor of *The Eisenhower Diaries*, put it: "Conner had taught him all he needed to know." In June 1926, Dwight Eisenhower graduated from the Command and General Staff College at Leavenworth ranked first among the 245 officers in his class—a remarkable accomplishment for an officer who had not attended his branch school.[29]

As a direct result of Fox Conner's professional guidance—and bureaucratic maneuvering—Dwight Eisenhower evolved from a mediocre football coach who had faced a court-martial in 1921 into one of the Army's rising stars by 1926. "Had I been denied the good fortune of knowing Fox Conner," Eisenhower wrote," the course of my career might have been radically different."[30]

Contemporary Army officers have criticized Conner's favoritism of Eisenhower as "the type of mentorship [that] cannot be condoned in the Army," and as an "example of what senior leaders should not do."[31] Eisenhower admitted that "to the cynic, all this may seem proof of 'it's not what you know, it's who you know.'" Referring to General Conner, Eisenhower also recognized: "because I did know him, I did go to Leavenworth," which became what the future general and president termed the "watershed in my life."[32]

Eisenhower would learn that Conner was not yet done helping him.

The Army's infantry branch, no longer led by General Farnsworth in 1926, did accept Leavenworth's top graduate back into its ranks. The new chief of infantry, Major General Robert H. Allen, then promptly assigned Eisenhower to Fort Benning, where Farnsworth had initially sent him.[33] In June 1926, Eisenhower took command of a battalion in the 24th Infantry. According to Eisenhower biographer Jean Edward Smith, the Army treated the 24th Infantry (manned by African-American troops) as a "penal regiment for white officers who had screwed up." Eisenhower also again coached football, at no extra pay. General Farnsworth may have been gone, but the infantry had not forgotten the Conner–Eisenhower end-run around its leader.

More positively for Eisenhower, the War Department granted his application to attend the Army War College class, set to convene in autumn 1927. No evidence exists that Conner intervened to secure the War College appointment, or needed to, given Eisenhower's strong showing at Leavenworth. But Conner again brought his influence to bear to secure a choice assignment for his protégé as he awaited the start of the War College course.

In 1927, the retired John J. Pershing headed the American Battle Monuments Commission, which established cemeteries and other monuments in France to the Americans who had fought and died there. Pershing decided to produce a travel guide that would not only direct visitors to the memorials, but also provide detailed information on the battles the AEF had waged. As the 10th anniversary of America's declaration of war approached, Pershing needed an efficient and hard-working assistant to write the book quickly and accurately. On Fox Conner's recommendation, Pershing chose Major Eisenhower.[34]

In *A Guide to the American Battle Fields in Europe*, Eisenhower condensed several voluminous postwar reports into a readable and informative history of the fighting waged in the areas of the French countryside where the monuments were built. Eisenhower's 1927 guidebook bears strong resemblance, in both style and content, to Fox Conner's 1919 Operations Section report. Eisenhower included casualty figures and wartime photographs to instill a greater appreciation of the sacrifices made by America's soldiers. For practicality, he provided turn-by-turn driving instructions along a designated tour route, information on available hotels, an explanation of French road signage, and a chart for converting kilometers and liters into miles and gallons.

Eisenhower's brief assignment with Pershing's commission provided him an important entrée to the ex-Chaumont clique in which his mentor, Conner, circulated. Eisenhower also developed an important ally in Pershing, who wrote Chief of Infantry Allen to tout Eisenhower's "splendid service," "unusual intelligence," and "constant devotion to duty." As biographer Jean Edward Smith wrote, Eisenhower had been "admitted to the ranks of the chosen few"—a status he would not have achieved without Fox Conner.

The years 1926 and 1927 clearly marked an important turning point for Dwight Eisenhower. Fox Conner's career also took some interesting turns.

In September 1926, General Hines stepped down from the chief of staff position. Conner, who still served as the Army's deputy chief of staff, emerged as a candidate to replace Hines.[35] Others under consideration included Dennis Nolan, who had served as the AEF's chief of intelligence, and Conner's classmate Malin Craig. Charles P. Summerall and Douglas MacArthur, two field generals with whom Conner had clashed during the war, made the short list as well.

Several factors operated in favor of Conner's appointment. Dwight F. Davishad become Coolidge's secretary of war following the death of John Weeks in 1925.[36] Conner and Davis each held a chief of operations position during the war—Davis for the 35th Division and Conner for the AEF. Since Conner's return to Washington, the two men had worked together in the war department, particularly once Conner had become the de facto chief of staff due to General Hines' absences. Conner provided an option to maintain continuity in the Army's leadership during a challenging period. President Coolidge's 1924 appointment of Hines had also established the precedent of elevating the deputy chief over more senior generals.

None of that mattered.

On Secretary Davis' recommendation, Coolidge appointed Charles P. Summerall, the Army's most senior general, as chief of staff. *Time* magazine noted that Secretary Davis was a "staunch believer in the seniority rule." The *New York Times* praised Summerall's appointment, as well as the general's "unsurpassed record" as a field commander during the war. The newspaper opined that "no staff officer knows the Army better than he does"—a veiled swipe at the Chaumont men, Nolan and Conner.

Summerall's appointment also reflected the decline of John J. Pershing's influence upon President Coolidge, who could not have been pleased with the performance of Pershing's last candidate, General Hines. The *New York Times* reported that Pershing had not been consulted about the choice to replace Hines. *Time* magazine expressed delight that "the Pershing crowd" in the War Department, which had been "so potent" at the time of Hines' appointment, had failed to place "another Pershing favorite" in control of the Army.

If President Coolidge intended to clean house in the American Army's high command, he chose the right man in General Charles P. Summerall.

In notes made around 1950, Summerall observed that the former Chaumont staff officers who held most of the general staff's top positions at the time of his appointment "held the prejudice of GHQ against me as being only a "combat officer." Summerall was not among friends, and he knew it. "No doubt they resented my selection," he wrote in his notes. The new chief also resented the failure of the assistant chiefs to attend department meetings. "It was manifest that they came reluctantly and, no doubt, felt that they need not come at all."[37]

Fox Conner and Charles Summerall, simply put, intensely disliked each other. The mutual loathing dated back to their heated argument in 1917 over divisional artillery strength, and had continued through incidents such as the Race for Sedan in 1918 and Conner's 1926 Governors Island proposal to relocate Summerall's Second Corps Area headquarters. As Bug Conner diplomatically put it, the two men were "fundamentally uncongenial." Although Conner remained the nominal deputy chief of staff, his status within the general staff had dramatically changed once General Summerall became chief of staff. For example, Fox Conner had accompanied President Coolidge on Armistice Day 1925 to a wreath-laying ceremony at the Tomb of the Unknown Soldier. In 1926, Conner marked the occasion with a speech to a Boy Scout troop; nonetheless, Conner delivered an eloquent address, which was printed, between poems by Rupert Brooke and Edith Wharton, in a 1927 anthology of patriotic writings.

The new chief "did not expect full loyalty" from his new subordinates, nor did he show it. Throughout early 1927, Summerall replaced three of the four assistant chiefs, plus the head of the War Plans Division, with this own cohorts. For example, Major General Frank Parker, who had led the almost-disastrous Race for Sedan in compliance with Summerall's wartime orders, replaced Malin Craig as the Army's G-3.

Fox Conner was also gone by April 1927.[38] Summerall named his "loyal friend," Major General Briant H. Wells, to replace Conner as deputy chief of staff. Wells had been Omar Bundy's chief of staff and one of the key figures duped by Conner in the Belfort Ruse. Not everyone in the Army, though, shared Summerall's disdain for his departed deputy. One service journal praised Conner's "impartiality and fairness" in making difficult financial decisions. "His devotion to the multiple tasks accruing to the Deputy Chief of Staff have [sic] made 'hard work' and 'Conner' synonymous in Army circles."

Fox Conner had already devised an exit strategy. In March 1927, the New York Times reported that Conner would take command of the Fifth Corps Area in the Upper Midwest, an assignment he had arranged before General Summerall took office. But within a week of the article's publication, Conner received different orders to take command of the 1st Division, based at Fort Hamilton, New York. Conner's only previous field command had been over his undermanned brigade in Panama. Although no specific documentation exists, it is plausible that Chief of Staff Summerall (who had commanded a full battle corps during the Great War) blocked Conner's effort to obtain a corps area command without his having first commanded at least a division.[39]

Fortunately for Conner, an attractive divisional command—in Hawaii—would become available later in 1927. Until that time, he and Bug settled in for a brief stay at Fort Hamilton, where they had begun their married life. The assignment also placed the Conners near to Brandreth Lake and to their son Tommy, who had both graduation from West Point and a wedding upcoming.

Chief of Staff Summerall delivered the commencement address at Tommy Conner's graduation on June 14, 1927.[40] Summerall discarded his prepared remarks in favor of a rousing extemporaneous speech honoring aviator Charles Lindbergh, who had returned the previous day from his historic transatlantic flight. The New York Times reported that the audience burst into applause and cheers that lasted several minutes. No record exists of Fox Conner's thoughts as he watched his rival bask in the limelight at Tommy's West Point graduation.

Following Tommy Conner's wedding to Muriel Macpherson on July 6, 1927, General and Mrs. Conner spent the rest of the summer on leave in the Adirondacks. Bug recalled that her husband "was in an exhausted and irritable state" at that time and "badly needed his two months at Brandreth."[41]

Fox Conner had indeed weathered a tumultuous period. In the summer of 1926, Conner had been in effective control of the Army's general staff and a serious candidate to be named its top officer. By the summer of 1927, he had been removed from the general staff in a widespread purge of officers who had served in Pershing's inner circle. Conner had also been denied a prominent corps-level command, and he had watched a man he detested assume control of the Army. His new assignment in Hawaii, however, offered an opportunity to distance himself from General Summerall and to enhance his own credentials as a field commander.

Fox Conner also had time on his side. The 60-year-old Summerall would face mandatory retirement in four years, when Conner would be only 56, and in prime position for appointment as the Army's chief of staff, particularly if the nation elected a president other than Coolidge in 1928.

As he had done in the long years before the Great War, Fox Conner needed to bide his time. He now had a paradise in which to do it. In September 1927, Fox and Bug Conner, accompanied by their youngest daughter Florence, sailed for Hawaii.

CHAPTER 12

THIRD TIME THE CHARM?

America stands today, in a military way, not among the great powers of the earth, but seventeenth on the list. I have repeatedly said of late, and I say again: It is no time to further emasculate the forces behind the flag.

—Fox Conner, May 19, 1934[1]

The Conners passed through the Panama Canal on their way to Hawaii in 1927. By then, the Army had abandoned Camp Gaillard, but Fox and Bug spoke briefly with old acquaintances, who greeted them as their vessel made its way through the locks.[2]

Other friends welcomed the Conners to Hawaii on October 7, 1927. George and Beatrice Patton met the ship, then escorted Fox, Bug, and Florence to their new station on the island of Oahu, home of the American naval base at Pearl Harbor. Conner assumed command of the Army's Hawaiian Division, a component of the 14,000-strong Hawaiian Department.[3] Conner served briefly as division commander before the War Department promoted him to command the entire Hawaiian Department on January 25, 1928. The *Honolulu Star-Bulletin* described an "impressive" ceremony in which General Conner strode between double rows of sentries and into department headquarters at Fort Shafter as marching music played and a salute gun boomed.

America's Pacific strategy centered upon holding Pearl Harbor. "As long as we hold Oahu," Conner said in one speech, "no enemy can operate in the Pacific." But America's war plans presumed the existence of 90,000 reinforcements the Army did not actually have. In February 1928, a joint Army–Navy planning board warned that the "present garrison of Hawaii cannot secure Oahu against capture by a strong expeditionary force." The board also pointed out the possibility of a "sudden raid" against Pearl Harbor.[4]

Conner's troops participated in joint training maneuvers with the Navy in the spring of 1928.[5] Conner watched from the bridge of the battleship USS *California* as aircraft launched from the USS *Langley*, the nation's first aircraft carrier, simulated an attack on Pearl Harbor.[6] The *New York Times* reported that "swarms of planes" from the *Langley* left before daylight. The aircraft achieved the element of surprise and, with support from a powerful naval bombardment, destroyed the American fleet at anchor in Pearl Harbor—an ominous portent of things to come.

In Conner's view, the 1928 maneuvers starkly illustrated the deficiencies in national defense caused by the previous 10 years of inadequate funding—a topic he addressed in a 1928 article on Army conditions in Hawaii. Conner pointed out the Army's inability, due to lack of money, to carry out needed training exercises and to supply adequate housing for troops.[7]

Conner also addressed the inadequacy of military spending in a 1928 article titled "The National Defense." True to form, Conner grounded his thesis in history, beginning with the War of 1812 and proceeding through the Mexican War, Civil War, Spanish–American War, and the recently concluded Great War. Conner quoted each era's leading lawmakers, who had all argued—shortly before the outbreak of war—that military spending constituted an unnecessary waste. Conner pointed out that the same views prevailed in the America of the 1920s, again imperiling the nation's defense.[8]

Whenever visiting dignitaries such as the secretary of war and members of Congress arrived on "inspection" trips to Hawaii, Conner pressed his case for increased funding, particularly to implement the 1926 Air Corps Act that his testimony had helped shape. Conner's efforts bore modest success. The Hawaiian Department obtained more modern aircraft and upgraded its aviation facilities. Conner also improved the department's barracks, hospital buildings, and mess halls. His troops performed well in 1929 maneuvers during which Conner presented increasingly complex tactical scenarios to assess the initiative of his subordinate commanders.[9]

Apart from having to attend obligatory social functions, which the general avoided whenever possible, Fox and Bug Conner embraced life in Hawaii.[10] The Conners particularly enjoyed the Army's "rest camp" for officers, which was located in the volcanic mountains of the Big Island of Hawaii. They also rented a cottage on Oahu's Kailua Beach, where they gathered with friends to enjoy the surf on the weekends, as well as *okolehau*, a native alcoholic spirit distilled from the root of the ti plant.

The years in Hawaii from 1927 through 1930 brought memorable events to the Conner family.[11] Bug's parents died within six weeks of each other in the spring of 1928. The Conners also welcomed four grandchildren: twin granddaughters Virginia and Beatrice Vida, born to Betsey and Frank Vida, and grandsons Fox Conner, III and Macpherson Conner, the sons of Muriel and Tommy Conner.

Another significant event in the Conner family occurred in June 1929 when Tommy Conner resigned his officer's commission.[12] Neither Tommy nor Muriel wanted to live the transient life on Army posts that Tommy had known as a boy. After leaving the service, Tommy first went to work for Radio Corporation of America (RCA), where James G. Harbord served as president. Tommy's employment by his father's former Chaumont colleague suggests at least Fox Conner's acquiescence, if not influence. Tommy later became president of Allcock Manufacturing, the Brandreth family's company, and moved to Ossining.

Florence Conner suffered a scare in Hawaii when she awoke one night to the sight of an intruder in her bedroom. After sentries apprehended the man (one of Conner's soldiers), the enraged father said, in a voice that Bug described as "enough to curdle anyone's blood": "You can thank your God that I did not catch you in my daughter's room." Florence had a much more pleasant encounter in Hawaii with Lieutenant Edgar "Joe" Gans, one of her father's aides. Like her sister Betsey, Florence fell in love in the tropics with a young officer under her father's command. Florence and Joe wed in 1931.[13]

Fox and Bug Conner also grew close to another of the general's aides, Lieutenant Trimble Brown, whom Tommy Conner had known in boarding school. The socially adept lieutenant helped offset the general's dislike of entertaining. Brown lived in the Conner residence and, according to Bug, became "like a son" to the Conners.[14]

★ ★ ★ ★ ★

While in Hawaii, Fox Conner continued to promote the career of George Patton. In 1928, Conner wrote letters backing Patton's effort to have the Army adopt his invention of a sled-mounted machine gun. As Patton's commanding officer, Conner also bestowed on his old friend a glowing performance evaluation. According to Patton biographer Martin Blumenson, Conner's support proved "exceedingly important" to Patton's career in the era following the Great War.[15]

Dwight Eisenhower's career also progressed steadily in the late 1920s.[16] Following his June 1928 War College graduation, Eisenhower had the choice either to serve within the War Department or to rejoin Pershing's American Battle Monuments Commission—this time in France. "My choice was easy," Eisenhower wrote. As the Conner family had done in 1911, the Eisenhowers spent a year in Europe.

In France, Eisenhower studied the areas of the Western Front he had written about in 1927; he then revised his guidebook. According to historian Carlo D'Este, "Eisenhower's sense of history had been so well honed by Fox Conner," that he was able to fully grasp the significance of the sites. According to biographer Piers Brendon, when Eisenhower saw the tens of thousands of graves in the military cemeteries, his mentor's prediction of a new war in Europe came to mind. "Fox Conner must be wrong," Eisenhower pondered. "Men can't be that crazy so soon again."

In late summer of 1929, Eisenhower received orders to report to the War Department in Washington, D.C. as an assistant to Brigadier General George Van Horn Moseley, another former member of the Chaumont inner circle. In mid-September 1929, the Eisenhower family sailed home on the *Leviathan*, the same liner that had borne Fox Conner home from the war.

★ ★ ★ ★ ★

In October 1929, the American stock market crashed to spawn the tumult of the Great Depression. Fox and Bug Conner sharply felt its effects. For years, they had saved money to build a retirement home at Brandreth Lake, only to lose most of it in 1929.[17]

The silver lining was that the 55-year-old Conner was not ready to retire. In July 1930, the War Department announced Conner's promotion to commanding general of the First Corps Area, headquartered in Boston—a move that placed him among the ranks of the Army's top field commanders.[18] The Army chief of staff position would also come open in November 1930 when General Summerall retired.

President Herbert Hoover, elected in 1928, would appoint the next chief. As the Great Depression worsened in 1930, Hoover focused mostly on economic policy. He left the selection of the next chief of staff to his secretary of war, Patrick J. Hurley, who had served in the AEF as an assistant to First Army's chief of artillery.[19]

In 1930, Douglas MacArthur held seniority among the major generals who could serve a full four-year term as chief of staff. MacArthur's appointment, though, was far from assured. Hoover believed that "the choice of chief of staff by seniority led only to dead ends." MacArthur had disappointed Hoover the previous year when the general declined the president's request to oversee comprehensive flood-control projects as chief of the Army Corps of Engineers. Secretary Hurley also had his qualms. According to MacArthur biographers Clayton James and William Manchester, Hurley thought poorly of MacArthur's being divorced and said: "A man who couldn't hold his woman shouldn't be chief of staff."

Fox Conner emerged as an alternative to Douglas MacArthur for the chief of staff position. Conner offered impeccable general staff credentials, having served as *de facto* head of the Army under Hines. By contrast, except for a term as West Point superintendent from 1919 through 1922, MacArthur's service had been entirely as a field commander. MacArthur lacked Conner's experience in waging the type of war that mattered at the time—the battle of the budget.

Conner also enjoyed the support of John J. Pershing. Following the Great War, Pershing had assisted the European food relief work that had first brought Herbert Hoover to national prominence. The two enjoyed a good relationship. But Pershing was preoccupied with his battle monuments work; he had also begun work on his memoirs. Pershing did not meet personally with either Hoover or Hurley to push Conner's candidacy.

Meanwhile, MacArthur's backers, including former chief of staff Peyton March, actively lobbied Secretary Hurley. MacArthur helped his own cause by sending the secretary a telegram praising his Philippine policy as "the most statesmanlike utterance that has emanated from the American Government in many decades." In August of 1930, Secretary Hurley decided to appoint MacArthur.

Only then did Pershing meet with Hoover and Hurley. In response to Pershing's request that the secretary reconsider his decision, Hurley responded that, during the war, he had served under a "brilliantly successful expeditionary forces commander who tolerated no interference in the selection of subordinate commanders." He would do the same. Pershing could only smile and admit to Hoover: "Mr. President, he's one of my boys all right. While I don't agree with him, we will probably have to let him make his own mistakes."

According to historian Robert Ferrell, a strained relationship had continued to exist, even after the war, between MacArthur and the "so-called Chaumont crowd, the officers such as Fox Conner."[20] Once again, mutual animosity would separate Conner from the chief of staff who commanded him.

The Conner family, accompanied by aide Trimble Brown, sailed from Hawaii on August 9, 1930. On their way to Boston, they toured the Canadian Rockies and Montreal, where Bug made Fox go shopping for a new suit. "Much against his will, we dragged him from store to store," Bug recalled, "but when he put on his new clothes, even he was well satisfied."[21]

After a leave at Brandreth Lake, General Conner took command of the First Corps Area on October 7, 1930. Because of financial restrictions, the Army did not provide quarters for the commanding general, so the Conners found an apartment in Cambridge, near Harvard University and an Episcopal monastery. Bug made friends with one of the cowl-wearing monks, but she recalled that "Fox used to shudder when some of these novitiates passed him on the street."

Fox Conner soon learned that he, as a high-ranking military officer during the 1930s, was almost as removed from the American mainstream as were his monastic neighbors. As noted in historian Russell Weigley's *History of the United States Army*, a "gloomy, negative kind of pacifism, automatically hostile to any measure which might improve the Army" prevailed in the nation during the Great Depression. Bug recalled that when her husband opened a bank account, the teller "eyed him with great suspicion" and "was not impressed." Despite a number of public appearances by Conner that were covered by the *The Boston Daily Globe* newspaper, Bug wrote that "the Proper Bostonians [did] not even know we were there."

Worse than the Army's low social standing, its military capability had further eroded. President Hoover's fundamental defense policy was to take advantage of "the great ocean moats between us and possible enemies," and to rely upon a "small skeleton army capable of quick expansion." Hoover, who favored international disarmament, was unsympathetic to the voices within the Army who called for greater military preparedness. An editorial in *The Boston Daily Globe* observed: "With no units of the Regular Army left in Massachusetts more than a few caretakers and a clerical force, Maj. Gen. Fox Conner, commandant of the First Corps Area, must have plenty of time to ponder the days when he was chief of staff [*sic*] to an Army of about 2,000,000 men."[22]

But Conner did not look back to the last war. He continued to urge preparedness for the next one. Whenever possible, whether speaking to soldiers, veterans' groups, social organizations, and even high school students, Fox Conner argued that the nation's fervent desire to avoid war would not prevent one. "We want no war," he told one group, "but we won't avoid it by lying down."[23]

Conner did what he could to prepare his troops.[24] He conducted regular inspections of training camps and bases. In July 1931, National Guard forces under Conner's command underwent training exercises that *The Boston Daily Globe* described as "the most exacting military problem ever given a National Guard organization to solve." In September, General Conner commanded one of the forces in Regular

Army maneuvers held in Vermont. He secured twenty-eight new tanks for his corps—no small accomplishment given the financial constraints of the times. Conner also arranged for professors at Harvard to present a series of eight lectures to his troops on subjects such as world economics and international trade.

Conner also continued to deliver his own lectures. He addressed the 1931 Army War College in a wide-ranging question-and-answer session, reminiscent of his Socratic discussions with Eisenhower in Panama.[25] One of the AEF's chief planners told the class that "the only way of avoiding changes in a plan is to plan to stay at home." He also spoke of the psychological importance of quickly replacing combat losses, so that the surviving soldiers would become "heroes" to the new men rather than allowing the veterans to ruminate over how they "saw their buddy's brains blown out and all smeared with blood."

Conner's views also reflected what Professor Weigley described as the "sense of helplessness and resignation" that hung over the American Army in the early 1930s. For example, in response to one question, Conner doubted that the Army would "ever have tanks enough to use along the whole front." He told his audience that "in the state that motorization is in now, everything, with the exception of staff cars in the division, should be animal drawn." In response to a question on the proper method to overcome enemy machine guns, he demurred: "I am proposing to the young men who are going to fight the next war that *they* find some way to overcome them."

Conner's reference to "the next war" proved timely. He addressed the War College on September 18, 1931—the same day that Japanese and Chinese troops clashed in Manchuria to ignite the Asian war that engulfed the United States 10 years later.

As the presidential election neared in 1932, the Army and Conner were challenged anew. President Hoover cut military spending by 10 percent, which shrunk the nation's army to the world's seventeenth largest (Portugal had a larger army). Soldiers took a 15 percent pay cut.[26] That same year, Conner's health problems recurred. He underwent surgery for removal of a tumor in his sinuses. During the summer, he suffered acute abdominal pain, weakness, and weight loss. Bug recalled that Fox lost a pound each day. Although Conner feared he had stomach cancer, his doctors could not determine a cause.

★ ★ ★ ★ ★

Dwight Eisenhower noted Fox Conner's health problems in his 1932 diary. Eisenhower also wrote that Conner had "held a place in my affections for many years that no other, not a relative, could obtain." According to Ike's son John S.D. Eisenhower, "Conner's aura was felt in the Eisenhower household for a long time"; whenever his father referred to "The General," he always meant Fox Conner.[27]

Although Conner lived in Boston and Eisenhower in Washington, D.C., the two had not resumed frequent personal contact after Conner's return from Hawaii. Eisenhower had, instead, begun to gravitate into the inner circle of Conner's rival, Douglas MacArthur.

As he had in Panama, Eisenhower developed a strong personal relationship with his superior officer, General George van Horn Moseley. "Among the senior officers in the Army," Eisenhower wrote in his diary, Moseley had become not only "a true friend," but also his "most intimate friend." In 1930, Chief of Staff MacArthur had elevated General Moseley to the deputy chief of staff position that Fox Conner once held. By 1932, Eisenhower had become a top assistant to MacArthur himself. "As long as he stays in the Army," Eisenhower wrote of MacArthur, "I am one of the people he has earmarked for his gang."

Douglas MacArthur made headlines in the summer of 1932 when war veterans converged on Washington, D.C. to demand early payment of a cash bonus due them in 1945. When some of the "bonus marchers" attempted to occupy federal buildings, Hoover directed the Army to restore order. MacArthur, who believed that a communist revolution was imminent, sent cavalry commanded by George Patton to drive out the veterans.[28] The chief of staff donned his dress uniform to command the action personally. Photographs of mounted cavalry routing unarmed civilians, who may have been their former comrades-in-arms, became a public relations nightmare for President Hoover, who faced an already difficult re-election bid against his Democratic challenger, Franklin D. Roosevelt.

"Well, Felix," Roosevelt told his aide Felix Frankfurter, "this will elect me."

★ ★ ★ ★ ★

Roosevelt trounced Hoover. Upon taking office in March 1933, President Roosevelt appointed Utah Governor George H. Dern as his secretary of war. Dern had no military experience of any kind. "I haven't any plan about anything," the new secretary told the *Army and Navy Journal* in March 1933. "I didn't come in with any idea of putting ideas of my own into effect."

In mid-March, Secretary Dern flew to Boston to meet Fox Conner and to inspect nearby Fort Devens. *The Boston Daily Globe's* coverage of the inspection included a photograph of General Conner and Secretary Dern striding toward a solider in the honor guard, who was struggling with his rifle. "The secretary seems to see the humor of the situation," the caption read, "but the General apparently is thinking some good old Army cuss-words."[29]

Roosevelt's campaign theme song had been "Happy Days Are Here Again," but the slogan did not apply to the United States Army.[30] To fund the president's New Deal's domestic spending programs, Roosevelt's budget office announced plans to slash military spending by one-third (approximately $90,000,000). In a heated confrontation, Chief of Staff MacArthur told the new president: "When an American boy, lying in the mud with an enemy bayonet through his belly and an enemy foot on his dying throat, spat out his last curse, I want the name not to be MacArthur but Roosevelt." MacArthur tendered his resignation, but Roosevelt would not accept it.

Military spending in the first year of the Roosevelt Administration plummeted to $225,000.00, which crippled the American Army. In 1933—the same year that Adolf Hitler came to power and began the rapid rearmament of Germany for his *blitzkrieg* (lightning war) conquest of Europe—lack of funds caused the American Army to halt development of its own air and motorized ground forces. Army units could not afford to conduct field training, or even target practice. To save ammunition, Fox Conner discontinued the customary thirteen-gun salute given him when he arrived at a military post.

With the United States Army unable to function as an effective military force, President Roosevelt converted it into an instrument of his domestic relief programs.

In April 1933, the Roosevelt Administration established the Civilian Conservation Corps (CCC) to shift hundreds of thousands of unemployed young men off welfare rolls and into government-paid public works jobs. As implied by its name, the corps was organized on a military model: employees were "inducted" at military recruiting stations; they received preliminary "physical training;" the men were grouped into "companies" at army-style "camps" operated by the military. The New Dealers would get their money's worth from MacArthur's army by requiring it to build and operate the CCC. By July 1933, 275,000 men had been inducted into the work force—considerably more than the 180,000 recruits mustered into service over a similar period after the 1917 declaration of war.[31]

Fox Conner, who had begun his military career in 1898 by training raw recruits in New England, embraced the Army's new role.[32] Conner oversaw the formation and operation of eighty-seven CCC camps in New England, including "Camp Conner" in Connecticut. According to one newspaper article, Conner kept a schedule that "would have exhausted many a younger man." He inspected each of the camps, several of which required treks into remote forest locations. Conner ate with the men to assure the quality of their rations; he also took the time to ask questions and listen to answers. On one project in Connecticut, Conner spoke at length with war veterans, some of whom had been bonus marchers the year before. Each expressed his appreciation for the opportunity to work.

For Thanksgiving 1933, Conner saw to it that employees in the CCC camps feasted on the same turkey and trimmings dinner served to his First Corps Area soldiers. *The Boston Daily Globe* reported that the general advanced the travel expenses for some young men who had gone home for Christmas but could not afford to return, purportedly because "they went broke buying presents for Ma and Pa." Conner even took interest in the romantic affairs of one worker. At the request of a Massachusetts congressman, the general offered to transfer the man to a camp closer to his fiancée. According to Conner, the man had replied that he preferred to stay where he was.

In late 1933, the CCC introduced educational courses for its employees. The War Department's chief liaison to the CCC (an officer named Colonel Major) opposed the initiative in the belief that the men in the camps needed to be taught "how to do an honest day's work," rather than listening to "long-haired men and short-haired women." Fox Conner, ever the son of two teachers, held a different view of the educational programs. Conner hired eighty-one instructors, who taught a variety of evening classes, from basic reading, writing, and arithmetic for those with little education, to what he termed "cultural courses," including foreign language, sociology, psychology, philosophy, and, of course, history.

Conner also revisited the Great War history he had helped make—with an ulterior agenda in mind.

Although the Great War had ended 15 years earlier, the feud between John J. Pershing and the Army's wartime chief of staff Peyton C. March had not. Even in their retirements, the two men continued to snipe at each other. In his 1932 book, *The Nation at War*, March had criticized Pershing's "preposterous demands" for troops during the war, as well as his "ignorance or disregard" of War Department instructions. A *New York Times* reviewer observed that "one cannot escape the impression that General March suffers from internal injuries because of a nation's forgetfulness or unawareness that as Chief of Staff he was General Pershing's superior officer."[33]

Pershing did not respond in kind; he had surrogates such as Fox Conner do it for him. For instance, in one 1933 article in which Conner primarily focused on the need for "radical reorganization" of the Army's division structure (as he had unsuccessfully attempted to accomplish in 1920), he also criticized passages from General March's book as "wholly incorrect," and failing to provide the "true and complete story" of the success of the AEF divisions in France.

Pershing was particularly irked by March's charge that the AEF commander-in-chief had displayed "profound ignorance" in his belief that the French Army preferred to operate on the defensive. March expressed incredulity that "such an entire misconception of the genius of the French Army was possible."

On Pershing's behalf, Conner countered with a 1934 article titled "The Genius of the French Army—Criticism of a Criticism." To demonstrate that France had indeed become primarily defensive in its military strategy, Conner traced the effects of the Austro-Prussian War of 1866, the Franco-Prussian War of 1870–71, the Franco-Russian alliance of 1891, the Anglo-Boer war from the turn of the 20th century, and the Russo-Japanese War of 1904–05 upon the development of French military doctrine. "There is not one fact," Conner argued, "to justify any single point of General March's criticism." In several letters, an appreciative Pershing praised Conner's "splendid" article, which, he thought, had left March without "the shadow of a leg to stand on."

Fox Conner also considered a writing project of a different nature. In April 1934, George Marshall arranged a meeting between Conner and an executive with the Little, Brown and Company publishing house, who asked Conner to write a book on the inner workings of the AEF general staff. "I do not quite visualize just how that is to be accomplished," Conner wrote Marshall on April 23. "Please give me some advice. I need it badly."[34]

In response, Marshall expressed pleasant surprise that Conner would "weaken on the writing business," which implies that Conner had declined prior opportunities to write a book. Marshall offered encouraging words: "With your literary ability, your general military knowledge and your comprehensive knowledge of affairs in France, coupled with your ability to reduce things to simplicities, you are better prepared to write such a book than anyone else I know in the Army."

Conner pursued the project. He had Dwight Eisenhower provide him with War Department records. Marshall sent Conner an outline of possible chapter headings, along with some advice: "You can make your book a best seller," Marshall counseled, "if you tell the truth about what happened." But Marshall warned Conner that "many toes would be tread on," and that much "yapping" would result from such a book. "Just how pleasant you would find this aspect," Marshall told Conner, "I do not know."

Perhaps in heed of Marshall's cautionary advice, Conner never wrote the book. Other events in 1934 also occupied Fox Conner's attention.

In September 1934, a strike by textile workers in Rhode Island turned violent.[35] After Rhode Island National Guardsmen killed one man and wounded several others in the town of Woonsocket on September 11, an enraged mob of thousands looted and burned the town's business district. As police and guardsmen struggled to maintain order, President Roosevelt warned that continued violence would lead to "direct intervention" by Army troops. As commander of the corps area that included Rhode Island, Fox Conner began to ready his force for deployment.

Conner assembled more than a thousand troops at Fort Devens, near Boston. Trucks commandeered from CCC camps lined up to transport the men. The general also converted a light tank company into a "flying squadron" of motorcycles armed with machine guns. On September 13, Conner told *The Boston Daily Globe* that his force stood "in readiness for instant mobilization"; they would be in Rhode Island within four hours once the president gave the order.

The astute politician Roosevelt, elected with the strong support of organized labor, dreaded the prospect of using troops against strikers. Instead, the president dispatched General Conner and Secretary Dern to personally assess the conditions in Woonsocket. On September 14, Roosevelt left Washington aboard the yacht *Nourmahal*, bound for Narragansett Bay near Newport, where he had previously planned to watch the America's Cup sailing races. While at sea, the president received radio updates from Dern and Conner as to the situation in Rhode Island.

On September 15, 1934, General Conner met President Roosevelt aboard the *Nourmahal* to discuss the president's options. They conferred near Fort Adams, where Conner had begun his career 36 years earlier. Conner, who leaned Republican in his politics, did not share Roosevelt's liberal views. The general, who in one speech had warned of the dangers of "internationalism, pacifism, sovietism, and all the isms man can utter," had no sympathy for the radical element of the American labor movement.[36] Conner's troops were prepared. So was his recommendation on what the president ought to do.

Conner advised Roosevelt to enjoy the boat races and let local authorities manage the situation.

A relieved Roosevelt concurred, and he invited Conner to remain aboard the *Nourmahal* to watch the races with him. The president had other business to discuss with the general.

A rocky relationship remained between President Roosevelt and Chief of Staff MacArthur, whose term would expire in November 1934. On September 9, the *New York Times* had included Fox Conner's name among a list of generals considered "more or less as dark horses" for MacArthur's position.[37]

The odds for Conner's selection ran higher than the newspaper knew. Roosevelt had created a handwritten list headed "Chief of Staff to succeed MacArthur." The list included the Army's major generals, in order of seniority, with Roosevelt's annotations beside each general's name. Conner ranked fourth in seniority. Roosevelt had ruled out the three men ahead of him on the list (Dennis Nolan, Johnson Hagood, and William Connor), none of whom could serve a complete four-year term due to mandatory retirement. The president had written "4 years" beside the name of 59-year-old Conner, who had the greatest seniority among the candidates eligible to serve a full term.

Other factors supported Fox Conner's selection. Conner's embrace of his CCC duties reflected well in the eyes of Franklin Roosevelt, as did his handling of the Rhode Island crisis. No officer offered greater general staff credentials. Also, by 1934, Franklin Roosevelt had come to view Douglas MacArthur as a potential political rival. Roosevelt could count on Fox Conner—who was certainly no MacArthur man—to prevent MacArthur from continuing to vicariously wield power through a malleable successor.

For the third time in his career, Conner stood on the verge of becoming the nation's highest-ranking soldier.

But this time, Conner turned down the job.

According to Dwight Eisenhower, who received a letter dated September 18, 1934 from Conner on the subject, Conner told Roosevelt that he did not wish to become the Army's next chief of staff. More plainly, Conner let the president know that he preferred to resign rather than return to the realm of Washington politics. Journalist Charles Brown, who interviewed Eisenhower in 1964, wrote that Conner recommended his longtime friend and colleague, Malin Craig, for the position. James G. Harbord later wrote Conner to express regret that "due to your own disinclination for it, you were never made Chief of Staff." A 1939 article in *Collier's* magazine referred to Conner as "the only man who ever was offered the appointment of Chief of Staff of the Army and turned it down."

President Roosevelt accordingly amended his list of generals: he wrote "NO" beside Fox Conner's name. Conner surely understood that he would never again have the opportunity to become the Army's chief of staff.

Conner left no record of his specific reasons for declining the opportunity to become the Army's chief of staff. In his 1964 article, Charles Brown speculated that the politically conservative Conner had no desire to join Roosevelt's New Dealers. Conner's family members have suggested that the general preferred to stay in Boston, and closer to Brandreth Lake in the Adirondacks, rather than spend the last four years of his career fighting unwinnable funding battles in Washington, D.C.

According to Dwight Eisenhower, though, Conner wanted to remain in command of troops. As Germany rearmed under Adolf Hitler and Japan continued to encroach upon China, Fox Conner became more certain of the inevitability of a new world-wide conflict. If—when—war came to the United States, Conner preferred the chance to become the nation's next Black Jack Pershing in the field rather than its Peyton March in Washington.

World events soon demonstrated that Fox Conner's chance might arise.

CHAPTER 13

THE ZENITH OF FOX CONNER

Whenever we got together, we went back to those same old subjects. Hitler had come in.
Now it was getting closer; he was getting more definite in his conviction of
what would happen.

—Dwight Eisenhower, 1964[1]

In late December 1934, Japan announced its intention to abrogate a 1922 international treaty designed to control the balance of naval power in the Pacific. Secretary of War George Dern, in response to President Franklin D. Roosevelt's directive to outline the "urgent needs of the Military Establishment," recommended substantially increased military spending to upgrade the Army's air power, motorized forces, ammunition, and housing—as officers such as Fox Conner had argued for years.[2]

In March 1935, Congress raised military appropriations by more than 25 percent. The generally isolationist lawmakers granted a spending increase greater than Roosevelt's budget office had asked for. The *New York Times* explained the extraordinary jump in spending as "being a result, at least in part, of the prevalent war talk."

Fox Conner also began to hear the talk of an awakening public. On March 29, 1935, he attended the annual Army–Navy dinner in Worchester, Massachusetts. The event's featured speaker, war correspondent and author Frederick Palmer, predicted the onset of a new world war within five years, a war "more bitter, with less quarter shown, than any of its predecessors." Conner offered his own advice to the audience: "We had better follow Theodore Roosevelt's advice. "Speak softly and carry a big stick."

The additional military appropriations enabled the American Army to resume field maneuvers. In August 1935, Fox Conner commanded his First Corps Area troops in the largest peacetime maneuvers held to that time in the United States. Conner's "Blue" force faced the "Red" army formed by Major General Lucius Holbrook's Second Corps Area troops. In all, more than 55,000 men participated in the exercises at the Army's Pine Camp training area in northern New York.[3]

The first phase of the exercise involved the concentration, transportation, and encampment of the troops. Conner's staff, which included his aide Trimble Brown and son-in-law Joe Gans, arranged the details to transport 10,000 soldiers more than 400 miles by rail, while the remainder formed what the The Boston Daily Globe termed "the largest fleet of army motor transportation ever to take the road." Conner praised his units for completing their mobilization on schedule. "We only learn when we make mistakes," Conner told the New York Times, "and there have been no mistakes."

The first engagement of the mock battle occurred in the triple-digit heat of August 23, 1935, when Conner's corps attacked southward across heavily wooded terrain. Holbrook's larger force stopped Conner's advance and then slowly pushed the Blue army back. The Boston Daily Globe observed that Conner's men gave ground "only after bitterly contesting each stubborn inch," and that Holbrook's superior force had been slowed to a "snaillike advance." According to maneuver umpires, though, Conner's forces also suffered heavy casualties—a fact that may not have surprised his wartime critics.

Conner's Blue force fared better in its August 26 attack, in which its commander fully exploited his motorized units. Trucks rushed reserves to the front to maintain the push against Holbrook's defenses. Conner sent tanks and halftracks to attack a ridge defended by machine guns and artillery. Journalist Hanson Baldwin of the New York Times wrote that Conner's tanks "smashed (theoretically) across machine-gun nests and sprayed a leaden hail into the Red lines."[4] By the end of the day, when heavy rain stopped the exercises, Conner's troops had advanced to their counterpart's final line of defense.

Generals Conner and Holbrook held a press conference on August 28 to critique the results of the maneuvers. Both found significant problems in communication between headquarters and field units. More positively, Conner thought the exercises had "developed very clearly the strategic value of motorization," particularly the Army's ability to transport large bodies of troops quickly to distant regions. Despite his corps' successful deployment of tanks on the last day of the maneuvers, Conner said he was "not so cocksure as some officers seem to be" as to the usefulness of mechanized weaponry on the battlefield. In Conner's view, the exercises, which had involved 1,337 animals but only thirty tanks and fifty-five tractors, had not given "any indication whatever of the tactical value of motorization and mechanization." As Conner phrased it: "I can't see yet in actual warfare how you can make prompt and effective reconnaissance from a station wagon."

In December 1935, Conner met with Brigadier General Frank Andrews, commander of the Army Air Corps, to plan air maneuvers designed to assess the Air Corps' ability to function in cold-weather environments.[5] Conner and Andrews chose a time of the year when frigid weather in New England could be almost guaranteed. During the first two weeks of February 1936, more than sixty aircraft participated from opposing airfields located in Vermont and New Hampshire. The weather cooperated: 12in. of snow fell on the runways one day. The planes flew a combined 300,000 miles and 2,000 hours with no engine failures. Take-off and landing exercises demonstrated that aircraft tires performed well on icy runways and that skis were not needed. The airmen learned that cold weather did not affect machine-gun performance but did lessen the performance of bomb release equipment.

The New England air exercises in 1936 formed one of several modernization efforts implemented by Army Chief of Staff Malin Craig, whom Conner had recommended for the position when he had declined it in 1934. President Roosevelt found in General Craig a chief of staff whose résumé resembled Fox Conner's—from their West Point graduation in 1898, to their service as key AEF staff officers, to their command of corps areas after the war. Throughout 1936, Chief of Staff Craig implemented measures to improve the Army's readiness.[6]

The year also brought a steady deterioration of the world's stability.

On March 7, 1936, German troops marched without opposition into the Rhineland (the industrial heartland of Germany located between the Rhine River and the French border). Hitler's action violated both the 1919 Treaty of Versailles and the separate 1925 Locarno Treaty. The inaction of the wartime Allies to stop or reverse the occupation emboldened the German *Führer*. Italy completed its conquest of Abyssinia (Ethiopia), which had begun the previous year with no effective response from the League of Nations to stop it. In July 1936, civil war erupted in Spain. Germany and Italy aided the fascist Nationalist forces while the Soviet Union backed the left-wing Republican government. On October 25, 1936 Italy and Germany formed the Rome–Berlin Axis.[7]

As the world edged toward the war Fox Conner had long forecast, Conner himself moved closer to a top field-command position if the conflict reached America. Conner, as the senior corps area commander in the eastern United States, also took command of the American First Army on May 1, 1936. First Army existed only on paper at the time, but in the event of mobilization for war, Conner would become one of four army-level field commanders, with overall command of all troops in the First, Second, and Third Corps areas.[8]

In late autumn 1936, General Conner went on leave to go hunting at Brandreth, where he and Bug had built a complex of cabins dubbed "Conner's Corner." The general had been in the chilly Adirondacks for several weeks when his son, Tommy, received a telephone call from a caretaker at the property. Something was not right with the general. On November 20, Tommy Conner drove through ice and snow from Ossining to Brandreth to check on his father. A physician went with him. The *New York Times* and *The Boston Daily Globe* newspapers each reported on November 22 that Conner had developed a "severe cold" while hunting.

In truth, Fox Conner had suffered an acute cerebral hemorrhage and a stroke.[9]

Army physicians determined the hemorrhagic stroke to have been "slight," and its cause "undetermined," in that era when the link between smoking and cardiovascular disease was not well understood. The general stayed at his son's home in Ossining—and out of public view—until he returned to duty on January 12, 1937. No reference to the true nature of Conner's illness appeared in any newspapers.

General Conner eased back into his duties through the first half of 1937. In July, he hosted, at Harvard University, a conference of CCC educational advisors at which college professors lectured on the latest theories on adult education. The general also visited the Citizens Military Training Camp at Fort Devens near Boston that summer.[10] Conner watched as 600 young men sweated in the sun while waiting to be processed and uniformed, as he had done at West Point 44 years earlier.[11]

Fox Conner also hearkened back to his Leavenworth and War College days during "command post maneuvers" designed to assess the ability of his First Army generals and their staffs to work from maps and to issue orders.[12] Conner related to reporters who covered the exercises how the lessons he had learned by working with maps of the Metz area made in the 1870s had been of great value to him during the Great War. "Division, corps, and army commanders must be capable of sitting in front of a map and dictating a complete field order," Conner proclaimed.

For two weeks that began August 23, 1937, the commanding generals and staff officers of the First, Second, and Third Corps areas waged a war, entirely on paper, against a hypothetical coalition of foreign powers that had landed troops in New England. As First Army commander, Conner oversaw the exercises. The eighteen generals and 351 staff officers at the corps, division, and brigade levels worked under wartime pressures, including sleep deprivation and rapidly changing conditions.

The 1937 exercises revealed some of the same deficiencies shown by the 1935 Pine Camp maneuvers. Slow communication between headquarters and field units continued to concern Conner. The *New York Times* and *The Boston Daily Globe* each reported his suggestion—perhaps made facetiously, perhaps not—that the Army should return to galloping couriers on horseback, as in the days of Napoleon, until the military developed more effective radio technology.

The command post maneuvers also demonstrated the vulnerability of the local civilian population to air attack—as had happened 4 months earlier in Spain. On April 26, 1937, German and Italian warplanes bombed and strafed civilians on a busy market day in the Republican town of Guernica. During First Army's exercises, enemy planes surprised an Air Corps base on August 31, and would have destroyed most of the American aircraft on the ground had the action been real. Germany's military attaché to the United States, Lieutenant General Friedrich von Boetticher, was at First Army headquarters, as an official observer, when the surprise air raid occurred.

International developments such as the Guernica bombing in 1937, as well as Japan's brutal conquest of China, prompted Congress to increase military spending to its highest level since 1921. On October 5, 1937, President Roosevelt called for a "quarantine" of the world's aggressive nations. Congress amended the nation's Neutrality Act to allow the president discretion to provide some forms of aid to belligerent nations on a "cash and carry" basis.[13]

As Roosevelt began to position the United States for a more active and flexible role should war occur, the War Department called upon Fox Conner to help do the same for the Army's infantry divisions.

In the autumn of 1937, Conner spent several weeks at Fort Sam Houston, Texas to observe tests of a new division structure.[14] Since 1920, the Army had maintained a 22,000-strong "square" division structure (formed by four regiments grouped into two brigades) in the model of the AEF's divisions during the Great War. Although Fox Conner had been a primary architect of the square AEF divisions, he thereafter came to favor a smaller "triangular" division composed of three regiments with no brigade organization. Conner had acknowledged in a 1931 address that the square division structure had "led to a great many unnecessary losses" during the war because of lack of mobility, and that such divisions were "ill-suited to the next war." In 1933, Conner had written that he was "heartily ashamed" of having signed the 1920 report that had maintained the square division structure.

The 2nd Division, based at Fort Sam Houston, served as the test division for a smaller 13,500-man structure designed by the division's chief of staff, Brigadier General Lesley McNair. McNair eliminated one regiment to create a triangular structure. He also pared the division's size by removing engineering, anti-aircraft, and anti-tank crews from the division's control and "pooling" those services at the corps level. He planned to maintain the division's firepower with more modern weaponry.

Conner supported McNair's initiatives, but he told the *The Boston Daily Globe* that a division of 13,500 was "still too large" for modern warfare. He recommended that artillery, medical, and supply services also be moved from the division to corps-level control, to further reduce the division's size to 10,000. Hanson Baldwin of the *New York Times* predicted that the smaller division size suggested by Conner was "an almost certain result" of the tests; Baldwin also identified Conner as a possible chairman of the committee to make final recommendations on the issue.

In late December 1937, Chief of Staff Craig did appoint a panel to make final recommendations regarding divisional reorganization. The board would be composed of only three officers: Fox Conner, George Marshall, and Lesley McNair.[15] In a December 21, 1937 letter, Marshall referred to the board as a "stacked deck" in favor of the smaller, triangular division structure. In a January 7, 1938 letter, Marshall reminded Fox Conner of "the struggle you and I made to get a small division in 1920." Marshall also asked Conner to provide information on Fort Sam Houston tests in advance of the panel's February meeting.[16]

But the board never met.

In late January 1938, Conner developed a prostate problem that required surgery. Following the February 21, 1938 procedure, Conner went on extended medical leave to recuperate. As Hitler's *Anschluss* expanded the Nazi empire into Austria in March 1938, Conner could only look forward to resuming his work of readying the American First Army for the task which he believed was ahead. In an April 1 letter to Pershing, Conner reported a steady recovery from his surgery; by April 26, Conner felt well enough to sit at the head table of a Boston Chamber of Commerce luncheon.

Then calamity struck.

On May 22, 1938, Fox Conner suffered a second, and much more severe, stroke. His physicians also diagnosed a "coronary thrombosis, acute"—a heart attack.[17] Conner survived, but the stroke left him debilitated. Conner spent the next eight weeks in a hospital bed at the Army's

Walter Reed Hospital in Washington, D.C. Black Jack Pershing, also recovering from heart failure, occupied the room across the hall.[18]

Conner's condition stabilized, then slowly improved. His strength began to return, and he regained some ability to walk. After nearly two months at Walter Reed, Conner left the hospital on July 16, 1938.

He also left the Army's list of active duty officers.

On August 8, Major General Fox Conner appeared before an Army retirement board which found him "incapacitated for active service." The panel concluded that Conner's disability had begun with his 1936 stroke and was "an incident of the service." The board set a retirement of September 30, 1938.[19]

Words of praise poured in as news spread through the Army of Conner's medical retirement.[20] Brigadier General William Wilson, Conner's chief of staff at First Corps, wrote to commend Conner's "sterling worth as a commander and a man." James G. Harbord, the AEF's first chief of staff, complimented Conner as "the ablest officer in the Army." Referring to Conner's decision to decline the chief of staff position in 1934, Harbord told him: "After all, though, what is the position of Chief of Staff of a small army in time of peace compared to the real power you exerted in your great function as Chief of Operations of the American Army in France?"

John J. Pershing issued a public statement praising Conner as "a brilliant soldier" and "one of the finest characters our Army has ever produced." Pershing also expressed his "affectionate esteem" in a personal letter to Conner. George Marshall wrote that he was "deeply sorry, both personally and officially, to see you leave the active list."

Fox Conner officially retired from the United States Army on September 30, 1938. That same day, Great Britain and France signed the Munich Agreement with Germany and Italy, which delivered a portion of Czechoslovakia to the Nazis in a vain attempt to appease Adolf Hitler's further territorial claims in Europe.

★ ★ ★ ★ ★

No longer needed in Boston, Fox Conner moved with Bug to Washington, D.C. to be near Walter Reed Hospital. At first, Bug dreaded the "long, dreary afternoons" of her husband's convalescence until Fox became more active.[21]

The stroke had impaired Conner's mobility and strength, but not his mind and speech. On February 10, 1939, Conner delivered a lengthy lecture to the Army War College titled "The Allied High Command and Allied Unity of Direction." After a visit from Conner, Black Jack Pershing wrote Bug on May 19 that Conner's "mind seems to be working perfectly." Pershing's letter also suggests that Conner had discussed another writing project with his former commander. "I am quite anxious to have Fox write his recollections of the war," Pershing wrote, "as, from my point of view, he is more familiar with the working of the AEF from top to bottom in all its phases than any other man."

By the summer of 1939, Conner's physical condition had improved. He wrote George Marshall in August that he was "in much better shape" and was able to work in his garden at Brandreth for several hours a day. Conner also thanked Marshall for sending him a letter written by a fellow officer who had praised Conner's work. "It is very pleasant to feel that one is not forgotten even though he is on the shelf," Conner confessed.[22]

George Marshall was a man on his way up in the summer of 1939. Chief of Staff Craig had made Brigadier General Marshall the Army's deputy chief of staff in October 1938. As Craig's mandatory retirement approached in 1939, he and Secretary of War Harry Woodring lobbied President Roosevelt to elevate Marshall to the position of chief of staff, although several major generals outranked him. The president heeded their advice. On September 1, 1939—the day Germany invaded Poland to trigger World War II in Europe—George Marshall became the Army's chief of staff. Marshall's appointment reflected the president's selection of yet another general in the mold of Fox Conner lead the Army.[23]

With Europe and Asia both at war, Chief of Staff Marshall continued Malin Craig's efforts to ready the Army for war—including measures that reflected Fox Conner's earlier work. In 1940, Marshall ordered the conversion of all Army and National Guard divisions to the smaller, triangular configuration that Fox Conner and he had advocated since 1920. In the summer of 1940, as the Nazi *blitzkrieg* conquered Europe from Norway to France, the War Department also activated the General Headquarters structure, which Conner had devised in the early 1920s, so that the Army would have a functioning general staff prepared to function immediately in the event of war.[24]

At the time of Conner's retirement in 1938, George Marshall had comforted his ailing friend by writing: "You have a great deal yet to give the Army out of that wise head of yours." In 1940, no longer able to wield a sword, Conner turned to a pen to make his contribution.[25]

Conner wrote a newspaper article that encouraged citizens to support the government's military preparedness efforts. "The idea that the United States is exempt by Providence from the rigors of war is not new to the isolationists of 1940," he wrote. Conner told the story of a Virginia congressman, who, in 1810, had persuaded his fellow lawmakers to limit military spending on the basis that the Atlantic Ocean would insulate the United States from European armies. Within 3 years, British troops had landed in that congressman's home state on their way to burn Washington, D.C.

The Boston Daily Globe published a 1940 article by Conner which praised legislation before Congress to implement a peacetime military draft. He pointed out that, in 1917, the armies of Britain and France had afforded the United States the luxury of letting 5 months pass between America's declaration of war and the induction of its first draftee. By the time Conner's article appeared, however, France had already surrendered to Germany, and Great Britain was barely surviving the battering of the aerial Battle of Britain. Conner warned that any further delay in mobilizing America's forces in advance of war "might well prove fatal" to the United States. In September 1940—as President Roosevelt sought an unprecedented third term in office—Congress passed the Selective Service Act of 1940, which the president immediately signed into law.

Conner also wrote an unflattering review of First Army's August 1940 maneuvers. In making the point that the Army's mobility had increased but its fighting effectiveness had not, Conner wrote: "There was far more Blitz than Krieg about these maneuvers." The poor performance of First Army's staff work particularly galled Conner, who had emphasized staff training in his 1937 command-post exercises. "It is said that we learn more from our mistakes than from the things we do well," Conner wrote. "If this be so, the maneuvers of the First Army in 1940 were an unqualified success."

Conner forwarded a copy of his article to Chief of Staff Marshall on September 15, with a note that began: "I know you have little or no time, to say nothing of patience, to hear the views of a Has Been." Conner proceeded to tell Marshall that First Army's performance had been "pretty awful." He added: "Had I been writing an official report, I would have been far more critical." Marshall promptly responded on September 20 to assure Conner: "We are never too busy to listen to the views of one who has been through the mill."[26]

In May 1941, the *Infantry Journal* published Conner's detailed article titled "Replacements: Life Blood of a Fighting Army." Conner recounted the AEF's chronic shortage of replacements, which "gave GHQ more headaches than any other one thing." He analyzed data from the AEF's seven most active divisions to demonstrate the numerous reasons, many unrelated to combat, that caused those divisions to experience an almost total turnover of personnel by the war's end. Conner therefore proposed the "safe and simple rule" of assigning one soldier to a replacement pool of soldiers for every soldier sent to a division. He also emphasized the need to properly train replacement troops. "We shall do well to stop any search after false gods," Conner wrote, "and accept a six months' training as the absolute minimum to be given men before throwing them into the hell of modern battle."[27]

By mid-1941, much of the world had descended into that hell. Having overrun most of Europe, Hitler then invaded the Soviet Union in June 1941. British troops moved into Iraq, Syria, and Iran to block an advance toward India. Japan continued its campaign in China and also invaded French Indochina (Vietnam, Laos, and Cambodia). In August 1941, the United States imposed an embargo to halt the sale of oil to Japan.

American naval vessels also began to escort merchant vessels bound for Britain through waters patrolled by German submarines. On October 31, 1941, a German U-boat sank the destroyer USS *Reuben James*, killing 115 American sailors off the coast of Iceland. Chief of Naval Operations

Harold Stark proclaimed: "Whether the country knows it or not, we are at war."[28]

As Fox Conner hunted in the Adirondacks in November 1941, he had reason to believe that Chief of Staff Marshall, his longtime friend and colleague, would find a way for the Army's chief of operations in its previous world war to make a meaningful contribution to the coming one. Conner's May article on replacements had demonstrated his enduring analytical acumen. More than 3 years after his stroke, Conner had also regained much of his strength.

Then Tommy Conner received another phone call from Brandreth Lake.

On November 17, 1941, the general's car got stuck in the mud on a logging road in the woods. Frank Carey, a Brandreth caretaker, placed firewood beneath the car's tires to provide traction. To lessen the weight in the vehicle, Conner got out and stood behind the vehicle. But as the car's wheels spun, one of the logs shot out from beneath the car and slammed directly into Conner's skull.

Fox collapsed into the mud, bleeding and unconscious—but alive. Carey frantically stopped a lumber truck, which brought Conner's limp form to the nearest train station. Carey and the truck driver laid the stricken general flat on his back in a freight car bound for Utica, New York. The station agent alerted the hospital in Utica.[29]

Dr. Fred Douglas, who represented the Utica area in Congress, met the train to accompany the still-unconscious Conner to the hospital. When Tommy arrived in Utica, he learned that the accident had badly fractured his father's skull. Dr. Douglas feared fatal brain damage. The next few days would be critical.

Tommy then broke the news to his mother, who took the next train for Utica. "This made the third time I had run to my dying husband's bedside," she wrote in her memoir. Mrs. Conner arrived at the hospital the next day. Expecting the worst, she entered her husband's sickroom.

"Hello Bug, where did you come from?" her husband asked cheerfully. Mrs. Conner wrote that her husband, whose head was swathed in bandages, "did not in the least look like a man about to die." Conner's cognitive functioning, though, was decidedly impaired. He did not understand where he was or what had happened to him. He lapsed in and out of consciousness. When awake, he became combative. Conner was alive, but far from well.

Chief of Staff Marshall learned of Conner's injury on November 19. Despite the tumult of his own work in late November 1941, Marshall immediately sent Bug Conner a telegram to express his sympathy; Marshall also asked that she apprise him of Fox's condition. Bug received several calls from Washington, offering to transport Conner by air to Walter Reed Hospital, but she decided to keep him in Utica. On December 1, Marshall received an update from Bug: "Fox is still unconscious but today seemed better ... We had one pretty poor day but there seems to be a decided change for the better today."

Six days later, the nation's fortunes dramatically changed for the worse.

On December 7, 1941, Japanese warplanes surprised American forces at Pearl Harbor, Hawaii. Bombs and torpedoes sunk most of America's Pacific Fleet at anchor, including the battleship *California*, from which Conner had observed a similar result during 1928 maneuvers. The Japanese also destroyed America's warplanes in the Philippines.

Fox Conner learned about Pearl Harbor from a hospital nurse who ran into his room on the afternoon of December 7 screaming news of the attack. Mrs. Conner recalled that her husband showed no anger; instead he perceived a call to duty. Bug recalled Fox's words: "Get me back to Washington as soon as you can, for the old man will need me." According to Mrs. Conner, though, her husband still did not understand his surroundings: "He was back in World War I, General Pershing's right hand man."

At Fox's insistence, the Conners left the hospital with what Bug described as "a long and ugly cut" on Fox's unbandaged head. They travelled by train to New York City, where a second train bound for Washington waited for the Conners to board. A nurse accompanied them. According to Bug, as soon as Fox entered their sleeping compartment, she and the nurse gave him a "stiff drink of whiskey" and put him to bed. Conner slept most of the way to Washington.

Once back in the capital, Fox Conner was reunited with Black Jack Pershing—in Walter Reed Hospital, where the 81-year-old Pershing occupied a suite of rooms as a retirement home. Although Fox Conner had gone south to a hospital bed and a permanent place on the shelf, he would nonetheless leave an imprint upon World War II, through the work of his protégé.

★ ★ ★ ★ ★

In late 1941, Dwight Eisenhower served as Third Army's chief of staff. Eisenhower had distinguished himself earlier in the year during large-scale maneuvers in Louisiana. According to historian Robert Ferrell, Eisenhower's plans for the Louisiana Maneuvers, "compounded from the instruction of Conner years before," had succeeded spectacularly. Eisenhower's performance in Louisiana merited promotion to the rank of brigadier general; more importantly, Eisenhower had impressed Chief of Staff George Marshall.[30]

Within a week of Pearl Harbor, Marshall summoned Eisenhower to Washington.[31] Eisenhower recounted the meeting in his 1948 memoir, in which he noted that the chief of staff showed "many of the characteristics of Fox Conner." Marshall outlined the Army's perilous position in the Philippines, where Eisenhower had served under Douglas MacArthur from 1935 through 1938. The chief of staff then suddenly asked Eisenhower a single question: "What should be our general line of action?" Eisenhower recognized that Marshall's question presented a test that required a prompt, brief, and logical response. "A curious echo from long ago came to my aid," Eisenhower wrote. "No oratory, plausible argument, or glittering generality would impress anyone entitled to be labeled genius by Fox Conner."

Eisenhower's plan, which centered upon holding Australia as a base for operations to relieve the Philippines, passed Marshall's test. The chief of staff first appointed Eisenhower, in December 1941, as an assistant in the general staff's War Plans Division, with responsibility for planning Asian operations. On February 16, 1942, Marshall placed Eisenhower in charge of the entire War Plans Division, which Fox Conner had structured in the 1920s.

In March 1942, Marshall reorganized his General Headquarters; the War Plans Division became the Operations Division (OPD). Marshall explained that Eisenhower, as his Operations Division chief, held the authority of a "subordinate commander" with the prerogative to deploy troops without clearing each decision with him—the same power Fox Conner had exercised as head of the AEF's Operations Section during World War I.

As OPD chief, Eisenhower devised plans for an eventual invasion of France from bases in Great Britain. Marshall then dispatched Eisenhower to London in May 1942 with orders to assess the suitability of the existing American commander and his staff. Marshall later acknowledged to his biographer that he had sent Eisenhower across the Atlantic "so the British could have a look" at him. Once home, Eisenhower directed a memorandum to Marshall that detailed the attributes and responsibilities required of the theater commander who would execute his plans. Upon receipt of the memo Marshall told his OPD chief: "You may be the man who executes it."

George Marshall made it official on June 11, 1942, when he appointed Major General Dwight Eisenhower to the position of Commanding General, United States Forces, European Theater. Eisenhower boarded an airplane on June 23 bound for London—and his place in history.

As Fox Conner had envisioned, the planner—who turned out to be his protégé—had indeed become the commander.

★ ★ ★ ★ ★

Conner stayed at Walter Reed Hospital for nearly 3 months as he recuperated from his severe head injury. He left the hospital in February 1942. Mrs. Conner, although hoping her husband would regain full clarity of mind, learned that Fox would never completely recover. That, she wrote, was "the hardest moment I ever lived through."[32]

When the weather warmed in 1942, Fox and Bug returned to Conner's Corner at Brandreth Lake. To help with chores, the Conners hired 19-year-old Sam Black, who spent the summer at the lake as he awaited entry into the Marine Corps.[33] The general and the recruit became companions. For hours each day, Black patiently rowed a boat as the retired general trolled for trout. In a 2012 interview, Sam Black recalled that Conner had a "way of bridging" to a "kid who was wide-eyed and delighted to be included in the conversation." Black described easy-going discussions, "interrupted by loon calls and the occasional smack of a mosquito." They discussed the flora and fauna of the Adirondacks. Conner spoke with pride of his father's Confederate service. Mostly, according to Sam Black, Conner enjoyed the beauty and tranquility of the lake.

They also discussed the war that Sam would soon join. Black recalled Conner's pride in the accomplishments of his former assistant, General Eisenhower. One mid-summer day in 1942, as their boat glided across Brandreth Lake, Fox reached into his pocket and removed an envelope. He encouraged his young friend to read the letter from London, which began:

> Dear General,
>
> More and more in the last few days my mind has turned back to you and to the days when I was privileged to serve intimately under your wise counsel and leadership. I cannot tell you how much I would appreciate, at this moment, an opportunity for an hour's discussion with you on problems that constantly beset me …

EPILOGUE

*I have no doubt that time will concede to you more fame
than has yet come to you from the work you did.*
—James G. Harbord to Fox Conner, July 12, 1938[1]

Four of Conner's West Point classmates, including Malin Craig, returned
to active duty during World War II. So did other retired officers, such
as John McAuley Palmer. Fox Conner, though, spent most of the war
years of 1942 through 1945 in the Blue Ridge Mountain village of
Flat Rock, North Carolina, near Asheville. In addition to the benefits
of scenery and climate, the North Carolina property generated rental
income during the summers, when Fox and Bug returned to Brandreth
Lake.[2]

Daughters Betty Vida and Florence Gans also moved to North Carolina
after their husbands left for wartime duty. Colonel Frank Vida served as
a training officer at Fort Benning, Georgia. Colonel Joe Gans took part
in the Normandy operation as an artillery officer until captured by the
Germans; Gans spent the rest of the war in a POW camp in Poland.
Grandson Fox Conner Vida joined the Navy. However, the Conners'
son, Tommy, did not reenter the Army; he instead oversaw the family's
business, which converted its plant from manufacturing animal traps to
making bulletproof shields for aircraft fuel tanks.

Fox Conner followed the war's progress through newspaper accounts—
augmented by extra insights. He and General Eisenhower exchanged
a few letters in the summer of 1942. Conner urged Eisenhower on
July 20 to open a second front in Europe to relieve pressure on the

Soviets. "When that is done, the fate of the paper hanger is sealed," Conner wrote in reference to Adolf Hitler. Conner closed his letter to Eisenhower "with all best wishes, and great pride in you." Eisenhower, in his August 21 reply, concurred with Conner's views. "I have never had any trouble getting academic concurrences," Eisenhower explained, "but there are plenty of difficulties to be encountered when you bring up questions of actual operations." The former AEF chief of operations could certainly empathize.[3]

No other wartime letters between Fox Conner and Dwight Eisenhower have survived. Eisenhower's son, John, while a cadet at West Point in 1943, visited Conner. He described the man known to his family as "The General" as "very quiet, perhaps conscious that he was very much on the shelf." In a 1943 Christmas greeting to Bug Conner, General Eisenhower sent his mentor a message: "Tell him that I still long for opportunities to sit down with him in front of a wood fire and discuss this damnable business of war."

By then, Eisenhower had well-learned his business, including the lessons Fox Conner had taught him in Panama two decades earlier. Eisenhower skillfully managed the multinational military coalition that successfully opened a second front against Axis forces in North Africa in late 1942, then invaded Sicily and Italy in 1943. As Supreme Commander of Allied Expeditionary Forces, Eisenhower successfully marshaled the forces of the United States, Great Britain, Canada, and other allied nations during the successful invasion of Normandy in June 1944 and the eventual push eastward into Germany to help win the war in 1945. Eisenhower wrote in 1948: "Allied unity, and the ways and means of attaining it, constituted the principal war lesson"—as Fox Conner had told him it would be. In a 1967 interview with historian Stephen Ambrose, Eisenhower credited his many discussions with Conner, as well as his own reading on the history of coalition warfare, as the keys to his success in effective allied unity.

In his memoir, Eisenhower wrote: "Success in such organizations rests ultimately upon personalities." One wonders whether Eisenhower may have consulted a treatise on applied psychology, as his mentor did in Panama, to manage the egos of figures such as Winston Churchill,

George Patton, British Field Marshall Sir Bernard Law Montgomery, and French General Charles de Gaulle.[4]

Chief of Staff George Marshall also stayed in touch with his friend, Fox Conner, during World War II.[5] On November 13, 1942, Marshall invited Conner to a meeting in Washington of retired generals, at which the chief of staff presented a confidential briefing on the Army's wartime operations. By then, Conner had moved to North Carolina and could not attend. In his November 17 reply, Conner lauded Marshall's "magnificent work" in managing the American war effort. When Marshall visited the Conners in April 1943, he found Fox quietly reading history and "Mrs. Fox talking in the usual tone of voice." Conner family members report that Marshall sometime consulted Conner on Army personnel decisions. In 1944, Conner asked Marshall to intervene so that Trimble Brown, Conner's former aide, could remain in the United States after two years in combat.

George Patton also corresponded with Conner during World War II.[6] On December 17, 1944—the day after the Battle of the Bulge had begun—Patton wrote Conner that the German offensive reminded him of Germany's March 1918 offensive in World War I. "I intend to put on quite a violent show," Patton wrote. He later sent Conner a detailed account of the American Army's successful operations in Bastogne, Belgium—one of the pivotal actions in the Battle of the Bulge.

The Conners and the Eisenhowers remained in contact after the war as well. The two couples had dinner at the Eisenhowers' home in 1947. When Eisenhower accepted the presidency of Columbia University in 1948, he invited Conner to the installation ceremony. Later that year, Eisenhower sent Conner a copy of his memoir, *Crusade in Europe*, with the handwritten inscription: "For Maj. General Fox Conner—to whom I shall always be indebted." Conner sent a thank-you note that also expressed his and Bug's "love to you and Mamie." Eisenhower replied that the thanks "should have been from me to you, for I doubt very much that I should ever have been in a position to prepare such a memoir, had it not been for the guidance and counsel I got from you."[7]

Conner continued to enjoy his summers at Conner's Corner in the Adirondacks. Macpherson Conner recalled that his grandfather would

248 • GENERAL FOX CONNER

leave his camp in the morning—while Bug practiced her violin—to visit with family and friends at the lake. He enjoyed working in his vegetable garden. Once up from an afternoon nap, the old general lounged in an Adirondack chair as he read or smoked or simply watched the water. Fox also spent time at Brandreth in his personal library, which held more than a thousand books. As a teenager, Macpherson Conner thumbed through works written in French to find the risqué books he had overheard his grandmother mention.[8]

To the general's delight, Macpherson Conner followed in the footsteps of his father and grandfather to become the third generation of Conners to attend West Point. Mac Conner recalled his grandfather's enthusiasm, as well as his hope in the summer of 1951, to be well enough to attend his West Point graduation in June 1952.

Fox Conner did not live to see Mac's graduation. On October 13, 1951, at age 77, General Conner died at Walter Reed Hospital in Washington, D.C. Conner did not succumb either to the cardiovascular disease that had plagued him or to complications from his head injury. He died of lung cancer. According to Mac Conner, even as his grandfather lay dying in an oxygen tent, he kept asking for cigarettes.[9]

The Conner family spread the general's cremated ashes along his favorite hunting trail at Brandreth. Memories of Fox Conner's service soon spread to the winds as well. According to Tommy Conner, his father's longtime aide, Trimble Brown, burned Conner's papers—as directed by the general himself.[10] Bug Conner's 1951 memoir, *What Father Forbad*, focused mostly upon her own life story. Perhaps in honor of her husband's wishes, Mrs. Conner left little record, before her death in 1960, of any private insight into her husband's public career.

Despite Dwight Eisenhower's several laudatory references to his mentor in his late-life writings, such as *At Ease*, Fox Conner faded into obscurity. As Eisenhower put it in 1967, Conner had become a "more or less invisible figure." Mamie Eisenhower noticed in 1971 that Conner was misidentified on a display that mentioned him at her late husband's presidential library and museum. A 1975 article in *Parameters*, the Army War College's journal, identified Eisenhower's mentor as

"William D. 'Fox' Connor," beneath a photo of Conner's nemesis from his plebe days, William Connor.[11]

A gradual resurgence of interest has begun in Fox Conner, prompted mostly by biographers of Dwight Eisenhower. Pam McPhail, a high school history teacher who lives near Slate Springs, Mississippi, has tirelessly worked to promote local remembrance of Calhoun County's most famous son. In 1994, the State of Mississippi inducted Fox Conner into its Hall of Fame. Fort Leavenworth recognized Conner as a member of the school's own Hall of Fame in 2014. Norm MacDonald, the general's grandson-in-law, who has also done much to preserve the history of Fox Conner's life and career, spoke at the Leavenworth ceremony. Mr. MacDonald noted that Fox Conner remained "an enigmatic figure whose influence and impact is probably still not fully understood."

Macpherson Conner expressed a similar view in a 2007 essay written to record his own thoughts and memories of his grandfather. "He operated behind the scenes, so to speak," Mac Conner wrote. "The general public was and is unaware of his value to the military and to the country … his true legacy stretched far beyond his own wonderful military career."

The legacy of this quintessential man-behind-the-scenes indeed endures. As Black Jack Pershing's chief of operations and Dwight Eisenhower's mentor, Fox Conner left an unmistakable imprint upon his nation's military history. Were they alive today, Pershing and Eisenhower, as well as George Marshall and George Patton—all titans of 20th-century American military history—would each offer eloquent testimony that Conner's memory belongs within their ranks. As Eisenhower said of Conner in a 1964 interview: "In sheer ability and character, he was the outstanding soldier of my time."[12]

NOTES

A note on abbreviations used

The following sources were extensively relied upon. Their abbreviated endnote references are more fully identified as follows:

CMPR	Conner, Fox Military Personnel Records, National Archives and Records Administration, National Personnel Records Center, St. Louis, Missouri. [Further identification of the specific records are in the *Bibliography*.]
Conner AGO File	Office of the Adjutant General Document File, RG94, Box 569, File 76804. [Further identification of the specific records are in the *Bibliography*.]
Conner Notes (A)	Conner, "Notes on Operations—A, The American Expeditionary Forces Prior to July 15, 1918." RG120, Entry 267, Box 3156, Folder 1113.
Conner Notes (B)	Conner, "Notes on Operations—B, Vicinity of Château-Thierry and the Vesle River." RG120, Entry 267, Box 3156, Folder 1114.
Conner Notes (C)	Conner, "Notes on Operations—C, Reduction of the St. Mihiel Salient." RG120, Entry 267, Box 3152, Folder 1085.
Conner Notes (D)	Conner, "Notes on Operations—D, The Meuse–Argonne Operation." RG120, Entry 267, Box 3156, Folder 1115.
Eisenhower Library	Dwight D. Eisenhower Presidential Library.
G-3 Report	"Report of the Assistant Chief of Staff, Third Section, General Staff." RG120, Entry 268, Box 3174.
Marshall Library	George C. Marshall Research Library.
MDAH	Mississippi Department of Archives and History.
RG120	Records Group 120. [Further identification of the specific entry, box, and folder numbers are in the *Bibliography*.]

Roosevelt Library	Franklin D. Roosevelt Library.
USAHEC	U.S. Army Heritage and Education Center, Carlisle, PA.
USAWW	*United States Army in the World War 1917–1919,* Historical Division, Department of the Army, Washington, D.C., 1948. [Numerical references in the endnotes are to the specific volume numbers set forth in the *Bibliography*.]
USMA	United States Military Academy. *The West Point Guidebook, 29th Annual Edition.* West Point, NY: Wm. H. Tripp & Company, 1928.
WDAR	War Department Annual Reports.
WPA	West Point Archives.
09/25/1917 Strategical Study	"Strategical Study of the Employment on the A.E.F. against the Imperial German Government," 09/25/1917. RG120, Entry 267, Box 3113, Folder 683.

Prologue

1. Eisenhower, Dwight D. (1967), p.61; Ferrell (1981), p.69.
2. Ferrell (1981), pp.64–65, 69–70; D'Este (2002), p.319; Ambrose (1970), pp.54–55.
3. Eisenhower to Conner, 07/04/1942, Eisenhower Library (3).
4. Pershing to Conner and Pershing press release, both 08/05/1938, MDAH (1).
5. Eisenhower, Dwight D. (1967), p.187; Brown (1987), p.200, 204; Eisenhower, John (2003), p.6.
6. Puryear (2007), p.168.

Chapter 1: Calhoun County

1. Conner Biographical Sketch, MDAH (1).
2. Conner, Macpherson unpublished essay (1), p.2; Conner, Virginia, p.81; McCain, pp.10–12, 114–15; Groom, pp.15–20; Cunningham, pp.421–24.
3. Conner, Macpherson unpublished essay (1), p.2. Other sources indicate that Robert Conner was blinded at the Battle of Shiloh. See: Brown (1987), p.203; Conner, Virginia (1951), p.81.
4. Conner Biographical Sketch, MDAH (1).
5. Conner, Macpherson unpublished essay (1), pp.2–3; Macpherson Conner Collection photographs; McCain (1975), p.115; Conner Biographical Sketch, MDAH (1); Rowland (1907), pp.694–95; Kirwan (1951), pp.41–42.
6. Conner, Macpherson unpublished essay (1), p.2; Norm MacDonald Collection photographs; McCain (1975), p.115; Conner Biographical Sketch, MDAH (1).

7. Conner, Macpherson unpublished essay (1), p.3; Conner letter to sister, undated, MDAH (1); Harris (1979), pp.333–34, 702–04; Garner (1901), pp.366–71; Lowry and McCardle (1891), p.423.
8. Conner, Virginia (1951), p.81.
9. Conner Biographical Sketch, MDAH (1).
10. *Ibid.*; Thompson, Lovell et al. (1954), v, x, pp.422–27, 474–77, 494–511, 516–23, 620–23; Cutts (1972), v–xii; Kelly (1984), pp.510–11.
11. Conner Biographical Sketch, MDAH (1).
12. *Ibid.*
13. Cutts (1972), vii; Thompson, Lovell et al. (1954), p.396.
14. McCain (1975), pp.10–12, 114–15.
15. Conner, Macpherson unpublished essay (1), p.4; Conner Biographical Sketch, MDAH (1).
16. WPA (4), p.33.
17. WPA (11), section referencing "Candidates for Admission 1893."
18. *Biographical Directory of the American Congress*, p.966; Rowland (1907), p.742.
19. *Biographical Directory of the American Congress*, p.966, 1,424; Rowland (1925), p.437; Rowland (1907), p.742. Kirwan (1951), p.88, 107, 148–52; Cresswell (2006), p.28.
20. WPA (4), p.33, and (11), section referencing "Candidates for Admission 1893;" Conner, Macpherson unpublished essay (1), p.4; Conner Biographical Sketch, MDAH (1).

Chapter 2: West Point

1. Conner to parents, 01/24/1897, MDAH (1).
2. Sources regarding Conner's 1893 attendance at West Point are in WPA (4), pp.35–38; (11) section referencing "Candidates for Admission 1893" p.54; and (15), pp.347–48, 384–89.
3. WPA (15), p.456; Linnerud (1998), I–18.
4. Sources regarding Conner's introduction to West Point's culture of hazing are in Conner to parents, 06/16/1894; WPA (1), pp.17–18; Todd (1955), pp.12–14, 69; DuRant and Carroll (2007), p.24, 34, 46; USMA, pp.10–12; Simpson (1982), p.95, 99–101, 113, 200; Palka and Malinowski (2008), p.137, 168; Ambrose (1966), pp.220–28; Pappas (1993), photos between pp.181–85.
5. Sources regarding Conner's first summer encampment are in Conner to parents, 06/16/1894, MDAH (1); WPA (1), p.17, (5), p.38, and (8), p.51; Farrow (1899), p.65; Simpson (1982), p.114, 128; USMA, p.12; Palka and Malinowski (2008), p.34; DuRant and Carroll (2007), pp.47–48.
6. Sources regarding Conner's initial academic work at West Point are in Conner to parents, 06/16/1894, 10/6/1894, 10/12/1894, 11/04/1894, 03/03/1895,

MDAH (1); WPA (5), p.30, 38 and (11), p.56; Linnerud (1998), I–18 *et seq.*; Cox (2011), p.12–14; Simpson (1982), p.115, 118–19; USMA, pp.17–18; DuRant and Carroll (2007), p.35; Palka and Malinowski (2008), p.72, 117, 150.

7. Conner to parents and sister, 10/06/1894, 10/12/1894, 10/14/1894, 11/04/1894, 03/03/1895, 10/10/1896, and undated letters, MDAH (1); WPA (5), p.38; McCain (1975), p.121; Ambrose (1966), p.227; Farrow (1899), p.116; DuRant and Carroll (2007), p.39–40; Simpson (1982), p.163.

8. WPA (16), pp.53–54, 136–38, 151–52, and (5), pp.16–18.

9. *Ibid.*; DuRant and Carroll (2007), p.47.

10. Conner to parents, 07/07/1895, 07/14/1895, and undated MDAH (1); Conner to parents 07/28/1895 (Macpherson Conner Collection); WPA (5), p.38; Simpson (1982), p.164; Palka (2008), p.14. Among other notable achievements, the author of *The Last Days of Pompeii*, Sir Edward Bulwer-Lytton, coined the phrase "the pen is mightier than the sword;" Bulwer-Lytton also began his *Paul Clifford* novel with the much-quoted phrase: "It was a dark and stormy night."

11. WPA (3), (6), pp.14–15, 30–31, and (16), p.291, 312–13; Conner to parents, 04/26/1896 and undated to sister, MDAH (1).

12. Conner to parents, 06/06/1894, 11/04/1894, 03/03/1895, and undated, MDAH (1); Author interview (1).

13. Conner to parents, 01/17/1897, 01/24/1897, MDAH (1); WPA (6), p.38; Linnerud (1998), I–37; Cox (2011), p.12; DuRant and Carroll (2007), p.24.

14. Sources regarding Conner's West Point demerits and punishments are in WPA (14), (9), p.21, 130–31, 176, 231, (6), pp.14–15, and (10), p.119, 123, 131, 142–46, 157, 158, 162, 168; Todd (1955), p.14; USMA, p.15; Farrow (1899), p.99; Ambrose (1966), p.221; Smythe (1973), p.42; DuRant and Carroll (2007), p.74–76; Conner, Macpherson unpublished essay (1), p.14.

15. Conner to parents and sister, 03/04/1896, MDAH (1).

16. Farrow (1899), pp.70–71; Conner to parents, 03/04/1896, MDAH (1); Cox (2011), p.14.

17. Conner to parents, 09/06/1896, MDAH (1).

18. WPA (7), p.31; Farrow (1899), pp.71–72.

19. Conner to parents, 01/17/1897, MDAH (1); WPA (3) and (16), p.354.

20. Conner to parents, 01/17/1897, 04/11/1897, MDAH (1); WPA (16), pp.353–57 and (8), p.31.

21. Conner to parents and siblings, 10/10/1896 and 01/24/1897 and other undated letters, MDAH (1).

22. Conner, Macpherson unpublished essay (1), p.5; Conner Biographical Sketch, MDAH (1).

23. Conner to parents, 03/04/1896, 05/16/1897, Conner to sister, undated, MDAH (1); Todd (1955), p.7; USMA, p.30, 34; Dupuy (1951), p.3; Palka and Malinowski (2008), p.199.

24. WPA (3); (16), pp.441–43, 462; (7), p.12.

25. WPA (8), p.26, 42–43, 150.
26. Conner to sister, undated, MDAH (1); WPA (3); (8), p.32 and (15); Farrow (1899), p.77.
27. WPA (2); WPA (8), p.26, 29; Farrow (1899), p.86.
28. Conner to parents, 12/05/1897, MDAH (1); WPA (9), p.231 and (10), p.259; Smythe (1973), pp.40–45; Smythe (1967), pp.40–45, 48; Smith, Gene (1998), pp.48–49.
29. Smythe (1967), p.40, 47–48; Smythe (1973), pp.43–44; Farrow (1899), p.86.
30. Smythe (1967), pp.44–46; Smythe (1973), pp.41–42; WPA (8), p.47.
31. O'Toole (1984), pp.11–12, 20–24, 34, 77–78, 126–27, 142–43, 148; Musicant (1998), pp.132–36, 140, 144, 150, 167. Subsequent forensic analyses of the explosion, including one undertaken by Admiral Hyman Rickover in the 1970s and another by the Smithsonian Institute in the 1990s, have reached differing conclusions as to whether the explosion resulted from a Spanish mine versus a spontaneous combustion of coal within the ship. See: Keenan (2001), pp.219–20.
32. Conner AGO File (25); Spiller et al. (1984), p.198; *New York Times*, 04/26/1898 and 04/27/1898; Farrow (1899), p.77; O'Toole (1984), pp.169–71; Musicant (1998), pp.184–87, 189–90; Ambrose (1966), p.238.
33. WPA (17), pp.95–97; Linnerud (1998).
34. Weigley (1984), pp.290–98, 305; Musicant (1998), p.162, 195–96, 235–37.
35. WPA (12), p.49.

Chapter 3: Biding Time

1. Conner AGO File (22).
2. Sources regarding Conner during the Spanish–American War, and the war generally, are in Conner AGO File (7), (25), (26), (27), (43); CMPR (1); Cullum (1901), Vol. IV, pp.646–57; Spiller et al. (1984), p.198; Aldrich (1993), p.4; Adjutant-General of the State of New York (1900), p.68; Musicant (1998), pp.249–53, 58; O'Toole (1984), pp.12–18, 299, 314–17, 328–30; Vestal (1922), p.199, 215–17; Keenan (2001), p.317; Weigley (1984), p.298.
3. Sources regarding Conner's Cuban service are in Conner AGO File (8); Conner to parents, 07/03/1899, and photographs in the Macpherson Conner Collection; CMPR (1); Spiller et al. (1984), p.198; WDAR (1), pp.311–14; Keenan (2001), pp.49–50, 99–100; Conner, Virginia (1951), pp.11–17; Author interview (2); Potter and Potter (2011), p.125.
4. Sources regarding the Fox Conner–Virginia Brandreth romance are in Conner, Virginia (1951), pp.17–19. The poem is excerpted from Virginia Conner's scrapbook in the Macpherson Conner Collection.
5. Sources regarding Franklin Brandreth and his introduction to Fox Conner are in Conner, Virginia (1951), p.7, 11, 21; Potter and Potter (2011), pp.1–3, 48, 94;

Norm MacDonald interview of Fox Brandreth Conner, October 1982 (Norm MacDonald Collection).

6. *New York Times*, 06/05/1902; Conner, Virginia (1951), pp.21–23.

7. Sources regarding the Conners' time at Fort Hamilton are in Conner, Virginia (1951), pp.21–23; McCain (1975), pp.115–16.

8. Sources regarding Conner's appointment to the Leavenworth Staff College are in Conner AGO File (10), (11), (12), (13), (32); Spiller et al. (1984), pp.198–99; *Regulations for the Army of the United States, 1901*, pp.320–23; Staff College Press (1906), *Annual Report*, pp.35–38 and *Staff College*, pp.3–4; Nenninger (1978), pp.53–60; Hewes (1975), pp.6–12; Weigley (1984), pp.312–17; Cox (2011), p.30.

9. Sources regarding Conner's service at the Staff College are in Conner AGO File (14), (41); CMPR (1); Staff College Press (1906), *Staff College*, Appendix E, p.1, 7 and *Annual Report*, p.36; Conner, Virginia (1951), pp.23–25; Nenninger (1978), p.46, 71–72, 75–77, 94–95, 105; Reardon (1990), p.3; Holley (1982), p.25, 185–86; Grande (2009), p.7, 108.

10. Conner, Fox (1906), p.170.

11. Sources regarding Conner's War College service are in Conner AGO File (16), (17), (18), (35), (38), (46), (50); Conner, Fox (1910), p.790; Conner, Fox (1934), p.327; CMPR (1); *Journal of the United States Artillery*, Vol. 34, pp.111–12; Spiller et al. (1984), p.199; Conner 1920 Congressional Testimony, p.1,692; Conner, Virginia (1951), p.26; Reardon (1990), p.57–58; Aldrich (1993), pp.8–10; Hewes (1975), p.12, 384; Linn (1997), pp.87–88; Norm MacDonald interview of Betty Conner Vida, 10/11/1987, (Norm MacDonald Collection); Holley (1982), pp.186–87, 201–02.

12. Conner, Virginia (1951), p.26; McCain (1975), p.115; photograph of Robert Conner's grave monument (Pam McPhail Collection).

13. Conner AGO File (1), (37), (51); Conner, Virginia (1951), pp.26–27; Spiller et al. (1984), p.199.

14. Ambrose (1983), pp.38–41; Eisenhower, Dwight D. (1967), pp.104–08.

15. Sources regarding Conner's service in the French regiment are in Conner, Virginia (1951), pp.27–34; Conner, Macpherson unpublished essay (1), p.7; Conner AGO File (20); Cox (2011), pp.41–42; Tuchman (1962), pp.28–32.

16. In 1912, Chinese revolutionaries overthrew the feudal Manchu Dynasty which had ruled China for more than a thousand years. Since proponents of the 1912 law curtailing general staff service viewed the legislation as forestalling the creation of a self-perpetuating dynasty of officers, they dubbed the new law limiting general staff service the "Manchu Law."

17. Conner AGO File (2), (3), (29), (49); CMPR (1); Conner, Virginia (1951), p.39; Weigley (1984), pp.332–33, n.33; Garber (1936), p.192.

18. Sources regarding Conner's second tour of duty at Fort Riley are in Conner AGO File (20), (21), (30), (52); CMPR (1); Conner, Virginia (1951), p.49, 59–63; Cullum (1920), Vol. VI-A, p.833; Eisenhower, Dwight D. (1967), p.169; Cox (2011), pp.45–46.

19. Keegan (2000), pp.48–50, 65–69, 112–26; Tuchman (1962), pp.414-15, 435–38.
20. Also known as World War I.
21. Sources regarding Conner's service at Fort Sill are in Conner AGO File (22), (23), (31), (53); Conner, Fox (1916), pp.305–06; CMPR (1), (2), and (3); Cox (2011), pp.48–50; Bryden (1916), p.51; Orlemann (2003), pp.28–30;
22. Sources regarding Conner's 1915 health crisis are in Conner, Virginia (1951), pp.75–77; CMPR (1), (2), and (3).
23. Sources regarding the Punitive Expedition into Mexico are in Welsome (2006), p.340; Stout (1999), pp.35–38; Cullum (1920), Vol. VI-A, p.837; Smith, Gene (1998) p.92, 129–31; D'Este (1995), pp.164–65.
24. Sources regarding Conner's 1916 service in the Inspector General's Bureau are in Conner AGO File (24), (39); WDAR (4), pp.297–302; CMPR (1), (3); Conner, Virginia (1951), p.77; Cox (2011), p.45; Blumenson (1972), p.347; D'Este (1995), pp.175–77; Owen (1918), p.58.
25. CMPR (3); Whitehorne (1998), pp.73–74.
26. Eisenhower, Dwight D. (1967), p.12, 112–13, 118–25; Ambrose (1983), pp.57–59; Cullum (1920), Vol. VI-B, p.1,754.
27. Weigley (1984), p.352; Heckscher (1991), pp.426–41.

Chapter 4: Getting Started

1. Réquin (1919), p.31.
2. Conner, Virginia (1951), p.78; Daniels (1922), pp.1–2; Traxel (2006), p.273; Cottman (1920), pp.3–6.
3. Conner Notes (A); Keegan (2000), pp.326-31; March (1932), pp.20–22; Harbord (1925), p.47; Pershing (1931) Vol. I, pp.69–70; Vandiver (1977), pp.741–42.
4. Conner Notes (A).
5. G-3 Report, p.108; Joffre (1932), p.566; Keegan (2000), p.311, 321; Vandiver (1977), p.682.
6. Conner, Fox (1933), p.174; Brown (1987), p.207; Coffman (1968), p.47; Cox (2011), p.37.
7. Sources regarding Joffre's mission are in Conner, Fox (1933), pp.173–74; G-3 Report, p.17–19; Conner, Virginia (1951), p.78; Joffre (1932), pp.565–68; Réquin (1919), pp.5–9; Coffman (1968), p.47; Vandiver (1977), p.682, New York Times, 05/10/1917; Halsey (197), pp.49–50; Horne (1993), pp.20–21; Holley (1982), pp.270–71.
8. "Long live the United States!"
9. The United States Army was organized into progressively larger units of platoons, companies, battalions, regiments, brigades, divisions, corps, and armies.
10. Conner, Fox (1933), p.173; Conner 1920 Congressional Testimony, p.1,692; Conner Notes (A); G-3 Report, p.8; Holley (1982), p.271; Réquin (1919), p.17.

At the time of the United States' declaration of war, the Regular Army numbered approximately 127,000 officers and men. The National Guard contained between 150,000 and 200,000 soldiers. See: Weigley (1984), pp.357–58.

11. Cooke (1997), p.4; Smith, Gene (1998), p.139; March (1932), p.372.

12. Conner, Fox (1933), pp.173–74; Aldrich (1993), pp.23–24; Holley (1982), pp.271–72; Coffman (1968), p.47.

13. Sources regarding Pershing's appointment as AEF commander-in-chief are in Pershing (1931) Vol. I, pp.18–19; Smythe (1986), pp.3–4; Vandiver (1977), p.683; Holley (1982), pp.272–73.

14. Sources regarding Pershing's assembly of his initial staff are in Fox Conner Lectures (3), p.1; Fox Conner Lectures (4), p.1; Pershing (1931) Vol. I, pp.18–19; Weigley (1984), pp.349–50; Réquin (1919), p.18, 22; Holley (1982), p.274, 280, 324, 330; Cooke (1997), pp.5–6; Reardon (1990), p.201; *USAWW*, Vol. 16, p.1; Brown (1987), p.207; Vandiver (1977), p.684, 689, 696; Blumenson (1972), p.387–90.

15. Sources regarding Pershing's inclusion of Conner on the initial staff are in *USAWW*, Vol. 16, p.1; Cullum (1920), Vol. VI-A, p.833; Pershing (1931) Vol. I, p.20 (n.1); Conner, Virginia (1951), p.79; Coffman (1968), p.267; Pershing to Lester, 05/26/1934 and Pershing to Virginia Conner, 05/19/1939, both in the Macpherson Conner Collection.

16. Eisenhower, Dwight D. (1967), p.26; Ambrose (1983), pp.60–61; Cullum (1920), Vol. VI-B, p.1,754; Smythe (1986), p.5.

17. Sources regarding Conner's departure from home are in CMPR (1), (3); Fox Conner to Virginia Conner, 05/23/1917 and Norm MacDonald interview of Fox Brandreth Conner, October 1982 (both in the Norm MacDonald Collection); Conner, Virginia (1951), p.79; Crowell and Wilson (1921), pp.388-89; Holley (1982), p.275; Blumenson (1972), p.389.

18. Sources regarding the departure of the *Baltic* are in Conner, Virginia (1951), p.79; Pershing (1931) Vol. I, p.42, 78; Harbord (1925), pp.5–7; Cooke (1997), p.7; Holley (1982), p.275; Smythe (1986), p.13; Crowell and Wilson (1921), pp.388–89; March (1932), p.3; Blumenson (1972), p.390.

19. Sources regarding work done aboard the *Baltic* are in Fox Conner Lectures (2), p.2; Fox Conner Lectures (4), p.2; G-3 Report, pp.8–9; Conner 1920 Congressional Testimony, pp.1,679–80; Pershing (1931) Vol. I, pp.38–40, 43, 52, 78; Holley (1982), pp.277–79; Harbord (1925), pp.7–20; Vandiver (1977), p.702; Smythe (1986), pp.14–15; Cooke (1997), p.7.

20. Sources regarding the AEF staff's arrival in England are in Conner 1920 Congressional Testimony, p.1,651; Holley (1982), pp.282–83; Pershing (1931) Vol. I, pp.44–53; Harbord (1925), pp.20–21; Smythe (1986), pp.14–17.

21. Sources regarding the AEF staff's arrival in France are in Pershing (1931) Vol. I, pp.58–59; Holley (1982), pp.282–83; Smythe (1986), p.20.

22. Conner Notes (A); G-3 Report, p.16; Pershing (1931) Vol. I, p.59.

23. Sources regarding the conditions under which the initial AEF staff functioned are in Fox Conner Lectures (3), pp.1–2; Conner Notes (A); G-3 Report, p.12; Conner 1920 Congressional Testimony, p.1,669; Pershing (1931) Vol. I, p.71, 100, 103; Holley (1982), pp.293–95; Harbord (1925), p.280; Fiske (1940), pp.5–6; Réquin (1919), pp.5–6; Vandiver (1977), p.734; Smythe (1986), p.17.

24. Conner 1920 Congressional Testimony, p.1,679–80; Fox Conner Lectures (2), p.2; Conner, Fox (1933), p.175; G-3 Report, p.12; Réquin (1919), pp.66–69.

25. Conner, Fox (1933), p.175; Conner, Fox (1934), p.329; Pershing (1931) Vol. I, p.199; *American Armies and Battlefields in Europe* (1938), p.501.

26. Sources regarding formation of the 28,000-strong "square" AEF division structure are in Conner, Fox (1933), pp.173–75; "Informal Talk by Chief of Operations, AEF" 10/22/1918, RG120, Entry 267 (7); Harbord (1936), pp.103–04; Holley (1982), pp.302–03; Pershing (1931) Vol. I, p.101, n.1; Smythe (1986), pp.37–38.

27. Sources regarding selection of Lorraine as the AEF's area of operations are in Conner Notes (A); Fox Conner Lectures (2); Conner memo, 11/08/1917, RG120, Entry 267 (3); G-3 Report, pp.10–11; Conner 1920 Congressional Testimony, pp.1,701–02; *American Armies and Battlefields in Europe* (1938), p.4, 16; Smythe (1986), p.27.

28. Holley (1982), pp.186–87.

29. Sources regarding the facilities offered by France to the AEF are in "Report of Board Considering Questions in the Zone of the Army," 06/28/1917, RG120, Entry 267 (3); G-3 Report, p.10; Conner 1920 Congressional Testimony, p.1,702; Holley (1982), pp.298–99; Vandiver (1977), p.742.

30. G-3 Report, p.17; Bland and Ritenour (1981), p.111; Vandiver (1977), pp.723–24, 733; Smythe (1986), p.33.

31. Sources regarding the involvement of the Chauncey Baker Board are in: Conner, Fox (1933), p.174; Fox Conner Lectures (3), p.2; G-3 Report, pp.8–9, 94; Harbord (1925), pp.56–57, 93; Harbord (1936), pp.100–01; Pershing (1931) Vol. I, p.100; Nenninger (2010), pp.106–07; Holley (1982), pp.302–04; Smythe (1986), pp.36–37; Cullum (1910), Vol. V, p.487.

32. Holley (1982), pp.301–06.

33. Hofmann (2006), pp.55–57.

34. Pershing (1931) Vol. I, p.100, 103; Holley (1982), pp.308–11; Harbord (1936), pp.97–98, 100; Pogue (1963), p.149.

35. Holley (1982), pp.307–08, 312, 316–17; Harbord (1925), p.200.

36. Holley (1982), p.278; Cullum (1920), Vol. VI-A, pp.629–30, 833.

37. Sources regarding the AEF's move to Chaumont are in G-3 Report, p.13; Pershing (1931) Vol. I, p.128, 156, 163; Harbord (1925), pp.139–40; Fiske (1940), pp.5–6; Bishop (1919), pp.1–4; Hanson (1922), pp.90–93; *American Armies and Battlefields in Europe* (1938), p.494.

38. Blumenson (1972), p.398, 403, 415; D'Este (1995), p.196, 200.

39. See: 09/25/1917 Strategical Study, pp.1–6, 10–21.

40. Sources regarding Conner's September 1917 hospitalization are in CMPR (2); Conner, Virginia (1951), p.80; Pershing (1931) Vol. I, p.23; Scott (1923), p.299; Blumenson (1972), p.430.
41. CMPR (2); Holley (1982), p.325, n.19, 727.
42. Repington (1920), pp.87–90.
43. Sources regarding Conner's discussions with Patton concerning the tank service are in Blumenson (1972), pp.427–34, 473–74; D'Este (1995), pp.205-08, 220–24; Aldrich (1993), p.228; Pershing (1931) Vol. I, p.168; Hofmann (2006), pp.55–57.
44. Eisenhower, Dwight D. (1967), pp.131–33; Perret (1999), pp.66–67; Cullum (1920), Vol. VI-B, p.1,754; Nenninger (1978), p.74.
45. Pogue (1963), pp.154–56; Coffman (1968), pp.139–40; Harries and Harries (1997), pp.3–5; Vandiver (1977), pp.808–10; Pershing (1931) Vol. I, pp.217–18; Smythe (1986), p.59.
46. Conner Notes(A); G-3 Report, 15–17; Pershing(I), 205–207; Holley, 325; Keegan, 340–341, 347–350.
47. "Memorandum for Operations Section," 11/05/1917, RG120, Entry 267 (3).
48. Cullum (1920), Vol. VI-A, pp.629–30; Center of Military History (1988), p.1.
49. G-3 Report, p.17; Holley (1982), pp.325–26.
50. Conner memo, 11/05/1917, RG120, Entry 267 (14).
51. Harbord (1936), p.97; Smythe (1986), p.34; Vandiver (1977), p.944; Ambrose (1983), p.73.

Chapter 5: The War within the War

1. Conner Notes (A).
2. *American Armies and Battlefields in Europe* (1938), p.502.
3. Conner memo, 11/06/1917, RG120. Entry 267 (2).
4. Conner memo, 11/09/1917, RG120, Entry 267 (3); Conner 1920 Congressional Testimony, p.1,703; Vandiver (1977), p.787, 871; Keegan (2000), p.394.
5. All references to the 11/15/1917 "Strategical Study" are in RG120, Entry 267 (3). See also Conner memo, 01/07/1918, RG120, Entry 267 (3).
6. Sources regarding Conner's proposal to convert the 42nd Division into a replacement division are in Conner memo, 11/10/1917, *USAWW*, Vol. 3, p.664, 666–67; Conner memo, 11/22/1917, *USAWW*, Vol. 3, pp.667–68; G-3 Report, p.17, 94; Smythe (1986), pp.61–62; Coffman (1971), p.45; Coffman (1968), pp.149–52; Cullum (1920), Vol. VI-A, pp.1,013–14; Hunt (1954), p.71.
7. Sources regarding the Conner–MacArthur relationship during World War I are in Hunt (1954), pp.70–71; Bland et al. (1991), p.243; Pogue (1963), pp.164–65; Cray (1990), p.81; Weintraub (2007), p.87; Eisenhower, John (2001), pp.292–93.
8. Holley (1982), pp.333–34; Center of Military History (1988), p.1.
9. Bland and Ritenour (1981), p.129; Cooke (1997), p.20, 47; Harbord (1925), p.202.

10. *The Boston Daily Globe*, 03/15/1931.
11. Sources regarding Conner's analysis of the British shipping proposal are in Conner memo, 12/16/1917, RG120, Entry 267 (2); Conner Notes (A); G-3 Report, p.19; Conner 1920 Congressional Testimony, p.1,656, 1,661.
12. Harbord to Conner, 01/01/1918 and Conner memo, 01/07/1918, both in RG120, Entry 267 (3); G-3 Report, p.19.
13. All references to Conner's 01/07/1918 Strategical Study are in Conner memo, 01/07/1918, RG120, Entry 267 (3); G-3 Report, pp.22–23.
14. Conner memo, 03/28/1918, *USAWW*, Vol. 3, pp.74–75.
15. Conner memo, 01/06/1918, *USAWW*, Vol. 3, pp.460–61; Conner memo, 01/15/1918, RG120, Entry 267 (12); Conner 1920 Congressional Testimony, p.1,655.
16. Conner memo, 01/19/1918, *USAWW*, Vol. 3, p.467; G-3 Report, pp.23–24; Liggett (1925), pp.19–21; Cullum (1920), Vol. VI-A, p.402.
17. Fox Conner Lectures (3), p.2; Reardon (1990), p.58; Cullum (1920), Vol. VI-A, p.402.
18. Bland and Ritenour (1981), pp.129–31.
19. Sources regarding Conner's 02/9/1918 shrapnel wound are in CMPR (1), (2); Conner, Virginia (1951), pp.81–82; Anon. "Our Gallery of Illustrious" (1935), p.1.
20. Conner memos, 02/17/1918, 02/18/1918, and 02/19/1918, all in RG120, Entry 267 (3).
21. March (1932), p.3, 34; G-3 Report, p.41; Harbord (1925), p.152; Smythe (1986), pp.46–49; Trask (1961), pp.30–33; Heckscher (1991), pp.461–62.
22. Eisenhower, Dwight D. (1967), pp.136–37, 150; Ambrose (1983), pp.61–62; Perret (1999), p.67. Regarding the nickname of Eisenhower's firstborn son, Doud Dwight Eisenhower, some have used the spelling "Ikky." The spelling used herein is taken from Eisenhower's own memoir, *At Ease*.
23. G-3 Report, p.26.
24. Conner memo, 03/18/1918, RG120, Entry 267 (8); G-3 Report, p.24.
25. Conner 1920 Congressional Testimony, p.1,664; Vandiver (1977), pp.863–69; Harbord (1925), pp.247–48.
26. Sources regarding Germany's March 1918 Operation *Michael* are in Fox Conner Lectures (2); G-3 Report, pp.26–27, 41; Keegan (2000), pp.394–02; Vandiver (1977), p.871; Pershing (1931), Vol. I, p.368; Smythe (1986) pp.96–98.
27. Keegan (2000), pp.402–03; Trask (1993), pp.49–51.
28. Conner memo, 03/25/1918, *USAWW*, Vol. 3, p.277.
29. Conner memo, 03/26/1918, *USAWW*, Vol. 3, pp.278–79; Trask (1993), p.53; Smythe (1986), pp.98–99.
30. G-3 Report, p.27, 41; Keegan (2000), pp.402–03; Trask (1993), pp.49–51, 55; Trask (1961), pp.63–64.
31. *See previous note. Also:* Foch to Pershing, 04/10/1918, *USAWW*, Vol 3, pp.283–84; Smythe (1986), p.101; *American Armies and Battlefields in Europe* (1938), pp.25–26.

32. Conner memo, 04/01/1918, RG120, Entry 267 (2); G-3 Report, p.43; "Informal Talk by Chief of Operations, AEF," 10/22/1918, RG120, Entry 267 (7); Pershing (1931), Vol. I, p.367.

33. Fox Conner Lectures (2), p.4; G-3 Report, pp.26–27, 31–32; Keegan (2000), p.394, 404; Tuchman (1962), p.32, 365; Trask (1993), pp.51–53.

34. Sources regarding Conner's analysis of Lord Reading's proposal are in Conner memo, 04/6/1918, RG120, Entry 267 (2); Pershing (1931), Vol. I, pp.382–83; Smythe (1986), pp.103–04; Keegan (2000), pp.395–404.

35. Conner memo, 04/9/1918, RG120, Entry 267 (2); Smythe (1986), p.108.

36. *Ibid.*

37. Details of Conner's 04/9/1918 meeting with General Ragueneau are in Conner memo, 04/09/1918, RG120, Entry 267 (2).

38. Sources regarding Germany's April 1918 Operation George are in G-3 Report, p.27; Keegan (2000), pp.405–06; Pershing (1931) Vol. II, p.31, 34.

39. Conner memo 04/09/1918 and 04/10/1918, *USAWW*, Vol. 3, pp.650–51; Conner memo, 04/12/1918; *USAWW*, Vol. 4, p.260.

40. Sources regarding the April 1918 London Conference are in Conner memo, 01/07/1918, RG120, Entry 267 (3); G-3 Report, pp.44–45; Pershing (1931), Vol. II, pp.5–8; Smythe (1986), pp.108–10. In a 1931 lecture discussing intra-Allied agreements for shipping priorities, Conner stated: "aside from the Chief of Staff, G-3 was the only one who accompanied the C. in C. to the various conferences and who was therefore fully cognizant of the complicated questions and policies involved." See: Fox Conner Lectures (3), p.3.

41. Conner Notes (A); G-3 Report, p.32.

42. G-3 Report, p.47; Pershing (1931), Vol. II, p.31.

43. Sources regarding the May 1918 Abbeville Conference are in G-3 Report, pp.45–46, 55–56; Pershing (1931), Vol. II, pp.21–34; *The Boston Daily Globe*, 03/15/1931. See also Conner memo, 12/16/1917, RG120, Entry 267 (2), and Conner memo, 01/07/1918, RG120, Entry 267 (3).

44. Conner memo, 05/07/1918, *USAWW*. Vol. 2, pp.384–86; Conner memo, 05/06/1918 and 05/12/1918, *USAWW*, Vol. 3, p.128, 133; G-3 Report, p.33.

45. Harbord (1925), pp.278–79; Pershing (1931), Vol. II, p.38; Smythe (1986), pp.120–21; Cooke (1997), p.84.

46. Cullum (1901), Vol. IV, p.463; Cullum (1910), Vol. V, p.419; Cullum (1920), Vol. VI-A, p.463; Smythe (1986), pp.120–21; Harbord (1925), pp.278–79, 281–82; Cooke (1997), p.84.

47. The Woëvre region encompasses the plain between the Meuse and Moselle rivers in Lorraine.

48. G-3 Report, p.56, 66; Conner Notes (C).

49. Conner memo, 05/24/1918; *USAWW*. Vol. 3, p.303; Liggett (1925), p.21.

50. Conner memo, 05/25/1918, *USAWW*. Vol. 3, pp.303–04; G-3 Report, pp.33–35; Pershing (1931), Vol. II, p.47; *American Armies and Battlefields in Europe* (1938), p.515; Thompson, Holland (1921), Vol. XIII, Appendix B, ii, iv.

51. Conner 1920 Congressional Testimony, p.1,704; G-3 Report, p.27; Smythe (1986), pp.120–21.

Chapter 6: Fighting with the French

1. Bland et al. (1991), p.240.
2. Griscom (1940), p.395. Lloyd C. Griscom, Pershing's personal representative to the British War Office, was in Chaumont at the time of the Cantigny operation and the May 1918 German offensive.
3. Sources regarding the details of the Cantigny operation are in: G-3 Report, p.32; Society of the First Division (1922), pp.77–86; Millet in Heller and Stofft (1986), pp.165–79; Pershing (1931) Vol. II, pp.54–55; Trask (1993), pp.66–67; Pogue (1963), p.166; Coffman (1968), p.158.
4. Sources regarding the details of the German offensive of May 1918 are in: G-3 Report, pp.27–28; Pershing (1931), Vol. II, pp.60–61; Trask (1993), pp.69–70; DeWeerd (1968), pp.289–92; *Guide to the American Battle Fields of Europe* (1927), p.22.
5. Conner's 1920 Testimony, p.1,704.
6. Grant to Conner, 05/29/1918, *USAWW*, Vol. 4, pp.167–68.
7. Translation: "It's terrible! It's awful! The Boche [Germans] have arrived at the Marne. Help!" All references to Conner's discussions of 05/27/1918 are from Griscom (1940), pp.394–96.
8. Conner Notes (A).
9. G-3 Report, pp.33–34; Conner memo, 05/24/1918, *USAWW*, Vol. 3, pp.303–04.
10. Conner memo, 05/28/1918 and 05/29/1918, both in *USAWW*, Vol. 4, pp.167–68.
11. Cullum (1920), Vol. VI-A, p.852; Linnerud (1998), pp.1–40.
12. G-3 Report, p.32.
13. Conner Notes (A); G-3 Report, p.32.
14. Conner Notes (A).
15. Memos to and from Conner, 05/29/1918 through 06/01/1918, all in *USAWW*, Vol. 4, pp.167–72, 187–88; Conner Notes (A).
16. Conner Notes (A); Harbord (1925), pp.288–90; Harbord (1936), p.283; Trask (1993), p.70; Simmons (1976), pp.110–11; Stallings (1963), p.88.
17. Conner memo, 05/29/1918, RG120, Entry 267 (3).
18. Sources regarding the Versailles conference of 06/01/1918–06/02/1918 are in Conner Lectures (3), p.5; Conner memo, 06/11/1918, *USAWW*, Vol. 2, p.461; G-3 Report, pp.47–49; Pershing (1931), Vol. II, pp.70–79; Griscom (1940), pp.414–15; Smythe (1986), pp.133–36; Trask (1993), pp.74–75.
19. Eisenhower, Dwight D. (1967), pp.139–47; Perret (1999), p.68; Korda (2007), pp.139–41; D'Este (1995), pp.205–10.

20. Conner Lectures (3), p.5; G-3 Report, p.36.

21. Sources regarding the Belleau Wood operation generally are in: Grant to McAndrew, 06/12/1918, *USAWW*, Vol. 4, pp.448–49; Coffman (1968), pp.214–22; Stallings (1963), p.89, 100; Vandiver (1977), pp.896–97; Smythe (1986), pp.134–40; Millet in Heller and Stofft (1986), p.180.

22. Harbord to Bundy, 06/11/1918, "Operations Reports No. 1 and No. 2"; Grant to McAndrew, 06/12/1918; Lejeune memo 12/31/1918, all in *USAWW*, Vol. 4, pp.236–38, 437–39, 448–49.

23. Vandiver (1977), p.898; Stallings (1963), pp.100–01. Stallings co-wrote the play *What Price Glory*, later made into a John Ford film adaptation starring James Cagney.

24. Robert C. Richardson eventually rose to the rank of lieutenant general during World War II and became the Commanding General of U.S. Army forces in the Central Pacific.

25. Report of Conner–Richardson conversation, 06/12/1918 and Grant memo to McAndrew, 06/12/1918, both in *USAWW*, Vol. 4, pp.448–49, 450–51.

26. Grant to Conner, 06/13/1918, *USAWW*, Vol. 4, pp.466–67; Conner order and Conner pencil note, both in *USAWW*, Vol. 4, p.430, 464.

27. Brown memo, 06/12/1918 and Bundy memo, 06/13/1918, both in *USAWW*, Vol. 4, p.453, 459.

28. Note of Conner–Richardson conversation, 06/13/1918, *USAWW*, Vol. 4, p.464.

29. Duchene to General Staff, 06/10/1918 and order, both in *USAWW*, Vol. 4, p.430, 464; G-3 Report, p.28; Coffman (1968), p.222.

30. Conner Notes (D); Grant to Conner, 06/13/1918, *USAWW*, Vol. 4, pp.466–67; Coffman (1968), p.219, 221–24; Smythe (1986), pp.139–40.

31. Warthin and Walker (1919), pp.32–33; Gillet (2009), pp.306–07; Fries and West (1921), pp.167–79. Amos Fries served as Chief of the AEF Chemical Warfare Section. He was also a classmate of Fox Conner's in the West Point Class of 1898.

32. Sources regarding the 06/14/1918 German mustard-gas bombardment in Belleau Wood are in memos to and from Conner, 06/15/1918, *USAWW*, Vol. 4, p.485, 490–91; Bundy to Pershing, 06/14/1918, *USAWW*, Vol. 4, p.470; Coffman (1968), p.221.

33. Hamilton and Corbin (1919), p.17.

34. Degoutte to General Staff, 06/14/1918; memos to and from Conner, 06/15/1918 (with 06/16/1918 addendum), all in in *USAWW*, Vol. 4, pp.476–77, 485, 490–91.

35. Conner and Short had served together at Fort Sill. Like his fellow liaison officer Robert C. Richardson (see footnote *supra*), Walter C. Short's career also reached its pinnacle in World War II, but under less favorable circumstances. Lieutenant General Walter C. Short commanded Army forces in Hawaii at the time of the Pearl Harbor attack, and much of the blame for the military's failure to anticipate and prepare for the attack fell upon him. Short was recalled to Washington, demoted in rank, and retired in early 1942.

36. Memos of Short and Eltinge to Conner, 06/25/1916 and 06/26/1918, *USAWW*, Vol. 4, p.559, 625; G-3 Report, p.37.
37. Conner memos, 05/24/1918 and 05/25/1918, both in *USAWW*, Vol. 3, pp.303–04; Grant to Conner, 06/15/1918, *USAWW*, Vol. 4, pp.490–91; Ferrell (2009), p.86.
38. G-3 Report, p.28, 37; Coffman (1968), p.222.
39. All references to Conner's 06/22/1918 memo are in *USAWW*, Vol. 3, pp.323–24.
40. Pétain to Commanding Generals, 06/19/1918, *USAWW*, Vol. 4, pp.511–12.
41. G-3 Report, p.33; Ragueneau to Conner, 06/29/1918, *USAWW*, Vol. 4, p.638; Ferrell (2009), p.88.
42. *See previous note. Also:* G-3 Report, p.56; Liggett (1925), pp.30–31.
43. Conner memo, 06/18/1918, *USAWW*, Vol. 2, pp.470–71; Pershing (1931), Vol. II, pp.10407, 118–23.
44. Sources regarding the 07/10/1918 conference are in Conner memos of 07/11/1918 (*USAWW*, Vol. 3, pp.333–34) and 07/14/1918, RG120, Entry 267 (3); Conner Notes (B), G-3 Report, p.51, 60–61, 74; Pershing (1931), Vol. II, p.138, 144–45.
45. All references to Conner's 07/14/1918 memo are in RG120, Entry 267 (3).
46. *Ibid.*; 09/25/1917 "Strategical Study," p.6, 10.
47. Sources regarding Marshall's transfer to, and early service in, the Chaumont GHQ are in Marshall (1976), pp.116–21; Bland and Ritenour (1981), p.144; Pogue (1963), pp.164–65, 168, 387; Payne (1951), pp.69–70; Frye (1947), p.147–48; Nenninger (1978), p.145.
48. Sources regarding the German offensive of 07/15/1918 are in Conner Notes (A); Conner Notes (B); G-3 Report, pp.28–29; Pershing (1931), Vol. II, p.153; *Guide to the American Battle Fields of Europe* (1927), pp.23–24.
49. Sources regarding the 07/18/1918 Allied counterattack at Soissons are in Conner Notes (B); G-3 Report, p.52; Pershing (1931), Vol. II, pp.158–60; Harbord (1925), pp.323–26; Liggett (1925), p.35, 49–51; *Guide to the American Battle Fields of Europe* (1927), p.56; Millet in Heller and Stofft (1986), p.180.
50. "Informal Talk by Chief of Operations, AEF," 10/22/1918, RG120, Entry 267 (7).
51. Conner Notes (B); G-3 Report, p.52; Drum to Conner, 08/7/1918, *USAWW*, Vol. 8, p.20; Pershing (1931), Vol. II, pp.160–61; Marshall (1976), p.117.
52. "Informal Talk by Chief of Operations, AEF," 10/22/1918, RG120, Entry 267 (7); Conner Notes (B).
53. Conner Notes (B); Conner Notes (C); G-3 Report, p.38; Pershing (1931), Vol. II, p.2, 171; McAndrew to Liggett, 07/11/1918, *USAWW*, Vol. 3, p.334; Liggett to McAndrew, 07/16/1918 and Hitt to Conner, 07/16/1918, both in *USAWW*, Vol. 5, p.32, 87–88.
54. *See preceding note. Also:* Drum to Bullard, 07/29/1918 and Conner to Liggett, 07/29/1918, both in *USAWW*, Vol. 5, pp.267–68; memos exchanged between

Conner and Drum, 07/29/1918 and 08/08/1918, both in *USAWW*, Vol. 8, p.120.

55. Conner Notes (C); Pershing (1931), Vol. II, p.172.
56. Sources regarding the preliminary planning for the St. Mihiel operation are in Conner Notes (C); Conner Notes (D); Conner memo, 08/03/1918, and telegrams and memos exchanged between Conner and Drum, 08/25/1918 and 08/28/1918, all in RG120, Entry 267 (5); Fox Conner Lectures (3), p.1; G-3 Report, p.54, 58–60; Marshall (1976), p.133; Pogue (1963), pp.172–74; Hallas (1995), p.22.
57. Conner memo, 08/16/1918, *USAWW*, Vol. 8, p.131; Conner memo, 08/18/1918 and Simonds to Conner, 08/23/1918, both in *USAWW*, Vol. 3, pp.174–80; G-3 Report, p.60; Marshall (1976), p.124; Hallas (1995), p.15.
58. Simonds to Conner, 08/23/1918, *USAWW*, Vol. 3, pp.179–80; Sherburne 1920 Congressional Testimony, p.1,848.
59. Marshall (1976), pp.125–26, 156; Bland and Ritenour (1981), pp.155–56; Cray (1990), p.69.
60. Sources regarding the 08/30/1918 meeting between Foch and Pershing are in G-3 Report, p.61, 74; Pershing (1931), Vol. II, pp.243–47.
61. Translation: "Do you wish to take part in the battle?"
62. Sources regarding the American response to Foch's 08/30/1918 proposal are in G-3 Report, pp.61–62; Pershing (1931), Vol. II, p.241, 244–50; *The Boston Daily Globe*, 03/15/1931.
63. Sources regarding the meetings of 08/31/1918–09/02/1918 are in G-3 Report, p.62, Pershing (1931), Vol. II, p.241, 253–54; *The Boston Daily Globe*, 03/15/1931; Johnson (1928), pp.44–45, 51–52. While Johnson credited Conner as a source for his book, he did not credit either Pershing or McAndrew. Presumably, Conner was Johnson's source for what transpired at these meetings.
64. Pershing (1931), Vol. II, pp.254–55.
65. Weigley (1984), p.388.

Chapter 7: Our Seat at the Table

1. G-3 Report, p.29.
2. Mott to Conner, 08/31/1918, RG120, Entry 267 (5); Pershing (1931), Vol. I, p.391.
3. Fox Conner Lecture (2); Herwig (2009), pp.74–77; Tuchman (1962), p.186, 188; Horne (1993), p.36, 44.
4. Pétain memo, 08/22/1918, *USAWW*, Vol. 8, pp.25–26; Coffman (1968), p.269; Pershing (1931), Vol. II, p.239.
5. Sources regarding the Belfort Ruse are in excerpts from letter written by Colonel Arthur S. Conger, 11/25/1926, *USAWW*, Vol. 8, pp.62–64; Conner Notes

(C); Conner memo, 08/26/1918, *USAWW*, Vol. 8, p.165; Conner memo, 08/28/1918, RG120, Entry 267 (5) [see also: *USAWW*, Vol. 8, p.34]; Bundy to Conner, 09/01/1918, and Conner memo, 09/01/1918, both in *USAWW*, Vol. 8, pp.44–45; Conner memo, 09/04/1918, RG120, Entry 267 (5); excerpt from report of French Military Mission, 9/12/1918 and excerpt from German Intelligence Report, 09/10/1918, both in *USAWW*, Vol. 8, pp.62–64, 297; Ludendorff to von Gallwitz, 09/04/1918; Group of Armies von Gallwitz to Group of Armies Duke Albrecht, 09/10/1918; and von Gallwitz to Supreme Headquarters, 09/21/1918, all in *USAWW*, Vol. 8, p.290, 298, 323–24; Pershing (1931), Vol. II, pp.239–40; Hallas (1995), p.44; Hallas in Venzon (1995), pp.70–71; Smythe (1986), pp.152–53; Stallings (1963), p.207; Coffman (1968), pp.269–70.

6. Historian James Hallas suggests the Belfort Ruse may have been "the seed of the whole fictitious army created 26 years later before the Normandy invasion of World War II," an assessment echoed by author Thaddeus Holt, who noted that Dwight D. Eisenhower's appreciation of the value of military deception in World War II "perhaps ... reflected memories of Conner's accounts of the operation." See: Hallas in Venzon (1995), pp.70–71; Holt, Thaddeus (2004), p.247.

7. Conner Notes (C); G-3 Report, pp.66–70; "Informal Talk by Chief of Operations, AEF," 10/22/1918, RG120, Entry 267 (7); Marshall (1976), p.130, 143–47; Liggett (1925), p.68; Johnson (1928), pp.91–96; Hallas (1995), pp.261–62, n.7; D'Este (1995), pp.232–34, 246, n.69; Smythe (1986), p.187; Coffman (1968), p.283; *American Armies and Battlefields in Europe* (1938), p.109; von Gallwitz to Hindenburg, 09/21/1918, *USAWW*, Vol. 8, pp.323–24.

8. Conner Notes (D); order of battle, *USAWW*, Vol. 9, p.1; Marshall (1976), pp.137–39.

9. Conner Notes (D); Marshall (1976), p.149.

10. Conner memo, 09/15/1918, *USAWW*, Vol. 2, pp.602–03.

11. Sources regarding the German defenses on the Meuse–Argonne Front are in Conner Notes (D); G-3 Report, pp.77–78, 87; Marshall (1976), p.159; Pogue (1963), pp.179–80; Cooke (1997), p.126; *Guide to the American Battle Fields of Europe* (1927), p.124; Johnson (1928), p.93.

12. Bland and Ritenour (1981), pp.360–61. Dennis E. Nolan served as Pershing's chief of intelligence (G-2) throughout the war.

13. G-3 Report, p.75; Conner to McAndrew, 09/15/1918, *USAWW*, Vol. 2, pp.602–03.

14. Conner Notes (D); Marshall (1976), p.151; Cray (1990), p.74; extract from Ludendorff's 09/22/1918 memorandum, *USAWW*, Vol. 9, p.509.

15. Sources regarding the beginning of the AEF's Meuse–Argonne offensive are in Conner Notes (D); G-3 Report, pp.78–81; Liggett (1925), pp.91–92; Marshall (1976), pp.162–63; Smythe (1986), p.190; Coffman (1968), pp.300–01; Cooke (1997), p.132, n.17; "Notes Made By the Inspector General, AEF During Active Operations From 12th September 1918 to 11th November 1918," p.1, RG120,

Entry 268 (18); McCullough (1992), pp.128–29; D'Este (1995), p.254, n.18, 256–63.

16.   Conner memo, 09/29/1918, *USAWW*, Vol. 2, pp.614–15; Conner Notes (D); G-3 Report, p.81.

17.   G-3 Report, p.91; Pogue (1963), pp.181–82; extract from Ludendorff memo of 09/29/1918 and von der Marwitz order of 10/01/1918, both in *USAWW*, Vol. 9, p.523, 531.

18.   Conner Notes (D);   Conner 1920 Congressional Testimony, p.1,710; Ferrell (2009), p.170; Cooke (1997), pp.133–35.

19.   Conner Notes (D); Ferrell (2007), p.80; Ludendorff to Gallwitz, 10/10/1918, *USAWW*, Vol. 9, p.549.

20.   Conner 1920 Congressional Testimony, p.1,680.

21.   Conner, Fox (1941), p.4; Conner Notes (D); G-3 Report, p.82, 94–95; Conner memo, 09/15/1918, *USAWW*, Vol. 2, pp.602–03.

22.   Sources regarding the AEF's reorganization are in Conner Notes (D); G-3 Report, p.82; Bland and Ritenour (1981), xxix, pp.430–31; Cooke (1997), p.133.

23.   Conner Notes (D); Cooke (1997), p.133; Smythe (1986), pp.214–16; *Guide to the American Battle Fields of Europe* (1927), pp.124–25; Ferrell (2009), p.171, 179.

24.   Pershing (1931), Vol. II, p.355; Smythe (1986), pp.216–17; March (1932), p.261.

25.   All references to the 10/22/1918 "Informal Talk by Chief of Operations, AEF" are in RG120, Entry 267 (7). See also: Johnson (1928), pp.288–92.

26.   Sources regarding planning for the AEF's November attack are in Conner Notes (D); Liggett (1925), pp.110–11; Ferrell (2009), pp.178–81, 184–85; Smythe (1986), p.223; Cooke (1997), p.134, n.1.

27.   Conner Notes (D); Keegan (2000), p.416; Lowry, Bullitt (1996), pp.148–49, 189.

28.   Sources regarding Pershing's proposal for an unconditional German surrender are in Brown (1987), pp.210–11; G-3 Report, p.86; Pershing (1931), Vol. II, pp.359–67; Lowry, Bullit (1996), pp.71–73, 97, 117–20; *New York Times*, 08/13/1944.

29.   Sources regarding the AEF's November 1918 attack are in Conner Notes (D); G-3 Report, p.29, 84; Conner 1920 Congressional Testimony, p.1,711, 1,716; Marshall (1976), p.159, 184, 191; Liggett (1925), pp.112–15; Harbord (1936), p.455, 459; Cooke (1997), p.139, n.1.

30.   Marshall (1976), p.191.

31.   Tuchman (1962), p.29; Liggett (1925), p.116; Smythe (1986), p.227.

32.   Pershing (1931), Vol. II, p.381; Ferrell (2007), p.140; Harbord (1936), p.455; Liggett (1925), p.116; Marshall (1976), pp.189–90.

33.   Sources regarding the "Race for Sedan" are in Murphy to Conner, 11/08/1918, *USAWW*, Vol. 8, p.111; Conner to Liggett, 11/10/1918, *USAWW*, Vol. 9, p.409; Marshall (1976), pp.189–92; Bland and Ritenour (1981), pp.165–68; Ferrell (2007), p.140; Ferrell (2009), p.189; Coffman (1968), pp.349–53; Harbord (1936), pp.457–60; Smythe (1986), pp.228–29; MacArthur (1964), p.68; Manchester

(1978), p.109; Cooke (1997), pp.135–36; Society of the First Division (1922), pp.447–48; Pershing (1931) Vol. II, p.381.

34. Conner Notes (D); G-3 Report, p.85; Conner 1920 Congressional Testimony, p.1,722.

35. *Ibid.*

36. Keegan (2000), pp.416–18; Lowry, Bullitt (1996), pp.149–51.

37. *Ibid.*; Conner Notes (D); *American Armies and Battlefields in Europe* (1938), pp.507–09.

38. Conner 1920 Congressional Testimony, pp.1,712–15; Pershing (via Drum) to Corps Commanders, 11/08/1918, *USAWW*, Vol. 9, pp.400–01.

39. Conner Notes (D); G-3 Report, p.85, 88–89; Smythe (1986), p.227, n.20.

40. Conner 1920 Congressional Testimony, pp.1,714–16; Liggett (1925), p.126.

41. Conner 1920 Congressional Testimony, pp.1,713–16; Conner Notes (D); Smythe (1986), p.231.

42. Eisenhower, Dwight D. (1967), pp.147–48, 151; Perret (1999), p.69; Ambrose (1983), p.65.

43. Conner Notes (D).

44. Sources regarding communication and acceptance of the armistice terms are in Conner 1920 Congressional Testimony, p.1,711, 1,714–21, 1,731; Keegan (2000), pp.417–19; Lowry, Bullitt (1996), p.149, 158–59; Coffman (1968), p.355.

45. Twenty-two years later, Adolf Hitler accepted the surrender of France in World War II in the same rail car and at the same location in the Compiègne Forest.

46. Conner Notes (D); Smythe (1986), pp.231–32.

47. Coffman (1968), p.299; Ferrell (2007), xi; Lengl (2008), p.419.

48. G-3 Report, p.87; Conner Notes (D).

49. Liggett (1925), p.125.

50. Conner, Virginia (1951), p.81. The photographs and sketches referenced are in the Macpherson Conner and Norm MacDonald collections.

51. CMPR (1).

52. Pershing to Conner, 08/05/1938, MDAH (1).

Chapter 8: Home Again

1. Conner 1920 Congressional Testimony, p.1,724.

2. CMPR (1); Brown (1987), p.21; Smythe (1986), p.259; March (1932), p.47.

3. Conner memo, 11/15/1918, RG120, Entry 267 (13); Fox Conner Lecture (3), p.5; G-3 Report, pp.100–03; Marshall (1976), pp.204–05; Nenninger (2010), p.156.

4. CMPR (1); Pogue (1963), pp.190–92, 389–90; Bland and Ritenour (1981), pp.175–82; Payne (1951), p.94.

5. Pershing to Conner, 11/29/1918, MDAH (1); Cullum (1930), Vol. VII, p.493, 833; Smythe (1986), p.254.

6. CMPR (2); Patton to Conner, 02/24/1919, MDAH (1).
7. Conner letter, 03/11/1919, RG120, Entry 267 (16); G-3 Report, p.33, 109–10.
8. Vandiver (1977), p.1,022; *American Armies and Battlefields in Europe* (1938), p.13, 509–10.
9. Conner, Virginia (1951), p.12; Eisenhower, Dwight D. (1967), p.195; Miller, Merle (1987), p.210.
10. Fox Conner to Virginia Conner, 06/02/1919, Norm MacDonald Collection; Conner, Virginia (1951), p.80.
11. Sources regarding Conner's return home are in CMPR (1); Conner, Virginia (1951), pp.81–86; Smythe (1986), pp.259–61. See also: photographs of Conner, Pershing, and Marshall on board the Navy launch that took them from the *Leviathan* to shore, in the Norm MacDonald Collection and also in the photographic insert to Marshall's memoir.
12. October 1982 interview of Fox Brandreth Conner by Norm Macdonald (Norm MacDonald Collection).
13. Nannie Conner letter to Virginia Conner, 07/03/1919 (Norm MacDonald Collection).
14. Conner, Virginia (1951), p.88.
15. Sources regarding the October 1919 trip to Brandreth Lake are in Conner, Virginia (1951), pp.88–63; Potter and Potter (2011), pp.113–16; Pogue (1963), p.207; Bland et al. (1991), p.247; Bland and Ritenour (1981), p.576; Vandiver (1977), p.1,045, n.15. See also: photographs from Virginia Conner's scrapbook (Macpherson Conner Collection).
16. Holley (1982), pp.402–03, 410, n.24–25; Conner, Virginia (1951), p.88; Bland and Ritenour (1981), pp.182–83; March (1932), p.331, 336–37; Coffman (1966), p.176.
17. Pogue (1963), p.207; Cooke (1997), p.198.
18. Sources regarding hearings on the Baker–March bill are in March (1932), pp.331–40; Coffman (1966), pp.189–98; Smythe (1986), pp.260–61; Cooper (2001), pp.198–99; Lowry, Bullitt (1996), pp.145–46.
19. Sources regarding Pershing's testimony on the Baker–March bill are in Bland and Ritenour (1981), p.194; Bland and Ritenour (1996), pp.587–88; Smythe (1986), pp.262–63; Vandiver (1977), p.1,045; Coffman (1966), p.202; Anon. (1919–20), "The Month in the United States."
20. Pogue (1963), p.210; Coffman (1966), pp.202–09; Smythe (1986), p.263; Heckscher (1991), pp.618–19.
21. Sources regarding the early Eisenhower–Patton relationship at Camp Meade are in Eisenhower, Dwight D. (1967), pp.169–73; Manuscript, 2nd draft, PATTON, 08/25/1967, Collection of Articles (1), B7, Augusta-Walter Reed Series, Eisenhower Library (2), p.3; Eisenhower, Susan (1996), p.64; D'Este (2002), pp.146–53; D'Este (1995), p.285, 289.
22. A verbatim quotation from an August 25, 1967 manuscript draft written by Eisenhower, who did not use expletives in the document.

23. Blumenson (1972), p.733; Smythe (1986), pp.264–66, 271; Vandiver (1977), p.1,047–49, 1,052; Pogue (1963), pp.210–12.
24. Cooper (2001), p.200; Heckscher (1991), pp.619–20; Huelfer (2003), p.49; *American Armies and Battlefields in Europe* (1938), p.515; Davis (1945), p.184.
25. Conner 1920 Congressional Testimony, p.1,651; *American Armies and Battlefields in Europe* (1938), p.505.
26. Conner 1920 Congressional Testimony, p.1,661–62, 1,691, 1,706–09.
27. *Ibid.*, p.1,717–20, 1,723–27.
28. *Ibid.*, pp.1,723–24, 1,728–30.
29. Sherburne 1920 Congressional Testimony, p.1,831, 1,834, 1,840–45, 1,848.
30. *Ibid.*
31. *Ibid.*, p.1,851.
32. *Ibid.*, pp.1,841–43.
33. Ferrell (2007), p.147, n.29.
34. Smythe (1986), pp.269–73; Vandiver (1977), pp.1,051–54.
35. Sources regarding Conner's War College restructuring plan are in Conner memos, 04/01/1920 and 04/03/1920, both at RG120, Entry 267 (1).
36. *Ibid.*; Pogue (1963), pp.213–14; Coffman (1966), p.206, 210, 226; Odom (1999), pp.16–17; Killigrew (1979), pp.1–2; Weigley (1984), p.400.
37. Conner, Fox (1933), pp.173–76; Bland et al. (1981), pp.572–73, 576; Lane (1921), p.486; Parker (2005), p.93, n.16, citing Conner "Notes on Organization" (Carlisle Barracks, PA; Military History Institute, 04/24/1920, typescript 1-22, UA25C565). The "square" 28,000-man AEF infantry division was formed of four regiments grouped into two brigades. Conner and Marshall favored a smaller "triangular" division of three regiments with no brigade-level command.
38. CMPR (1); USAHEC Records (3); Coffman (1966), p.311, n.103; Smythe (1986), p.275; Vandiver (1977), p.1,053.
39. Sources regarding Eisenhower and Patton in late 1920 are in Eisenhower, Dwight D. (1967), pp.174–80; Ambrose (1983), p.67; Perret (1999), p.82; D'Este (2002), p.150; D'Este (1995), pp.300–02.

Chapter 9: Unlike Ike

1. Eisenhower, John (2003), p.6.
2. Eisenhower, Dwight D. (1967), p.178; D'Este (2002), pp.146–47.
3. While Eisenhower discussed his first meeting with Conner in his 1967 memoir *At Ease*, he did not provide a specific date, or even a year, of that meeting. His son, John S.D. Eisenhower, wrote that the initial meeting was in 1920, a date which is also provided in certain Eisenhower biographies. See: Eisenhower, John (2003), p.6; Ambrose (1983), p.73; Perret (1999), p.83; Korda (2007), pp.153–54; Perry (2007), p.43. Sources on Conner also place the meeting in

1920. See: Kingseed (1980), p.26; Cox (2011), xiv. However, other sources indicate the initial meeting was in 1919. See: D'Este (2002), p.163, n.6; Puryear (2007), p.162, McCann (1952), p.77; Davis (1945), p.188; Parker (2005), p.92. John S.D. Eisenhower had unparalleled access to information from his father. Also, it is much more likely that Conner would have sought out a potential executive officer for a field assignment in late 1920, once his position as AEF chief of staff had been eliminated, than in the autumn of 1919 when Conner spent much of that time with Pershing at Brandreth Lake preparing Pershing for his congressional testimony.

4. Sources regarding Eisenhower's introduction to Conner are in Eisenhower, Dwight D. (1967), p.178; Eisenhower, Dwight D. (1948), p.95; Conner, Virginia (1951), p.109; Brown (1987), p.211; Eisenhower, John, (2003), p.6; Perret (1999), p.83; D'Este (2002), pp.146–47; Miller, Merle (1987), p.187.

5. Sources regarding Eisenhower's article are in Eisenhower, Dwight D. (1920), pp.453–57; Eisenhower, Dwight D. (1967), p.173; Manuscript, 2nd draft, PATTON, 08/25/1967, Collection of Articles (1), Box 7, Augusta-Walter Reed Series, Eisenhower Library (2), p.4; D'Este (2002), p.152; Perret (1999), pp.80–82; Hewes (1975), p.392.

6. Sources regarding the death of Eisenhower's son are in Eisenhower, Dwight D. (1967), pp.180–82; Eisenhower, Susan (1996), p.68; D'Este (2002), p.156, n.47.

7. Author interview (2); McCain (1975), p.s115.

8. Sources regarding Conner's 1921 *The Cavalry Journal* article are in Conner, Fox (1921), pp.11–18; Coffman (1966), p.227, n.104, 311.

9. Sherburne 1920 Congressional Testimony, p.1,844; Miller, Merle (1987), p.209.

10. Vandiver (1977), pp.1,056–57; Coffman (1966), p.225.

11. Sources regarding Secretary Weeks' views on Conner's War College restructuring proposal are in *New York Times*, 04/22/1921; Vandiver (1977), p.1,057; Smythe (1986), p.273, n.30; Pogue (1963), p.217; Coffman (1966), pp.225–27.

12. Sources regarding the fishing vacation taken by the Conners and the Pattons are in Conner, Virginia (1951), pp.96–107; Prioli (1991), pp.108–09. There is a slight variation in the language of the Patton poem quoted by Mrs. Conner in her book and by Dr. Prioli in his. The version printed in Mrs. Conner's book is quoted herein, although Dr. Prioli accurately quoted the language of a typed version of the same poem, bearing a June 1921 date, found in George Patton's papers on file at West Point.

13. Sources regarding Conner's work on the army reorganization board are in USAHEC Records (1–5); Hewes (1975), p.384.

14. Sources regarding Pershing's restructuring of the general staff corps are in USAHEC Records (6); Smythe (1986), p.275; Vandiver (1977), p.1,058; Pogue (1963), p.218; Hewes (1975), pp.389–90.

15. CMPR (1); Brown (1987), p.212.

16. Conner, Virginia (1951), pp.112–13.

17. *National Defense Act Approved June 3, 1916, As Amended Through June 30, 1921,* p.9.
18. Conner, Fox (1921), p.15; Conner AGO File (17); Williams (1922), p.602; Major (1993), p.177, 180, n.70; Vandiver (1977), p.1,054; Smythe (1986), p.272; Wells Senate Testimony, p.580, 591–93, 602.
19. CMPR (1); Coffman (1966), p.229; D'Este (2002), p.149; Vandiver (1977), p.1,054.
20. Vandiver (1977), p.1,059; Sherburne Congressional Testimony, pp.1,841–44; Ferrell (2007), p.147, n.29.
21. Eisenhower, Dwight D. (1967), p.178; Brown (1987), p.211.
22. Eisenhower, Dwight D. (1967), pp.178–79.
23. $250.67 in 1921 dollars equates to more than $3,000.00 in 2016 dollars.
24. Sources regarding the army's effort to court-martial Eisenhower because of his improper expense reimbursement are in the following documents found in Eisenhower Library (1): Eisenhower to Adjutant General, 06/17/1921; Adjutant General's Office, "Report in the Case of Major Dwight D. Eisenhower, Inf. Tanks," received 06/21/1921(with subsequent indorsements through 10/21/1921); White to Adjutant General, 06/30/1921; Helmick to Adjutant General, 07/06/1921; Helmick to Adjutant General, 08/25/1921; Helmick to Assistant Chief of Staff, G-1 (McRae), 12/14/1921; and Helmick to Chief of Staff, 12/14/1921. See also: D'Este (2002), pp.161–62; Perret (1999), p.82; Miller, Merle (1987), pp.196–200.
25. CMPR (1).
26. Conner to Eisenhower, 10/06/1921, Eisenhower Library (3).
27. Pogue (1966), p.237; Eisenhower, Dwight D. (1967), p.208.
28. Hodges to Adjutant General, 10/24/1921 and Helmick to Adjutant General, 11/01/1921, both in Eisenhower Library (1); Miller, Merle (1987), pp.201–02; Perret (1999), p.617.
29. Adjutant General to Pershing, 11/16/1921, Eisenhower Library (1); Perret (1999), p.83, 617; Miller, Merle (1987), p.203.
30. CMPR (1).
31. Helmick to Assistant Chief of Staff, G-1(McRae), 12/14/1921, Eisenhower Library (1); Miller, Merle (1987), p.204; Perret (1999), p.617.
32. McRae to Adjutant General, 12/14/1921; Adjutant General to Eisenhower (through the Chief of Infantry), 12/16/1921, both in Eisenhower Library (1); Miller, Merle (1987), p.204; D'Este (2002), p.162, n.1.
33. Eisenhower, Dwight D. (1967), p.182.
34. *Ibid.*
35. Pugh to Conner, 04/16/1918 and Conner to Pugh, 04/18/1918, both in RG120, Entry 267 (13).
36. Conner AGO File (13); Conner, Virginia (1951), pp.26–27; Whitehorne (1998), pp.73–74, 116; Cullum (1920) Vol. VI-A, pp.505–06.
37. Ambrose (1983), p.65; D'Este (2002), p.137.

38. Helmick to Assistant Chief of Staff, G-1 (McRae), 12/14/1921, Eisenhower Library (1).

Chapter 10: Panama

1. Eisenhower, Dwight D. (1967), p.185.
2. Sources regarding the Conner family's arrival in Panama are in CMPR (1); Conner, Virginia (1951), p.109, 113–14; Betty Conner Vida interview 10/11/1987, Norm MacDonald Collection; Eisenhower, Susan (1996), p.76.
3. Sources regarding Dwight and Mamie Eisenhower's arrival in Panama are in Eisenhower, Dwight D. (1967), pp.183–85; Brown (1987), p.206; Perret (1999), pp.84–85; Eisenhower, Susan (1996), pp.74–77; Brandon (1954), pp.128–30.
4. Sources regarding the condition of the troops at Camp Gaillard when Conner took command are in Conner, Virginia (1951), p.115; Betty (Betsey) Conner to Fox Brandreth (Tommy) Conner, 04/24/1997 (Macpherson Conner Collection); D'Este (2002), p.149; Miller, Merle (1987), p.209; Weigley (1984), pp.400–01; Finlayson (2001), pp.72–73; Major (1993), p.180; WDAR (4), p.200; WDAR (6), p.156; Wells Senate Testimony, p.580, 593.
5. Chynoweth later rose to the rank of brigadier general. He commanded American forces in the central Philippines at the time of the Japanese conquest of the islands in 1942. Chynoweth was taken prisoner and spent the remainder of the war in a Japanese POW camp.
6. Sources regarding the efforts of Conner and Eisenhower to improve the brigade's discipline and performance are in Betty (Betsey) Conner to Fox Brandreth (Tommy) 04/24/1997, and Conner, Macpherson unpublished essay (1), p.2, (both in the Macpherson Conner Collection); Anon. (1922), "Rifle Marksmanship in the Canal Zone," pp.620–621; Brown (1987), p.212; Conner, Virginia (1951), p.115; Chynoweth (1975), pp.99–105, 192–200; USAHEC Records (8), pp.22–23; D'Este (2002), p.172; Miller, Merle (1987), pp.208–09; Puryear (2007), p.162, n.10, 413; Korda (2007), p.161; Goodman (1922), p.272.
7. Jones (1922), *Foreword*; Betty (Betsey) Conner to Fox Brandreth (Tommy) Conner (Macpherson Conner Collection).
8. Eisenhower, Dwight D. (1967), p.39, 185; Brown (1987), p.205; Eisenhower, John (2003), p.8; Korda (2007), pp.128–29.
9. Eisenhower, Dwight D. (1967), p.185; Brown (1987), pp.205–06; Betty Conner Vida interview 10/11/1987 (Norm MacDonald Collection); Chynoweth (1975), p.100.
10. Eisenhower, Dwight D. (1967), p.185.
11. Eisenhower, Dwight D. (1967), pp. 185–87; Nye (1986), p.31, 150–53.
12. *The Times-Picayune* (New Orleans), 04/01/1969, MDAH (1); Puryear (2007), p.381, n.3, 427.

13. Eisenhower, Dwight D. (1967), p.185; Conner to parents, undated, MDAH (1).

14. References to *The Exploits of Brigadier Gerard* are in Conan Doyle (1896), p.1, 43–46, 87, 110–15, 130–34, 145, 269, 278, 312. See also: Ambrose (1983), p.65; Perret (1999), p.70.

15. References to *The Long Roll* are in Johnston (1911), p.27, 85, 102–03, 145, 165–68, 680.

16. References to *The Crisis* are in Churchill (1901), p.39, 82–83, 232–34, 227, 243, 397–98, 406.

17. Sources regarding Conner's efforts to further develop Eisenhower's interest in history are in Eisenhower, Dwight D. (1967), pp.185–86; Kingseed (1980); Miller, Merle (1987), p.210; *New York Times*, 10/11/1965.

18. Sources regarding Mamie Eisenhower's difficulties in Panama are in Conner, Virginia (1951), pp.120–21, 153; Eisenhower, Susan (1996), p.77; Eisenhower, Dwight D. (1967), p.184; Miller, Merle (1987), p.208, 214–15; Perret (1999), pp.85–86.

19. Sources regarding Virginia Conner's activities in Panama are in Betty Conner Vida interview 10/11/1987 and Mamie Eisenhower letter to Mrs. Conner, 05/17/1952 (both in the Norm MacDonald Collection); Conner, Virginia (1951), p.63, 114–15, 129, 153; Eisenhower, Dwight D. (1967), p.184; Eisenhower, Susan (1996), p.78; Miller, Merle (1987), p.221.

20. Sources regarding Betty Conner's romance with Frank Vida are in Conner, Virginia (1951), p.110, 115–18, 127–29; McCain (1975), p.115.

21. Conner, Virginia (1951), p.142, 147.

22. Sources regarding the relationship between Conner and his son while in Panama are in the October 1982 interview of Fox Brandreth Conner by Norm Macdonald (Norm MacDonald Collection); Author interview (2); Miller, Merle (1987), p.208; Conner, Virginia (1951), p.133.

23. Sources regarding the development of the personal aspects of the Conner–Eisenhower relationship are in Eisenhower, Dwight D. (1967), pp.186–87; Brown (1987), p.205, 212; Holt and Leyerzapf (1998), pp.226–27; Conner, Virginia (1951), p.120; Ambrose (1983), p.76; Miller, Merle (1987), p.208; USAHEC Records (9), pp.4–5; Brendon (1986), p.50; Brandon (1954), p.146; Burk (1986), p.31; D'Este (1995), p.294.

24. Sources regarding Eisenhower's progression in Panama to a more advanced level of military study are in Eisenhower, Dwight D. (1967), pp.186–87; Eisenhower to Olive Ann Tambourelle, 03/02/1966, Eisenhower Library (2), Special Names, Box 8; Brown (1987), p.205, 208; Miller, Merle (1987), p.211, 687; D'Este (2002), p.168, 604 (n.34); D'Este (1995), p.120, 317; Bassford (1994), pp.160–61; Kingseed (1980); Lovelace (1944), p.62; Reardon (1990), pp.88–89, 109, 112–13.

25. Sources regarding the Conner–Eisenhower discussions on studying the humanities are in Eisenhower, Dwight D. (1967), pp.185–87; Brown (1987), p.206; *The*

Times-Picayune (New Orleans), 04/01/1969, MDAH (1); Golomb and Wistrich (2002), pp.301–03.

26. Eisenhower, Susan (1996), pp.83–84; Conner, Virginia (1951), pp.120–21; Lovelace (1944), p.62.

27. Sources regarding George Marshall's visit to Panama and Conner's views on Marshall are in Eisenhower, Dwight D. (1967), p.195; Eisenhower, Dwight D. (1948), pp.18–19; Bland et al. (1991), p.611; Bland and Ritenour (1981), pp.259–60; Miller, Merle (1987), p.213; Puryear (2007), p.80, n.55, 168, 408; Ambrose (1983), p.77; Conner to Eisenhower, 10/06/1921, Eisenhower Library (3). See also D'Este (2002), p.737, n.2 which includes a quote from Marshall that "Fox Conner never hinted to me that I made such an impression on him."

28. Sources regarding Conner's 1920s prediction of a second world war are in Eisenhower, Dwight D. (1967), p.195; Eisenhower, Dwight D. (1948), pp.18–19; Brown (1987), p.210; Conner, Virginia (1951), pp.120–21; October 1982 interview of Fox Brandreth Conner by Norm Macdonald, (Norm MacDonald Collection); Conner, Fox (January 1928), p.1; Miller, Merle (1987), p.210; *New York Times*, 10/11/1965.

29. On August 23, 1939, the foreign ministers of Nazi Germany and the Soviet Union signed a "non-aggression pact," which created a de facto alliance between the two totalitarian dictatorships. The pact remained in effect until Germany invaded the Soviet Union on June 22, 1941.

30. Sources regarding the Conner–Eisenhower discussions on management of international military coalitions are in Eisenhower, Dwight D. (1967), p.195; Eisenhower, Dwight D. (1948), pp.18–19; Brown (1987), pp.208–09; Miller, Merle (1987), p.210; Puryear (2007), p.382; *New York Times*, 10/11/1965. See also the October 1982 interview of Fox Brandreth Conner by Norm Macdonald (Norm MacDonald Collection).

31. Perret (1999), p.89; Lovelace (1944), p.62.

32. Sources regarding Chynoweth's views of Conner and Eisenhower are in Chynoweth (1975), pp.99–103, 106, 165, 181–85, 194–95; USAHEC Records (8), p.1, 23–24; USAHEC Records (9), p.11; D'Este (2002), 173; Finlayson (2001), p.112.

33. Eisenhower, Dwight D. (1948), pp.18–19; Brown (1987), pp.205–06.

34. CMPR (1).

35. Major (1993), p.188; Eisenhower, Dwight D. (1967), p.185; USAHEC Records (7). The Army condemned Camp Gaillard in 1927. It eventually slid entirely into the Panama Canal.

36. CMPR (1); 09/02/24 correspondence of Captain George Randolph, Pam McPhail Collection.

37. Bender (1990), pp.14–15; Perret (1999), p.89.

38. *Ibid.*; Miller, Merle (1987), p.224.

39. Eisenhower, Dwight D. (1967), pp.195–96.

Chapter 11: Climbing Their Ladders

1.   Conner, Virginia (1951), p.147.
2.   CMPR (1).
3.   Cooke (1997), pp.149–50; *New York Times*, 08/13/1924 and 10/03/1926.
4.   Sources regarding Conner's adjustment to his G-4 duties are in Fox Conner Lecture (2), p.1; Conner, Fox (1926), pp.219–21; *Hearings before the President's Aircraft Board*, Vol. 1 (1925), p.1,516; Conner, Virginia (1951), p.147.
5.   Ferrell (1998), pp.167–68; McCoy (1967), p.147, 306; Odom (1999), pp.82–84; Linn (1997), pp.253–54; *American Armies and Battlefields in Europe* (1938), p.505, 509–10.
6.   Fox Conner Lecture (4), pp.2–6. The Army Industrial College educated both military officers and business leaders as to the issues involved in industrial mobilization and supply in time of war. See: Weigley (1984), p.407.
7.   Eisenhower, Dwight D. (1967), p.173, 196–200; Brown (1987), p.213; D'Este (2002), pp.175–76; Hewes (1975), p.392.
8.   Now named the Eisenhower Executive Office Building.
9.   Sources regarding Eisenhower's appointment to the Leavenworth program are in Brown (1987), pp.213–14; Eisenhower, Dwight D. (1967), pp.198–201; Smith, Jean (2012), pp.70–72; Puryear (2007), p.163, 413; Perret (1999), pp.91–93; Ambrose (1983), p.79; Davis (1945), pp.202–03; Cooke (1997), p.85; Korda (2007), p.69; Gunther (1951), p.60; Miller, Merle (1987), p.225; D'Este (2002), p.178.
10. D'Este (2002), pp.176–78, 732 (n.6).
11. Hurley (1964), pp.67–70, 84–85, 91–102; Odom (1999), pp.88–89. In December 1925, General Mitchell was convicted and dismissed from the service.
12. Hurley (1964), pp.99–102; Odom (1999), p.89. The President's Board is sometimes referred to as the "Morrow Board," in recognition of its chairman, Dwight Morrow.
13. *Hearings before the President's Aircraft Board*, Vol. 1 (1925), p.1,514, 1,516, 1,519–22, 1,526–27, 1,534–35. See also: Linn (1997), pp.253–54.
14. Hurley (1964), pp.105–06; McCoy (1967), p.305; Linn (1997), pp.253–54.
15. Blumenson (1972), pp.800–01.
16. Conner 1925 Congressional Testimony, pp.271–75.
17. Conner 1926 Congressional Testimony, pp.552–57.
18. Conner, Fox (1926), pp.219–24.
19. CMPR (1); Pershing to Conner, 10/16/1925, MDAH (1).
20. Sources regarding the Conner–Hines relationship are in *New York Times*, 11/12/1925; Conner, Virginia (1951), pp.147–50; D'Este (2002), p.174, 732; Cooke (1997), p.150; Miller, Merle (1987), p.224.
21. The national holiday presently known as Veteran's Day was originally named Armistice Day, in commemoration of the armistice which ended the fighting in World War I on November 11, 1918.

22. Conner, Virginia (1951), p.151; Author interview (2); Eisenhower, Dwight D. (1967), p.216; Smith, Jean (2012), p.79.

23. Sources regarding Conner's Governors Island proposal are in *New York Times*, 04/19/1926 and 04/27/26.

24. Fiorello LaGuardia later served as the Republican mayor of New York City from 1934 through 1945. LaGuardia Airport in New York City is named in his honor.

25. *New York Times*, 08/09/1926; Rice (2004), pp.74–80; Odom (1999), p.82, 88–89.

26. Betros (2012), pp.44–46; Conner, Virginia (1951), p.145.

27. Blumenson (1972), pp.800–01; Hewes (1975), pp.390–92.

28. Eisenhower, Dwight D. (1967), p.212; Brown (1987), p.214; Smith, Jean (2012), p.72; D'Este (2002), p.179 (n.13), 181; Ambrose (1983), p.80; Bender (1990), p.16; Nenninger (1994), pp.225–26, 231.

29. Ferrell (1981), p.6; Smith, Jean (2012), pp.72–73; D'Este (2002), pp.733–34; Ambrose (1983), p.81; Bender (1990), p.18.

30. *Ibid.*

31. Bagnal et al. (1985), pp.16–17; USAHEC Records (9), pp.14–15.

32. Eisenhower, Dwight D. (1967), p.200.

33. Sources regarding Eisenhower's Fort Benning service are in Eisenhower, Dwight D. (1967), pp.203–04; Cullum (1930), Vol. VII, p.1,076; Smith, Jean (2012), pp.74–76; Brandon (1954), p.158; Perret (1999), p.98 (n.5); Hewes (1975), p.392.

34. Sources regarding Eisenhower's work on the 1927 battlefield guidebook are in Eisenhower, Dwight D. (1967), p.204; Smith, Jean (2012), pp.76–80; Ambrose (1983), p.82; D'Este (2002), p.190; Perret (1999), p.98; Holt and Leyerzapf (1998), p.59. See also *Guide to the American Battle Fields of Europe* (1927), generally and at vi, p.17, 33, 76, 131, 167, 268–71.

35. Sources regarding Conner's 1926 candidacy for the Army chief of staff position are in *New York Times*, 09/07/1926, 09/22/1926, 09/23/1926; Bell (2003), p.116; Mead (1921), p.250; Anon. (1923) "Dwight F. Davis Assistant Secretary of War," p.240; Hewes (1975), p.54.

36. Davis is best known for founding the Davis Cup international tennis competition.

37. Sources regarding the Conner–Summerall relationship are in Nenninger (2010), vii, p.129, 194; Conner, Virginia (1951), p.153; Sanford and Shauffler (1927), pp.276–78; Hewes (1975), pp.389–92; *New York Times*, 04/19/1926; Cooke (1997), p.151.

38. Hewes (1975), p.389; Nenninger (2010), p.194; WPA (18); Brown (1987), p.213.

39. Sources regarding Conner's assignment to command the 1st Division are in *New York Times*, 03/22/1927, 04/05/1927, and 05/02/1927; Conner, Virginia (1951), pp.153–54; Cullum (1930), Vol. VII, p.463.

40. *New York Times*, 06/15/1927.

41. CMPR (1); Conner, Virginia (1951), p.154; McCain (1975), p.116.

Chapter 12: Third Time the Charm?

1. Fox Conner speech, 05/19/1934 (Norm Macdonald Collection).
2. Sources regarding Conner's arrival in Hawaii are in CMPR (1); Conner, Virginia (1951), p.156; USAHEC Records (7), p.15; *Honolulu Star-Bulletin*, 10/07/1927 and 01/25/1928; Linn (1997), pp.253–54; Killigrew (1979), pp.1–2.
3. The National Defense Act of 1920 organized the American Army into nine "corps areas" in the continental United States and three territorial "departments" in Hawaii, the Philippines, and Panama.
4. Sources regarding America's Pacific strategy in the late 1920s are in Linn (1997), pp.85–88, 169–74, 222–23, 289; Fox Conner (1921), p.15; *New York Times*, 06/07/1929; article titled "Function of Army of Oahu" (Macpherson Conner Collection).
5. *New York Times*, 05/18/1928, 06/10/1928.
6. The *California* was one of the American battleships sunk at Pearl Harbor on December 7, 1941.
7. Conner, Fox (October 1928).
8. Conner, Fox (January 1928), p.1, 3, 6, 11.
9. Conner, Fox (October 1928); Whitehorne (1998), p.343; *New York Times*, 06/07/1929.
10. Conner, Virginia (1951), p.157, 169–73, 180.
11. *Ibid.*, p.156, 165; McCain (1975), pp.115–17.
12. Author interview (2); October 1982 interview of Fox Brandreth Conner by Norm Macdonald (Norm MacDonald Collection); Cullum (1930), Vol. VII, pp.2,043–44.
13. Conner, Virginia (1951), pp.167–69; Author interview (2); McCain (1975), p.118.
14. Conner, Virginia (1951), pp.166–67, 172–76; Author interview (3).
15. Blumenson (1972), pp.820–21, 837; Spiller & al. (1984), pp.198–99.
16. Cullum (1930), Vol. VII, p.1,075; Eisenhower, Dwight D. (1967), pp.205–07, 210; Ambrose (1983), p.85; D'Este (2002), pp.191–97; Smith, Jean (2012), pp.80–82, 88–92; Brendon (1986), pp.56–57; Perret (1999), p.102; Cooling (1975), p.26 *et seq.*
17. Conner, Virginia (1951), p.214.
18. *New York Times*, 07/18/1930.
19. Sources regarding the 1930 chief of staff appointment are in Hoover (1952), pp.338–39; Lohbeck (1956), pp.71–72, 101–02; Smythe (1986), pp.276–77; Smith, Jean (2012), p.62; Perret (1996), pp.141–43; Hunt (1954), pp.126–28; James (1970), pp.343–44, 674–75 (n.19); Bane and Lutz (1943), pp.490–92; Cullum (1930), Vol. VII, p.576.
20. Ferrell (1981), p.7.
21. Sources on Conner's early service in Boston are in CMPR (1); *New York Times*, 07/18/1930; Conner, Virginia (1951), pp.180–82; Weigley (1984), pp.402–05; *The Boston Daily Globe*, 10/11/1930, 10/15/1930, 10/21/1930.

22. Conner, Fox (January 1928), p.11; Hoover (1952), pp.338–39; *The Boston Daily Globe*, 03/18/1931; Weigley (1984), pp.402–03.

23. *The Boston Daily Globe*, 11/14/1930, 01/22/1931, 02/02/1931, 05/30/1931, 07/22/1931.

24. *The Boston Daily Globe*, 07/8/1931, 07/12/1931, 07/15/1931, 08/26/1931, 10/03/1931, 10/29/1931, 02/26/1932, 03/25/1932.

25. Fox Conner Lecture (3), p.1, 7–11; Weigley (1984), p.403; Li (2012), p.183.

26. Killigrew (1979), V-11-19; Coffman (2004), p.234; Odom (1999), p.82, 98–99; Finlayson (2001), p.99, 153 (n.1); Pogue (1963), p.184; CMPR (2); Conner, Virginia (1951), p.183.

27. All references to Eisenhower's diary are in Holt and Leyerzapf (1998), pp.225–27; See also: Brown (1987), p.214; Eisenhower, John (2003), p.10; Ambrose (1983), pp.91–93; Hewes (1975), p.389.

28. Lohbeck (1956), pp.102–18; Killigrew (1979), VII-8-14; Burner (1979), pp.309–12; MacArthur (1964) pp.,93–97; Eisenhower, Dwight D. (1967), pp.216–17; Ambrose (1983), pp.96–98; James (1970), p.403. Felix Frankfurter was later appointed by Roosevelt to the United States Supreme Court, where he served from 1939 to 1962.

29. Killigrew (1979), X-7-8; James (1970), p.443; *The Boston Daily Globe*, 03/18/1933, 03/19/1933.

30. Killigrew (1979), X-8-16, 21, 26; MacArthur (1964), p.101; Hunt (1954), pp.151–52; Finlayson (2001), p.99; *The Boston Daily Globe*, 07/15/1933, 08/17/1933, 09/28/1933, 02/27/1934.

31. Salmond (1967), p.4, 8, 12, 31; Killigrew (1979), XII-6, 10-21, XIII-19-20; Pogue (1963), pp.274–76, 279; *The Boston Daily Globe*, 04/7/1933, 04/09/1933; *New York Times*, 10/20/1935, 12/20/1936.

32. Sources regarding Conner's work with the Civilian Conservation Corps (CCC) are in Brown (1987), p.215; Conner, Virginia (1951), p.183; Salmond (1967), pp.47–52, 127–28, Killigrew (1979), XII-11; Patton, Thomas (2005), p.163, 168, 185 (n.1), 187 (n.28); *The Boston Daily Globe*, 07/22/1933, 08/04/1933, 09/01/1933, 09/23/1933, 10/07/1933, 10/18/1933, 10/20/1933, 10/30/1933, 11/29/1933, 01/03/1934, 01/23/1934, 12/12/1934; *New York Times*, 10/20/1935, 08/02/1936. See also undated article in the Norm MacDonald Collection.

33. Sources regarding Conner's responses to General March's book are in March (1932), pp.253–54, 269–70, 285, 291; Conner, Fox (1933), pp.173–76; Conner, Fox (1934), pp.327–29; Coffman (1966), p.238-39 (n.55); Smythe (1986), p.294. See also letters from Pershing to Conner (Macpherson Conner Collection).

34. Sources regarding Conner's 1934 book project are in Bland et al. (1991), pp.428–31; Eisenhower to Conner, 04/27/1934, Eisenhower Library (3).

35. Sources regarding the 1934 labor unrest in Rhode Island and Conner's role in the response are in Salmond (2002), p.45, 52, 66–67, 84, 92–100; Gerstle (1989),

pp.127–37; *New York Times*, 09/14/1934, 09/15/1934, 09/16/1934; *The Boston Daily Globe*, 09/15/1934, 09/16/1934.

36. *The Boston Daily Globe*, 11/04/1930, 07/22/1931, 01/18/1934, 05/20/1934, 07/15/1934; Author interview (2).

37. Sources regarding Conner's opportunity to have become chief of staff in 1934 are in Roosevelt Library (1), (2); Eisenhower to Conner, 09/24/1934, Eisenhower Library (3); *New York Times*, 09/09/1934; Smith, Jean (2012), p.62; Shrader (1993), p.160; Harbord to Conner, 07/12/1938, MDAH (1); *Collier's* [magazine], 07/1/1939 (copy in the Macpherson Conner collection); Author interview (2); Conner, Macpherson, unpublished essay (2), p.11; Potter and Potter (2011), p.117; Farley (1948), p.55; Perret (1996), pp.174–75; James (1970), pp.435–41; Hunt (1954), pp.159–60; Brown (1987), pp.214–15. Charles Brown's article, written after his 1964 interview with Eisenhower, was not published until 1987, in a version edited by Professor John Ray Skates. The reference to Conner's recommendation of Craig appears in the original 1964 manuscript by Brown, but not in the published version edited by Skates.

Chapter 13: The Zenith of Fox Conner

1. Brown (1987), p.215.

2. Sources regarding America's response to international events in late 1934–early 1935 are in Lamb and Tarling (2001), p.103; Finlayson (2001), p.121; Killigrew (1979), XIV-15-19, 26-37, Appendix 1.

3. Sources regarding the 1935 Pine Camp maneuvers are in *The Boston Daily Globe*, 05/12/1935, 08/04/1935, 08/05/1935, 08/11/1935, 08/19/1935, 08/24/1935, 08/26/1935, 08/27/1935, 08/29/1935 and *New York Times*, 08/11/35, 08/20/1935, 08/28/1935, 08/29/1935.

4. In 1943, Hanson Baldwin won the Pulitzer Prize for his wartime reporting from the Pacific.

5. Sources regarding the 1936 New England air maneuvers are in *The Boston Daily Globe*, 12/07/1935, 01/28/1936, 02/16/1936.

6. Spiller et al. (1984), pp.212–15; Killigrew (1979), XV, 14–16.

7. Lamb and Tarling (2001), pp.99–102, 114–17.

8. *The Boston Daily Globe*, 08/14/1937; *Official Annual 1937, First Corps Area, Fifth CCC District*, p.7.

9. Sources regarding Conner's 1936 stroke are in CMPR (2); Conner, Virginia (1951), pp.213–16; Conner, Macpherson, unpublished essay (1), p.9; *The Boston Daily Globe*, 11/22/1936; *New York Times*, 11/22/1936.

10. The CMTC was established by the National Defense Act of 1920 to form a volunteer army reserve force.

11. *The Boston Daily Globe*, 07/09/1937, 07/10/1937.

12. Sources regarding the 1937 First Army command post exercises are in *The Boston Daily Globe*, 08/14/1937, 08/15/1937, 08/22/1937, 08/24/1937, 08/26/1937, 08/29/1937, 08/31/1927, 09/04/1937, 09/05/1937, 09/09/1937; *New York Times*, 08/29/1937.
13. Odom (1999), p.82; Killigrew (1979), Appendix 1; Pogue (1963), pp.312–13.
14. Sources regarding Conner's contribution to pre-World War II divisional restructuring are in Conner, Fox (1933), p.176; Fox Conner Lectures (3), p.7; Weigley (1984), pp.461–65; Finlayson (2001), p.102 (n.24), 129; Odom (1999), pp.112–13; *The Boston Daily Globe*, 10/03/1937; *New York Times*, 11/15/1937.
15. Lieutenant General Lesley McNair served as the commanding general of all army ground forces in World War II until he was killed at the front in France in 1944 as the result of an errant bomb dropped by an American airplane.
16. Bland and Ritenour (1981), pp.572–73, 576; Pogue (1963), p.314.
17. Conner's medical records also contain reference to the same "acute" condition occurring on June 13, 1938. It is unclear as to whether this represents a second heart attack or an error as to the date.
18. Sources regarding Conner's 1938 stroke and other health problems are in CMPR (2); Conner, Macpherson, unpublished essay (1), p.9; Bland and Ritenour (1981), p.614.
19. CMPR (2).
20. Letters regarding Conner's retirement are in MDAH (1); Macpherson Conner Collection; Marshall Library.
21. Sources regarding Conner's 1939 activities are in Fox Conner Lectures (1); Conner, Virginia (1951), p.199; Pershing's letter to Virginia Conner of 05/19/1939 in the Macpherson Conner Collection; letters of 08/11/1939 and 08/17/1939 in the Marshall Library.
22. *"On the shelf" is an idiom referring to things or people thought to be no longer of use.
23. Cray (1990), pp.137–40; Parrish (1989), pp.86–87, 95–98; Pogue (1963), p.328.
24. Wiegley (1984), p.424 (n.8), 429; Cray (1990), p.147.
25. Marshall to Conner, 09/09/1938, Marshall Library. The 1940 newspapers articles are found in the Macpherson Conner collection.
26. Conner's letter of 09/15/1940 and Marshall's 09/20/1940 response, both in Marshall Library.
27. Conner, Fox (1941).
28. Blair (1996), p.375.
29. Sources regarding Conner's 1941 head injury are in Conner, Virginia (1951), pp.207–10; Potter and Potter (2011), p.136; telegrams and letters exchanged between George Marshall and Virginia Conner, Marshall Library.
30. Sources regarding Eisenhower's prewar service in 1941 are in Ferrell (2007), p.39; Pogue (1966), pp.162–63; Perret (1999), pp.140–43.
31. Sources regarding Eisenhower's service in Marshall's GHQ at the beginning of World War II are in Eisenhower, Dwight D. (1967), pp.249–50; Eisenhower,

Dwight D. (1948), pp.14–28, 31, 49–52; Ferrell (2007), p.48, 52, 58, 62; Perret (1999), pp.146–47; Bland et al. (1991), p.470; Ambrose (1983), p.134, 144–46; Pogue (1963), p.218; Pogue (1966), p.317, 339.
32. Conner, Virginia (1951), p.211.
33. Author interview (1).

Epilogue

1. Harbord to Conner, 07/12/1938, MDAH (1).
2. Sources regarding Conner and his family during World War II are in Conner, Virginia (1951), p.66, 212; Potter and Potter (2011), pp.198–200; Linnerud (1998), 1-23 through 1–39.
3. Sources regarding contact between the Conner and Eisenhower families during World War II are in letters dated 07/04/1942, 07/29/1942, 08/21/1942, 12/26/1943, all in Eisenhower Library (3); Eisenhower, John (2003), pp.10–12.
4. Eisenhower, Dwight D. (1948), pp.18–19, 30, 452; Ambrose (1970), p.80, 676; Brown (1987), pp.208–09.
5. See letters and telegrams exchanged between Conner and Marshall dated 11/13/1942, 11/17/1942, 11/16/1944, 11/18/1944, all in Marshall Library; Bland and Ritenour (1991), pp.663–64; Potter and Potter (2011), p.117; Author interviews (2), (3).
6. Patton to Conner, 12/17/1944 and 03/13/1945, MDAH (1).
7. See letters exchanged between Conner and Eisenhower dated 10/07/1948, 12/28/1948, 01/03/1949; Conner, Virginia (1951), pp.121–23; Eisenhower's book inscription to Conner is in the Norm MacDonald Collection.
8. Sources regarding Conner's final years in retirement are in Conner, Macpherson, unpublished essay(1), p.11; Author interviews (2), (3); Norm MacDonald's 05/08/1914 address delivered at the Fort Leavenworth Hall of Fame induction ceremony.
9. CMPR (4); Author interview (2).
10. Letters of Fox B. (Tommy) Conner to Edward Coffman, 03/06/1970 and to Edwin A. Thompson, 05/05/1970 (both in the Macpherson Conner Collection); Author interviews (2), (3).
11. Photo of Mamie Eisenhower, with caption, Macpherson Conner Collection; Cooling (1975), pp.27–29.
12. Sources regarding Conner's legacy are in Eisenhower, Dwight D. (1967), p.187; Brown (1987), p.204; Ferrell (1981), p.6; Norm MacDonald's 05/08/1914 address delivered at the Fort Leavenworth Hall of Fame induction ceremony; Conner, Macpherson, unpuplished essay (2), p.12.

BIBLIOGRAPHY

Published Materials

Adjutant-General of the State of New York. *New York In the Spanish–American War*, Vol. II. Albany, NY: James B. Lyon, State Printer, 1900.

Aldrich, William F. "Fox Conner: An Individual Study Project." United States Army War College Military Studies Program Paper, Carlisle Barracks, PA, 1993.

Ambrose, Stephen E. *Duty, Honor, Country: A History of West Point*. Baltimore, MD: The Johns Hopkins University Press, 1966.

_____ *The Supreme Commander: The War Years of General Dwight D. Eisenhower*. Garden City, NY: Doubleday & Company, Inc. 1970.

_____ *Eisenhower*, Vol. 1: *Soldier, General of the Army, President-Elect, 1890–1952*. New York: Simon & Schuster, 1983.

Anon. "Formation of the U.S. Field Artillery Association." *Journal of the United States Artillery*, Vol. 34 (1910).

_____ "The Month in the United States." *Current History: A Monthly Magazine of the New York Times*, Vol. XI (October 1919–March 1920).

_____ "Rifle Marksmanship in the Canal Zone." *Infantry Journal*, Vol. XX, No. 1 (January 1922).

_____ "Dwight F. Davis Assistant Secretary of War." *Army Ordnance—Journal of the Army Ordnance Association*, Vol. III, No. 17 (March–April 1923).

_____ "Our Gallery of Illustrious." *Reserve Officer*, Vol. XII, No. 1 (January 1935).

Bagnal, Charles W., Earl C. Pence, and Thomas N. Meriwether. "Leaders as Mentors." *Military Review*, July 1985.

Bane, Suda Lorena and Ralph T. Lutz (eds.) *Organization of American Relief in Europe, 1918–1919.* Palo Alto, CA: Stanford University Press, 1943.

Bassford, Christopher. *Clausewitz in English: The Reception of Clausewitz in Britain and America 1815–1945.* Oxford, UK: Oxford University Press, 1994.

Bell, William Gardner. *Secretaries of War and Secretaries of the Army: Portraits & Biographical Sketches.* Washington D.C.: Center of Military History United States Army, 2003.

Bender, Mark C. "Watershed at Leavenworth: Dwight D. Eisenhower and the Command and General Staff School." Command and General Staff College Combined Arms Research Library, March 1990.

Betros, Lance. *Carved From Granite: West Point Since 1902.* College Station, TX: Texas A&M University Press, 2012.

Bishop, Ernest G. "Rural Community Life in the Haute Marne." Southern California Sociological Society, University of Southern California, *Studies in Sociology Sociological Monograph No. 12*, Vol. III, No. 4 (May 1919).

Blair, Clay. *Hitler's U-Boat War: The Hunters 1939–1942.* New York: Random House, 1996.

Bland, Larry and Sharon Ritenour (eds.) *The Papers of George Catlett Marshall*, Vol. 1: *"The Soldierly Spirit" December 1880–June 1939.* Baltimore, MD: The Johns Hopkins University Press, 1981.

_____ *The Papers of George Catlett Marshall*, Vol. 3: *"The Right Man for the Job" December 7, 1941–May 31, 1943.* Baltimore, MD: The Johns Hopkins University Press, 1991.

_____, Jolleen K. Bland and Sharon Ritenour Stevens (eds.) *George C. Marshall: Interviews and Reminiscences for Forrest C. Pogue.* Lexington, Virginia: George C. Marshall Research Foundation, 1991.

_____ and Sharon Ritenour (eds.) *The Papers of George Catlett Marshall*, Vol. 4: *"Aggressive and Determined Leadership" June 1, 1943–December 31, 1944.* Baltimore, MD: The Johns Hopkins University Press, 1996.

Blumenson, Martin. *The Patton Papers: 1885–1940.* Boston, MA: Houghton-Mifflin Company, 1972.

Brandon, Dorothy. *Mamie Doud Eisenhower: A Portrait of a First Lady.* New York: Charles Scribner's Sons, 1954.

Brendon, Piers. *Ike: His Life and Times.* New York: Harper & Row, 1986.

Brown, Charles H. "Fox Conner: A General's General." Edited by John Ray Skates. *Journal of Mississippi History*, Vol. XLIX, February–November 1987.

Bryden, William. "Notes on the Recent Tractor Test at Fort Sill, Oklahoma." *Field Artillery Journal*, Vol. VI, No. 1 (January–March 1916).

Bulwer-Lytton, Sir Edward. *The Last Days of Pompeii.* New York: John Wurtele Lovell, 1880.

Burk, Robert F. *Dwight D. Eisenhower: Hero and Politician.* Boston, MA: Twayne Publishers, 1986.

Burner, David. *Herbert Hoover: A Public Life.* New York: Alfred A. Knopf, 1979.

Center of Military History, United States Army. *Order of Battle of the United States Land Forces in the World War: American Expeditionary Forces.* Washington, D.C., 1988.

Churchill, Winston. *The Crisis.* New York: The Macmillan Company, 1901.

Chynoweth, Bradford Grethen. *Bellamy Park.* Hicksville, NY: Exposition Press, 1975.

Coffman, Edward M. *The Hilt of the Sword: The Career of Peyton C. March.* Madison, WI: The University of Wisconsin Press, 1966.

_____ *The War to End All Wars: The American Military Experience in World War I.* New York: Oxford University Press, 1968.

_____ "The American Military Generation Gap In World War I: The Leavenworth Clique in the A.E.F." *Command and Commanders in Modern Warfare*, United States Air Force Academy, 1971.

_____ *The Regulars: The American Army 1898–1941.* Cambridge, MA: Harvard University Press, 2004.

Conan Doyle, Sir Arthur. *The Exploits of Brigadier Gerard.* New York: D. Appleton and Company, 1896.

Conner, Fox. "The Siege and Fall of Port Arthur." *Journal of the United States Cavalry Association*, Vol. XVII (July 1906).

_____ "Field Artillery in Cooperation with the Other Arms." *Journal of the United States Infantry Association*, Vol. VI (May 1910).

"Notes on Lost Motion and Jump." *International Military Digest Annual: A Review of Current Literature of Military Science* (1916).

"The Relations That Should Exist Between the War Department and Forces in the Field." *The Cavalry Journal*, Vol. XXX, No. 122 (January 1921).

"Supply Division of the General Staff." *Military Engineer*, Vol. XVIII, No. 99 (May–June 1926).

_____ "The National Defense." *North American Review* (January 1928).

_____ "Problems of Hawaiian Department Outlined." *Army–Navy Journal*, Vol. LXVI, No. 9 (October 27, 1928).

_____ "Divisional Organization." *Coast Artillery Journal*, Vol. 76, No. 1 (January–February 1933).

_____ "The Genius of the French Army—Criticism of a Criticism." *Army Ordnance—Journal of the Army Ordnance Association*, Vol. XIV, No. 84 (May–June 1934).

_____ "Replacements: Life Blood of a Fighting Army." *Infantry Journal*, Vol. XLVIII, No. 5 (May 1941).

Conner, Virginia. *What Father Forbad*. Philadelphia, PA: Dorrance & Company, Inc., 1951.

Cooke, James J. *Pershing and His Generals: Command and Staff in the A.E.F.* Westport, CT: Praeger Publishers, 1997.

Cooling, Benjamin Franklin, "Dwight D. Eisenhower at the Army War College, 1927–1928." *Parameters: Journal of the U.S. Army War College*, Vol. V, No. 1 (1975).

Cooper, John Milton, Jr. *Breaking the Heart of the World: Woodrow Wilson and the Fight for the League of Nations*. Cambridge, UK: Cambridge University Press, 2001.

Cottman, George. *Jefferson County in the World War*. Madison, IN: The Jefferson County Historical Society, 1920.

Cox, Edward. *Grey Eminence: Fox Conner and the Art of Mentorship*. Stillwater, OK: New Forums Press, Inc., 2011.

Cray, Ed. *General of the Army: George C. Marshall, Soldier and Statesman*. New York: Cooper Square Press, 1990.

Cresswell, Stephen. *Rednecks, Redeemers, and Race: Mississippi after Reconstruction, 1877–1917.* Jackson, MS: University Press of Mississippi, 2006.

Crowell, Benedict and Robert Forrest Wilson. *How America Went To War: The Road to France II—The Transportation of Troops and Military Supplies 1917–1918.* New Haven, CT: Yale University Press, 1921.

Cullum, George W. *Biographical Register of the Officers and Graduates of the U.S. Military Academy at West Point, Supplement, Vol. IV (1890–1900).* Cambridge, MA: The Riverside Press, 1901.

_____ *Biographical Register of the Officers and Graduates of the U.S. Military Academy at West Point, Supplement, Vol. V (1900–1910).* Saginaw MI: Seeman and Peters, Printers, 1910.

_____ *Biographical Register of the Officers and Graduates of the U.S. Military Academy at West Point, Supplement, Vol. VI-A (1910–1920).* Saginaw MI: Seeman and Peters, Printers, 1920.

_____ *Biographical Register of the Officers and Graduates of the U.S. Military Academy at West Point, Supplement, Vol. VI-B (1910–1920).* Saginaw MI: Seeman and Peters, Printers, 1920.

_____ *Biographical Register of the Officers and Graduates of the U.S. Military Academy at West Point, Supplement, Vol. VII (1920–1930).* Chicago, IL: R.R. Donnelley & Sons Company, Lakeside Press, 1930.

Cunningham, O. Edward, Gary D. Joiner and Timothy B Smit (eds.) *Shiloh and the Western Campaign of 1862.* New York: Savas Beatie, LLC, 2009.

Cutts, Richard. *Index to The Youth's Companion 1871–1929.* Metuchen, NJ: The Scarecrow Press, Inc., 1972.

Daniels, Josephus. *Our Navy at War.* New York: George H. Doran Company, 1922.

Davis, Kenneth S. *Soldier of Democracy: A Biography of Dwight Eisenhower.* Garden City, NY: Doubleday, Doran & Company, Inc., 1945.

D'Este, Carlo. *Patton: A Genius for War.* New York: Harper Collins, 1995.

_____ *Eisenhower: A Soldier's Life.* New York: Henry Holt and Company, 2002.

DeWeerd, Harvey A. *President Wilson Fights His War: World War I and the American Intervention.* New York: The Macmillan Company, 1968.

Dupuy, R. Ernest. *Men of West Point: The First 150 Years of the United States Military Academy*. New York: William Sloane Associates, 1951.

DuRant, Maureen Oehler and Peter E. Carroll. *West Point*. Charleston, S.C.: Arcadia Publishing, 2007.

Eisenhower, Dwight D. "A Tank Discussion." *Infantry Journal*, Vol. XVII (November 1920).

_____ *Crusade in Europe*. Baltimore, MD: The Johns Hopkins University Press, 1948.

_____ *At Ease: Stories I Tell to Friends*. Garden City, N.Y.: Doubleday, 1967.

Eisenhower, John S.D. and Joanne Thompson Eisenhower. *Yanks: The Epic Story of the American Army in World War I*. New York: Free Press (A Division of Simon & Schuster, Inc.), 2001.

_____ *General Ike: A Personal Reminiscence*. New York: Free Press (A Division of Simon & Schuster, Inc.), 2003.

Eisenhower, Susan. *Mrs. Ike: Memories and Reflections on the Life of Mamie Eisenhower*. New York: Farrar, Strauss and Giroux, 1996.

Farley, James A. *Jim Farley's Story: The Roosevelt Years*. New York: Whittlesey House (A Division of the McGraw-Hill Book Company, Inc.), 1948.

Farrow, Edward S. *West Point and the Military Academy*. New York: J.S. Ogilvie Publishing Company, 1899.

Ferrell, Robert H. *The Eisenhower Diaries*. New York: W.W. Norton & Company, 1981.

_____ *The Presidency of Calvin Coolidge*. Lawrence, KS: The University Press of Kansas, 1998.

_____ *America's Deadliest Battle: Meuse–Argonne, 1918*. Lawrence, KS: University Press of Kansas, 2007.

_____ *In the Company of Generals: The World War I Diary of Pierpont L. Stackpole*. Columbia, MO: University of Missouri Press, 2009.

Finlayson, Kenneth. *An Uncertain Trumpet: The Evolution of U.S. Army Infantry Doctrine, 1919–1941*. Westport, CT: Greenwood Press, 2001.

Fiske, H.B. "General Pershing and his Headquarters in France'. *Command and General Staff School Military Review* (September 1940).

Fries, Amos Alfred and Clarence Jay West. *Chemical Warfare*. New York: McGraw-Hill Book Company, Inc., 1921.

Frye, William. *Marshall: Citizen Soldier*. Indianapolis, IN: The Bobbs-Merrill Company, 1947.

Garber, Max B. *A Modern Military Dictionary: Ten Thousand Terms Ancient and Modern, American and Foreign*. Washington, D.C., Max Garber, 1936.

Garner, James Wilford. *Reconstruction in Mississippi*. New York: The Macmillan Company, 1901.

Gerstle, Gary. *Working-Class Americanism: The Politics of Labor in a Textile City 1914–1960*. Cambridge, UK: Cambridge University Press, 1989.

Gillet, Mary C. *The Army Medical Department 1917–1941*. Washington, D.C.: U.S. Government Printing Office, 2009.

Golomb, Jacob and Robert S. Wistrich (eds.) *Nietzsche, Godfather of Fascism?: On the Uses and Abuses of a Philosophy*. Princeton, NJ: Princeton University Press, 2002.

Goodman, Herman. "The Anti-Venereal Disease Campaign in Panama." *Western Medical Times*, Vol. XLII, No. 1 (July 1922).

Grande, Peter J. *Images of America: United States Disciplinary Barracks*. Charleston, SC: Arcadia Publishing, 2009.

Griscom, Lloyd C. *Diplomatically Speaking*. New York: The Literary Guild of America, Inc., 1940.

Groom, Winston. *Shiloh 1862*. Washington, D.C.: National Geographic Society, 2013.

Gunther, John. *Eisenhower: The Man and the Symbol*. New York: Harper & Brothers, Publishers, 1951.

Hallas, James M. *Squandered Victory: The American First Army at St. Mihiel*. Westport, CT: Praeger Publishers, 1995.

Halsey, Francis W. (ed.) *Balfour, Viviani and Joffre: Their Speeches and Other Public Utterances in America*. New York: Funk & Wagnalls Company, 1917.

Hamilton, Craig and Louise Corbin (eds.) *Echoes From Over There: By the Men of the Army and Marine Corps Who Fought In France*. New York: The Soldiers Publishing Company, 1919.

Hanson, Joseph Mills. *The Marne: Historic and Picturesque*. Chicago, IL: A.C. McClung & Co., 1922.

Harbord, James G. *Leaves From a War Diary*. New York. Dodd, Mead & Company, 1925.

_____ *The American Army in France 1917–1919*. Boston, MA: Little, Brown, and Company, 1936.

Harries, Meirion and Susie Harries. *The Last Days of Innocence: America at War 1917–1918*. New York: Random House, 1997.

Harris, William C. *The Day of the Carpetbagger: Republican Reconstruction in Mississippi*. Baton Rouge, LA: Louisiana State University Press, 1979.

Heckscher, August. *Woodrow Wilson: A Biography*. New York: Collier Books, Macmillan Publishing Company, 1991.

Heller, Charles E. and William A. Stofft (eds.) *America's First Battles 1776–1965*. Lawrence, KS: University Press of Kansas, 1986. [The chapter entitled "Cantigny, 28–31 May 1918" was written by Allan R. Millet.]

Herwig, Holger H. *The Marne, 1914: The Opening of World War I and the Battle That Changed the World*. New York: Random House, 2009.

Hewes, James E., Jr. *From Root to McNamara: Army Organization and Administration, 1900–1963*. Washington, D.C.: United States Army Center for Military History, 1975.

Hofmann, George F. *Through Mobility We Conquer: The Mechanization of U.S. Cavalry*. Lexington: University Press of Kentucky, 2006.

Holley, I.B., Jr. *General John M. Palmer, Citizen Soldiers, and the Army of a Democracy*. Westport, CT: Greenwood Press, 1982.

Holt, Daniel D. and James W. Leyerzapf (eds.) *Eisenhower: The Prewar Diaries and Selected Papers, 1905–1941*. Baltimore MD: The Johns Hopkins Press, 1998.

Holt, Thaddeus. *The Deceivers: Allied Military Deception in the Second World War*. New York: A Lisa Drew Book/Scribner, 2004.

Hoover, Herbert. *The Memoirs of Herbert Hoover: The Cabinet and the Presidency 1920–1933*. New York: The Macmillan Company, 1952.

Horne, Alistair. *The Price of Glory: Verdun 1916*. London: Penguin Books, 1993.

Huelfer, Evan Andrew. *The "Casualty Issue" in American Military Practice: The Impact of World War I*. Westport, CT: Prager, 2003.

Hunt, Frazier. *The Untold Story of Douglas MacArthur*. New York: The Devin-Adair Company, 1954.

Hurley, Alfred F. *Billy Mitchell: Crusader for Air Power.* New York: Franklin Watts, Inc., 1964.

James, D. Clayton. *The Years of MacArthur*, Vol. I: *1880–1941.* Boston MA: Houghton Mifflin Company, 1970.

Joffre, Joseph J.C. *The Personal Memoirs of Joffre: Field Marshal of the French Army*, Vol. II. New York: Harper and Brothers Publishers, 1932.

Johnson, Thomas M. *Without Censor: New Light on Our Greatest World War Battles.* Indianapolis: The Bobbs-Merrill Company, 1928.

Johnston, Mary. *The Long Roll.* Boston, MA: Houghton Mifflin Company, 1911.

Jones, Ralph Edward. *Principles of Command.* Des Moines, IA: Riker's Booksellers, 1922.

Keegan, John. *The First World War.* New York: Vintage Books (A Division of Random House, Inc.), 2000.

Keenan, Jerry. *Encyclopedia of the Spanish–American & Philippine–American Wars.* Santa Barbara, CA: ABC-CLIO, Inc., 2001.

Kelly, R. Gordon. *Children's Periodicals of the United States: Historical Guides to the World's Periodicals and Newspapers.* Westport, CT: Greenwood Press, 1984.

Killigrew, John W. *The Impact of the Great Depression on the Army.* New York: Garland Publishing, Inc., 1979.

Kingseed, Cole C. "Mentoring General Ike." *Military Review* (October 1980).

Kirwan, Albert D. *Revolt of the Rednecks: Mississippi Politics 1876–1925.* Lexington, KY: University of Kentucky Press, 1951.

Korda, Michael. *Ike: An American Hero.* New York: Harper-Collins, 2007.

Lamb, Margaret and Nicholas Tarling. *From Versailles to Pearl Harbor: The Origins of the Second World War in Europe and Asia.* New York: Palgrave, 2001.

Lane, A.W., "Tables of Organization." *Infantry Journal*, Vol. XVIII (January–June 1921).

Lengl, Edward G. *To Conquer Hell: The Meuse–Argonne, 1918.* New York: Henry Holt and Company, 2008.

Li, Xiaobing (ed.) *China at War: An Encyclopedia.* Santa Barbara, CA: ABC-CLIO, LLC, 2012.

Liggett, Hunter. *Commanding an American Army: Recollections of the World War*. Boston, MA: Houghton Mifflin Company, 1925.

Linn, Brian McAllister *The U.S. Army and Counterinsurgency in the Philippine War, 1899–1902*. Chapel Hill, NC: The University of North Carolina Press, 1989.

_____ *Guardians of Empire: The U.S. Army and the Pacific, 1902–1940*. Chapel Hill, NC: The University of North Carolina Press, 1997.

Linnerud, Susan. "The Spanish War Class." *1998 Register of Graduates and Former Cadets*, Association of Graduates, USMA, West Point, NY, 1998.

Lohbeck, Don, *Patrick J. Hurley*. Chicago, IL: Henry Regnery Company, 1956.

Lovelace, Delos W. *General "Ike" Eisenhower*. New York: Thomas Y Crowell Company, 1944.

Lowry, Bullitt. *Armistice 1918*. Kent, OH: The Kent State University Press, 1996.

Lowry, Robert and William H. McCardle. *A History of Mississippi: From the Discovery of the Great River by Hernando DeSoto, Including the Earliest Settlement Made by the French, Under Iberville, To the Death of Jefferson Davis*. Jackson, MS: R.H. Henry & Co. 1891.

Major, John. *Prize Possession: The United States and the Panama Canal 1903–1979*. Cambridge, UK: Cambridge University Press, 1993.

MacArthur, Douglas. *Reminiscences*. New York: McGraw-Hill Book Company, 1964.

Manchester, William. *American Caesar: Douglas MacArthur 1880–1964*. Boston, MA: Little, Brown and Company, 1978.

March, Peyton C. *The Nation at War*. New York: Doubleday, Doran & Company, Inc., 1932.

Marshall, George C. *Memoirs of My Services in the World War 1917–1918*. Boston, MA: Houghton Mifflin Company, 1976.

McCain, William D. *Eight Generations of the Family of Henry Fox (1768–1852) and His Wife, Sarah Harrell Fox (1772–1848) of South Carolina, Tennessee, Alabama, and Mississippi*, Vol. I. Hattiesburg, MS, 1975.

McCann, Kevin. *Man from Abilene*. New York: Doubleday & Company, 1952.

McCoy, Donald R. *Calvin Coolidge: The Quiet President*. New York: The Macmillan Company, 1967.

McCullough, David. *Truman*. New York: Simon & Schuster, 1992.

Mead, Frederick S. (ed.) *Harvard's Military Record in the World War*. Boston, MA: The Harvard Alumni Association, 1921.

Miller, Merle: *Ike the Soldier: As They Knew Him*. New York: G.P. Putnam's Sons, 1987.

Miller, Stuart Creighton. *"Benevolent Assimilation": The American Conquest of the Philippines, 1899–1903*. New Haven, CT: Yale University Press, 1982.

Musicant, Ivan. *Empire by Default: The Spanish–American War and the Dawn of the American Century*. New York: Henry Holt and Company, 1998.

Nenninger, Timothy K. *The Leavenworth Schools and the Old Army: Education, Professionalism, and the Officer Corps of the United States Army, 1881–1918*. Westport, CT: Greenwood Press, Inc., 1978.

_____ "Leavenworth and Its Critics: The U.S Army Command and General Staff School, 1920–1940." *Journal of Military History*, Vol. 58 (April 1994).

The Way of Duty, Honor, and Country: The Memoir of General Charles Pelot Summerall. Lexington, KY: The University Press of Kentucky, 2010.

Nye, Roger H. *The Challenge of Command: Reading for Military Excellence*. Wayne, NJ: Avery Publishing Center, 1986.

Odom, William O. *After the Trenches: The Transformation of the U.S. Army, 1918–1939*. College Station, TX: Texas A&M University Press, 1999.

Orlemann, Eric C. *The Caterpillar Century*. St Paul, MN: Motorbooks International, 2003.

O'Toole, G.J.A. *The Spanish War: An Epic—1898*. New York: W.W. Norton & Company, 1984.

Owen, Allison. "History of the Washington Artillery." *Publications of The Louisiana Historical Society, Proceedings and Reports 1917*, Vol. X (1918).

Palka, Eugene and Jon C. Malinowski. *Historic Photos of West Point*. Nashville, TN: Turner Publishing Company, 2008.

Pappas, George S. *To the Point: The United States Military Academy, 1802–1902*. Westport, CT: Praeger Publishers, 1993.

Parker, Jerome H. "Fox Conner and Dwight Eisenhower: Mentoring and Application." *Military Review* (July–August 2005).

Parrish, Thomas. *Roosevelt and Marshall: Partners in Politics and War*. New York: William Morrow and Company, Inc., 1989.

Patton, George S., Jr. "Tanks in Future Wars." *Infantry Journal*, Vol. XVI, No. 11 (May 1920).

Patton, Thomas W. "When The Veterans Came to Vermont: The Civilian Conservation Corps and the Winooski River Flood Control Project." *Vermont History*, Vol. 73 (Summer/Fall 2005).

Payne, Robert. *The Marshall Story: A Biography of General George C. Marshall*. New York: Prentice-Hall, 1951.

Perret, Geoffrey *Old Soldiers Never Die: The Life of Douglas MacArthur*. New York: Random House, 1996.

———— *Eisenhower*. New York: Random House, 1999.

Perry, Mark. *Partners in Command: George C. Marshall and Dwight D. Eisenhower in War and Peace*. New York: The Penguin Press, 2007.

Pershing, John J. *My Experiences in the First World War*, 2 vols. New York: Frederick A. Stokes Company, 1931.

Pogue, Forrest C. *George C. Marshall: Education of a General 1880–1939*. New York: The Viking Press, 1963.

———— *George C. Marshall: Ordeal and Hope 1939–1942*. New York: The Viking Press, 1966.

Potter, Orlando B. III and Donald Brandreth Potter. *Brandreth: A History of Brandreth Park 1851–2010*. Bennington, VT: Two Loons Media, 2011.

Prioli, Carmine A. (ed.) *The Poems of General George S. Patton, Jr.: Lines of Fire*. Lewiston, NY: The Edwin Mellen Press, 1991.

Puryear, Edgar F., Jr. *Nineteen Stars*. Washington, D.C.: Coiner Publications, Ltd., 2007.

Reardon, Carol. *Soldiers and Scholars: The U.S. Army and the Uses of Military History, 1865–1920*. Lawrence, Kansas: University Press of Kansas, 1990.

Repington, Charles à Court. *The First World War 1914–1918: Personal Experiences of Lieut. Col. C. à Court Repington*. Boston, MA: Houghton Mifflin Company, 1920.

Réquin, Edouard. *America's Race to Victory*. New York: Frederick A. Stokes Company, 1919.

Rice, Rondall R. *The Politics of Air Power: From Confrontation to Cooperation in Army Aviation in Civil-Military Affairs*. Lincoln, NE: University of Nebraska Press, 2004.

Rowland, Dunbar *Mississippi: Comprising Sketches of Counties, Towns, Events, Institutions, and Persons, Arranged in Cyclopedic Form*, Vol. I. Atlanta: Southern Historical Publishing Association, 1907.

_____ *History of Mississippi: The Heart of the South*, Vol. II. Chicago–Jackson: The S.J. Clarke Publishing Company, 1925.

_____ *Military History of Mississippi 1803–1898*. Spartanburg, SC: The Reprint Company, 1978.

Salmond, John A. *The Civilian Conservation Corps, 1933–1942: A New Deal Case Study*. Durham, NC: Duke University Press, 1967.

The General Textile Strike of 1934: From Maine to Alabama. Columbia, MO: The University of Missouri Press, 2002.

Sanford, A.P. and Robert Haven Shauffler (eds.) *Armistice Day*. New York: Dodd, Mead and Company, 1927.

Scott, James Brown. Robert Bacon: Life and Letters. New York: Doubleday, Page & Company, 1923.

Shrader, Charles Reginald (ed.) *Reference Guide to United States Military History 1865–1919*. New York: Sachem Publishing Associates, Inc. 1993.

Simmons, Edwin H. *The United States Marines 1775–1975*. New York: The Viking Press, 1976.

Simpson, Jeffrey. *Officers and Gentlemen: Historic West Point in Photographs*. Tarrytown, NY: Sleepy Hollow Press, 1982.

Smith, Gene. *Until the Last Trumpet Sounds: The Life of General of the Armies John J. Pershing*. New York: John Wiley & Sons, Inc., 1998.

Smith, Jean Edward. *Eisenhower In War and Peace*. New York: Random House, 2012.

Smythe, Donald. "Pershing at West Point, 1897–1898." *New York History—The Quarterly Journal of the New York State Historical Association*, Vol. XLVIII, No. 1 (January 1967).

_____ *Guerilla Warrior: The Early Life of John J. Pershing*. New York: Charles Scribner's Sons, 1973.

_____ *Pershing: General of the Armies.* Bloomington, IN: Indiana University Press, 1986.

Society of the First Division. *History of the First Division During the World War 1917–1919.* Philadelphia, PA: The John C. Winston Company, 1922.

Spiller, Roger, Joseph G. Dawson, III, and T. Harry Williams (eds.) *Dictionary of American Military Biography*, Volume I: *A–G.* Westport, CT: Greenwood Press, 1984.

Staff College Press, *Annual Report of the Commandant U.S. Infantry and Cavalry School, U.S. Signal School, and Staff College For the School Year Ending Aug. 30, 1906.* Fort Leavenworth, KS, 1906.

Stallings, Laurence. *The Doughboys: The Story of the AEF, 1917–1918.* New York: Harper & Row Publishers, 1963.

Stout, Joseph A., Jr. *Border Conflict: Villistas, Carrancistas and the Punitive Expedition, 1915–1920.* Fort Worth, TX: Texas Christian University Press, 1999.

Thompson, Holland (ed.) *The Book of History: The World's Greatest War from the Outbreak of the War to the Treaty of Versailles,* Vol. XIII. New York: The Grolier Society, 1921.

Thompson, Lovell, M.A. DeWolfe Howe, Arthur Stanwood Pier, and Harford Powel (eds.) *The Youth's Companion.* Boston: Houghton Mifflin Company, 1954.

Time [magazine]. "Army and Navy: Chief of Staff." October 4, 1926.

Todd, Frederick P. *Cadet Gray: A Pictorial History of Life at West Point As Seen Through Its Uniforms.* New York: Sterling Publishing Co., Inc., 1955.

Trask, David F. *The United States in the Supreme War Council: American War Aims and Inter-Allied Strategy, 1917–1918.* Middletown, CT: Wesleyan University Press, 1961.

_____ *The A.E.F. and Coalition Warmaking, 1917–1918,* Lawrence, KS: University Press of Kansas, 1993.

Traxel, David. *Crusader Nation: The United States in Peace and the Great War 1898–1920.* New York: Alfred A. Knopf (A Division of Random House), 2006.

Tuchman, Barbara W. *The Guns of August*. New York: Random House Publishing Company, 1962.

United States Military Academy. *The West Point Guidebook, 29th Annual Edition*. West Point, NY: Wm. H. Tripp & Company, 1928.

Vandiver, Frank. *Black Jack: The Life and Times of John J. Pershing*, Vol II. College Station, TX: Texas A&M University Press, 1977.

Venzon, Anne Cirpriano (ed.) *The United States In the First World War: An Encyclopedia*. New York: Garland Publishing, 1995. [The passages on Hunter Liggett and the Belfort Ruse were written by Paul F. Braim and James Hallas, respectively.]

Vestal, S.C. "Field Service of the Coast Artillery in War," *Journal of the United States Artillery* Vol. 56, No. 3 (March 1922).

Warthin, Alfred Scott and Carl Vernon Walker. *Mustard Gas Poisoning*. St. Louis, MO: C.V. Mosby Company, 1919.

Weigley, Russell F. *History of the United States Army*. Bloomington, IN: Indiana University Press, 1984.

Weintraub, Stanley. *15 Stars: Eisenhower, MacArthur, Marshall—Three Generals who Saved the American Century*. New York: Free Press (A Division of Simon & Schuster, Inc.), 2007.

Welsome, Eileen. *The General and the Jaguar: Pershing's Hunt for Pancho Villa—A True Story of Revolution and Revenge*. New York: Little, Brown and Company, 2006.

Whitehorne, Joseph W.A. *The Inspectors General of the United States Army 1903–1939*. Washington, D.C.: Office of the Inspector General and Center of Military History, 1998.

Williams, Dion. "Co-Ordination in Army and Navy Training." *United States Naval Institute Proceedings*, Vol. 1 (January 1922).

United States Congress: Congressional testimony

Conner 1920 Congressional Testimony and Sherburne 1920 Congressional Testimony

U.S. Congress, House. *Hearings before Subcommittee No. 3 of the Select Committee on Expenditures in the War Department, 66th Cong.* 01/05/1920–01/08/1920.

Conner 1925 Congressional Testimony
U.S. Congress, House *Hearings Regarding War Department Appropriations Bill, FY 1927*. 12/11/1925.

Conner 1926 Congressional Testimony
U.S. Congress, House. *Hearings Regarding War Department Appropriations Bill, FY 1927*, 01/08/1926.

Wells Senate Testimony
U.S. Congress, Senate, *Hearings before Subcommittee of the Committee on Appropriations, 67th Cong.* 04/17/1922.

United States Government Printing Office Publications

A Guide to the American Battle Fields of Europe, 1927.
American Armies and Battlefields in Europe: A History, Guide, and Reference Book. Washington, D.C., 1938.
Biographical Directory of the American Congress, 1774–1971.
Hearings before the President's Aircraft Board, Vol. 1, 1925.
National Defense Act Approved June 3, 1916, As Amended Through June 30, 1921.
Regulations for the Army of the United States 1901, With Appendix.
United States Army in the World War 1917–1919, Historical Division, Department of the Army. Washington, D.C.: 1948.
   Vol. 2: *Policies.*
   Vol. 3: *Training and Use of American Units with the British and French.*
   Vol. 4: *Military Operations of the American Expeditionary Forces.*
   Vol. 5: *Military Operations of the American Expeditionary Forces.*
   Vol. 8: *Military Operations of the American Expeditionary Forces.*
   Vol. 9: *Military Operations of the American Expeditionary Forces.*
   Vol. 16: *General Orders G.H.Q., A.E.F.*

War Department Annual Reports:
(1) *Report of the Military Governor of Cuba on Civil Affairs.* Vol. I, Part S: *Fiscal Year Ending June 30, 1900.*

(2) *Report of the School of Application for Cavalry and Field Artillery*, 1907, Vol. IV.
(3) *Report of the Chief of Staff, 1910*, Vol. I.
(4) *Report of the Inspector General, 1916*, Vol. I.
(5) *Report of the Surgeon General U.S. Army to the Secretary of War, Fiscal Year Ended June 30, 1921.*
(6) *Report of the Secretary of War to the President, Fiscal Year Ended June 30, 1922.*

Unpublished material

Author Interviews:
(1) Black, Sam, December 23, 2012.
(2) Conner, Macpherson, June 1, 2013.
(3) MacDonald, Norm, June 2–3, 2013.

Conner, Fox Military Personnel Records:
National Archives and Records Administration, National Personnel Records Center, St. Louis, Missouri.
(1) Conner Military Personnel Records (Service).
(2) Conner Military Personnel Records, Veterans Administration Form 3101, dated June 8, 1938 (Medical Information).
(3) Conner Military Personnel Records, Form No. 697 (Expense Reimbursements).
(4) Report of Death.

Conner, Macpherson, unpublished essays in the Macpherson Conner Collection:
(1) "General Conner Out of Uniform."
(2) "Major General Fox Conner."

Dwight D. Eisenhower Presidential Library

(1) Eisenhower's 201 File.
(2) Post-Presidential Papers, 1961–69.
(3) Pre-Presidential Papers; Box #27; Folder Title: "Conner, Fox."

Franklin D. Roosevelt Library

(1) Graph titled "General Officers of the Regular Army: Date of Retirement;" Official File 25, War Department: 1934 (Box 1).

(2) Undated handwritten FDR note: "Chief of Staff to Succeed McArthur;" Official File 25, War Department: 1935 (Box 1).

George C. Marshall Research Library

Marshall Papers, Box 18, Folder 41.

Mississippi Department of Archives and History, Jackson, Mississippi:

(1) Subject File, Conner, Fox, 0–1979

(2) Subject File, Conner, Fox, 1980—

National Archives I, Washington, D.C.

Office of the Adjutant General (AG) Document File, RG94, Box 569, File 76804:

(1) AG to Conner, 07/05/1911.

(2) AG to Conner, 07/24/1912.

(3) AG to Conner 7/25/12.

(4) Assistant Secretary of War to Secretary of State, 03/25/1911.

(5) Assistant Secretary of War to Secretary of State, 04/01/1911.

(6) Bell to AG, 01/18/1908.

(7) Efficiency Report, 06/30/1899.

(8) Efficiency Report, 06/30/1900.

(9) Efficiency Report, 06/30/1901.

(10) Efficiency Report, 06/30/1902.

(11) Efficiency Report, 06/30/1903.

(12) Efficiency Report, 06/30/1904.

(13) Efficiency Report, 06/30/1905.

(14) Efficiency Report, 06/30/1906.

(15) Efficiency Report, 06/30/1907.

(16) Efficiency Report, 06/30/1908.

(17) Efficiency Report, 06/30/1909.

(18) Efficiency Report, 06/30/1910.

(19) Efficiency Report (Individual Service Report), 12/31/1911.

(20) Efficiency Report, 1912.

(21) Efficiency Report, 1913.

(22) Efficiency Report, 1914.

(23) Efficiency Report, 1915.

(24) Efficiency Report, 1916.

(25) Conner to AG, 05/28/1898, with endorsements.

(26) Conner to AG, 06/24/1898.

(27) Conner to AG, 07/24/1898, with endorsements.

(28) Conner to AG, 03/26/1899, with endorsements.

(29) Conner to AG, 07/9/1912, with endorsements.

(30) Conner to AG, 12/12/1912.

(31) Conner to AG, 01/2/1914 (*sic* 1915).

(32) Conner to Army Military Secretary, 01/29/1907.

(33) Conner to Secretary, School of Application for Cavalry and Field Artillery, 06/24/1907, with endorsements.

(34) Conty to Bacon, 06/08/1911.

(35) Duvall to Assistant Secretary of War, 04/23/1907.

(36) Extracts from Reports of Commanding General and General Staff Observer at the Camp of Instruction, Fort Riley, Kansas, 1906.

(37) Liggett and Wotherspoon to Chief of Staff, 07/01/1911.

(38) Macomb to AG, 04/07/1907, with endorsements.

(39) Report of an Examining Board, 04/07/1913.

(40) Rodgers to AG, 10/22/1901, with endorsements.

(41) Swift (Eben), correspondence of 01/28/1907.

(42) Unknown to Secretary of War, 06/28/1911.

(43) War Department Special Orders, 1898, No. 192, 08/16/1898.

(44) War Department Special Orders, 1901, No. 254, 11/02/1901.

(45) War Department Special Orders, 1906, No. 147, 06/21/1906.

(46) War Department Special Orders, 1907, No. 106, 05/06/1907.

(47) War Department Special Orders, 1907, No. 152, 06/29/1907.

(48) War Department Special Orders, 1907, No. 189, 08/15/1907.

(49) War Department Special Orders, 1912, No. 174, 07/25/1912.

(50) Wood to AG, 06/23/1911.

(51) Wood to AG, 07/03/1911.

(52) Wotherspoon to AG, 12/02/1912.

Fox Conner-edited.docx(53) Wotherspoon to AG, 10/19/1914.

National Archives II, College Park, Maryland:

Records Group (RG) 120:

Entry 267:

(1) Box 3105, Folder 594.

(2) Box 3113, Folder 682.

(3) Box 3113, Folder 683.

(4) Box 3113, Folder 683 [09/25/1917 Strategical Study].

(5) Box 3152, Folder 1081.

(6) Box 3152, Folder 1085 [Conner Notes (C)].

(7) Box 3155, Folder 1106 [Conner's Informal Talk to the Press].

(8) Box 3155, Folder 1108-A.

(9) Box 3156, Folder 1113 [Conner Notes (A)].

(10) Box 3156, Folder 1114 [Conner Notes (B)].

(11) Box 3156, Folder 1115 [Conner Notes (D)].

(12) Box 3205, Folder 1814.

(13) Box 3210, Folder 1904.

(14) Box 3211, Folder 1907.

(15) Box 3211, Folder 1917.

Entry 268:

(17) Box 3174 (G-3 Report).

(18) Box 3206, Folder 1826.

(19) Box 3223, Folder 2704.

National Archives—Affiliated Archives

Records on Deposit at U.S. Military Academy Archives, West Point, NY
  (Record Group 404—West Point Archives):

(1) A Brief Narrative of the Life of Guy V. Henry, Jr.

(2) Adjutant, USMA, Consolidated Monthly Conduct/Merit Rolls (By
  Class), January 1894–April 1907, Box 4 of 4.

(3) Adjutant, USMA, Semi-Annual Conduct/Merit Rolls (By Subject)
  June 1894–June 1902, Box 3 of 3.

(4) Official Register of the Officers and Cadets, June 1894.

(5) Official Register of the Officers and Cadets, June 1895.

(6) Official Register of the Officers and Cadets, June 1896.
(7) Official Register of the Officers and Cadets, June 1897.
(8) Official Register of the Officers and Cadets, June 1898.
(9) Register of Delinquencies No. 3.
(10) Register of Punishments No. 9.
(11) School History of Candidates, No. 1 1880–1899.
(12) *The Howitzer* 1896 (yearbook).
(13) *The Howitzer* 1897 (yearbook).
(14) *The Howitzer* 1898 (yearbook).
(15) U.S. Military Academy Staff Records, No. 14.
(16) U.S. Military Academy Staff Records, No. 15.
(17) U.S. Military Academy Staff Records, No. 16.
(18) Folder #3825 Conner, Fox, Miscellaneous information.

Official Annual 1937, First Corps Area, Fifth CCC District
U.S. Army Heritage and Education Center, Carlisle, PA (USAHEC)

USAHEC Records:

(1) "War Department Special Orders, No. 155-0," July 7, 1921, Appointing Board of Officers.
(2) "Minutes of a Meeting of Board of Officers," 07/08/1921.
(3) "Minutes of a Meeting of Board of Officers," 07/13/1921.
(4) Conner, Palmer, and DeWitt to Harbord, 07/13/21, "Reasons for establishing the Nucleus of G.H.Q. within the War Department General Staff."
(5) Conner, Palmer, and DeWitt to Harbord, 07/14/1921, "Supplemental on Reasons for Establishing the Nucleus of G.H.Q. within the war Department General Staff."
(6) Harbord to Chief of Staff, August 1921, "Report of Board of Officers appointed by Paragraph 25, Special Orders 155-0, War Department, July 7, 1921."
(7) Excerpt on Camp Gaillard from Sullivan, Charles J. *Army Posts and Towns: The Baedeker of the Army* (1926), p.15.
(8) Chynoweth to Pappas, 10/24/1967.
(9) Bodner, Diana L. "The Relationship Between Fox Conner and Dwight Eisenhower." *Army War College Strategy Research Project*, 04/09/2002.

Fox Conner Lectures on file at USAHEC:

(1) "The Allied High Command and Allied Unity of Direction." Lecture to the Army War College, Washington, D.C. 02/10/1939 [West Point Library.]
(2) "G-4 from a G-3 A.E.F. Point of View." Lecture to the Army War College, Washington, D.C., 01/06/1925 [G-4 Course 4, 1924–25.]
(3) "Organization and Functioning of G-3, A.E.F." Lecture to the Army War College, Washington, D.C. 09/18/1931 [G-3 Course 8, 1931–32 and 1933–34.]
(4) "Problems of Supply from the View Point of the General Staff." Lecture to the Army War College, Washington, D.C., 06/20/1925.

Private collections

(1) Macpherson Conner Collection, Bardonia, New York.
(2) Norm MacDonald Collection, Ossining, New York.
(3) Pam McPhail Collection, Slate Springs, Mississippi.

INDEX